W9-BYH-945

When should I travel to get the best airfare?
Where do I go for answers to my travel questions?
What's the best and easiest way to plan and book my trip?

frommers.travelocity.com

Frommer's, the travel guide leader, has teamed up with **Travelocity.com**, the leader in online travel, to bring you an in-depth, easy-to-use resource designed to help you plan and book your trip online.

At **frommers.travelocity.com**, you'll find free online updates about your destination from the experts at Frommer's plus the outstanding travel planning and purchasing features of Travelocity.com. Travelocity.com provides reservations capabilities for 95 percent of all airline seats sold, more than 47,000 hotels, and over 50 car rental companies. In addition, Travelocity.com offers more than 2,000 exciting vacation and cruise packages. Travelocity.com puts you in complete control of your travel planning with these and other great features:

> **Expert travel guidance from Frommer's** - over 150 writers reporting from around the world!

> **Best Fare Finder** - an interactive calendar tells you when to travel to get the best airfare

> **Fare Watcher** - we'll track airfare changes to your favorite destinations

> **Dream Maps** - a mapping feature that suggests travel opportunities based on your budget

> **Shop Safe Guarantee** - 24 hours a day / 7 days a week live customer service, and more!

Whether traveling on a tight budget, looking for a quick weekend getaway, or planning the trip of a lifetime, Frommer's guides and Travelocity.com will make your travel dreams a reality. You've bought the book, now book the trip!

Travelocity.com
A Sabre Company

Frommer's

A New Star-Rating System & Other Exciting News from Frommer's!

In our continuing effort to publish the savviest, most up-to-date, and most appealing travel guides available, we've added some great new features.

Frommer's guides now include a new **star-rating system.** Every hotel, restaurant, and attraction is rated from 0 to 3 stars to help you set priorities and organize your time.

We've also added **seven brand-new features** that point you to the great deals, in-the-know advice, and unique experiences that separate travelers from tourists. Throughout the guide, look for:

Finds	Special finds—those places only insiders know about
Fun Fact	Fun facts—details that make travelers more informed and their trips more fun
Kids	Best bets for kids—advice for the whole family
Moments	Special moments—those experiences that memories are made of
Overrated	Places or experiences not worth your time or money
Tips	Insider tips—some great ways to save time and money
Value	Great values—where to get the best deals

Frommer's®

Newfoundland and Labrador

1st Edition

by Dawn Chafe
&
Doreen Pendgracs

WILEY

John Wiley & Sons Canada, Ltd.

About the Author

Dawn Chafe is an entertaining writer, accomplished interviewer, sharp editor and dedicated researcher. A proud Newfoundlander, Chafe resisted the siren call of outmigration to live and work in her home province. Career highlights include stints in the social policy and post-secondary arenas, as well as a four-year term as a small town mayor. She and her husband Karl, along with their two sons, make their home in Petty Harbour, NL. Since 1998, Dawn has been editor of Atlantic Canada's premier business publication, *Atlantic Business Magazine*.

Published by:

John Wiley & Sons Canada, Ltd.

6045 Freemont Boulevard
Mississauga, ON L5R 4J3

Copyright © 2004 John Wiley & Sons Canada, Ltd. All rights reserved. No part of this work covered by the copyright herein may be reproduced or used in any form or by any means—graphic, electronic or mechanical without the prior written permission of the publisher. Any request for photocopying, recording, taping or information storage and retrieval systems of any part of this book shall be directed in writing to The Canadian Copyright Licensing Agency (Access Copyright). For an Access Copyright license, visit www.accesscopyright.ca or call toll free 1-800-893-5777.

FROMMER'S is a registered trademark of Arthur Frommer. Used under license.

National Library of Canada Cataloguing in Publication Data

Chafe, Dawn, 1968-
    Frommer's Newfoundland and Labrador / Dawn Chafe. — 1st ed.

Includes index.
ISBN 0-470-83223-1

1. Newfoundland and Labrador—Guidebooks. I. Title.

FC2157.C53 2003   917.1804'4   C2003-900259-4

General Manager: Robert Harris
Editor: Michelle Marchetti
Publishing Services Director: Karen Bryan
Cartographer: Mapping Specialists, Ltd.
Cover design: Kyle Gell
Front cover photo: Getty Images / Eastcott Momatiuk / A Pair of Atlantic Puffins
Back cover photo: John Sylvester Photographer / The Narrows, St. John's, NF, CAN
Text layout by IBEX Graphic Communications Inc.
Printer: Tri-Graphic Printing Ltd.

Special Sales

For reseller information, including discounts and premium sales, please call our sales department: Tel: 416-646-7992. For press review copies, author interviews, or other publicity information, please contact our marketing department: Tel: 416-646-4584, Fax: 416-236-4448.

2 3 4 5 6 7 8 9 10

Manufactured in Canada

Contents

List of Maps

Acknowledgments

I'd like to acknowledge the patience and support of my husband and children for sacrificing countless family activities and part of our summer vacation so that I had the time to research and write this book. Also, thanks to the tourism operators in Newfoundland and Labrador for providing the perfect accoutrements to this timeless setting.

An Invitation to the Reader

In researching this book, we discovered many wonderful places—hotels, restaurants, shops. And more. We're sure you'll find others. Please tell us about them, so we can share the information with your fellow travelers in upcoming editions. If you were disappointed with a recommendation, we'd love to know that too. Please write to:

Frommer's Newfoundland and Labrador, 1st Edition
John Wiley & Sons Canada, Ltd. • 22 Worcester Road • Etobicoke, ON M9W 1L1

An Additional Note

Please be advised that travel information is subject to change at any time—and this is especially true of prices. We therefore suggest that you write or call ahead for confirmation when making your travel plans. The authors, editors, and publishers cannot be held responsible for the experiences of readers while traveling. Your safety is important to us, however, so we encourage you to stay alert and be aware of your surroundings. Keep a close eye on cameras, purses and wallets, all favorite targets of thieves and pickpockets.

New! Frommer's Star Ratings & Icons

Every hotel, restaurant and attraction listing in this guide has been ranked for quality, value, service, amenities, and special features using a star-rating scale. In country, state, and regional guides, we also rate towns and regions to help you narrow down your choices and budget your time accordingly. Hotels and restaurants in the Very Expensive and Expensive categories are rated on a scale of one (highly recommended) to three stars (exceptional). Those in the Moderate and Inexpensive categories rate from zero (recommended) to two stars (very highly recommended). Attractions, towns, and regions are rated according to the following scale: zero stars (recommended), one star (highly recommended), two stars (very highly recommended), and three stars (must-see).

In addition to the rating system, we also use seven icons to highlight insider information, useful tips, special bargains, hidden gems, memorable experiences, kid-friendly venues, places to avoid, and other useful information:

(Finds   (Fun Fact   (Kids   (Moments   (Overrated   (Tips   (Value

The following abbreviations are used for credit cards:

AE	American Express	DISC	Discover	V	Visa
DC	Diners Club	MC	MasterCard		

FROMMERS.COM

Now that you have the guidebook to a great trip, visit our website at **www.frommers.com** for travel information on nearly 2,000 destinations. With features updated regularly, we give you instant access to the most current trip-planning information available. At Frommers.com, you'll also find the best prices on air fares, accommodations, and car rentals—you can even book travel online though our travel booking partners. At Frommers.com you'll find the following:

- Daily Newsletter highlighting the best travel deals
- Hot Spot of the Month/Vacation Sweepstakes & Travel Photo Contest
- More than 200 Travel Message Boards
- Outspoken Newsletters and Feature Articles on travel bargains, vacation ideas, tips & resources, and more!

Here's what the critics say about Frommer's:

"Amazingly easy to use. Very portable, very complete."

—Booklist

"The only mainstream guide to list specific prices. The Walter Cronkite of guidebooks—with all that implies."

—Travel & Leisure

"Complete, concise, and filled with useful information."

—New York Daily News

"Hotel information is close to encyclopedic."

—Des Moines Sunday Register

"Detailed, accurate and easy-to-read information for all price ranges."

—Glamour Magazine

The Best of Newfoundland & Labrador

You've done the Florida sun, the European tour, the Caribbean cruise, and the all-inclusive resort, but what you really want is something different. You want to experience something natural and untamed, to relax and rejuvenate without resorting to laziness. You want to create your own vacation memories, not reenact someone else's itinerary. You yearn for a place unlike any other, somewhere that hasn't been sanitized and packaged for official tourist consumption. Well, now you've found it: Newfoundland & Labrador, the Far East of the Western world.

Here, in Canada's youngest and most easterly province, untold adventure awaits your discovery. What's around the next bend in the highway? Could it be a double rainbow? A breaching humpback? A glistening iceberg? A beaming lighthouse? There's no script or schedule here, so you never know what you'll find when you start to explore. The key word here is "explore"—some of your most treasured memories will be found on the roads less traveled.

The rustic majesty that is Newfoundland & Labrador can be summed up in two words: "people" and "place." Both are unforgettable. The inhabitants of this isolated locale are as real as it gets. They are unpretentious, thoughtful, and witty. They'll charm you with their accents and their generous spirit. Though their lifestyle is neither opulent nor lavish, they will never hesitate to help a person in need. It comes from living in a harsh environment where a helping hand can make the difference between survival and some other, ugly, alternative.

Newfoundland & Labrador's landscape and its animal inhabitants are equally remarkable. There are fjords and mountain vistas of stunning beauty. Places where sky meets horizon in blazing color, and where stands of spruce flow in an evergreen sea. Here, salmon launch themselves against the current and traffic slows for road-hopping rabbits. It is a place where howling winds have blown trains off their track and arctic air chills your backbone. As any local will tell you, this is the most blessedly cursed union of land, sea, air, and sky in creation. Come here once, and you'll have a perpetual longing to return.

Up until the last decade, Newfoundland was virtually undiscovered as a tourist destination. Even most Canadians hadn't been to "the Rock." But over the past 10 years, the province has put great effort into promoting itself throughout North America and on the global stage. Newfoundland & Labrador has only recently revealed itself to the world as an exciting destination.

So be patient as you make your way throughout Newfoundland & Labrador, understanding that tourism is a new industry for the province and that services are not as abundant as they are in certain other locales. And really, isn't that why you're coming here in the first place?

Note: The following pages are designed to give you a quick overview of the best Newfoundland & Labrador has to offer. Wherever possible, I have included at least one attraction per category for every region of the province.

(Moments A Contagious Spirit

This is a true story about the potent influence of the Newfoundland character. While traveling on a Toronto subway, a family of four were chatting amongst themselves. Their lilting Irish-English accents signaled that they were obviously from Newfoundland, as did their friendly smiles and greetings to fellow commuters. Surprisingly, that jaded throng of usually sullen subway riders smiled back. Some even nodded in return. It wasn't long before someone asked if they were from Newfoundland. The affirmative response encouraged the stranger to ask if they were on vacation, and if they had yet seen a Toronto Blue Jays baseball game. Hearing that they hadn't, he explained that his company had season tickets set aside for its employees. He said no one was using the tickets for the next day's game, and offered them to the Newfoundland family because they had brightened up his day. He then gave them his business card so they could arrange to pick up the tickets later that evening. A whole subway car full of people actually took the time to acknowledge each other as individuals, one of them even extending his hand in a spontaneous act of generosity, all because a small group of Newfoundlanders had followed their natural instinct to greet their fellow travelers.

1 The Best Travel Experiences

- **Walk the streets of St. John's:** St. John's is one of the most interesting and visually exciting cities I've ever been to. The city is relatively small, and many of the top sights can be found within a four-block radius of the harbor. See chapter 3.

- **Stand on top of Signal Hill:** You literally have a city at your feet when you stand at the base of Cabot Tower (walk around the tower to the other side and you'll be gazing down at the broad expanse of the Atlantic Ocean). It's one of those must-see pilgrimages for any visitor to the capital city, and even for a good many local residents. See chapter 3, p. 67.

- **Watch the sun come up at Cape Spear:** On this, the most easterly point in North America, a spectacular sunrise, swirling surf, and picturesque lighthouse make Cape Spear the perfect location for an unforgettable marriage proposal. Find your inner romantic; see chapter 3, p. 64.

- **Put the wind in your sails on board the *Scademia*:** Head out through the Narrows of St. John's harbor on a 27-m (90-ft.), full-rigged schooner. If that doesn't have you feeling like a true Newfoundlander, the "screech-in" ceremony ought to do the trick. See chapter 3, p. 73.

- **Dance the night away on George Street:** With the most nightclubs per capita in North America all clustered together on a two-block stretch, it's like visiting a northern New Orleans. There's something for everyone on George Street (rap, jazz, traditional, contemporary, and more). Find your favorite nighttime hotspot in section 10, "St. John's After Dark," in chapter 3.

Spirit of Newfoundland *(Value)*

You'll have an unforgettable evening of first-class food and entertainment with **Spirit of Newfoundland Productions** ★★★, the province's best dinner theater experience. Talented singers and actors retain their comic characters throughout the night, even when pressed into service as waiters and waitresses. You may even find yourself spontaneously transformed from passive audience member to unsuspecting active participant! Some of the shows are quintessentially Newfoundland, others, such as tributes to Frank Sinatra and Patsy Cline, have broader appeal. All this plus a delicious three-course meal for just C$45 (US$32). Spirit of Newfoundland Productions take place at two St. John's venues, both located on Duckworth Street. To find out about the latest show, or to make a reservation, call ✆ **709/579-3023**, or go to www.spiritof newfoundland.com.

- **Find your lucky rock at Middle Cove Beach:** Just outside St. John's, this stony beach is covered with striped treasures. If you find a stone with a complete white circle around it, that's your lucky rock. If you find one with a double white circle (like I did), you've got double the luck! It's a cheap way to have some fun, and maybe pick up a few inexpensive souvenirs for friends or family back home. See chapter 3, p. 66.

- **Enjoy a bird's-eye view of Bird Rock:** I felt as though I was sitting on top of the world on that cliff overlooking Bird Rock at **Cape St. Mary's Ecological Reserve.** Imagine gazing into the eyes of thousands of squawking gannets nearly within arm's reach! See chapter 4, p. 92.

- **Get sprayed by the Spout:** A natural geyser that shoots saltwater more than 60m (197 ft.) into the air. You'll be wet, cold, and tired by the time you get there . . . and you won't even notice. You'll be too awestruck by every step along this spectacular seacoast journey. For directions, see chapter 4, p. 81.

- **Experience an active archaeological dig at the Colony of Avalon:** Walk the oldest cobblestone street in North America and see artifacts from a 16th-century settlement. You'll learn about ancient battles for property ownership, and skirmishes with marauding privateers. See chapter 4, p. 90.

- **Dig into history at Bell Island:** It's just a 30-minute boat ride from Portugal Cove, but a giant step back in time when you explore the abandoned iron-ore mines of Bell Island. Or step back even further with a scuba diving expedition to the wreckage of sunken ships that surround the island's perimeter. Find out how you can organize your own Bell Island adventure in chapter 4, p. 102.

- **Explore Cape Bonavista:** This remarkable place at the northern tip of the Bonavista Peninsula has something for everyone. You'll find a colorful lighthouse with a striking view, learn some interesting maritime history, and have a chance to get close to Atlantic puffins. When your eyes have had their fill, head to the nearby town of Bonavista for lunch. See chapter 5, p. 116.

- **Race to the finish at the Clarenville Dragway:** If you enjoy the smell of burning rubber and the sound of roaring engines, you'll thrill over the full-throttle antics of these hot rods, muscle cars, and motorcycle maniacs. It's not the Indy 500, but it's still adrenaline-pumping action. See chapter 5, p. 109.
- **Get carried away by Rising Tide:** Here's professional theater in both indoor and outdoor venues, in the heart of Newfoundland's most visually historical community. Whether it's the comedic characters of the Trinity Pageant, or the haunting tragedy of a more serious dramatic production, you're sure to be impressed by the Rising Tide theater company. Not to be missed! To reserve your seats, see chapter 5, p. 113.
- **Float on a sea of contentment with Mag-Ami Kayaking:** Take some first-class kayak instruction with expert guides who know all the best spots for seeing seabirds, icebergs, caves, and whales. And, even though you'll feel like you could paddle forever, you'll be only mildly disappointed when it's time to stop for a break. That's when your guides break out the kettle for a traditional Newfoundland beach boil-up. See chapter 5, p. 114.
- **Light up your day with a trip to the Cape Bonavista Lighthouse:** This step back in time is informative, introspective, and breathtakingly beautiful. Inside, you'll be greeted by costumed interpreters and a realistic portrayal of life as it once was for the lighthouse keeper and his family. Outside, you'll be equally enraptured by the surrounding countryside and flowing seascape. See chapter 5, p. 116.
- **Chart a course for the Aviation Museum:** Experience the history of Gander's love affair with flight, as depicted through storyboards, scale model displays, and actual decommissioned aircraft. And if you've ever dreamed of becoming a pilot, you can move a step closer to that dream when you park yourself in the cockpit of a DC-38. See chapter 6, p. 133.
- **Applaud enthusiastically for the A.N.D. Company's Summer Theatre Festival:** The only thing you'll forget about this theater company is that the actors are amateurs—such is the range of their repertoire and talent. Your ticket not only gets you access to a great show, but also brings the satisfaction of knowing you're supporting local youth. See chapter 6, p. 134.
- **Cruise the South Coast:** Visit the most isolated communities on the island portion of the province. These rare gems of outport perfection are accessible only by coastal boat. They might not have pavement, but they're also free of traffic jams and road rage. A trip to the South Coast is the best way to get up close and personal with the best (people) and worst (isolation) of rural Newfoundland. See chapter 6, p. 141.
- **Set sail on a Viking adventure:** Take your place at the oar on board a replica Viking *knarr* with Viking Boat Tours. It's a full-fledged Viking-style ocean-going adventure: you can even dress in traditional garb for a more authentic experience. Still, I doubt the Vikings would have approved —only good, clean fun is allowed on this ship. For information on how to book your Nordic adventure, see chapter 7, p. 154.

- **Leave the world behind on Quirpon Island:** This isolated island retreat is the perfect escape from techno-society. Amenities include hearty home-cooked meals, endless waves, iceberg views, and conversations with whales. It's just you and your thoughts for company. See chapter 7, p. 157.
- **Plan an extreme adventure with Driftwood Inn and Backcountry Adventures:** Hidden far from the blacktop is a different kind of highway. Instead of tractor trailers and bumper-to-bumper traffic, this "roadway" is accessible only by snowmobile in winter and ATV in summer. Along the way through this spectacularly mountainous region, you'll cross paths with moose, black bear, and wandering fox. See chapter 7, p. 158.
- **Visit the province's last pocket of French settlement, on the Port au Port Peninsula:** It's the only place in the province where French displaces English as the native language. *Ici, on parle français.* Language, however, is just one part of a larger cultural dynamic. Here you'll find a more overt Roman Catholic heritage, and a genuinely French *joie de vivre*—singularly unique in a society of primarily English and Irish descent. See chapter 7, p. 166.
- **Sail the fjords of Gros Morne:** It's a truly magnificent feeling to sail across **Western Brook Pond** in Gros Morne National Park, as you pass countless waterfalls and feel at peace with nature. All of Gros Morne is a must-see, but for me this was the highlight. See chapter 8, p. 176.
- **Get ringside seats for the best light show on Earth:** Standing on the deck of the St. Barbe–Blanc Sablon ferry, you'll witness the aurora borealis—a celestial fireworks display of unparalleled beauty. The night sky will be lit with random flickers of cascading brilliance, in ever-changing shades of red, gold, and green. As if that weren't enough, you'll get double impact in the water-reflected glory. To book your front-row seat, see chapter 9, p. 185.
- **Climb the lighthouse tower at Point Amour:** Even though my knees didn't especially like it, I truly enjoyed the steep climb to the top of the tallest lighthouse in Atlantic Canada. You'll get a spectacular view (including a bird's-eye view of some of the oldest fossils found in North America), learn quite a bit about naval history and shipwrecks, and have the chance to hike the Raleigh Trail when you're done. See chapter 9, p. 194.

2 The Best Spots for Observing Wildlife & Nature

- **The Fluvarium:** This interesting facility is in the heart of St. John's and next to one of its nicest parks, making it easily accessible to those using public transport and very convenient to campers next door in Pippy Park. The Fluvarium offers a firsthand look at the underwater world of brook trout and other creatures that inhabit Newfoundland's many freshwater ponds. See chapter 3, p. 64.
- **See fish in action at the Ocean Sciences Centre:** It's the unofficial star of Logy Bay, an impressive scientific research facility (open only at certain hours, and via guided tour) that has an outdoor seal tank (no set schedule, drop by anytime). You'll be entertained for

hours by the comical antics of the resident seals as they splash and dive in their own private pool. If you're lucky, you may even see them interacting with Centre staff—and being rewarded for their efforts with a tasty fish. See chapter 3, p. 65.

- **Route 10, The Irish Loop:** Head south of St. John's and you'll find a number of the province's best nature attractions within close proximity. At **Bay Bulls/Witless Bay Ecological Reserve** seabirds abound, numbering more than 2.5 million, including 500,000 Atlantic puffins. The waters are also full of playful humpback whales. A herd of caribou can often be seen from the highway near Trepassey, and if you're really lucky you may be able to watch the humpbacks feeding off the beach at St. Vincent's—the whales actually heave their massive bodies out of the water and snare mouthfuls of food during their descent. See chapter 4, p. 94.

- **Visit a wilderness zoo at the Salmonier Nature Park:** At this temporary retirement/recovery home for aging and wounded animals, you'll see moose, fox, hare, lynx, and more in their natural environment (or almost natural—the holding areas are securely fenced enclosures). The Nature Park is a pleasant walk and education expedition combined with a rare opportunity to view reclusive animals. See chapter 4, p. 91.

- **Communicate with some of the biggest mammals on Earth with Ocean Contact Ltd.:** Join Dr. Beamish and learn how to talk (or the next best thing) with the whales. You'll be spellbound watching Beamish maneuver his Zodiac in and around these graceful giants. To book your tour, see chapter 5, p. 115.

- **Watch salmon return to their annual spawning grounds at the Salmonid Interpretation Centre:** Here you'll get both a surface and an underwater view of these homeward-bound fish as they make their annual against-the-current pilgrimage. See chapter 6, p. 134.

- **White-water raft with Red Indian Adventures:** Your exhilarating ride through breathtaking scenery just might include passing a black bear or moose. You'll see the province in a way you never thought possible from the highway. See chapter 6, p. 139.

- **Twillingate and Iceberg Alley:** This is the place to be if you're thrilled by the sight of towering icebergs and massive whales. Icebergs are visible here from May through July—they seem to linger a bit longer in the bay near Twillingate than they do elsewhere around the province. Humpback whales are in abundance from June through September. See chapter 6, p. 136.

- **The Great Northern Peninsula:** Anyone looking for a moose is bound to spot one here. This remote and rugged part of northwestern Newfoundland is home to many of the province's 150,000 big, brown, beautiful creatures. You'll often see them on or along the highway at dusk or dawn, especially during the fall. See chapter 7, p. 144.

- **Sail amid the glacial castles of the sea with Northland Discovery Tours:** You'll marvel at the cracks and colors in 10,000-year-old icebergs while traveling alongside playful dolphins, whales, and seabirds in their natural environment. To learn how you can get a taste of Northland Discovery's unique eco-tourism adventure (not to mention the purest water on Earth), see chapter 7, p. 153.

- **The Tablelands:** Students of geology already know that there's no better place to be than Newfoundland & Labrador, commonly known as the Rock. And there's no more spectacular example of the world's natural geological forces than this particularly scenic part of Gros Morne National Park, just south of Woody Point. The park has been named a UNESCO World Heritage Site in consideration of this natural wonder. See chapter 8, p. 175.

- **Gros Morne Adventures:** Guided sea kayaking tours through the sheltered waters of Bonne Bay give you a sea-level view of bald eagles, terns, and other wildlife. You'll be gliding through one of the most scenic areas of the province: mountains, fjords, and glacial deposits are just a few of the features you'll encounter along your paddling adventure. See chapter 8, p. 176.

- **Pinware River Provincial Park:** Most of the Labrador Straits area is open, barren land with just a few stands of tuckamore for color. Not here. In Pinware Park you'll find a verdant spruce carpet in a sheltered valley, as well as abundant freshwater fish and extreme kayaking conditions (for experts only!). To learn more about the park, see chapter 9, p. 190.

- **Trans Labrador Highway:** If you're traveling across Labrador, keep a sharp eye on the side of the road. You never know what may cross your path. It could be a porcupine or even a caribou. If you're watching carefully, you just might catch a glimpse of a rare double or triple rainbow. Be extra careful driving the highway at night, though—you're likely to be so entranced by the aurora borealis that you might end up in a ditch! *Note:* The "best of" rating is for what you'll see along the way. It is not an endorsement of the highway itself. See chapter 9.

3 The Best Scenic Drives

- **Cape Spear Road:** Just a 15-minute drive south of St. John's, Cape Spear is the most easterly point in North America, a National Historic Site, and site of the Cape Spear Lighthouse. Be sure to bring a sweater, as Cape Spear is often windy and considerably colder than the city of St. John's. If you're enjoying the drive, continue a little farther south toward the scenic fishing village of Petty Harbour. It won't take you more than an hour to drive the complete circle from St. John's to Cape Spear–Petty Harbour–Goulds–Kilbride and back to St. John's (2 hours if you stop at Cape Spear). See section 5, "Exploring St. John's," in chapter 3.

- **Middle Cove to Pouch Cove** (pronounced "pooch cove"): In the opposite direction from Cape Spear and Petty Harbour are the close-knit communities of Logy Bay–Middle Cove–Outer Cove, Torbay, Flat Rock, and Pouch Cove (follow routes 30 and 20). There's an interesting contrast along the drive: nestled in between the farmland and obviously rural lifestyle are some of the most prestigious properties on the island, evidence of the growing prosperity in this part of the province. See chapter 3.

- **The Irish Loop:** A 4-hour round-trip drive through the heart of Newfoundland's Irish heritage and caribou country. You'll see beautiful coastal communities for all but a short strip between Salmonier and the Trans-Canada Highway. The rest of the drive is a panorama of rugged shore and outport loveliness. Follow Route 10 south of St. John's. If you stay on the same route (the name changes to Route 90 about halfway), only turning right when you reach the Trans-Canada, you'll be carried back to the capital city. See section 2, "The Irish Loop," in chapter 4.

- **The Baccalieu Trail:** This stretch of road gets my vote for the most scenic drive in the province. The tiny outport communities that line the shores of this finger of the Avalon Peninsula between Trinity and Conception bays are simply beautiful. Routes 80 and 70 will take you to inviting communities such as Heart's Delight, Heart's Content, and Harbour Grace. But remember to get off the highway and drive right into the villages in order to truly enjoy the beauty. See section 4, "The Baccalieu Trail," in chapter 4.

- **Route 230 from Trinity Bight to Bonavista:** Beautiful in any season, this stunning stretch of highway is especially breathtaking when cloaked in early fall foliage. You'll find yourself wanting to pull over at every bend in the road so you can really appreciate the incredible views. The shining stars of the journey are the towns of Trinity and Bonavista and the striking landscape seen from the end of the road at Cape Bonavista. See chapter 5.

- **The foot of the Heritage Run:** If you look at the Burin Peninsula on a map, you'll notice it resembles a leg with a foot on the end. The long "leg" of the Heritage Run has some memorable

moments, though for the main it doesn't qualify as a scenic drive. But the loop journey from the ankle to the toe and back (routes 222, 220, and 213) is a different story. Here you'll follow a coastal trail with an obvious maritime theme. Highlights of the trip are the lobster pots, fishing boats, and immaculate wharf facilities you'll spot along the side of the road. See chapter 5.

- **The Kittiwake Coast:** It's a long drive from Gambo through the assorted towns and villages along the north coast (routes 320–330) before heading back to the Trans-Canada at Gander, but it's so worth the effort. En route are picture-perfect picnic spots, a sandy beach (rare in this part of the world), and the community known as the "Venice of Newfoundland." See chapter 6.

- **The Viking Trail:** At the community of Deer Lake you can get on Route 430, which will take you north along the western shore of the Great Northern Peninsula. You'll pass through Gros Morne National Park, Port au Choix National Historic Site, L'Anse aux Meadows National Historic Site, and the town of St. Anthony, where you're likely to see an iceberg or two. In between all these spectacular highlights, the road takes you through some handsomely rugged and remote countryside. See chapter 7.

- **Port au Port Peninsula:** Just west of Stephenville on the west coast of Newfoundland is the last pocket of predominantly French settlement on the island. Here you'll see religious icons and ancient war relics, as well as the largest wooden structure and the highest mountain in the province. See chapter 7.

- **The Straits Highway:** Route 510 takes you from the ferry at Blanc Sablon, Quebec, to the captivating outport of Red Bay, Labrador. It's a good paved road (one of the few in Labrador, so take advantage of it) and gives you a chance to tour the interesting communities and many historical attractions found on the Labrador Straits. Highlights include a sunken ship, a 7,500-year-old burial mound, and the tallest lighthouse in Atlantic Canada. See chapter 9.

4 The Most Picturesque Villages

- **Petty Harbour** (Greater St. John's): Just 15 minutes south of St. John's, this peaceful and quaint fishing village has been the backdrop for a number of films. With its aging fishing sheds, wooden slipways, and cliff-hugging houses tucked within a protective hillside embrace, its attraction as a movie set is readily apparent. It's amazing to find such a picturesque and well-preserved piece of traditional Newfoundland culture just minutes from the capital city. See chapter 3, p. 67.

- **Quidi Vidi Village** (Greater St. John's): Pronounced "kiddee viddee," this historical fishing village has managed to stop time in its tracks. You're not more than 5 minutes' drive from the traffic of St. John's, yet Quidi Vidi has the oldest cottage in North America, horses grazing on the cliffs overlooking the peaceful lake, and timeless fishing sheds snuggling up to the granite cliffs that guard its sheltered harbor. See chapter 3, p. 66.

- **Brigus** (Avalon Peninsula): This tiny fishing village has won a "Tidy Towns Award" for its pristine appearance. You'll see lots of beautiful flowers and overhanging trees lining the narrow streets that lead to the harbor, and an abundance of heritage-style homes that give the town a real step-back-in-time feel. If you're looking to make the modern world go away for a while, Brigus is the perfect retreat. See section 4, "The Baccalieu Trail," in chapter 4.

- **Dildo** (Avalon Peninsula): If the name alone isn't enough to spark your curiosity, you might be attracted by this historical fishing village's proud seafaring history. And then there's its aesthetic beauty: it was named one of Canada's prettiest towns, and you're sure to agree when looking at the wonderful view of Trinity Bay. Green space and simple wooden fences add to Dildo's rustic charm. See section 4, "The Baccalieu Trail," in chapter 4.

- **Ferryland** (Avalon Peninsula): Aside from the unique lure of its ongoing archaeological dig (impressive as that is), the town of Ferryland is a strikingly attractive community. It flows down from the hills in graceful descent to sea level, layers of green grass and rocky knolls sprinkled amidst stubborn settlement. On the small peninsula extending out from Ferryland Harbour is a lighthouse, its blinking eye a haunting reminder of the tragedy that can befall unwary sailors. To plan your visit to Ferryland, see chapter 4, p. 85.

- **Trinity** (Bonavista Peninsula): Time seems to have stood still for this quaint fishing village that has preserved many of its 19th-century buildings. Or, if it hasn't stood still, there's certainly a concerted community effort to turn back the clock. If you climb the hill from Courthouse Road behind the Royal Bank just before sunset, you'll get one of the most beautiful views available anywhere. See chapter 5, p. 109.

- **Twillingate** (Central Region): Here is a community perfectly positioned for optimum iceberg viewing. With such impressive floating monoliths frequenting the shore every spring and early summer, you'll be forgiven if your attention wanders from the man-made beauty in and around the town. But rest assured, Twillingate is indeed a complementary composition of raw landscape and human construction. You'll find it at the northern tip of Route 340. See chapter 6, p. 136.

- **Francois** (Central Region): At the opposite end of the compass from Twillingate is an isolated outport village, accessible only by boat. It has neither paved road nor hotel, but that doesn't put Francois at a disadvantage. Majestic cliffs ring the little community, and wooden boardwalks serve as the local land highway (the real highway is the ocean). You'll have to work to find it, as it's hidden from view on a narrow strip of land at the head of a fjord. See chapter 6, p. 141.

- **Port aux Basques** (Western Region): An often under-appreciated community, Port aux Basques is more than a relay station for the Newfoundland–Nova Scotia ferry. It has both traditional architectural beauty and an impressive blasted-rock harbor entrance. It takes on a romantic ambiance in the twilight hours thanks to the guidelights used to illuminate the ferry terminal. And the outdoor amphitheater and waterfront shops invite you to stroll around the harbor. See chapter 7, p. 163.

- **Battle Harbour** (Labrador): This restored fishing village has 230-year-old buildings and a simple beauty that is nearly haunting. Take the half-hour boat ride over to Battle Island and escape the hustle and bustle of the modern world, whether for a full-day's visit or overnight in the nostalgic Battle Harbour Inn. See section 1, "The Labrador Straits," in chapter 9.

 Getting to Know Salvage

On the western edge of the Eastern Region, following Route 310 north of Glovertown, is one of the most picturesque (and most photographed!) fishing communities in the province. Salvage (pronounced "sal-*vage*") is a visual treat of stages, wharves, sheds, and slipways nestled in and around a granite shore. This, plus the never-ending ocean serenade and houses built in the unlikeliest of places, make Salvage an unforgettable destination.

5 The Best Hikes & Walking Tours

- **The Haunted Hike** (St. John's): Looking for something different? Try this evening stroll in St. John's with the Rev. Thos. Wyckham Jarvis, Esq. He'll take you on a rather eerie walk through some of the oldest graveyards in the city, and add quite a bit of theatrics along the way to keep your adrenaline pumping. See chapter 3, p. 74.

- **Signal Hill–Battery Trail** (St. John's): Not for the faint of heart! This walk starts at a pinnacle height towering over the capital city and follows a thigh-burning descent along a dizzying path less than 3m (10 ft.) from the edge of a 61-m (200-ft.) drop to the North Atlantic. Those brave enough to attempt it are rewarded with the most spectacular scenery in the city. See chapter 3, p. 68.
- **The East Coast Trail** (Avalon Region): This fantastic trail system is easily accessible from St. John's and takes you along the beautiful coastline of the Avalon Region. You can see whales and seabirds close to shore, and parts of the trail are easy enough for the beginner. It's divided into sections so you can do as much or as little as you like, tailoring your hike(s) to your time frame and skill level. See chapter 4, p. 79.
- **The Discovery Trail** (Eastern Region): Similar to the East Coast Trail, this is also organized into sections of varying difficulty. Choose your hiking route based on what you want to see (sea stacks? abandoned communities? rocky outcrops?) as well as the level of difficulty. See chapter 5, p. 115.
- **Port au Choix National Historic Site** (Western Region): A trio of excellent hiking trails, each with its own attributes, are at this intriguing site on the southern end of the Great Northern Peninsula. The **Phillips Garden Walking Trail** stands out because of its accessibility and its guided interpretive walks. See chapter 7, p. 147.
- **Gros Morne National Park:** It's impossible to select one particular trail from this park as the best; they're all very dynamic, and you can easily find one that meets your own abilities or interests. If you're an experienced hiker and enjoy the challenges of a difficult climb, you'll find that **Gros Morne Trail,** the trail that leads to the peak of Gros Morne Mountain, offers the most spectacular scenery. See chapter 8, p. 169.
- **Edible Trail Hike** (Terra Nova National Park): Ever wonder what you would live on if you were lost in the woods? You'll know the answer after you take part in this guided interpretive walk. Equally important, you'll know which plants to avoid! See chapter 8, p. 182.
- **The Raleigh Trail:** On this coastal hike at Point Amour, Labrador, you can find 500-million-year-old fossils, parts of a shipwreck, waterfalls, mouthwatering berries, and some interesting fauna without having to go too far off the beaten track. The trail begins at the site of the tallest lighthouse in Atlantic Canada. See chapter 9, p. 197.

6 The Best Family Activities

- **Fluvarium** (St. John's): A first-class interpretation facility where visitors can go beneath the surface to see trout and underwater species (the building boasts a glass-walled viewing area). Try to time your visit for the day's scheduled feeding. See chapter 3, p. 64.
- **Johnson Geo Centre** (St. John's): A geological display that's fun for the whole family. Adults will appreciate the educational interpretive program, while teenagers will be impressed by the oversized displays (and cool audiovisual presentation with simulated rain and volcanic eruptions). Younger children will entertain themselves for hours just squirting water at the exposed rock wall. See chapter 3, p. 65.

- **Railway Coastal Museum** (St. John's): If you like trains—and most everyone does—you'll appreciate the newest family attraction in the province's capital city. Don't miss the moving train mobile. See chapter 3, p. 69.

- **Avondale Railway Station Museum** (Avalon Region): The Trans-Canada Highway is a relatively new piece of infrastructure for the province, so it's not that long ago that trains played an important role in Newfoundland & Labrador. You can see just how important they were at the Avondale Railway Station Museum, the oldest railway station in the province. There are decommissioned cars on display, and during the summer months children can go for a ride on one of the museum's small rail cars. See chapter 4, p. 98.

- **Wilderness Newfoundland Adventures** (Avalon Region): Kayaking is fun for the young and the young-at-heart. Wilderness Newfoundland Adventures has specially designed kayaks so children too young to paddle on their own can ride with mom or dad. And, for beginners, there's expert on-shore instruction before heading out onto the water. See chapter 4, p. 82.

- **Terra Nova Golf Resort** (Eastern Region): Golfing, nature hikes, mini-golf, tennis, basketball, swimming, a comprehensive children's program . . . what more could you possibly want? There's something for every vacationer at Terra Nova Golf Resort. See chapter 5, p. 108.

- **Trinity Loop** (Eastern Region): This amusement/activity park features a working miniature train. The train does a loop around the park, overlooking the pond with its water-recreation facilities (paddle boats, kayaks, canoes, and rowboats) as well as the playground and Ferris wheel. See chapter 5, p. 113.

- **Frenchman's Cove Provincial Park** (Eastern Region): Children need downtime, too. So, instead of always trying to find activities to fill their day, choose a vacation destination that gives them ample amounts of unstructured playtime. Frenchman's Cove offers a pebble beach, playground, and freshwater pond for outdoor swimming. Don't worry, the adults won't find themselves at loose ends—they can always avail of the onsite Robert Heaslip–designed nine-hole golf course. See chapter 5, p. 124.

- **Splash-n-Putt** (Eastern Region): The largest waterpark in the province, with a 91-m (300-ft.) waterslide. Comes complete with bumper cars, go-karts, and mini-golf. See chapter 5, p. 126.

- **Norstead** (Western Region): This reenactment village depicts the everyday life of Norsemen—and women—from about A.D. 800 to 1000. Norstead's wonderful Discovery Program for kids offers a hands-on opportunity to participate in the various activities that would have been carried on in the settlement. Even the teens will be shocked out of their chronic boredom by the clanging swords and hand-to-hand combat of the mock battles. See chapter 7, p. 156.

- **Newfoundland Insectarium & Butterfly Pavilion** (Western Region): What kid doesn't like bugs or butterflies? This is a really neat facility where kids can have a great time watching honeybees buzzing about, stretching out their hands to catch a butterfly, getting some bug-related souvenirs to take home, and having an ice cream when they're done. See chapter 7, p. 159.

- **Marble Mountain** (Western Region): Winter fun for the whole family (except toddlers or infants). The 34 ski runs are of varying difficulty, making them suitable for everyone from expert to novice. For the younger set, there's certified ski instruction and a supervised play program, which means both parents and children get to enjoy the slope on their own terms. It's especially attractive to families traveling with teenagers. See chapter 7, p. 162.

- **Terra Nova National Park:** Terra Nova gets high marks for its family activities. The park has an excellent Junior Naturalist program, nice campgrounds, a sandy beach for sports and swimming, campfire concert series, great hands-on displays at Salton's Marine Interpretation Centre, and a fantastic educational boat tour. See chapter 8.

7 The Best Places to Discover Local History & Culture

- **Signal Hill** (St. John's): This National Historic Site offers the best view of St. John's, just a short ride from downtown up the hill and past the Geo Centre. It was here that Guglielmo Marconi received the first wireless transatlantic signal, using a kite to catch the faint transmission from Poldhu, England. Climb the Cabot Tower and time your visit to take in the Signal Hill Military Tattoo (at the Queen's Battery Interpretation Centre). See chapter 3, p. 67.

- **Newman Wine Vaults** (St. John's): It's an unassuming brick building on the outside, a near-solid rock structure on the inside. Learn how an accidental side trip led to Newman Port's return to this North Atlantic island for wine aging. See chapter 3, p. 63.

- **Basilica of St. John the Baptist** (St. John's): For years the largest and most imposing structure on the St. John's skyline, the Basilica was one of the few buildings to survive the Great Fires that plagued the capital city during the early part of the 20th century. A highlight of your visit will be a viewing of the Veiled Virgin statue. See chapter 3, p. 63.

- **Quidi Vidi Battery** (St. John's): In the early battles for control of this rich fishing colony, residents constructed heavy fortifications at strategic locations throughout the city. This quiet hill overlooking Quidi Vidi Harbour was one of them. Today, costumed interpreters explain the purpose of the installation as well as the number of people who resided there and the conditions under which they lived. See chapter 3, p. 66.

 Exploring St. John's Art Galleries

Artists are acknowledged mediums for the ideas and attitudes of their cultural generations. You can see (and buy) the work of some of the most talented artists in the province through one of several downtown art galleries: Christina Parker, Emma Butler, and Lane. The new provincial art gallery and museum, The Rooms, was not open at the time of writing but is scheduled to open in 2004. See chapter 3, p. 69.

- **James J. O'Mara Pharmacy Museum** (St. John's): Also known as Apothecary Hall, it displays the tools of the trade for pharmacists of yesteryear. Some of the items will look familiar, but others will leave you scratching your head in puzzlement. As in, they used that for *what?* See chapter 3, p. 68.
- **No. 2 Mine & Museum** (Avalon Region): Bell Island will be of special interest to anyone interested in mining. Just a short boat ride (which you catch in Portugal Cove, a short drive from St. John's) takes you a world away on a 1-hour tour of an abandoned underground iron-ore mine, where you'll examine interesting artifacts and photos depicting the people and tools used to tunnel under Bell Island and beneath the ocean floor. See chapter 4, p. 102.
- **Colony of Avalon** (Avalon Region): This independently run National Historic Site offers a world-class Interpretation Centre and the chance to have a firsthand look at an ongoing archaeological dig site. Archaeologists are continuing to uncover remnants of the first successful planned colony in Newfoundland, settled in 1621. See chapter 4, p. 90.
- **Hawthorne Cottage** (Avalon Region): The former home of famous Arctic explorer Captain Bob Bartlett includes intriguing insights into the life and times of the man and his family, as well as the struggles he faced on his Arctic expeditions. See chapter 4, p. 98.
- **Dildo Fisheries Interpretation Centre:** This is a fascinating facility if you're interested in the intricacies of a fish hatchery and want to learn more about the way of life for Newfoundlanders of the not-so-distant past as well as the

Native peoples who once inhabited Dildo Island. Plus, it comes with a replica of a giant squid that was caught in the area! See chapter 4, p. 98.
- **Woody Island** (Eastern Region): Experience life in a now-resettled Newfoundland community. Learn why it was so hard for people to leave their homes, despite promises of better jobs, health care, and community services. See chapter 5, p. 106.
- **Trinity Historical Properties** (Eastern Region): The entire community of Trinity is a living heritage village, with residents embracing their past as the route to future prosperity. Historical highlights include the Lester-Garland Premises, Hiscock House, Trinity Museum, Court House, and Green Family Forge. See chapter 5, p. 112.
- **Ryan Premises National Historic Site** (Eastern Region): This cluster of 19th-century buildings is a restoration of the merchant premises that served as the hub of a once-thriving fishing community. The Interpretive Centre has an excellent display about changes that have affected the province's fishery. Also check out the replica in the harbor of the *Matthew,* the three-masted 15th-century vessel sailed by John Cabot to Newfoundland in 1497. See chapter 5, p. 118.
- **Burin Heritage Museum** (Eastern Region): The communities of Grand Bank and Fortune are among the closest in the world to the rich fishing grounds of the Grand Banks. Through interpretive panels and traveling exhibits, this museum pays tribute to that heritage. See chapter 5, p. 126.
- **Barbour Living Heritage Village** (Central Region): Similar to the

Ryan Premises, but on a larger scale. It's not just a restored commercial property, but a series of reconstructed buildings typical of a 1900 fishing village. They're more than just historical monuments, however: these multi-purpose buildings also serve as the local museum, theater, and art gallery. See chapter 6, p. 137.

- **Boyd's Cove Beothuk Interpretation Centre** (Central Region): With all the hype about John Cabot discovering Newfoundland, and even the Vikings arriving a millennium ago, it's easy to forget that there were permanent residents here long before the Europeans arrived. Boyd's Cove is one of those sites that helps us remember. Although little is known about Newfoundland's now-extinct Beothuk inhabitants, Boyd's Cove sheds some light on who they were, how they lived, and why they were so fond of covering themselves and their tools with red ocher. See chapter 6, p. 138.

- **Dorset Soapstone Quarry** (Central Region): Even before the Beothuk, there were Dorset Indians on the island 2,000 years ago. Proof of their existence can be found in the province's earliest known mine, where the Dorset mined soapstone for use as bowls and cooking pots. See chapter 6, p. 140.

- **Conne River Mi'kmaq Reserve** (Central Region): Take part in a powwow celebrating the unique culture of the island's existing native population, the Conne River Mi'kmaq. The band is successfully integrating elements of modern culture into its traditional lifestyle. See chapter 6, p. 140.

- **Port au Choix National Historic Site** (Western Region): What is it about Port au Choix that has made it the location of choice for several different Native populations? Archaeologists are still trying to puzzle the answer from the clues left behind from past civilizations (including the Maritime Archaics, the Groswater, and the Dorset-Paleoeskimo, dating as far back as 5,500 years ago). See chapter 7, p. 147.

- **Grenfell Interpretation Centre** (Western Region): This is a recommended stop for anyone interested in the early medical history of northern Newfoundland & Labrador. Learn about Sir Wilfred Thomason Grenfell, the English doctor who became a local hero to the Inuit and early settlers of the region. See chapter 7, p. 153.

- **L'Anse aux Meadows National Historic Site** (Western Region): Around A.D. 1000, a group of Vikings settled at L'Anse aux Meadows on the northeastern tip of the Great Northern Peninsula. An excellent Visitor Centre guides you in your exploration of this site, where you'll walk among the remnants of a 1,000-year-old Viking village. Plus, there are reenactors on hand to demonstrate how these early settlers might have interacted with each other. See chapter 7, p. 156.

- **Battle Harbour National Historic District** (Labrador): Similar to the Ryan Premises of Bonavista but even older at about 230 years, this restored community tells the story of the local fishery and how Battle Harbour was once the hub of Labrador. Battle Harbour is the only intact salt-fishing village left in the province and can be reached by a 30-minute boat ride to Battle Island. See section 1, "Exploring the Labrador Straits," in chapter 9.

- **Red Bay National Historic Site** (Labrador): This remote outpost on the Labrador coast was once the whaling capital of the world. Rumor has it that the name itself came from the color of the water, which was supposedly so bright with whales' blood that it flowed red. Inside the interpretive center is a reproduction of a wooden whaling ship, surrounded by the mandible (jawbone) of a bowhead whale. The area wasn't treacherous just to whales, however; at least two ships are known to have gone down in the waters of Red Bay. For more information, see chapter 9, p. 195.

8 The Best Festivals & Special Events

- **Newfoundland & Labrador Folk Festival** (St. John's): This is an absolute must for all lovers of traditional music. The three-day event takes place in downtown St. John's during the first weekend of August and provides a good variety of music that includes folk, country, bluegrass, and Celtic. See chapter 3, p. 70.
- **St. John's Royal Regatta** (St. John's): This is the biggest event of the year for St. John's; its importance is recognized by its status as a municipal holiday. The oldest continuous sporting event in North America offers a day of fixed-seat rowing races and lots of fun for the whole family at Quidi Vidi Lake (such as games of chance and live entertainment). See chapter 3, p. 71.
- **George Street Festival** (St. John's): You'll enjoy the George Street Festival if you're young (or at the very least young-at-heart) and don't mind loud music and crowds. During the six-day event, a two-block stretch of the downtown street is closed off, and bars open up their doors and bring in a lineup of terrific entertainment. See chapter 3, p. 71.
- **Southern Shore Shamrock Festival** (Avalon Region): Traditional Irish-Newfoundland music mingles with some modern material in this popular annual event. Many of the province's best-known performers are from this part of the province, so the lineup is always guaranteed to impress. See chapter 4, p. 85.
- **NaGeira Theatre Festival** (Avalon Region): Newfoundland is famous for its high-quality, informal, community theatrical productions. If the thought of sitting in a beautiful seaside setting and being entertained appeals to you, you're quite likely to enjoy this festival held in Carbonear each summer. See chapter 4, p. 99.
- **Brigus Blueberry Festival** (Avalon Region): Arrive early, because there's always a crowd in Brigus for this popular event. It's an excellent venue for buying locally made products such as knitted goods, quilts, and, of course, blueberry products. See chapter 4, p. 95.
- **Summer in the Bight Theatre Festival** (Eastern Region): Each year between June and October, the **Rising Tide Theatre** puts on a number of professional shows that give poignant life to the Newfoundland character and lifestyle. Staged at both indoor and outdoor venues, Summer in the Bight includes the renowned **Trinity Pageant.** See chapter 5, p. 113.
- **Fish, Fun & Folk Festival** (Central Region): One of the largest and longest running folk festivals in Newfoundland, this event is

held the last full weekend of July in Twillingate. If you want to have a great time with the family and gain deeper insight into what makes Newfoundlanders tick, plan to take in this event. You're likely to see a few icebergs at the same time, because Twillingate is one of the best places in the province to spot bergs (even late in July). See chapter 6, p. 139.

- **Exploits Valley Salmon Festival** (Central Region): A five-day family event and salmon celebration held each July in Grand Falls–Windsor. Take time to enjoy a performance at the highly regarded **Summer Theatre Festival.** See chapter 6, p. 134.
- **Gros Morne Theatre Festival** (Gros Morne National Park Region): Treat yourself to a dinner theater production of excellent regional music, comedy, and drama while in the area of Gros Morne National Park between June and September. The festival is held in the northern part of the park. Twice weekly, you'll have the chance to enjoy a theatrical performance as well as taste some of the best pan-fried cod found anywhere. See chapter 8, p. 173.
- **Bakeapple Folk Festival** (Labrador): Time your visit to the Labrador Straits for the second weekend of August, when the bakeapple berries are ripe and the biggest summer event of the year is taking place. You'll get four days of fun, music, and merriment. See chapter 9, p. 196.

9 The Best Hotels & Resorts

- **The Fairmont Newfoundland** (115 Cavendish Square, St. John's; *℃* **800/441-1414** or 709/726-4980; www.fairmont.com): The best full-service property in the province. Although it lacks an outwardly Newfoundland style because of its size and branding, you will still find the unique island character in the personality of the caring and professional staff. See chapter 3, p. 51.
- **Murray Premises** (5 Beck's Cove, St. John's; *℃* **866/738-7773** or 709/738-7773; www.murray premiseshotel.com): This is my favorite smaller hotel in St. John's. You simply can't beat the attention to detail so evident at this beautifully decorated boutique hotel. The staff and management are top-notch, and although the hotel does not offer the full range of services you'll find at the Fairmont, everything they do offer—most notably an exceptional standard of service—will ensure your stay is enjoyable. See chapter 3, p. 52.
- **Celtic Rendezvous Cottages By The Sea** (Route 10 to Bauline East; *℃* **866/334-3341** or 709/334-3341; www.celticrendezvous cottages.com): Don't stay here if a long list of amenities is important to you. But if you're looking for a place where you can hear the surf pounding from inside your cabin or while sitting on the porch overlooking the rugged coastline, this is a great choice. The cabins provide a retreat-style atmosphere within 45 minutes' drive of St. John's. See chapter 4, p. 84.
- **The Wilds at Salmonier River** (Route 90, Salmonier Line; *℃* **866/888-9453** or 709/229-5444; www.thewilds.nf.net): Even Fido is welcome at this terrific family resort. The Wilds has self-contained cabins as well as hotel-style rooms in the main building. A great golf course is on-site, and you're just minutes from

Salmonier Nature Park. See chapter 4, p. 88.

- **Bird Island Resort** (Main Rd., St. Bride's; ℭ **888/337-2450** or 709/337-2450; www.birdislandresort.com): Fully equipped efficiency units ideal for traveling families. All-ages fun includes mini-golf, horseshoe pits, and fitness center. There are also laundry facilities on-site—essential for when wee ones make big messes. See chapter 4, p. 93.

- **Kilmory Resort and Trailer Park** (Route 210, Swift Current; ℭ **709/549-2410;** www.kilmory.nf.ca): If you were to imagine the perfect location for a cottage, you'd probably conjure up a location with privacy, alongside a pond or lake with timber-studded hills rising in the background. That's exactly what you'll find at Kilmory, along with a pool, playground, and rustic-luxe facilities. See chapter 5, p. 122.

- **Terra Nova Golf Resort** (Port Blandford; ℭ **709/543-2525;** www.terranovagolf.com): This fantastic full-service family resort offers a great kids' program, a championship golf course, and is ideally situated for touring the Discovery Trail as well as Terra Nova National Park. See chapter 5, p. 108.

- **BlueWater Lodge & Retreat** (Trans-Canada Highway near Gander; ℭ **709/424-4600;** www.relax-at-bluewater.ca): A wonderful place to stay while touring Notre Dame Bay and other points in the Central Region, the lodge has a private, serene setting on a small lake, making it a perfect retreat for anyone really wanting to get away from it all. See chapter 6, p. 136.

- **Vinland Motel** (West Street, St. Anthony; ℭ **800/563-7578** or 709/454-8843; www.vinlandmotel.com/vinland.htm): The Vikings never had it so good. You'll be surprised by the number and quality of amenities offered here, some of them usually available only in much larger establishments. Highlights include a sauna, hot tub, and massage therapist. See chapter 7, p. 152.

- **Marble Mountain Cabins** (Dogwood Dr., Steady Brook; ℭ **877/497-5673** or 709/634-2237; www.explorenewfoundland.com): It doesn't have the more exclusive ambiance of the official Marble Mountain Resort, and that's a good thing. I find these cabins are actually cozier and more inviting than their more expensive counterparts. The ample on-site amenities (sauna, fitness facility, playground) add even more value to the package. See chapter 7, p. 161.

- **Strawberry Hill Resort** (Exit 10 off Route 1 to Little Rapids; ℭ **877/434-0066** or 709/634-0066; www.strawberryhill.net): When previous guests include a former prime minister and royalty, you know it has to be exceptional. And it is. Outside the luxury of the resort itself, Strawberry Hill adjoins a teeming salmon river and scenic walking trails. See chapter 7, p. 162.

- **Shallow Bay Motel & Cabins** (Route 430, Cow Head; ℭ **800/563-1946** or 709/243-2471; www.shallowbaymotel.com): Here you'll find a kid-friendly place that takes some of the vacation stress off mom and dad. Beachcombing, all-ages theater, and mini-golf are among the many features that make Shallow Bay attractive to traveling families. See chapter 8, p. 172.

- **Bluestone Inn** (34 Queen's Rd., St. John's; © 877/754-9876 or 709/754-7544; http://theblue stoneinn.com): Modern chic blends effortlessly with classic architectural design for a one-of-a-kind B&B. This place has it all: splendid downtown location, an interesting history, superlative food, and spacious rooms. See chapter 3, p. 53.

- **Winterholme Heritage Inn** (79 Rennies Mill Rd., St. John's; © 800/599-7829 or 709/739-7979; www.winterholmeheritage inn.com): Bring your neck brace —you'll need it from constantly staring upwards at the ornately carved woodwork. If you're a real romantic, this may be the place for you—at least for one night, as the rates are pretty steep. See chapter 3, p. 54.

- **Hagan's Hospitality Home** (Route 10, Aquaforte; © 709/363-2688; www.haganshospitality. com): It's not luxurious by any means, but you'll feel like royalty under the attentive care of Rita Hagan. Features hearty home-made food and white-glove cleanliness. See chapter 4, p. 86.

- **Dogberry Hill B&B** (Portugal Cove–St. Philip's; © 709/895-6353; www.dogberryhill.com): Just 15 minutes' drive from St. John's, this beautifully designed B&B offers the finest linens and haute cuisine. If you don't mind paying a little more for that extra level of service and amenities, you'll really enjoy a stay at the Dogberry. See chapter 4, p. 101.

- **Inn By The Bay** (78 Front Rd., Dildo; © 888/339-7829 or 709/582-3170; www.innbythebay dildo.com): Who can resist staying in one of "Canada's 10 Prettiest Towns"? This lovely B&B has an attentive owner and a waterfront location, and it's right in the heart of Dildo, an odd-sounding but very beautiful fishing village. See chapter 4, p. 96.

- **Campbell House** (Trinity Bay; © 877/464-7700 or 709/464-3377; www.trinityvacations.com): This is a wonderful B&B in the scenic village of Trinity. Gover House is one of the buildings that make up Campbell House—and my favorite because of its large deck overlooking Trinity Bay. Not suitable for children. See chapter 5, p. 110.

- **Fishers' Loft Inn** (Mill Road, Port Rexton; © 877/464-3240; www.fishersloft.com): A short drive from Trinity, this remote property with an ethereal atmosphere is perfect for anyone seeking peace, tranquility, and really great food. See chapter 5, p. 111.

- **Humberview B&B** (11 Humberview Dr., Deer Lake; © 888/635-4818 or 709/635-4818; www.thehumberview.com): This B&B offers unparalleled modern luxury in an executive-style home, replete with Grecian columns and four-poster bed in the master suite. You'll wish you could pack it in your suitcase to take home with you. See chapter 7, p. 158.

- **Battle Harbour Inn** (Battle Island, Labrador; © 709/921-6957 or 709/921-6216; www. battleharbour.com): Looking to step back in time? This small inn will enable you to do just that. It has wood stoves and oil lamps, and the setting is in the oldest intact salt-fish community in the province. See chapter 9, p. 189.

- **The Bonavista** (Fairmont Newfoundland, St. John's; ✆ 709/726-4980): Every Friday, you'll find a terrific buffet-style "Jiggs Dinner"—a traditional Newfoundland meal of boiled beef and cabbage—that is so good, even the locals come here for it. The Fairmont is also home to **The Cabot Club,** a pricier restaurant with exquisite food and a dynamite view, for those extra-special evenings when you're looking for something more upscale. See chapter 3, p. 57–58.

- **Magnum & Steins** (284 Duckworth St., St. John's; ✆ 709/576-6500): Fine dining in eclectic, funky surroundings. A masterpiece of contemporary gastronomical delights—not to be missed! See chapter 3, p. 58.

- **The Bread Pig** (21 Queen's Rd., St. John's; ✆ 709/579-4788): This is a good place to come if you're looking for a casual bistro-style atmosphere. Lunches include gourmet pizzas, steamed mussels, and a variety of soups and sandwiches. The Bread Pig is also a bakery and chocolatier, so you're bound to find something to tempt you here. See chapter 3, p. 58.

- **Nautical Nellies** (201 Water St., St. John's; ✆ 709/738-1120): Great food, big portions, and reasonable prices in pub surroundings—that's what you'll find at Nautical Nellies. It's both small and very popular, making it hard to get a table. Sorry, they don't accept reservations. See chapter 3, p. 61.

- **Captain's Table Restaurant** (Route 10 to Mobile; ✆ 709/334-2278; www.captainstable.nf.ca): This is the place to go if you're looking for the best fish and chips or pan-fried cod on the Avalon Peninsula. You can get a good selection of Newfoundland favorites here, and the location is handy if you're driving the Irish Loop. See chapter 4, p. 84.

- **Colony Café** (Route 10, Ferryland; ✆ 709/432-3030; www.ferryland.com/colonycafe): A professional French chef waits to tempt your taste buds with succulent seafood and rich desserts. Situated next to the Colony of Avalon archaeological dig in Ferryland. See chapter 4, p. 86.

- **Skipper's Café** (42 Campbell St., Bonavista; ✆ 709/468-7150): It's worth the drive to this lovely waterfront restaurant in the historic village of Bonavista if you like seafood and don't want to pay big prices. You'll find terrific seafood chowder, cod au gratin, and other delectable dishes—a great reward after doing some touring of the historical sites in the village and at Cape Bonavista. See chapter 5, p. 118.

- **Alcock & Brown's** (Hotel Gander, 100 Trans-Canada Highway [Route 1]; ✆ 800/563-2988 or 709/256-3931): When you can't make up your mind between upscale and casual, head to Alcock & Brown's. It's both an intimate fine-dining room and a fun family restaurant—with the menu to match. See chapter 6, p. 132.

- **Norseman Restaurant & Gallery** (Route 436, L'Anse aux Meadows Harbour; ✆ 877/623-2018): A meal here can be a much-appreciated treat at the end of a long road. The Norseman is one of the better fine-dining restaurants in the province, with a similarly stellar wine list. See chapter 7, p. 154.

- **Deer Lake Irving Big Stop** (TCH Route 1, Deer Lake; ✆ 709/635-2129): This is by no means a fancy place, but if you're looking for solid fare at reasonable prices in the Deer Lake area, you can't beat Big Stop. Portions are ample and they offer traditional Newfoundland favorites, making it a popular choice for local residents. See chapter 7, p. 159.

- **Thirteen West** (13 West St., Corner Brook; ✆ **709/634-1300):** Nouvelle cuisine that would be just as much at home in Montreal as it is in Newfoundland's smallest city. See chapter 7, p. 162.

- **Harbour Restaurant** (Main Road, Port aux Basques; ✆ **709/ 695-3238**): You're in Port aux Basques, either just disembarking the ferry or preparing to leave. Either way, you have an hour or two before you begin the next leg of your journey. Where can you find the sustenance to help you continue on your way? The Harbour Restaurant, with delicious homestyle favorites as well as a very good selection of pizza and pub snacks, makes an excellent choice. See chapter 7, p. 165.

- **Anchor Pub & Dining Room** (Ocean View Motel, Rocky Harbour; ✆ **800/563-9887** or 709/458-2730): When you have a longing for lobster, they know how to serve it up right. The picturesque setting is a bonus. See chapter 8, p. 172.

- **Basque Dining Room** (Northern Light Inn, L'Anse au Clair; ✆ **800/563-3188** or 709/931-2332): Excellent value for delicious food, especially the seafood and traditional Labrador meals (like caribou). See chapter 9, p. 191.

- **Whaler's Restaurant** (Red Bay, Labrador; ✆ **709/920-2156**): Want the best fish and chips in the province? Head over to the Labrador Straits and try the Chalupa fish and chips at Whaler's. They're tasty, tangy, and value-priced. And the restaurant is located in historic Red Bay, where you can finally find the answer to the riddle, What is a Chalupa? See p. 192.

Planning Your Trip to Newfoundland & Labrador

A visit to Canada's most easterly province takes planning, but your efforts will be amply rewarded. You'll be taken with the warmth of the people, always quick with a smile and a friendly greeting. You'll enjoy spontaneous walks off the beaten path as you go exploring for migratory birds and follow the sounds of unseen waterfalls. But first you have to get here. The information on the following pages is designed to make your travel planning as informed as possible.

Canada's Far East

Newfoundland & Labrador is the official name for the province, which combines two very distinct regions. Newfoundland is an island, whereas Labrador is part of the mainland, adjacent to Quebec. The official abbreviation for the province is NL. A mere 3,050km (1,895 miles) from Ireland, Newfoundland is the closest point in North America to Europe. By comparison, the capital city of St. John's is double that distance from the border of Canada's most westerly province, British Columbia.

2 Visitor Information

Contact **Tourism Newfoundland & Labrador** to request a free *Travel Guide, Hunting and Fishing Guide,* or *Highway Map.* Reach them by mail at P.O. Box 8700, St. John's, NL A1B 4J6; call © **800/563-6353** or 709/ 729-2830; or find them on the Web at www.gov.nl.ca/tourism. This Frommer's guidebook will give you a more richly detailed, first-person perspective of travel throughout Newfoundland & Labrador. And because this guidebook follows the same regional divisions as the provincial *Travel Guide,* you can easily cross-reference the two.

Entry Requirements & Customs

ENTRY REQUIREMENTS
Like just about every jurisdiction in our world post–September 11, 2001, strict security surrounds entry into Canada. Photo identification is required, especially if traveling by air. Keep it on your person at all times so you can show it to authorities upon request.

U.S. citizens, who used to be able to come into Canada with just a photo ID and either a birth certificate or proof of citizenship, are now advised to bring passports. If you're driving into Canada, bring along your vehicle registration papers. Permanent U.S. residents who are not U.S. citizens must carry their Alien Registration Cards (green cards).

Atlantic Canada

Youth under age 18 must carry photo ID as well as a letter from a parent or guardian granting permission for the trip to Canada. More information concerning visa requirements can be obtained from www.cic.gc.ca.

CUSTOMS
WHAT YOU CAN BRING INTO THE COUNTRY

Customs regulations are fairly flexible with respect to most goods, provided they do not endanger the health of Canadian citizens, their industry, or their environment.

All guns must be declared. If you are a hunter bringing your own firearm, you should make advance arrangements with a local guide so you can provide proof of your intentions to Customs officials (see **Tourism Newfoundland & Labrador's** *Hunting & Fishing Guide* for a list of outfitters).

Household pets can be brought into the province accompanied by proof of rabies vaccinations within the previous 36 months. For more information concerning animals entering Canada, contact the Animal Health Division, Department of Forest Resources and Agrifoods, by mail at P.O. Box 7400, St. John's, NL A1E 3Y5, or call ✆ **709/729-6879.**

The legal age for alcohol consumption is 19, so anyone aged 19 and over can bring in 1.14 liters (40 oz.) of wine or liquor or 24 (12-oz.) bottles/cans of beer.

You are also allowed to bring in 200 cigarettes or 50 cigars without paying any tax or duty. You are permitted to bring gifts valuing C$60 (US$38) duty-free for Canadian residents.

For more information, contact the **Canada Customs and Revenue Agency** on the Web at www.ccra-adrc.gc.ca or call ✆ **800/461-9999.** You can also check with the **International Tax Services Office** toll-free from Canada or the U.S. ✆ **800/267-5177,** or ✆ 613/952-3741 from elsewhere (collect calls accepted).

WHAT YOU CAN TAKE HOME

U.S. residents should check with the **U.S. Customs Service** at ✆ **877/287-8667** or www.customs.gov. It's a good idea to request a copy of their brochure *Know Before You Go* (also available online), so you don't try to take something home that will not be allowed. After a 48-hour absence, your duty-free exemption includes US$400 worth of merchandise, 200 cigarettes and 100 cigars, and, if you are over 21 years of age, one liter (33.8 fl. oz.) of alcohol.

4 Money

CURRENCY

At the time of writing, the conversion rate between the U.S. and Canadian dollar remains very favorable for U.S. visitors, with US$1 equal to C$1.40.

To convert Canadian prices to U.S. dollars, use a conversion ratio of approximately .71, meaning an item you see for C$1 will cost approximately US.71¢.

Although many places accept American dollars, it's better to arrive with Canadian currency. This is especially true if you are coming from a country other than the U.S., as NL has no foreign currency house.

See the universal currency converter at www.xe.com for the most current conversions on global currencies.

Canada uses both paper money and coins. Paper bills start at $5 and go up from there to $10, $20, $50, and $100. Coins include denominations from the penny up to the two-toned $2 toonie. The $1 coin (called the loonie) is slightly smaller and is brass colored.

Tips Go for Small Change

When converting money into Canadian dollars, you'd be wise to request mostly $20 bills. Some businesses (especially corner stores and service stations) won't accept $50 or $100 denominations because of problems with counterfeiters.

The prices of most goods are similar to those in the U.S., the major exception being the cost of gasoline. Canada's fuel prices are significantly higher than those found in the U.S. Gas is sold by the liter, with 3.8 liters equaling the U.S. gallon. In the summer of 2003, the price of gasoline was as high as C.83¢ for a liter of regular unleaded, which would translate roughly into C$3.15 (or about US$2) for a gallon of gas.

Canadian prices are also higher for liquor and cigarettes, but you'll find prices for meals, accommodations, souvenirs, and clothing comparable to those in the U.S.

ATMS

Automated teller machines can be found both in bank branches and in some stores, the latter becoming more prevalent as you move into rural areas. While most ATMs are compatible with any bank, you'll want to be aware of additional charges when you use ATMs at other than your designated bank. You'll find branches of at least six major Canadian banks on Water Street in downtown St. John's, the largest concentration in the province.

CREDIT CARDS

Visa and MasterCard are widely accepted for nearly all goods and services. Other credit cards such as American Express and Diner's Club are also gaining popularity.

Be sure to bring along the international toll-free number from your credit card issuer so you can immediately report any loss or theft.

TRAVELER'S CHECKS

Although traveler's checks are becoming less common because of problems with counterfeiting, they are still generally accepted. Be sure to carry the sheet with your check numbers, along with the number you are to call in case of loss or emergency, separately from your checks.

TIPS AND TAXES

Tips of 15% are the norm in the cities and tourist centers. Ten percent is still acceptable in some of the smaller, more rural regions.

NL has a harmonized sales tax (HST) of 15%, which represents a combined 8% provincial tax and 7% federal goods and services tax (GST). The HST applies to most goods and services. Note that in the city of St. John's, an additional 3% hotel tax brings the tax on your hotel room to a total of 18%. Non–Canadian residents can apply for an HST rebate on items they are taking out of Canada, in addition to a rebate on taxes paid on any accommodations of at least C$50 before taxes, provided they stay less than one month at each establishment.

If you're departing by ferry, have receipts validated by Canada Customs when you leave the country. When departing by air, your boarding pass will be proof you have left Canada.

Call ✆ **800/668-4748** from within Canada, or ✆ 902/432-5608 from outside Canada, for more information on **Canada's Tax Rebate Program,** or visit www.ccra-adrc.gc.ca.

WHAT TO DO IF YOUR WALLET GETS STOLEN

Immediately block charges against your credit and debit card accounts when you discover a card has been lost or stolen. Then file a police report Your credit card company or insurer may require a police report number or record of the theft.

Almost every credit card company has an emergency toll-free number. They may be able to wire you a cash advance immediately, and in many places they can deliver an emergency credit card in a day or two. The issuing bank's toll-free number is usually on the back of your credit card—though, of course, if your card has been stolen that won't help unless you recorded the number elsewhere.

Citicorp Visa's U.S. emergency number is ℂ **800/336-8472.** American Express cardholders and traveler's check holders should call ℂ **800/869-3016.** MasterCard holders should call ℂ **800/307-7309**. Otherwise, call the toll-free-number directory at ℂ 800/555-1212.

If you need emergency cash, you can have money wired to you from **Western Union** (ℂ **800/325-6000;** www.westernunion.com). You must present valid ID to pick up the cash at the Western Union office. However, in most countries you can pick up a money transfer even if you don't have valid identification, as long as you can answer a test question provided by the sender. Be sure to let the sender know in advance that you don't have ID. If you need to use a test question instead of ID, the sender must take cash to his or her local Western Union office, rather than transferring the money over the phone or online.

Note: There is no Western Union agent in St. John's, and none of the available agents anywhere in the province are open on Sundays. In NL, Western Union agents are located in Goose Bay, Baie Verte, Deer Lake, Corner Brook, and Lewisporte.

What Things Cost in Newfoundland & Labrador	
Taxi from the airport to downtown St. John's	C$20/US$13
Taxi across town in St. John's	C$10/US$7
Metrobus within St. John's (no service to/from airport)	C$1.50/US$1
Local telephone call	C.25¢/US.16¢
Liter of gasoline	C.80¢/US.51¢
Pint of beer	C$5/US$3.20
Can of cola	C$1/US.65¢
Cup of coffee or tea	C$2/US$1.30
Standard 200 ASA Kodak camera film	C$9/US$5.75
Movie in St. John's (Monday to Thursday)	C$7/US$4.50
Movie in St. John's (Friday to Sunday)	C$10/US$6.40
Double room at the Fairmont Newfoundland (expensive)	C$150/US$96
Double room at the Guv'nor Inn (moderate)	C$80/US$51
Dinner for one at Aqua (expensive)*	C$50/US$32
Dinner for one at the Guv'nor Eatery (moderate)*	C$20/US$13
*Includes tax and tip, but not wine	

WEATHER

As they say locally, "If you don't like the weather, just wait five minutes—it'll change." So pack accordingly. Layered clothing and an oversized backpack or bag to carry your umbrella, rain gear, and an extra sweater are recommended.

You're apt to get the most stable weather, best whale watching, and greatest variety of special events during July and August, but you'll also hit the highest prices and tightest availability for accommodations. Some of the most visited places—such as St. John's and Trinity—book up well in advance during the summer, and especially in St. John's during the first week of August. That's when you'll find the Royal St. John's Regatta, the Newfoundland & Labrador Folk Festival, and the George Street Festival happening simultaneously.

If you're especially keen on seeing icebergs, May and June are the best times to visit. You'll see a few stragglers along the Northern Peninsula as late as the end of July, but you're nearly guaranteed a few sightings if you visit earlier in the season.

The island of Newfoundland has a temperate marine climate, with winters offering an average norm of 0°C (32°F) and summer temperatures with an average of 16°C (61°F).

Labrador has a harsher winter climate, but its summer temperatures regularly hit upward of 25°C (77°F)—albeit for shorter periods.

The following chart provides the temperature ranges and precipitation rates for the capital city, as well as for St. Anthony on the Northern Peninsula. For temperature ranges in other locations throughout the province, visit Environment Canada's website at www.climate.weatheroffice.ec.gc.ca.

St. John's Average Temperatures (°C/°F) & Precipitation (mm/inches)

	Jan	Feb	Mar	Apr	May	June	July	Aug	Sept	Oct	Nov	Dec
Avg. High	-1/34	-2/31	1/34	5/41	11/52	16/61	20/69	20/68	16/61	11/51	6/43	1/34
Avg. Low	-9/16	-9/15	-6/21	-2/28	2/35	6/43	11/51	11/51	8/46	3/38	-1/31	-6/22
Precip.	150/5.9	125/4.9	131/5.2	122/4.8	101/4.0	102/4.0	89/3.5	108/4.3	131/5.2	162/6.4	144/5.7	149/5.9

St. Anthony's Average Temperatures (°C/°F) & Precipitation (mm/inches)

	Jan	Feb	Mar	Apr	May	June	July	Aug	Sept	Oct	Nov	Dec
Avg. High	-7/19	-8/18	-3/26	1/34	6/33	12/54	17/62	17/62	12/54	6/43	1/34	-4/25
Avg. Low	-16/3	-16/4	-11/12	-5/23	-1/31	3/37	8/46	8/47	5/41	0/32	-5/24	-11/12
Precip.	107/4.2	90/3.5	101/4.0	87/3.4	89/3.5	114/4.5	410/4.1	120/4.7	126/5.0	117/4.6	119/4.7	124/4.9

HOLIDAYS

NL respects all national statutory holidays, including New Year's Day, Good Friday, Easter Monday, Victoria Day (third Monday in May), Canada Day (July 1), Labour Day (first Monday in September), Thanksgiving (second Monday in October), Remembrance/Armistice Day (November 11), Christmas Day (December 25), and Boxing Day (December 26).

Holidays specific to Newfoundland & Labrador include St. Patrick's Day (March 17—usually just government offices and banks are closed), St. George's Day (fourth Wednesday in April), Discovery Day (fourth Tuesday in June), Orangeman's Day (second Saturday in June), and Regatta Day (in St. John's, the first Wednesday in August, weather permitting).

Note: Check with the visitor information office of the place you are visiting; there may be holidays unique to that area.

Warning: Sunday shopping is not a given in NL. You will find most shops open on Sunday afternoons in the larger centers, but many retail establishments in the smaller communities are not open at all on Sundays.

CALENDAR OF EVENTS

January

Ocean Net's Annual Polar Bear Dip, Foxtrap, Conception Bay South, Route 60 (Avalon Region). Demonstrate your New Year's resolution with a chilly dip in the Atlantic Ocean! January 1. Call ℭ **709/685-4564** or visit www.oceannet.ca.

February

Conception Bay South Winterfest, Conception Bay South, Route 60 (Avalon Region). Break out of hibernation and into a sweat with free swims at the local pool, free skating, and a hockey tournament. Mid-February. Call ℭ **709/834-6534.**

Mount Pearl Frosty Festival, Mount Pearl, Route 60 (Avalon Region). The community comes alive for 10 days of fun for all ages: dances, choral demonstrations, a co-ed personality pageant, dart competitions, basketball tournaments, and more! Mid-February. Call ℭ **709/748-1008** or visit www.mtpearl.nf.ca.

Wintertainment, Clarenville, Route 1 (Eastern Region). A full week of activities including dances, dinners, sporting events, snow sculpting, ice-fishing, and tobogganing. Mid-February. Call ℭ **709/ 466-7937.**

Winterlude, Grand Falls–Windsor, Route 1 (Central Region). Warm up your winter by taking part in one of these lively events. Includes a hockey tournament, figure skating competition, teen dances, snow sculpting, a bowling tournament, cross-country skiing, and more. Mid-February. Call ℭ **709/489-0450.**

Grand Bank Winter Carnival, Grand Bank, Route 220 (Eastern Region). Ten days of winter fun for all ages including talent night, seniors' night, a scavenger hunt, torch-light parade, snow sculpting, snowman contest, skating party, cross-country skiing, and traditional Newfoundland music and food. Late February to early March. Call ℭ **709/832-2617.**

March

Newfoundland All-Breed Kennel Club Championship, St. John's, Route 1 (Avalon Region). A panel of experts judges more than 100 dogs representing 50 different breeds. Early March. Call ℭ **709/ 437-1785.**

Fishing Derby, Pasadena, Route 1 (Western Region). Competitive ice fishing and snowmobile races. Late March. Call ℭ **709/634-6758** or visit www.westernsnoriders.com.

April

Smokey Mountain Annual Slush Cup, Labrador City, Route 500 (Labrador). A wacky event to commemorate the end of the downhill skiing season. Includes a ski run across open shallow water. Mid-April. Call ℭ **709/944-2129** or see www.skismokey.com for more info.

May

Labrador City Polar Bear Dip, Labrador City, Route 500 (Labrador). Are you brave enough to take the dip into the frigid waters of Northern Lake? Late May. Call ℭ **709/ 944-3602** or e-mail recreation@labcity.nf.ca for more info.

June

Discovery Day, Bonavista, Route 230 (Eastern Region). Celebrate the discovery of Newfoundland in 1497 by Italian explorer Giovanni Caboto (aka John Cabot). There's a parade, games of chance, interesting food selections (moose burgers!), and a free tour of a Cabot ship replica. Late June. Call ☎ 877/468-1497 or 709/468-1493, or visit www.matthewlegacy.com.

National Aboriginal Day, Nain (Labrador). If sailing up the coast of Labrador is on your agenda, time your visit to coincide with this wonderful event. You'll participate in Inuit games and enjoy traditional foods. June 21 from 1pm to 10pm. Call ☎ 709/922-2842.

Franco-Fest, St. John's, Route 1 (Avalon Region). *Parlez-vous* fun? Enjoy this weekend celebration of francophone culture. Late June. Call ☎ 877/407-1055 or 709/726-4900.

Cow Head Lobster Festival, Cow Head, Route 430 (Western Region). Daily lobster feasts, an assortment of local crafts, and family entertainment. While in the area, take in the Gros Morne Theatre Festival, which runs all summer. Late June through July 1. Call ☎ 709/243-2471.

July

Bird Island Puffin Festival, Elliston, Route 238 (Eastern Region). This festival features live local entertainment and one of the largest Jiggs Dinners held in the province—prepared with vegetables from the town's historical root cellars. Mid-July. Call ☎ 709/468-7117 or see www.rootcellars.com.

Tri-Fest, Corner Brook, Route 1 (Western Region). For six consecutive years, Corner Brook has been one of just 11 venues worldwide to host an International Triathlon Union (ITU) World Cup. Not only does it claim to be the only triathlon festival in the world, it also claims to have the toughest course in the world. Late July. Call ☎ 877/874-6353 or 709/639-2000, or see www.triourworld.com.

Labrador West Regatta, Wabush, Route 503 (Labrador). A smaller version of the St. John's Regatta, this competition offers a series of Olympic-style rowing races combined with a fun day of games, food, and music. Late July. Call ☎ 709/944-5780.

August

Newfoundland & Labrador Folk Festival, St. John's, Route 1 (Avalon Region). The year's foremost celebration of traditional Newfoundland music, performed by some of the province's best-known musicians. First weekend in August. Call ☎ 709/576-8508 or see www.sjfac.nf.net.

Royal St. John's Regatta, Quidi Vidi Lake (Avalon Region). Join more than 20,000 regular attendees for the biggest event of the year for St. John's and the oldest continuous sporting event in North America. Enjoy a full day of fixed-seat rowing competition in addition to games of chance, pony rides, and live music. Second Wednesday in August, weather permitting. Call ☎ 709/576-8921 or see www.stjohns regatta.org.

George Street Festival, St. John's, Route 1 (Avalon Region). Serious party-goers will need to bank some ZZZs in preparation for this event. Six days of live music, two dozen bars, a closed street, and as much liquid refreshment as your wallet allows. Not to be missed! Early August. Call ☎ 709/576-5990.

Bakeapple Folk Festival, Forteau, Route 510 (Labrador). A 4-day, mouthwatering celebration of the bakeapple (a wild berry found in only two places in the world: this province and Norway). In addition to irresistible desserts, this event includes folk music, knitted crafts, embroidered goods, games of chance, children's activities, and fireworks. Early August. Call ✆ **709/931-2545**.

September

Festival of Colours, Corner Brook, Route 1 (Western Region). This celebration of fall's rich foliage includes craft fairs, storytelling, visual and performing arts, food fairs, dinner theater, and traditional music. Mid-September through mid-October. Call ✆ **709/637-1584** or see www.cornerbrook.com.

October

Christmas at the Glacier, Mount Pearl, Route 60 (Avalon Region). Just in time for the holidays, a prolific showcase of unique and reasonably priced handcrafted gifts. Late October. Call ✆ **709/738-1750** or see www.mtpearl.nf.ca/ComProfile/page77.html.

Grand Falls–Windsor Red Maple Festival, Grand Falls–Windsor, Route 1 (Central Region). Enjoy this 10-day community festival topped by a huge bonfire and fire-works display. Late October/early November. Call ✆ **709/489-0450** or see www.grandfallswindsor.com.

November

West Coast Craft Fair, Corner Brook, Route 1 (Western Region). The biggest and longest-running Christmas craft fair on Newfoundland's west coast has much to offer visitors. Early November. Call ✆ **709/753-2749** or see www.craftcouncil.nf.ca.

December

Bay Roberts Festival of Lights, Bay Roberts, Route 70 (Avalon Region). A month-long event that kicks off with a tree-lighting ceremony and continues with community caroling, mummering (see Fun Fact), and more. December 1 through early January. Call ✆ **709/786-2126** or see www.bayroberts.com.

New Year's Eve Celebration, St. John's, Route 1 (Avalon Region). Dress warmly and prepare for an abundance of goodwill smooches from complete strangers. St. John's is the first city in North America to ring in the New Year (it's 30 minutes ahead of Atlantic Standard Time). To commemorate that fact, the city hosts a popular fireworks display on the waterfront at the stroke of midnight. December 31. Call ✆ **709/576-8651**.

Fun Fact Any Mummers Allowed In?

If you're fortunate enough to be in NL during the Christmas season, don't be alarmed by a loud pounding on the door and the muffled cry of "Any mummers allowed in?" Mummering is a traditional working-class Christmas pastime. A group of people disguise themselves in outlandish costumes and visit various homes throughout the community, entertaining their delighted hosts with comic antics, energetic dancing, and music. The hosts join in the game by trying to guess the identity of their mysterious visitors. Mummers are often rewarded for their efforts with a drink of rum, and then they're off to the next house to continue the fun.

6 Package Tours

Tour operators offering NL packages are listed on the province's tourism website: www.gov.nl.ca/tourism.

One company, **Maxxim Vacations,** has 15 years' experience in packaging theme trips to NL that include visiting local movie sites; taking in a Viking Trail experience; immersing yourself in the traditional culture; visiting the offshore French islands; or participating in road races, golf, or skiing. Call © **800/ 567-6666** to request their brochure, or visit www.maxximvacations.com.

Elderhostel, the not-for-profit organization dedicated to providing learning adventures for people 55 and over, offers a good variety of inexpensively priced NL experiences. Visit www.elderhostel. org or call toll-free © **877/426-8056** to receive a copy of their catalog.

7 Getting There

More than a thousand years ago, Leif Eiriksson—acting on the rumored sighting of an unknown westward land—stocked the Viking-era equivalent of a cargo ship with provisions, cattle, and tools. With only the most rudimentary navigational aids (a notched bearing dial, a sunstone, and the stars), Eiriksson set out from Greenland. He and his crew braved the uncertain temper of the North Atlantic in an open longboat for almost 3 weeks before reaching their destination. Proof of their landing can be found in L'Anse aux Meadows, on Newfoundland's Northern Peninsula. Fortunately for today's travelers, while the destination is just as enticing as it was for Eiriksson, you no longer have to row your way across the Atlantic—unless you want to.

TRAVEL OPTIONS

You can get to the island by sea (a number of cruise lines include St. John's and Corner Brook as ports of call), air (the major airports are at St. John's on the east coast, Deer Lake on the west coast, Gander in the interior, and Goose Bay in Labrador), or by ferry (with two different routes from Nova Scotia).

Different options exist if your destination is Labrador. Travel here is severely impaired due to the lack of roads connecting communities. If you're arriving by road via Quebec, you can do a self-guided trip from Labrador City as far east as Happy Valley–Goose Bay. Because of the length and isolation of the Trans Labrador Highway, you need to be fully prepared in case of emergency— especially in winter (see "Winter Driving Survival Kit," below).

A good, paved road services communities of the Labrador Straits, but the two regions (Newfoundland and Labrador) are not currently connected by road. There is a ferry, however, from Blanc Sablon to the Northern Peninsula.

See www.roads.gov.nl.ca for detailed information on NL roads.

Tips Winter Driving Survival Kit

Include a scraper and brush; a shovel; booster cables; traction pads, sand, salt, or kitty litter (for traction on ice); a flashlight; flares; extra fuses, radiator hoses, and fan belts; blankets, sleeping bags, and extra winter clothing and footwear; a tow line or chain; an axe or hatchet; a supply of nonperishable foods; and a first aid kit. As an added precaution, make sure someone knows where you are traveling and when you expect to arrive at your destination.

TRAVEL BY AIR

Air Canada is the biggest player in the province, offering three flight options: Air Canada's regular air service, its regional carrier Jazz, and its discount carrier Tango. Call **Air Canada** at ✆ **888/247-2262** or visit them on the Web at www.aircanada.ca, www.flyjazz.ca, or www.flytango.ca.

CanJet is a low-fare, no-frills (not a huge sacrifice; none of the airlines offer many amenities anymore) carrier providing service to St. John's from Toronto, Ottawa, and Montreal, as well as Moncton, New Brunswick, and Halifax, Nova Scotia. Call ✆ **800/809-7777** or visit their website at www.canjet.com.

Jetsgo is a new discount carrier in NL, with regular stops at Gander and Goose Bay. Book your flight online at www.jetsgo.net or call ✆ **866/448-5888.**

WestJet is a low-fare airline from Western Canada that recently added Gander and St. John's to its route roster. To compare prices, see www.westjet.com, or call ✆ **877/952-4638**.

Conquest Vacations offers reasonably priced flights to NL from Toronto via Skyservice. Call ✆ **866/232-4722** or visit them on the Web at www.flyconquest.com.

Air Transat flies to St. John's. Call ✆ **866/847-1112** or visit their website at www.airtransat.com for details on their seasonally adjusted flight schedules.

Provincial Airlines offers service from St. John's and Halifax to many of the smaller communities throughout NL. Call ✆ **800/563-2800** or 709/576-1666, or visit them on the Web at www.provair.com.

Air Labrador offers service from St. John's, Stephenville, St. Anthony, and Goose Bay, with connections to 12 coastal Labrador communities. Call ✆ **800/563-3042** or visit them online at www.airlabrador.com.

ARRIVING BY SEA

Marine Atlantic offers service between North Sydney, Nova Scotia, and two points in NL. Those heading to the province's west coast can take the approximately 6-hour journey to Channel-Port-aux-Basques. Rates per small vehicle begin at C$69.75 (about US$45) one way. Ferry service on this route operates year round.

If your primary destination is St. John's, you can take the approximately 14-hour sailing to Argentia, which is a 1½-hour drive to the capital city. This is a seasonal service that operates from mid-June to mid-September. Rates per small vehicle begin at C$140.25 (about US$90) for a single trip.

Give serious consideration to the additional cost for a cabin on the ferry, as fog and high winds can easily extend those 14 hours into 16 or 18 very long hours at sea. The more moderately priced cots are not a good choice for those who like their privacy or are even mildly claustrophobic.

Advance reservations are recommended for all sailings, and a C$25 (about US$17) deposit, payable through a major credit card, is required for reservations booked more than 48 hours prior to departure.

Note: Reservations cannot be guaranteed unless you arrive 60 minutes in advance of scheduled departure. Smoking is not permitted while on board.

Contact the Marine Atlantic reservations bureau at ✆ **800/341-7981** or 902/794-5700, or visit the website at www.marine-atlantic.ca.

If you've only a limited amount of time yet would like to get to Labrador, taking the ferry to the Labrador Straits (a string of communities along the southeast coast) is a good plan.

Daily ferry service crosses the Strait of Belle Isle in summer between St. Barbe on Newfoundland's Viking Trail and Blanc Sablon, Quebec, on the Quebec–Labrador border. Crossing time aboard the MS *Apollo* is about 1½ hours and costs C$27.50 (about US$18) for one adult with an automobile.

For reservations and more information on schedules and rates, call the **Woodward Group Labrador Marine Inc.** toll-free at 🕾 **866/535-2567.** You'll receive confirmation of reservation upon their receipt of a nonrefundable C$5 (US$3) deposit. All traffic with reservations should be at dockside 1 hour prior to departure.

Coastal Labrador Marine Services, a subsidiary of the Woodward Group, operates a seasonal ferry service along the Labrador coast. The ferry service operates from mid-June to mid-September. June sailings can be delayed due to ice conditions. The ferry, which carries automobiles, docks at Cartwright and Happy Valley–Goose Bay. The one-way sailing takes about 12 hours. For reservations, call toll-free 🕾 **866/535-2567.**

Also, a coastal boat service departs from Cartwright, calling at some 40 isolated villages as far north as Nain, Labrador. The one-way trip takes about 4 days. This is a freighter service and does not carry automobiles. Contact Coastal Labrador Marine Services at 🕾 **709/535-6872.**

For more information on ferry service in and around NL, visit www.gov.nf.ca/ferryservices.

If your destination is the French islands of St. Pierre and Miquelon, you'll need to catch the ferry from the town of Fortune on the Burin Peninsula. **St. Pierre Tours Ltd.** offers walk-on passenger service only (no vehicles) to this little bit of France right off the coast of NL. It costs C$74.95 (about US$48) round-trip per adult. Call 🕾 **800/563-2006** for reservations or more information.

If you're interested in touring NL by cruise ship, a number of companies offer some interesting options. Visit the **Cruiseship Authority of Newfoundland & Labrador** at www.cruisenewfoundland.com for more information about which companies include NL among their ports of call.

Peregrine Adventures offers a compelling 9-day package called "Newfoundland Circumnavigation." Their small ship tours many of the top spots around the island, with an emphasis on national parks and historical sites.

You'll sail from St. John's to Terra Nova National Park, then on to St. Anthony and L'Anse aux Meadows National Historic Site on the Northern Peninsula. Then you'll cross the Strait of Belle Isle to historical Battle Harbour and Red Bay in Labrador.

As you head south along the west coast of Newfoundland you'll stop at Gros Morne National Park, followed by a visit to the remote island community of Ramea on Newfoundland's lovely South Coast and the nearby French islands of St. Pierre and Miquelon. The final stop before heading back to St. John's is the wonderful Cape St. Mary's.

This is a fantastic itinerary well worth the price tag of about C$2,240 (US$1,600). Peregrine's head office is in Melbourne, Australia, but you can book travel through several Canadian travel agents listed on their website at www.peregrineadventures.com.

Adventure Canada offers a similar itinerary, replacing Terra Nova National Park with Trinity and Bonavista. The prices are higher, probably because of the high-profile tour guides (they regularly include celebrity biologists, top photographers, and distinguished chefs). You'll pay at least C$3,220 (US$2,300) for a cabin on a 10-day voyage that begins in St. John's and ends in Halifax, Nova Scotia. If you're interested, call Adventure Canada at 🕾 **800/363-7566** or visit them online at www.adventurecanada.com.

If you're planning on sailing your own yacht to NL, you should contact the **Canadian Coast Guard** (Search & Rescue) at www.ccg-gcc.gc.ca/sar/main_e.htm.

The volunteer **Canadian Coast Guard Auxiliary** (CCGA) offers information on boating safety and regulations you need to know while sailing Canadian waters. Visit them on the Web at www.ccga-gcac.org for an online version of their *Safe Boating Guide.* The Newfoundland chapter of the CCGA can be reached by mail at P.O. Box 938, St. John's, NL A1C 5M3; ℰ **709/772-4074.**

ARRIVING BY RAIL

The island of Newfoundland is not accessible by train, nor does it have an internal rail service. Limited rail service is available in western Labrador.

You can travel by train between Sept-Îles, Quebec, and Labrador on the Quebec North Shore & Labrador Railway. The trip takes 10 hours. For information, contact **Quebec North Shore & Labrador Railway** at ℰ **418/968-7805** if calling from Quebec or **709/944-8205** if calling from Labrador.

8 Planning Your Trip Online

NL is not considered a major international destination, so it is unlikely you will encounter any big sales or super deals to help get you here.

Unless you are extremely savvy with respect to online bookings, you're best off putting your planning in the hands of a knowledgeable travel counselor or service that can help you with the logistics of getting to and around this deceivingly expansive and varied province. Plus, a travel agent can save you money by alerting you to special, unadvertised deals (such as vacancies on charter flights).

But if you've got a few online bookings under your belt and you have the time to thoroughly research the transportation segments that will be necessary in planning your trip, go for it! Here are a few resources that may help.

You'll find many travel websites, and each has an upper hand in certain aspects of service. Your first stop should be www.frommers.com (check out the online newsletter). Another site, www.smarterliving.com, offers weekly e-mail notification of special fares from your chosen city. As most flights to NL originate out of Toronto or Halifax, you're wise to subscribe to this service for those two cities. The only drawback is that you usually have to travel the same week as the posting, and last-minute travel doesn't work well in the summer when availability of accommodations is at a premium. Another great site is www.expedia.com (or www.expedia.ca, the Canadian version), which offers e-mail notification if a sale to your chosen destination becomes available.

9 Health & Insurance

Like all provinces in Canada, NL has its own provincial medical plan. Wise travelers will obtain sufficient medical insurance before leaving home. Even though prices for health care in Canada are significantly lower than in the U.S., they are still costly for those not covered by the provincial plan.

Most larger communities in the province have hospitals and full medical service. Travelers who have a preexisting medical condition may wish to stay in a community offering full medical services; the more remote regions may be too far from emergency care.

Traveling with a list of prescribed medications is a good idea. That way, if you lose your medication or it becomes damaged you can more easily refill your prescription while in the province.

BlueCross BlueShield is the most popular form of medical insurance in Canada and widely accepted at most, if not all, hospitals. Call © **800/810-2583** or find them on the Web at www.bluecares.com.

It's also recommended that you consider trip cancellation and lost luggage insurance before leaving home.

You'll need **collision damage waiver** insurance if you're renting a vehicle. If you have a gold or platinum credit card, chances are this coverage is included with your card. As long as you pay for the rental with the card, you won't have to purchase the expensive coverage offered by the rental company. If you're not certain whether your card offers this option, check with your credit card company before leaving home.

Driver's liability insurance is another matter. If you own a car at home, be sure to check with your insurer to determine whether you will be covered while driving a rental vehicle. If not, you're advised to purchase liability coverage from the rental company.

10 Tips for Travelers with Special Needs

FOR TRAVELERS WITH DISABILITIES

Newfoundland & Labrador may be a step behind some of the more populated Canadian centers in terms of providing service for persons with disabilities, but it is making progress. But part of the charm of visiting NL is having the opportunity to visit old, Victorian-style privately run inns, and many, if not most, of them are not accessible to people with mobility problems. Some locations may be "wheelchair friendly" and offer a room or two on the main floor, but the second- and third-floor rooms with their beautiful winding staircases will not be accessible.

In St. John's, the biggest event of the year, the Regatta, is not fully accessible by wheelchair. Much of the path around Quidi Vidi Lake is not paved, and pushing a wheelchair on gravel is never easy. One option is to rent a battery-operated scooter for the day. Eastern Medical Supplies © **709/754-7711** at 95 Military Road in St. John's rents battery-operated wheelchairs for about C$100 (US$64) and scooters for about C$120 (US$77) per month. Daily and weekly rentals are also available. Remember to call ahead, as most public services are closed on Regatta Day.

FOR SENIORS

Recognizing the importance of mature travelers to the tourism industry, most establishments will reward seniors' patronage with a special discount. However, just who qualifies for a seniors' discount is determined by each provider. Some companies offer seniors' rates to anyone over 50. For others, you must be 65. If you are 50 or older, don't hesitate to ask if you are eligible for a discount—it could add up to substantial savings.

FOR FAMILIES

The most important thing to remember when traveling with children is to put sunscreen on them regardless of the conditions outdoors. It is often foggy or overcast in NL, and that can be deceiving. You might think that's when UV rays are less intense, but in fact they are even more dangerous, especially near salt water.

Newfoundland weather changes quickly and can often be considerably different at locations separated by just a few kilometers, so it's best to pack clothes for all seasons and consider yourself lucky if you don't need them.

You won't find good signage along the roads in many areas, so if you have a young passenger who is anxious for a snack or a bathroom, don't hesitate to stop and ask anyone you see where you can find the nearest facilities. When driving, it's also best to travel with snacks, as services can be few and far between in some parts of the province.

FOR GAY & LESBIAN TRAVELERS

The gay lifestyle is fully accepted in Newfoundland. So much so that the province is developing a reputation as a destination for health-conscious same-sex couples. St. John's is gaining status as the San Francisco of the Eastern seaboard with its Victorian architecture, fresh climate, hilly terrain, and the welcoming acceptance of local residents.

One highly recommended gay/straight dance bar in St. John's is Liquid Ice, © **709/754-2190,** at 186B Water St. See www.liquidice.org.

To get detailed information on gay-friendly accommodations, bars, restaurants, and events, call Newfoundland Gays and Lesbians for Equality, Inc. at © **709/753-4297,** or e-mail new foundlandgay@yahoo.com.

11 Getting Around

The first thing you need to realize is that NL is big—very big—compared to the rest of Atlantic Canada. The island of Newfoundland alone stretches for 111,390 sq. km (43,442 sq. miles) —it's nearly as large as the three maritime provinces of Nova Scotia, New Brunswick, and Prince Edward Island combined. Add in the vast territory of Labrador at 294,330 sq. km (114,789 sq. miles) and the provincial total becomes a massive 405,720 sq. km (158,231 sq. miles).

To see highlights of the entire province, you'll likely need a month's stay. If you can't afford the time or resources for a lengthy visit, however, pick a couple of adjoining regions, allowing a week per region. Remember, the wonderfully slower pace of NL is best enjoyed if you don't have to rush through it.

Scenic winding roads, spectacular national parks, great camping opportunities, and a host of interesting things to see along the way make the island a dream destination for RVers. But remember that this is not currently true of Labrador, as paved roads and services are minimal outside the Labrador Straits region.

Life in Newfoundland has always been strongly tied to the sea, which is why all the original communities in the province were built along the extensive coastline. It's therefore no big surprise to learn that some parts of the province are accessible only by boat—most notably the very scenic **South Shore** of the Central Region.

That's also why it isn't unusual to meet Newfoundlanders who have never set foot outside the province. Many older folk grew up under the restrictions of regional isolation—which accounts for the distinctly different dialects throughout NL.

GETTING AROUND BY CAR

The **Trans-Canada Highway** (also known as Highway 1) starts in St. John's and heads west 905km (about 560 miles) across the province to Channel-Port-aux-Basques (about a 10½-hour drive), where you can hop the ferry to Nova Scotia.

Note: The Trans-Canada is just two lanes wide in many remote areas of the province. The volume of traffic doesn't warrant a more developed road system at this time.

Newfoundland & Labrador

Cape Chidley

Ungava Bay

Hebron

QUEBEC

Nain

Davis Inlet

Hopedale

Makkovik

ATLANTIC

OCEAN

502

Smallwood Reservoir

Rigolet

LABRADOR

Esker

Labrador City

501 Churchill Falls

520 *Lake Melville*

Cartwright

500

Churchill River

500

Happy Valley-Goose Bay

Wabush

Mud Lake

389

MEALY MOUNTAINS

Kenamu River

510

Pinware

Battle Harbour

L'Anse-au-Loup

Red Bay

L'Anse-Amour

Blanc-Sablon

St. Anthony

L'Anse-au-Clair

St. Barbe

Harrington Harbour

430

Englee

Sept-Iles

Gros Morne National Park

Baie Verte

Twillingate

Terra Nova National Park

Anticosti Island

330

Corner Brook

Deer Lake

1

Gander

Trinity/ Bonavista

Stephenville

Grand Falls

235

Gulf of St. Lawrence

NEWFOUNDLAND

Clarenville

230

80

St. John's

360

70

480

210

Channel-Port aux Basques

Grand Bank

100

Argentia

Havre-Aubert

90

10

St-Pierre

- - - - - Ferry

0   150 mi

0   150 km

However, there is a high volume of moose on the roads! NL has more than 150,000 of these mighty creatures roaming on and near its roadways. Extreme caution and reduced speeds are recommended when traveling any time between sunset and sunrise, as that's when the massive animals are most likely to be about.

You'll have the most fun—and meet the most interesting people—if you get off the Trans-Canada and take the smaller arteries into the coastal communities. Most, but not all, of these smaller roads are paved. Get yourself a good up-to-date highway map of the province to guide you, and keep it by your side at all times.

Warning: Driving conditions can be severely hampered by the weather. Fog and heavy rains can happen unexpectedly, and roads are fairly narrow, leaving little room for error. Call ✆ **900/451-3300** for road conditions anywhere in the province or ✆ **709/729-7669** for road conditions in St. John's or the Avalon Region. See www.roads.gov.nf.ca for updates on local road conditions.

A common—and valid—complaint is the inadequate highway signage. Don't expect anything like the 401 in Ontario, where signs regularly update you on your proximity to the next turnoff. Here you may find yourself making quick turns or lane changes when you suddenly realize that you've missed your intersection.

If you're adventuring into more remote areas, you'll find fewer service stations (and any you encounter may not necessarily be open), so always check your tank, oil, tires, and windshield wipers before leaving a populated area.

On car trips, remember to wear your seat belt or risk facing a hefty fine. Motorcyclists are legally required to wear helmets. And the use of radar detectors is prohibited.

RENTING A CAR

You'll find that most of the popular rental companies have counters at the St. John's airport. If you're coming in peak season (late July and early August), be sure to book your rental as far in advance as possible. The rental agencies have been known to run out of cars.

If you're doing a cross-province trek, you'll need to find a rental company that will permit pick-up in St. John's and drop-off at the Deer Lake airport. National Car Rental is one option, but you'll be subject to a hefty drop-off fee of C$100 (about US$71). National is also a good company to choose if you're looking for a rental in some of the smaller communities, such as St. Anthony.

Most rental companies do not offer unlimited kilometers in NL. You're generally looking at a rental price subject to a daily limit on kilometers driven. Deals change from time to time, so your best bet is to call them all and indicate whichever discounts you're eligible for.

Call **Hertz** at ✆ **800/263-0600** or visit them on the Web at www.hertz.com. **National Car Rental** can be reached at ✆ **800/227-7368** or online at www.nationalcar.com. Other local players include **Avis** (✆ **800/879-2847;** www.avis.com), **Budget** (✆ **800/268-8900;** www.budget.com), and **Rent-a-Wreck** (✆ **800/327-0116**).

GETTING AROUND BY BUS

DRL Coachlines Ltd. offers scheduled bus service along Route 1 from St. John's west across the province. Stops include Gander, Grand Falls–Windsor, Deer Lake, Corner Brook, and Channel-Port-aux-Basques. Call ✆ **888/263-1852** or ✆ **709/738-8088** for details. You'll also find them online at www.drlgroup.com/coachlines/nfsched.html. DRL buses offer comfortable seats, air-conditioning, and onboard washroom facilities.

GETTING AROUND BY FERRY

NL has ferries that will get you to the province, ferries from one community to the next, and ferries to the French islands offshore.

See the "Getting There" section earlier in this chapter for more info on traveling by ferry.

GETTING AROUND BY AIR

If your budget allows, you may choose to fly from one end of the province to the other. It takes about 12 hours to drive from St. John's to St. Anthony, but it only takes about an hour to make the same trip by air.

See the "Getting There" section earlier in this chapter for details on interprovincial air travel.

GETTING AROUND BY RAIL

While there is no railway system on the island, there is limited train service through the western part of Labrador via Quebec, from Schefferville south past Wabush and back into Quebec. (See "Getting There" earlier in this chapter for further details.)

 FAST FACTS: **Newfoundland & Labrador**

Area Codes　All of Newfoundland & Labrador uses the **709** area code.

ATMs　See "Money," earlier in this chapter.

Automobile Clubs　The Canadian equivalent of AAA is the **CAA** (Canadian Automobile Association), which does not have an office in NL. If you are a **CAA** or **AAA** member, call ℭ **800/222-4357** for emergency road assistance. Call ℭ **800/947-0770** for emergency roadside service if you are a member of the **Good Sam Club**. (If you're not a member but would like to join, call ℭ **800/842-5351**.) Both clubs' operators will connect you with appropriate local service providers.

Car Rentals　See "Getting Around," earlier in this chapter.

Climate　See "When to Go," earlier in this chapter.

Currency　See "Money," earlier in this chapter.

Documents　See "Entry Requirements & Customs," earlier in this chapter.

Driving Rules　See "Getting Around," earlier in this chapter.

Drugstores　These are more commonly referred to as "pharmacies" in Canada. Many of the larger grocery chains fill prescriptions. Be sure to bring a copy of any prescriptions along with you in case you lose your medication and need to have the prescription refilled.

Electricity　Electrical and phone outlets are the same as in the U.S.: 110–115 volts, AC, 60 cycles. No special adapters are necessary.

Embassies and Consulates　All embassies within Canada are located in Ottawa, Ontario, the national capital. The **U.S. embassy** is situated at 90 Sussex Dr., Ottawa, ON K1M 1M8 (ℭ **613/238-5335**). You can find a **U.S. consulate** in Halifax, Nova Scotia, at 2000 Barrington St., Suite 910, Scotia Square (ℭ **902/429-2485**). The **British consulate** can be found at 1 Canal St., Dartmouth, NS (ℭ **902/461-1381**.)

Emergencies　Call ℭ **911** in case of emergency to reach police, ambulance, or in case of a fire.

Internet Access　There are few true Internet cafes in NL. Larger bookstores, local libraries, and copy shops may provide computers for public use at a nominal fee. Some hotels in St. John's, such as the Fairmont Newfoundland, offer complimentary use of hotel computers to preferred guests (ask for a room on their Gold Floor). The Battery Hotel & Suites has a lobby computer that guests can use at a nominal fee for time online. You're wise to contact your local ISP in advance for its NL dial-up number to avoid long-distance charges. If you're toting a laptop, be sure to check with your ISP for details on dialing in while traveling, and check with any properties you're booking to ensure they offer in-room Internet access.

Liquor Laws   The legal drinking age is 19. Don't drink and drive, as Canadian laws are tough if you are caught impaired behind the wheel, and you will be charged under the Criminal Code.

Mail   It currently costs C.49¢ to mail a letter or card (weighing 30 grams or less) within Canada. It costs C.65¢ to mail that same letter or card to the U.S.

Newspapers & Magazines   The major newspaper in St. John's is *The Telegram*. There are also many community newspapers throughout the province. See www.thepaperboy.com for a full listing. The province's major lifestyle/nostalgia magazine is *The Downhomer.*

Religion   Many religions are practiced throughout NL. Check the phone book of the communities you are visiting for locations of your chosen house of worship.

Taxes and Tipping   You will pay 15% tax on most purchases. Tips of 15% are expected in larger cities such as St. John's, with 10–15% being more common in smaller centers. See "Money," earlier in this chapter.

Telephones   Pay phones cost C25¢ for local calls. You can purchase prepaid calling cards from local retailers if you find that your calling card from home doesn't work. You're unlikely to get digital cellphone service while in NL, but analog service will work in many places. Here's a local tip: If your cellphone doesn't work in one of the smaller coastal communities (which are all generally at sea level), you may be able to get service just a kilometer or two up the road if you head for higher ground.

Time Zones   NL has its own time zone, **Newfoundland time zone,** which runs a half-hour ahead of the rest of Atlantic Canada. Most of Labrador is in the Atlantic time zone, so be sure to check the time upon your arrival in Labradorian communities apart from the Labrador Straits, as chances are they're on Atlantic time. Daylight savings time is practiced throughout the province in summer.

Tobacco Laws   You must be at least 16 years of age to legally purchase cigarettes. Smoking is not allowed in most St. John's restaurants, but you can smoke and eat in liquor lounges. Outside of St. John's, most restaurants provide designated smoking areas. However, many of the smaller inns do not allow smoking at all. If you are a smoker, be sure to check with the establishment before making a booking or reservation.

Safety   Whether you're gay, elderly, of a visible minority, or a woman traveling alone, you will feel secure in NL. Street crimes are rare, but you still need to practice common sense. Lock your vehicle, don't leave your purse or backpack unattended, and be aware of your surroundings.

3

St. John's

St. John's is one of my favorite cities. It's full of old-world charm, new-world finesse, and the fresh salt smell of the sea. Stroll along its downtown residential streets and you're likely to be enchanted by the colorful row houses standing tall in various shades of red, brown, yellow, blue, and green. You don't often see that kind of architectural excitement in other parts of Canada.

St. John's is full of color. Not just in the buildings, but in its people, who seem to take time to greet everyone they meet on the street. In a small city of about 100,000 residents, it's a lot easier to get to know others than it would be in larger centers.

Yet the city's "townies"—the nickname for those who live in St. John's as opposed to the numerous outports throughout the province—are a special lot who seem to have treasured and preserved the art of knowing and caring about their neighbors more than many of us do.

The vistas and views in and around St. John's are spectacular. At the center of it all is the city's harbor. It was—and still is—the heart and soul of the city. Nothing has been more instrumental to its origin, growth, hard times, and return to prosperity than the city's connection to the sea. Yet it is not as truly beautiful a harbor as you'll find in other cities, whose harbors make you want to stroll along and just enjoy being there.

This is a working harbor, with cargo ships and piles of material lying about. All imported supplies come to St. John's via container ships. With an average of 20 ships arriving each week, it's an obviously busy port.

St. John' mystique comes from the wealth of history that looks down on the city from the surrounding cliffs. To one side, **Signal Hill** (now a National Historic Site), with its rich military history, stands proud overlooking the harbor. Just across the Narrows (the protective entrance to the harbor), the 1810 lighthouse and World War II gun batteries at nearby **Fort Amherst** are a reminder of past battles. And maritime history lives on in the fishermen and sailors who make their living much in the same way as their ancestors did over a century ago.

You are constantly reminded of that history every time you take a walk along the waterfront, or watch the ships come and go—more than 500 years after the first "tall ships" began rolling in to this very spot.

The goal of this chapter is to provide you with the tools to make your visit to St. John's a fun and fulfilling one. Just be sure to allow yourself a good stay in the city—especially if you visit during July and August, when St. John's is at its peak at both the George Street Festival and the Royal St. John's Regatta.

The cultural and music scene in St. John's is unparalleled for a city this size. Indeed, many larger and supposedly more metropolitan centers would find it hard to compete with the range and quantity of its homegrown talent.

At many places, you can catch free (or very inexpensively priced) live local entertainment of an excellent caliber.

Visitors are treated well in St. John's—much like long-awaited friends. And you'll find your fill of good restaurants where the service is more than friendly and the food a treat for any palate. The wide range of choices for accommodations should please nearly every budget. And plenty of activities are available without going more than an hour from the city. As one of the oldest cities in North America, St. John's boasts a history bursting with stories of pirate treasure, restless ghosts, and military prowess. Visit the "City of Legends" once and I guarantee you'll find a way to return.

1 Essentials

GETTING THERE

St. John's is a 3-hour flight from Toronto or Boston, a 4-hour flight from New York, and a 5-hour flight from London, England. But because the volume of air traffic to St. John's is considerably lower than to many other centers, prices are high. (For example, a flight from Winnipeg to St. John's can cost you more than one to Eastern Europe.)

However, upon arrival in St. John's you'll be pleased to find that from the newly refurbished airport it's just minutes (6km/4 miles) and a relatively inexpensive cab ride (less than C$20/US$13) to downtown.

Warning: If you're leaving St. John's on one of the early-bird flights (anywhere between 6am to 6:30am), you'll want to arrive at least 1.5 to 2 hours before your scheduled departure. That's usually the busiest time of the day at the airport, and arriving early will save you from getting caught in congestion at the airport security counter. The latest you should arrive at the airport for any flight is 1 hour prior to departure.

Taking the ferry from Nova Scotia to Newfoundland & Labrador is cheaper than flying, but it's a much more time-consuming endeavor. The trip that gets you closest to St. John's is a full 14-hour sailing from North Sydney to Argentia, followed by a 1½-hour drive to the city. But if you have the time, you can save a considerable chunk of change by sailing and driving your own car versus flying and then renting a car on arrival. (Find more detail in section 7, "Getting There," in chapter 2.)

Moments **Hospitality in the Face of Evil**

More than 70 airplanes were diverted here following the tragic events of September 11, 2001. Thirty-eight made emergency landings at Gander, 27 at St. John's International Airport, and the remainder at other smaller airports throughout the province. The warmth, caring, and hospitality of the local people was so notable and unexpected that it made world news. Since then, the number of U.S. tourists visiting Newfoundland & Labrador has been on a steady increase as the stranded passengers have not only returned to visit, but have also spread the word about the Newfoundland & Labrador hospitality.

Tips **How to Avoid Unnecessary Security Delays**

- Gifts may be opened by airport security. So save the wrapping until you reach your destination.
- Letter-openers, scissors, nail files, nail clippers, pointed tweezers, and other potentially dangerous goods will not be allowed through carry-on screening. If you do need to carry these items, pack them in your suitcase.
- All medications should be clearly labeled in their original containers.
- Never pack aerosols, household cleaners, or other potentially dangerous goods.
- Keep your photo ID handy. You may need it at check-in.
- Electronic devices will be examined. So make sure laptop computers, personal stereos, razors, cameras, and so on have fully charged batteries so you can demonstrate how they work.

VISITOR INFORMATION

The **Avalon Convention & Visitors Bureau** (ACVB) has a visitor information booth open 10am to midnight, 7 days a week, conveniently located on the main floor of the airport by the car-rental counter. Here you can pick up regional travel brochures, maps, and information.

Note: The Avalon Region includes and surrounds St. John's and comprises about half the province's total population and many of its major attractions. The Avalon Region outside of St. John's is covered in detail in chapter 4.

You can reach the airport location of the ACVB directly by calling ✆ 709/758-8515 if you have specific questions about the airport. Call their toll-free line at ✆ 877/739-8899 for general information or to have travel literature sent to you. The ACVB also has a comprehensive website that provides details on local businesses and services at www.canadasfareast.com.

Note: The **City of St. John's** previously had a visitor information office in an authentic railcar located on Harbour Drive. The railcar has now been moved to the old railway station as part of a museum exhibit and a new downtown information booth is under construction. You can pick up visitor information downtown on the second-floor annex at St. John's City Hall weekdays from 8:30am to 4:30pm, New Gower Street (✆ 709/576-8106).

2 Getting Around

From as far back as the early 1500s, life in St. John's has centered on its harbor. Indeed, in its early days, the city owed its existence to the British, Spanish, French, Portuguese, and other fleets whose annual arrival signaled the beginning of another fishing season—usually for cod. Shops and local businesses seemed to spring from the water itself, so close were they to the city's teeming waterfront. Even today, most everything you'll want to see in St. John's will either be on, or just off, one of four streets.

Harbour Drive, and Water, Duckworth, and George streets all run parallel to the waterfront. You'll find the boat tours, an opportunity to get close to all sorts of foreign ships, and most of the parking spaces in town along Harbour Drive,

Downtown St. John's

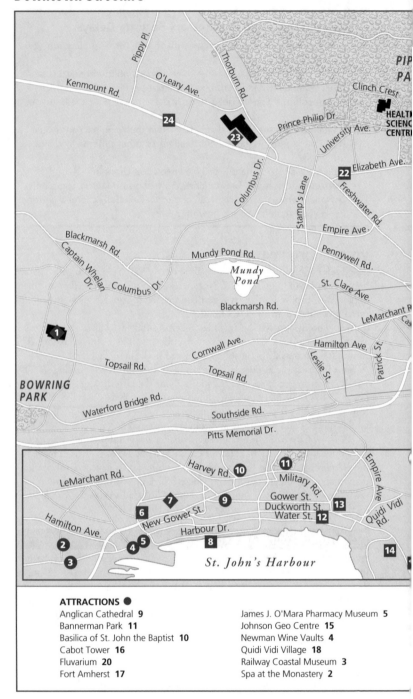

ATTRACTIONS ●

Anglican Cathedral **9**
Bannerman Park **11**
Basilica of St. John the Baptist **10**
Cabot Tower **16**
Fluvarium **20**
Fort Amherst **17**

James J. O'Mara Pharmacy Museum **5**
Johnson Geo Centre **15**
Newman Wine Vaults **4**
Quidi Vidi Village **18**
Railway Coastal Museum **3**
Spa at the Monastery **2**

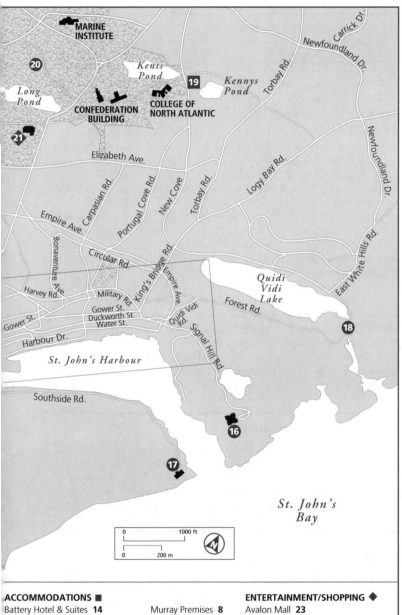

ACCOMMODATIONS ■

Battery Hotel & Suites **14**
Best Western Traveller's Inn **24**
Delta Hotel **6**
Fairmont Newfoundland **13**
The Guv'nor Inn **22**
Holiday Inn **19**

Murray Premises **8**
Quality Hotel **12**

ENTERTAINMENT/SHOPPING ◆

Avalon Mall **23**
Arts & Culture Centre **21**
Mile One Stadium **7**
Village Mall **1**

which runs adjacent to the harbor and is accessible off the Trans-Canada Highway leading into downtown from the west.

Most of the services (shops, financial institutions, post office, and so on) are on Water Street, the next street up from the waterfront, running the full length of the harbor. And you'll find the highest concentration of restaurants along Duckworth Street, one block farther up the hill. If you're looking for nightlife, about two dozen pubs can be found on George Street, a two-block stretch of excitement between Water Street and City Hall.

BY FOOT

The streets of St. John's are ideal for walking enthusiasts. Buildings throughout the downtown area (especially along Gower Street) have brightly colored, beautifully restored historical facades. It's a perfect area for wandering, the air is invigorating, and there are many interesting diversions along the way to wherever you're heading.

Warning: The city is built on a fairly steep incline, so if you have difficulty walking you may want to stick to Harbour Drive and Water Street, which are relatively flat. By the time you get to Duckworth Street, the incline gets more difficult to navigate. Between Duckworth Street and LeMarchant Road, there are places where you'd be grateful for a ski lift.

Another reason you may want to walk the city is that it's tricky navigating your way around by car. St. John's has many one-way streets, quite a few hidden intersections (the one turning on to Harbour Drive from the Quality Hotel on **Hill O'Chips** is especially tricky), and some crazy intersections where you have to do a roundabout to get where you want to go (watch out for one of these by the Fairmont). Plus, you may be so absorbed by the wildly colored and intriguingly named buildings (such as the **Bread Pig**) that the driving should be left to someone else.

Fun Fact Buried Treasure

Legend has it that in the 1940s, a dishonest bank employee stole tens of thousands of dollars and buried his loot in a laneway connecting New Gower and Water Streets. The criminal was charged, found guilty, and spent 4 years in jail for the deed—only to be released and discover that the laneway had been covered over with concrete during his incarceration. The money has never been recovered.

BY CAB

Cabs in St. John's are fairly priced. Most rides about town will cost you under C$10 (US$7.10). The biggest company is **Bugden's Taxi** (© 709/726-4400). Others include **Co-op Taxi** (© 709/726-6666) and **Gulliver's City Wide Taxi** (© 709/722-0003). If you're planning to pay by credit card, be sure to call ahead before you get in the cab to verify that credit cards—and your particular card—are accepted. Similarly, if you require an infant car seat make sure you ask for one when you call for a cab—most taxi companies have at least a couple of cars equipped with that option.

ⓘ Moments Unforgettable Stories

You'll find that, regardless of which company they work for, most taxi drivers are exceedingly friendly. Many of them have a delightful Irish brogue, a sure hint of a marvelous storyteller who needs just a little encouragement to get started. One driver, named Sean, noted the time a passenger—after a wee bit too much fun on George Street—stumbled into his cab and promptly fell asleep. On awakening the passenger to find out where he lived, the groggy man threw $20 on the seat, thanked Sean for the ride, and got out of the car right where he'd gotten in! It took some encouragement to get the man back in, and even more coaxing to find out where he lived, but Sean made sure his passenger was delivered safe at home.

BY BUS

As any experienced traveler knows, public transit is one of the cheapest and fastest ways to become acquainted with unfamiliar surroundings. St. John's doesn't have subways, streetcars, or passenger trains, but it does have an inexpensive public bus system, **Metrobus** (*©* **709/722-9400;** www.metrobus.com). Adults (including seniors) can ride for C$1.50 (US$1.06). Children ages 3 to 18 (with student card) can ride for C$1 (US71¢). Under age 3 is free. You may find one of the 10-ride passes to be a bit more economical if you're planning to use the bus a lot.

Warning: Metrobus operates with an exact–cash fare policy. Drivers do not carry change.

BY CAR

Get yourself a detailed city map and have your navigator guide you along the way, as driving in St. John's—despite the fact that it's a compact city—isn't the easiest. A lot of the streets in the capital city, as well as in most other communities throughout the province, are in desperate need of repair. According to some expert tellers of tall tales, there are potholes so big you could get lost in them. Unfortunately, after a few days driving around the municipal obstacle course, you start to believe them.

Warning: Beware of the multitude of one-way streets, hidden and roundabout intersections, and the fact that streets change names at whim from one block to the next. The good thing is that it's not that difficult to find your way back on track even if you do get lost or turned around, as the city isn't very large and traffic volumes are generally not a problem. Also, be aware that you may find a shortage of downtown parking during business hours and when there are special events taking place at Mile One Stadium.

3 Where to Stay

During peak season, which is generally late July to mid-August, the city books to capacity. This is when the Folk Festival, the George Street Festival, and the Royal St. John's Regatta all take place. If you like excitement, it's the best time to visit St. John's, but it can also be the most expensive and difficult time to secure accommodations. So plan well ahead whenever possible.

FAST FACTS: **St. John's**

ATMs   You'll find a number of financial institutions along **Water Street** in downtown St. John's. Check the phone book for other bank locations.

Business Hours   See the "Holidays" section in Chapter 2 for a detailed listing of days that stores would be closed. Most shops in the city are open weekdays for business from around 10am until 6pm, but individual store hours may vary. Malls are open 10am to10pm. The malls and some shops are open Sundays from noon to 5pm. Banks are generally open weekdays 10am to 4pm, although some close at 3pm while others are open until 5pm.

Car Rentals   Most of the major players have rental booths at the St. John's airport. Check the phone book for other locations.

Climate   St. John's has a temperate marine climate. See the "When to Go: Weather" section of chapter 2 for further details. Call ℂ **709/772-5534** for local updates on the weather while in town.

Emergencies   Call ℂ **911** in case of emergency to reach police, ambulance, or the fire department.

Internet Access   The only true Internet/cybercafe in St. John's is located in the **Wordplay Bookstore,** 221 Duckworth St. (ℂ **800/563-9100** or 709/726-9193). **Starbucks/Chapters** at 70 Kenmount Rd. (ℂ **709/726-0375**) also offers Internet access. As well, free Internet service is available at the following public libraries: **A. C. Hunter Library at the Arts and Culture Centre,** Allandale Rd. (ℂ **709/737-2133**); **Marjorie Mews Library,** 18 Highland Dr. (ℂ **709/737-3020**); and **Michael Donovan Library,** 655 Topsail Rd. (ℂ **709/737-2621**). The **Canada Post** office also offers free Internet access at 354 Water St. (ℂ **709/758-1003**).

Libraries   See "Internet Access," above.

Newspapers   The major newspaper in St. John's is *The Telegram.* Their online version (www.thetelegram.com) offers many useful local links.

Post Office   The main **Canada Post** office can be found at 354 Water St. (ℂ **709/758-1003**). You can also find postal outlets in most **Shoppers Drug Mart** stores, for example at 430 Topsail Rd. in the Village Shopping Centre (ℂ **709/368-6084**) and 141 Torbay Rd. (ℂ **709/722-6270**).

Safety   Whether you're gay, elderly, of a visible minority, or a woman traveling alone, you should feel secure walking the streets of St. John's. Street crimes are relatively rare.

Warning: Be aware that because so many pubs are on George Street, the area can get quite rowdy late in the evening and is best avoided if you're not a pub-goer. (If you are, it can be a lot of fun!) Be sensible and lock your vehicle when unattended anywhere in the city. Don't leave your purse or backpack unattended, and be alert to your surroundings as you would when visiting anywhere.

Taxes   An HST (harmonized federal and provincial sales tax) of **15%** is applicable to most purchases. St. John's has an **additional 3% tax on accommodations** within the city limits. See the "Tips & Taxes" section in chapter 2 for info on tax rebates.

Telephone   It costs **C.25¢** to make a local call from a pay phone. If you have a cellphone, you'll have no difficulty getting service while in St. John's. Call 𝄐 **411** for directory assistance.

Water   St. John's tap water is fine for drinking. Bottled water is provided in many hotels and is available for purchase throughout the city.

St. John's offers a rich choice of accommodations, everything from a modest room in a local resident's home to a small number of luxurious hotels, and quite a bit in between. The only category that you won't find is the massive or lavish resort-type accommodations found in, say, Las Vegas.

The listings in this guidebook include properties that stand out for a particular reason. For example, one is located next to the Folk Festival grounds; another is an aesthetic treat with its beautiful stained glass; and yet another is best known as a favorite hideaway for honeymooners. And to get away from strictly material amenities, one listing offers the friendliest hosts in the city. You get the picture.

Heritage "Inn" St. John's

Newfoundland & Labrador's capital city is unique for its incredible number of heritage inns. Most of these are classified under the Bed & Breakfast section in the province's online list of accommodations (www.gov.nf.ca/tourism/mainmenu/wheretostay/avalon/default.htm).

A simple bedroom for rent in someone's home may also fall into this same B&B category providing it has met certain government criteria. It's therefore very important to read the list of amenities carefully to ensure that you're getting not only what you're paying for, but also what you need to be comfortable.

Many people (myself included) do not especially like to share a bathroom with other travelers—or even with the owner of the home. In St. John's, you don't really have to worry about this as virtually all B&Bs offer private baths (at least for most of their rooms).

In the more remote communities throughout the province, however, accommodations with a shared bath become a reality and may be referred to as either a B&B or Hospitality Home.

Most of the B&Bs in St. John's are more like country or heritage inns and are in a higher price range than you may expect. The average price for one of the nicer ones is well over C$100 (US$71) per night for one of their better rooms. When making your reservations, be sure to ask about the amenities that are most important to you—especially if you have mobility problems, as many of these inns do not have an elevator to get you up the stairs.

If you're staying in St. John's for more than a few days, you may want to consider staying at more than one type of accommodation—say, a hotel and at least one heritage inn or B&B—to get a fuller flavor of the city's interesting range of offerings.

Type of accommodation may be more relevant in your decision-making process than strictly price, so I've grouped accommodations by type rather than price. I've used two broad categories to cover standard accommodations: **Hotels/Motels** and **Heritage Inns/B&Bs**. Depending on your individual preference, you can choose a particular property from within that category based on the price you want to pay and the amenities offered.

Information on camping in the St. John's area is also included. Remarkable camping is just a 10-minute drive from the city's downtown area—which makes St. John's an ideal destination for RVers and camping families.

HOTELS AND MOTELS

The Battery Hotel & Suites ⋆⋆
An all-white, sentinel-like structure, the Battery at night appears to be an almost spectral image suspended above the city. Located on the way up to Signal Hill and a 1-minute walk from the new Geo Centre, the Battery has a distinctive name and the best location in the city. And while it's a nice hotel, you can't help being disappointed because it has the potential to be a truly great hotel—if only the owners had dedicated themselves to creating a personality. They might have done a more thorough job of incorporating the facility's military namesake into its decor, or branded it as the city's preeminent luxury hotel. Instead, it follows the standard impersonal script found in the majority of mid-range hotels. The most striking amenities are the view (an unparalleled eagle's perspective of the harbor below), the natural Newfoundland courtesy of hotel staff, and a Sunday brunch stocked with a selection of food that requires some major belt loosening.

There's ample free parking, and a business center in the lobby with free computer use (except for modest online charges) that's available to all guests. There is no air-conditioning in the guest rooms but the windows do open. Some rooms have whirlpool baths, and suites are fully equipped with kitchenettes.

100 Signal Hill Rd., St. John's, NL A1A 1B3. ℭ **800/563-8181** or 709/576-0040. Fax: 709/576-6943. www.batteryhotel.com. 125 units. C$89–$189 (US$65–$137) double. AE, DC, MC, V. **Amenities:** Restaurant, bar; indoor pool; sauna; whirlpool; laundry & dry-cleaning services; walking trails. Pets welcome. *In room:* TV w/pay movies, coffeemaker, hairdryer, iron.

Best Western Traveller's Inn ⋆
Moderately priced, reliably clean, and uncomplicated accommodations that are perfect for the business traveler or the budget-conscious visitor. You'll find the Traveller's Inn makes a strategic base from which to plan excursions throughout the city. By car, it's just 15 minutes from downtown, less than 5 minutes from the largest shopping mall in the province, and no more than 10 minutes from Memorial University, a hospital, and the provincial government. Because it's situated on one of the busiest streets in St. John's, you'll want to ask for a room at the back of the building where the noise of passing traffic is less likely to keep you awake at night. The recently renovated guest rooms are spacious and comfortably, although not luxuriously, appointed.

199 Kenmount Rd., St. John's, NL A1B 3P9. ℭ **800/261-5540** or 709/722-5540. Fax: 709/722-1025. www.bestwestern.com. 88 units. C$79–$109 (US$57–$79) double. AE, DC, MC, V. **Amenities:** Restaurant, lounge; heated outdoor pool; billiard room; free parking; laundry service. *In room:* TV w/pay movies, coffeemaker, hairdryer, iron.

Delta St. John's Hotel & Conference Centre ⋆⋆
Situated on the Trans-Canada Highway arterial road that enters St. John's, and adjacent to the new Convention Centre and Mile One Stadium, the Delta is an ideal choice for the business or individual traveler attending a function at any of these venues. It's also one of the closest accommodations to downtown shopping and nightlife, so

you can shop 'til you drop, bring your parcels to your room, and be back in action within minutes.

Of special note for corporate travelers are the "Business Zone" rooms, which come specially equipped with in-room fax machine, printer, cordless phone, ergonomically designed chair, halogen lamp, 24-hour computer availability, and office supplies.

120 New Gower St., St. John's, NL A1C 6K4. *©* **800/268-1133** or 709/739-6404. Fax: 709/570-1622. www.deltahotels.com. 276 units. C$150–$315 (US$109–$228) double. AE, DC, DISC, MC, V. Underground, valet parking available for C$5/US$3 additional/day. **Amenities:** Restaurant; indoor pool; fitness center; children's program and babysitting; concierge; laundry/dry cleaning. *In room:* A/C, TV w/pay movies, minibar, coffeemaker, hairdryer, iron.

Fairmont Newfoundland ★★★ Still referred to as the "Hotel Newfoundland" among locals because of its longtime history under that name, the Fairmont Newfoundland stands alone as the best full-service hotel in town. Positives include everything from two fine restaurants (one very expensive and the other more moderately priced—see the "Where to Dine" section for reviews); a spa and fitness center; art gallery; gold-level service floor, complete with no-wait check-in, on-floor concierge, and lounge with computer for guest use; and the best view of the Narrows in the city. The only negatives are its lack of traditional charm and windows that don't open to provide you with a whiff of that fresh sea air.

With more than 300 guest rooms on 7 floors, the Fairmont is where royalty and other dignitaries stay while in St. John's. If you can spare the C$800 (US$580) it costs for a night, go for the lavish Admiral Suite and you can say you slept in the same room as the Queen of England. End-of-the-hall rooms with numbers ending in 00 offer the best panoramic views. The Junior Suites offer large porthole-style windows.

The Fairmont rewards you for planning ahead. With plenty of lead time, you can get a deluxe room with harbor view for as low as C$135 (US$98), even in peak season. That same room goes for C$300 (US$217) in periods of low availability with little or no advance booking, so the longer you wait to book, the more you'll pay.

115 Cavendish Sq. (P.O. Box 5637), St. John's NL A1C 5W8. *©* **800/441-1414** or 709/726-4980. Fax: 709/726-2025. www.fairmont.com/newfoundland. 301 units. C$199–$800 (US$144–$580) double. AE, DC, DISC, MC, V. Pets allowed for additional C$25/night. **Amenities:** 2 restaurants, lounge; indoor pool and fitness center; day spa; business center; babysitting; concierge; 24-hour room service. *In room:* A/C, TV w/pay movies and Sony PlayStation™, minibar, coffeemaker, hairdryer, iron, bathrobes.

⸨Fun Fact⸩ Remember When

The original Hotel Newfoundland opened in 1926. With its steam heating, ballroom, and luxury accommodations, it was heralded in the news of the day as the ultimate in "artistic taste." Rooms cost $18/night for double occupancy; running water cost an extra $7.

Guv'nor Inn ★ You'd miss the Guv'nor on a quick drive-by because of its modest exterior, but this isn't one of those hotels you visit for its ambiance. Its strongest feature is its location: minutes from Memorial University and within walking distance of the General Hospital Health Sciences Centre. It's a comfortable, convenient place to stay if you're visiting someone in hospital or have business at the university.

Note: The inn has no elevator, so anyone with heavy luggage or bad knees may have trouble with the stairs.

389 Elizabeth Ave., St. John's, NL A1B 1V1. ℭ **800/961-0092** or 709/726-0092. Fax: 709/726-5921. www. guvnor-inn.com. 38 units. C$80–$100 (US$58–$72) double; extra person C$7. AE, DC, MC, V. **Amenities:** Restaurant, pub. *In room:* TV, dataport, coffeemaker, hairdryer, iron.

Holiday Inn *Kids* With two groomed walking trails, a playground, and the best 18-hole mini-golf course in the city (Sir Admiral John's Green) all within a 5-minute walk, this hotel is the perfect accommodation for traveling families. If you request one of the motel-style rooms, you'll have the added bonus of being able to park your vehicle directly outside your room door (great when small children fall asleep on the drive—you can carry them straight to bed). That said, however, it is on the pricey side given its style and standard (typical Holiday Inn). Both smoking and nonsmoking floors are available.

180 Portugal Cove Rd., St. John's, NL A1B 2N2. ℭ **800/933-0506** or 709-722-0934. Fax: 709/722-9756. www.holidayinnstjohns.com. 250 units. C$125–$200 (US$91–$145) double. AE, DC, DISC, MC, V. **Amenities:** Restaurant, lounge, outdoor heated pool (open July–Aug only), salon, babysitting. *In room:* A/C, TV w/pay movies, dataport, minibar, coffeemaker, hairdryer, iron.

Murray Premises Hotel *Finds* A boutique hotel that gets top marks for its excellent service and distinctive character. You may find yourself slightly disoriented at first because the hotel lobby/check-in counter looks like a building directory/information desk. But, after an abbreviated ride in an elevator built for two (it's a *very* small elevator), you'll swear you're at an exclusive European chalet, complete with personal towel warmers and fireplace. The original beamed ceilings, columns, and timber-slanted roofs add a rustic, cozy feeling to the otherwise modern rooms.

If you can pull yourself away from the custom-made maple beds with gorgeous duvets and top-quality linens, you should take the time to discover the other businesses conveniently located under the same roof. The Murray Premises is a refurbished cluster of former warehouses that is now home to exclusive shops (I'm still drooling over the sleek, handcrafted, red leather shoulder bag I saw in the luggage store), offices, eating establishments, the best-stocked wine boutique in the province, and, of course, a hotel. It's accessible from Water Street and Harbour Drive, which means you have both the downtown shopping district and the waterfront on your doorstep.

5 Beck's Cove (P.O. Box 208) St. John's, NL A1C 6H1. ℭ **866/738-7773** or 709-738-7773. Fax: 709/ 738-7775. 28 units. www.murraypremiseshotel.com. C$129–$189 (US$93–$137) double. AE, DC, MC, V. **Amenities:** 2 restaurants, limited room service, all nonsmoking guest rooms. *In room:* A/C, TV, dataport, fridge, coffeemaker, hairdryer, iron, bathrobe.

Quality Hotel–Harbourfront Located as it is on Hill O'Chips, you'd think this hotel would be well known for its food—and you'd be right! It's lobby restaurant, Rumpelstiltskin's, has a business-casual atmosphere with well-prepared meals and reasonable prices (see the review in the "Where to Dine" section). The hotel itself is less memorable, although its harborside rooms offer a picturesque view of the Narrows. Because it's part of the Choice Hotels chain, you know what to expect before you arrive. Which means it doesn't have the personality of a boutique hotel, but at the same time you know you can depend on it for reliable service as well as clean and comfortable rooms. Its 42 Business Class rooms furnished with full-size desks and ergonomic chairs make it a popular choice with corporate travelers.

2 Hill O'Chips, St. John's NL A1C 6B1. ☎ **800/228-5151** or 709/754-7788. Fax: 709/754-5209. www.choice hotels.ca. 160 units. C$154–$169 (US$112–$122) double; kids under 18 stay free with an adult. AE, DC, DISC, MC, V. **Amenities:** Restaurant, lounge. *In room:* A/C, TV w/pay movies, dataport, fridge in some rooms, coffeemaker, hairdryer, iron.

HERITAGE INNS AND BED & BREAKFASTS

Banberry House ★★ One of the best things about Banberry House is Annie, the cook. She loves to be creative, and is bound to please and surprise you with such local breakfast delicacies as *toutons* (fried bread dough that tastes much better than it sounds, especially topped with molasses), salt cod cakes, and bread-stuffed bologna. Everything is made on-site, and guests are guaranteed not to get the same breakfast twice if they're staying for a week or less, as a different specialty is featured each morning.

Another great thing about this property is its location. When staying here, just a stone's throw from Bannerman Park where the Folk Festival is held each summer, you can actually sit on the patio amidst the potted plants and enjoy the music without ever leaving the yard—or getting too far from Annie's delights. Built in 1892, the Banberry House boasts wonderful stained glass by the same craftsman whose work adorns the nearby Catholic Basilica of St. John the Baptist.

The guest rooms at the Banberry exhibit carefully preserved historical authenticity. One of the rooms has an old-style four-poster bed and wood-burning fireplace. Some have the old-fashioned footed tubs as well as shower stalls. The main floor "Labrador Room" has an especially rugged feel to it. With your room rate, you get a complimentary gourmet breakfast and off-street parking. On-site dining is available at an additional charge.

116 Military Rd., St. John's, NL A1C 2C9. ☎ **877/579-8226** or 709-579-8006. Fax: 709/579-3443. www. bbcanada.com/banberry. 6 units.

C$119–$149 (US$86–$108) double; off-season rates available. AE, MC, V. **Amenities:** Nonsmoking rooms. *In room:* TV, private ensuite bathrooms.

Bluestone Inn ★★★ *Finds* This funky yet classic inn in downtown St. John's is tastefully decorated with a wonderful selection of original art mingled with historical embellishments. It took owner Neil Oates a year and a half to dig out the original stone wall, which adds an old-world atmosphere to "Excess Baggage," the name he's given this wonderful meeting/conference room.

The original building dates back more than 250 years, and is reported to be the oldest stone structure in the city. The location is fantastic—by foot, it's within minutes of restaurants, the Folk Festival grounds, shopping, and museums. And you're just a 10-minute drive (5km/3 miles) from St. John's International Airport.

For breakfast, you can enjoy local specialties such as partridgeberry pancakes. The lower-level breakfast nook doubles as a bar for guests later in the day and evening. To unwind at the end of the day, you can enjoy a glass of wine and share stories with fellow travelers here or out on the lovely street-front patio.

The guest rooms are spacious and above average in every way. High-quality bedding is used throughout. Room 1 is magnificent, with dark wood and more of a masculine feel. Some of the other rooms have a softer touch. All have Jacuzzis and many other amenities such as high-speed Internet and a hotel-style telephone system. Self-contained units are available for longer stays. For an additional charge, the owner can even arrange unique float-plane excursions.

34 Queen's Rd., St. John's, NL A1C 2A5. ☎ **877/754-9876** or 709/754-7544. Fax: 709/722-8626. http://the bluestoneinn.com. 4 units. C$139–$299 (US$101–$217) double; ask about off-season rates. AE, DC, MC, V. **Amenities:** Lounge, nonsmoking rooms, group-use space available. *In room:* TV, dataport.

Leaside Manor *A* A charming Tudor mansion situated in a quiet suburban location just minutes from downtown, Leaside Manor provides a peaceful and serene place to lay your head. The grounds are lovely, with gardens in full bloom if you're fortunate enough to visit during summer and early fall.

The most important thing about Leaside Manor is that the rooms vary considerably, both in rates and amenities. The Parker Suite is gorgeous, with a bedside Jacuzzi. The spacious Signal Hill apartment is also nice, with full kitchen, a Jacuzzi, and lovely furnishings. The Confederation Room, although nicely furnished and equipped with plenty of reading material as well as a VCR, has a phone booth–sized shower stall that doesn't meet the standards of the rest of the inn.

All rooms include a complimentary full breakfast and parking. Tour planning assistance is offered and fully equipped apartments are available for long-term stays at two additional locations.

39 Topsail Rd., St. John's, NL A1E 2A6. *C* 877/807-7245 or 709/722-0387. Fax: 709/739-1835. www.leaside.nf.ca. 8 units. C$99–$199 (US$73–$147) double. AE, DC, MC, V. **Amenities:** *In room:* TV/VCR, dataport.

Maunder Manor *A* *Value* What it lacks in glamor, Maunder Manor makes up for in warmth and hospitality. Don and Yvonne Bradbury are the dream hosts you hope for at every B&B you visit. They're helpful, considerate, and accommodating—particularly when it comes to solitary travelers.

All that, plus a terrific location (just around the corner from the Fairmont), and clean and inviting rooms make Maunder Manor a good choice for anyone on a budget or in search of traditional NL-style hospitality right in the heart of the city. You'll find a well-stocked reading room upstairs, and a comfortable sitting room with TV on the main floor. Your room rate includes a terrific made-to-order full breakfast.

29 Forest Rd., St. John's, NL A1C 2C2. *C* 709/726-5304. E-mail: mauman29@nf.sympatico.ca. 2 rooms. C$60 (US$44) double ensuite; C$50 (US$36) double with shared bath.

McCoubrey Manor *A* *A* This inn's terrific breakfast includes fresh fruit salad, muffins, loaves, homemade jams, and a choice of two hot entrees. McCoubrey Manor, built in 1904, is quaintly nostalgic with black-and-white photos of the original owners throughout the home. Antique furnishings and log-burning fireplaces make this a cozy choice—especially during the colder months. The warm colors used to decorate McCoubrey Manor provide a comfortable ambiance for the complimentary evening wine-and-cheese get-togethers hosted by the owners, Jill and Roy Knoechel. Some of the guest rooms have a view of the harbor; "Catherine's Haven" offers the romantic luxury of a double Jacuzzi.

6–8 Ordnance St., St. John's, NL A1C 3K7. *C* 888/753-7577 or 709/722-7577. Fax: 709/579-7577. www.mccoubrey.com. 4 units. C$89–$199 (US$64–$144) double. AE, DC, MC, V. **Amenities:** Laundry facilities, nonsmoking rooms. *In room:* A/C, TV/VCR w/CD player.

Winterholme Heritage Inn *A* *A* *A* *Finds* I'm a romantic at heart, so when owner Dick Cook told me that his inn is popular with honeymooners, my ears perked up. To my luck, a newlywed couple was checking out on my arrival. Needless to say, they were beaming. I think anyone would be after spending a night at Winterholme. It's a truly breathtaking property inside and out. The intricate woodwork, the lovely stained glass, and the spacious double-Jacuzzi rooms are all special touches, but it's the English oak staircase—appraised at C$250,000/US$194,000!—that will leave you in awe. It's a piece of artwork in itself.

Designated a National Historic Site, Winterholme is a wonderful example of Queen Anne Revival architecture—popular in Canadian house construction from the 1880s until about 1914. Anyone who appreciates fine craftsmanship and has a sense of history would enjoy staying here. Every guest room is different and offers its own charm, but all are extremely spacious and equipped with luxuries such as a double Jacuzzi and fireplace. A delicious full breakfast and parking are included in the rates.

79 Rennies Mill Rd., St. John's, NL A1C 3R1. ℂ 800/599-7829 or 709/739-7979. Fax: 709/753-9411. www.winterholmeheritageinn.com. 12 units.C$129–$199 (US$93–$144). AE, DC, MC, V. **Amenities:** Laundry facilities, fax machine, computer and printer, microwave. *In room:* Cable TV, dataport, coffeemaker, hairdryer.

HOSTELS AND CAMPING

C.A. Pippy R.V. Park   Whether you're camping in a tent or a fancy RV, Pippy Park provides a wonderfully treed setting close to Memorial University and within minutes of downtown St. John's. The Fluvarium is an educational attraction within the park (separate admission) and well worth investigating. The campground operates 94 fully serviced, 38 semi-serviced, and 26 unserviced sites.

Nagle's Place (P.O. Box 8861), St. John's, NL A1B 3T2. ℂ 877/477-3655, 709/737-3669, or 709/737-3655 off-season. Fax: 709/737-3303. www.pippypark.com. May 1–Sept 30 subject to weather conditions. C$23 (US$17) full service, C$20.70 (US$15) semi-serviced, C$16.10 (US$12) unserviced; tax included. Winter storage available Oct 1–Apr 30. MC, V. **Amenities:** Dumping station; electrical, sewer, and water hook-up; golf; hiking; pets allowed; playground; fully accessible shower and washroom facilities; kayak and canoe rentals at nearby Memorial University.

Hostel Accommodations, Memorial University *Value*   All budget-conscious travelers, both students and non-students, should know about the inexpensive accommodations available from May to August through the Conference Office at Memorial University. Rooms are standard dormitory issue (there are single and twin rooms; twin rooms have two beds, two desks, two chairs, and two closets) with communal, gender-specific bathrooms. The university residence is not only on a main bus route, but also within walking distance of the Pippy Park golf course, Aquarena fitness facility, the Arts and Culture Centre, and General Hospital Health Sciences Centre. All this in a quiet, park-like setting with mature trees and the added protection of campus security.

Conference Office, Rm 315, Hatcher House, Memorial University, St. John's, NL A1B 3P7. ℂ 709/737-7933. Fax: 709/737-3520. www.housing.mun.ca/conf/index.php?content=conf_summeraccom. C$16 (US$12) student/senior rate for double room, C$19.50 (US$14) for non-students, twin room. MC, V. **Amenities:** Coin-operated laundry facilites on-site; meals can be purchased in the cafeteria-style dining hall.

4 Where to Dine

For such a small city, St. John's has some wonderful restaurants and a great variety of culinary adventures to choose from: traditional NL meals, wild game, expertly prepared seafood, melt-in-your-mouth steak, sushi, haute cuisine—the list goes on. You could eat out every night for a month without dining at the same place twice. The most sophisticated independent eating establishments are on Duckworth or Water streets, but surprisingly several of the hotels also have great food.

Regardless of where you venture for finer dining, you have to have fish and chips at least a couple of times while in NL. St. John's has some excellent places that specialize in fish and chips. Freshwater Road is a popular location. The most famous is **Ches's,** but **Johnny's** and **Leo's** are also recommended. Some of the locals swear that **Chucky's Fish & Ships** at 10 King's Road (north of Duckworth Street E.) has the best *fi and chi* (pronounced "fee and chee"; that's waiter-speak for fish and chips). You'll find Newfoundlanders are definite connoisseurs of this particular dish, judging each establishment by the texture of the batter and the crispness of the fries.

I tried them all, but not being a native I couldn't identify any substantial differences between them. They're all visit-worthy, providing good value and sizable portions of battered cod served with french-fried potatoes. Just remember that when you're in NL, you automatically get cod when you order fish unless it's otherwise specified. And don't be surprised if someone asks if you want dressing and gravy with your fries. Just as Montrealers love their fries dipped in mayonnaise, many Newfoundlanders and Labradorians wouldn't want their fries unless they were smothered in dressing and gravy.

(Fun Fact What's "Dressing"?

As it relates to food, "dressing" in Newfoundland & Labrador usually means one thing: bread crumbs mixed with chopped onion, savory, and melted butter. Some people add diced celery as well. In addition to its use as a side dish for french fries, it's also the stuffing of choice for roast turkey and chicken.

If you have any room left for dessert, drop in to **Moo Moo's Dairy Bar** at 88 King's Road (near Rawlins Cross). Housed in a building boldly painted to look like a cow, Moo Moo's has excellent homemade ice cream. The orange pineapple flavor is especially refreshing on a hot summer's day, and I guarantee it's just about the creamiest ice cream you'll ever taste.

Note: Smoking is banned in any public places where children may be found, including restaurants. You can smoke and eat in bars where minors are prohibited. *Warning to parents:* Children under 16 aren't allowed in most of the pubs and even some of the restaurants because of the anti-smoking laws. It'll save time—and be less embarrassing—if you call ahead and see if children are allowed, rather than risk being turned away at the door.

EXPENSIVE

AQUA Restaurant & Bar ★★ ECLECTIC   Owner Alfred Hynes has put together a rather exotic menu for his intimate downtown restaurant. Specialties of the house include pistachio-encrusted goat cheese (made locally) served on mixed greens with a raspberry mango sauce and garlic crostini and locally grown island blue mussels served in a coconut cilantro broth; both are listed as starters, but combined they make a perfect and affordable meal. Be sure to try the flatbread coated with sea salt served at your table. Save room for dessert. Everything is made on-site and is fantastic, including the rich and creamy crème brûleé and the sour cream and coconut ice creams. The menu changes with the season. An interesting selection of black-and-white photography adorns the walls.

310 Water St. (℃) **709/576-2782.** www.aquarestaurant.ca. Reservations recommended, especially during summer weekends. Main courses C$18–$29 (US$13–$21). AE, DC, MC, V. Mon–Fri noon–2pm; Sun–Thurs 5:30–10pm, Fri–Sat 5:30–10:30pm.

Tips Dining Money Matters

You'll find a 15% harmonized sales tax added to your bill before tip, so at better establishments you're looking at 30% (for tip and taxes) on top of the base price of your bill. As well, wine prices tend to be higher than in other destinations. It's not uncommon to pay C$8–10 (US$6–7) for a good glass of wine with dinner. Another somewhat more adventurous alternative is to go with the house wine, which can be as much as C$3 (US$2.13) cheaper per glass.

Most of the downtown restaurants are in the C$20 (US$13) per person price range. If that's a bit steep for your budget, you can order a soup or salad followed by an appetizer as your entree, a more economical—yet satisfying—way to try the best restaurants without breaking the bank. Or you may want to save some of the more expensive places for lunch rather than dinner; if they're open, many of these establishments offer basically the same menu at lunch for a less prohibitive price.

Another tip: To try as many restaurants as possible when you're on a limited schedule, why not restaurant hop? Ordering a soup or salad with a glass of wine in one restaurant and then heading to another for a hot appetizer or entree (and another glass of wine!), and maybe a third for dessert and coffee is a terrific way to try the offerings of a greater number of places. This works especially well on Duckworth Street, where you'll find several very good—yet varied—restaurants all in a row.

The Bonavista *** CANADIAN   This informal dining room at the Fairmont Newfoundland is bright, cheery, and offers a more relaxed setting than its formal counterpart, The Cabot Club. The Bonavista is highly regarded among locals for its terrific "Jiggs Dinner" buffet, served every Friday at noon. Other menu highlights include the "Newfoundland Cod Corner," offering several different ways to have your cod prepared, and the "Pick a Pasta Delisioso," which gives you the opportunity to choose your pasta type, special ingredients, and serving size. The one thing I didn't like about the layout of this eating area is that it isn't fully enclosed, so that other people in the hotel can watch you eat as they walk past.

115 Cavendish Sq. © **709/726-4980.** Reservations not required. AE, DC, DISC, MC, V. Main courses C$18–$29 (US$13–$21); Friday noon buffet C$20.50 (US$15). Mon–Fri 6:30am–10pm; Sat–Sun 7:30am–10pm.

Fun Fact A Tasty Dish

Boiled corned beef and cabbage, along with potatoes, carrots, parsnip, turnip, and pease pudding (made from dried, split peas) was a dietary staple in NL in the days before modern refrigeration. It was also the favorite meal for Mr. Jiggs, a character in an American comic strip. Hence the nickname Jiggs Dinner.

The Cabot Club ⭐⭐⭐ CONTINENTAL   The harbor view in itself is worth the hefty prices you'll pay in this magnificent dining room at the Fairmont Newfoundland. Is it any wonder that the most elegant hotel in the city should be home to St. John's only four-diamond restaurant (so named by AAA/CAA)? It also boasts the honor of being named one of Canada's top 100 restaurants in the book *100 Best Restaurants of Canada* written by John McCann and published by Wanderlust Publications Ltd. You can be assured that the quality of service matches the impeccable quality of the food served at the Cabot Club. Menu selection includes everything from Alberta beef to a wonderful offering of Atlantic lobster in garam marsala aioli served with a squash and lentil stew. The desserts are so decadent that the locals order them to take home. If you're a chocolate lover, try the chocolate Italiano. It's truly magnifico!

115 Cavendish Sq. ℭ **709/726-4980.** Reservations recommended on weekends. AE, DC, DISC, MC, V. Main courses C$24–$37 (US$17–$27). Daily 6–10pm.

Chez Briann ⭐⭐ FRENCH   The food is great, with impeccable plate presentation. Depending on your mood, the decor could be considered either dark and somber or cozy and intimate. Situated in the heart of restaurant row on Duckworth Street, Chez Briann specializes in seafood and lamb with a French flair. Both the *fruits de mer Romesco* (tiger shrimp and scallops sautéed with roasted peppers, almonds, and garlic) and the *filet de saumon farci aux epinards* (medallions of salmon stuffed with spinach and ginger) were wonderfully flavored and of generous portion. The stairs leading from the front entrance to the second-floor dining area unfortunately make this a difficult venue for people with mobility limitations.

290 Duckworth St. (at Cathedral). ℭ **709/579-0096.** Reservations recommended. AE, DC, MC, V. Main courses C$11.95–$27.95 (US$9–$20). Daily 6–9:30pm.

Magnum & Steins ⭐⭐⭐ *Finds* CONTEMPORARY   It's one of those rare establishments that actually lives up to its promotional persona: Magnum & Steins bills itself as a creative dining experience. And it is. From your first glimpse of its audacious sidewalk presentation (oversized metal signage, two storeys of floor-to-ceiling windows) you immediately recognize that this restaurant is dramatically different from anything else in the city. The bold metallic accents continue inside, where a steel-plated winding staircase invites you to the upstairs dining room. But regardless of the artistic merit of your surroundings, they are no more (and no less!) than the perfect setting for the pièce de résistance: the food.

Each dish is a masterful creation, blending layers of subtle flavor with complementary colors and extraordinary plate arrangement. The result is gourmet. I went there with a couple of people, and we all ordered something different so that we could—what else?—sample each other's meals. The only problem was that we couldn't decide who had the best meal. I said it was my grilled striploin (so tender I could cut it with a fork) with jardiniere of vegetables, roasted new potatoes, and Madeira sauce. No, said another companion, it was her fresh salmon in its perfectly roasted garlic and potato crust. You're both wrong, said the third, it was his roasted game hen with cranberry and paté stuffing, drizzled with black currant reduction. In the end, it was an easy contest: we all won.

284 Duckworth Street. ℭ **709/576-6500.** Reservations recommended. Main courses C$19–$30 (US$14–$22). AE, DC, MC, V. Mon–Fri noon–2pm and 5–10pm; Sat 5–10pm; Sun 6–9pm.

NaGeira's Restaurant ★★ MODERN EUROPEAN   As if the suit of armor out front weren't enough, what makes NaGeira's really outstanding is its innovative menu selection. You can get everything from soup to nuts (meaning wild game, rabbit, veal, lamb, and the other usuals), but it's the seafood specialties that make this warm and inviting restaurant stand out. The baked Atlantic salmon stuffed with a shrimp and scallop mousse is delightful. Or try the spinach with chicken livers sautéed in Frangelico and molasses; though only an appetizer, it's ample enough for a light meal. If you're a smoker or on a budget, you can have a more reasonably priced lunch and lighter meals up in Finnigan's Wake, the upstairs lounge.

283 Duckworth St. (at Cathedral). ✆ **709/753-1924.** www.nageiras.com. Reservations recommended. Main courses C$16–$50 (US$12–$36). AE, DC, MC, V. Mon–Fri noon–2:30pm, daily 5–10pm.

MODERATE

The Bread Pig ★★ WHOLESOME LOCAL FARE   A casual bistro, bakery, and chocolatier, The Bread Pig is well worth a visit. They're best known for the bread they make from a 270-year-old starter brought over from France. Lunches include gourmet pizzas, steamed mussels, and a good variety of soups and sandwiches. Dinners include a host of seafood specialties. The "Champagne Brunch à la Bread Pig" offers selected favorites such as smoked salmon and scrambled eggs, a tasty breakfast burrito, and *toutons*—a traditional NL dish. You'll get all fresh ingredients here. Nothing is deep fried, and nothing is served from a tin. Live entertainment every Friday and Saturday. The kitchen closes at 9:30pm, but the bar and coffee service stay open later. Try the bread pudding for dessert. *Tip:* They even accept Canadian Tire money!

21 Queen's Rd. at Prescott (at the famous Rawlins Cross intersection). ✆ **709/579-4788.** http://thebread pig.com. Main courses C$10.75–$23.50 (US$6.90–$15). AE, DC, MC, V. Mon–Fri 11:30am–9:30pm; Sat 10am–10pm; Sun brunch 11am–3pm, dinner 3–9:30pm.

Chucky's Fish & Ships ★ REGIONAL   Chucky's provides casual dining specializing in regional seafood, wild game, and NL favorites such as seal flipper pie. They're one of the only places in town to have a live lobster tank (in season), and are known to have the best fish and chips as well as a selection of game dishes that includes moose and caribou stews. And you can't get fish any fresher. Much of the fish served at Chucky's is caught right off of Chuck's own boats. Try their seafood platter. If you prefer your fish broiled as opposed to fried, they will oblige. The fish and chips are reasonably priced, and you get two generous pieces of fish, homemade fries, and Chucky's special coleslaw.

10 King's Rd. (north of Duckworth Street E.). ✆ **709-579-7888.** Main courses C$16–$24 (US$10–US$15). AE, DC, MC, V. Mon–Fri 11:30am–3pm and 5–9pm; Sat 4:30–9pm. Closed Sun.

Oliver's ★★ CONTINENTAL   Here you'll find classic dishes served in Mediterranean-style comfort with cozy booths that are large enough for a group of friends and intimate enough for a romantic duo (although there are a couple of tables that are too close to their neighbor for comfort). The Cajun jambalaya pasta is a deliciously spiced medley of shrimp and chicken, served over perfect al dente pasta. And the jumbo scallops marinara is a low-fat menu choice so sinfully tasty that you won't feel the least bit deprived. But my personal favorite isn't a main dish at all: it's the mulligatawny soup—a curry cream concoction with vegetables that's just this side of addictive. One spoonful, and you won't look up again until the bowl is empty! Their wine list also deserves some attention.

Oliver's stocks more than 500 wines, and selects several different varieties to feature as their house wine of the day.

160 Water St. ℂ **709/754-6444**. www.olivers-cafe.com. Reservations recommended. Main courses C$12–$26 (US$9–$19). AE, DC, MC, V. Sun–Thurs 11am–10pm; Fri 11am–11pm; Sat 10am–11pm.

The Pepper Mill ★ NOUVELLE   Owner Eric Collins says his restaurant offers "Haute cuisine without the haute attitude." He's right! It's a casual, comfortable place, yet the food is second to none. The Pepper Mill specializes in soups and generally has five to choose from each day. Other healthy choices include a good assortment of salads (which come in two sizes). Try the prawns sautéed in white wine and garlic for a starter. The daily dinner specials include such delicacies as arctic char (farmed locally and served trout-style with a citrus sauce). If you come here in the winter, request a table in the back of the restaurant. Patrons closest to the door are apt to feel the draft.

178 Water St. ℂ **709/726-7585**. Reservations recommended. Main courses C$14–$20 (US$9–$13). AE, DC, MC, V. Daily noon–2:30pm; Sun–Thurs 5–9:30pm, Fri–Sat 5–10pm.

Rumpelstiltskin's ★ CANADIAN   A wonderfully casual and informal atmosphere, with a multi-page menu that has something for everyone: chicken, ribs, steak, pizza, stir-fry (seriously, if you can't find something you like here, you're not hungry). The prime rib (of beef) is done to perfection and served with tender-crisp vegetables and a baked potato. I also recommend the scrumptious chicken sizzle, but watch out for the cast-iron serving tray—it's hot! To end a great meal, try one of their excellent desserts. A favorite is the chocolate ganache, a truly decadent creation of several layers topped with a thick layer of chocolate icing. It left this chocolate lover smiling all the way to dreamland.

The same menu is available all day, which is kind of nice if you're looking for a larger meal at noon or smaller meal at dinnertime. You'll have to book your reservation early if you want one of the window seats overlooking the harbor; this eatery is very popular with the locals.

2 Hill O'Chips (Quality Hotel). ℂ **709/579-6000**. Reservations recommended. Main courses C$6.95–$19.95 (US$5–$14). AE, DC, MC, V. Sun–Thurs 7am–10pm; Fri–Sat 7am–10:30pm.

INEXPENSIVE

Green Sleeves Pub, Lounge & Restaurant ★ BAR AND GRILL   It's like having three restaurants in one, all offering the same menu but completely different dining experiences. The main floor is a pub—complete with boisterous patrons, video lottery terminals, and smoking. Upstairs is a more subdued, civilized environment with table linens and no smoking. Outside is a multi-level open-air deck; the preferred choice for mid-day relaxation on a sunny afternoon. If you're in the mood for finger food, try the wings. They're the best chicken wings in the city, with a secret dry-spice mix that's zesty on its own, or you can boost the zing with a mild, medium, or hot dipping sauce. For a more substantial main course, choose the chicken savoyarde (tender chicken breast with mushrooms and onions in a sour cream and bacon sauce, tossed with linguine). It's a house specialty.

14 George St. ℂ **709/579-1070**. Main courses C$6.95–$14 (US$5–$10). AE, DC, MC, V. Sun 10am–10pm, Mon 11am–10pm, Tues–Fri 11am–9:30pm, Sat 10am–9:30pm.

The Guv'nor Pub & Eatery ★ PUB FARE   You'll want to come here for the atmosphere of this very English-style pub. Although it can be moderately boisterous if a bunch of students are on hand (it's close to Memorial University), the comfortable booths give you enough space and privacy to still enjoy your meal. The lasagna (served with garlic toast) is exceptionally good for pub fare. And the soup of the day (a turkey-, chicken-, or beef-vegetable variation) has a tasty broth that'll have you swiping the bowl with your dinner roll. Menu selection is very broad, including local specialties such as rabbit and caribou pot pies. The Guv'nor also has a location downtown at 210 Water St., in the McMurdo Building (© **709/738-3018**). Until as recently as 2003, the service at the downtown location tended to be slow, even during the lunch hour when most people are looking for express meals. Now, however, the food, service, and ambience is every bit as good as at the Elizabeth Avenue location. Both locations are worthy of a visit.

389 Elizabeth Ave. (at the Guv'nor Inn). © **709/726-3053**. Main courses C$8–$16 (US$6–$12). AE, DC, MC, V. Sun–Mon 9am–11pm, Tues–Sat 9am–midnight.

Nautical Nellies ☆ *Value* PUB FARE   There are a surprising number of negatives to dining at Nautical Nellies. It's a small, dark establishment that doesn't take reservations, has slow service, is sweltering in the summer, and has ice on the windows in the winter. That said, it's always crowded—especially from the start of Friday happy hour until closing. And, as you can tell from a quick conversation with any of those with Scottish, British, or Australian accents seated at the bar, it's the preferred hangout of visiting oil industry personnel. Why? Because it's the ideal place to have an ale and unwind, a true pub where staff know their regulars by name and drink preference. The food is excellently prepared and generously portioned—even at lunch, where one meal is probably enough for two people. Their chicken quesadilla is the best I've ever had, with tender chunks of chicken in every bite. The curried pork tortilla horns and crab spring roll appetizers are similarly exceptional.

201 Water St. © **709/738-1120**. No reservations. Main courses C$14–$20 (US$9–$13). AE, DC, MC, V. Sun 11am–3pm, Mon–Thurs 11:30am–3pm and 5–9pm, Fri 11:30am–3pm, Sat 11:30am–3pm and 5pm–9pm.

5 Exploring St. John's

Many of the capital city's most well-known attractions are either in the downtown core, or less than an hour's drive from there.

Unless you have mobility problems, the best way to explore the downtown area is on foot. The motorists are courteous (they have to be, because NL pedestrians have a tendency to just walk into traffic—especially downtown), so you don't have to worry about taking your life in your hands when you step off the curb.

Another great thing is that walking doesn't cost anything, and many of the buildings you'll want to see or stop at have either no—or a very small—admission. So take your time and enjoy what's around you.

Also remember that parking meters downtown are strictly policed, so you're best off parking in a lot if you're unsure of the amount of time you'll need. The maximum amount of time you can buy on a meter is 2 hours. Parking meters are free on weekends and after 6pm weekdays.

Unless you're a very energetic and experienced hiker, you'll have to drive to get to Fort Amherst, Signal Hill, Cape Spear, or Quidi Vidi. They're outside the downtown loop, but not out of reach if you have wheels.

DOWNTOWN ATTRACTIONS

Anglican Cathedral of St. John the Baptist   This National Historic Site was built between 1843 and 1885, with some reconstruction necessary following the Great Fire of 1892. The massive cathedral's Gothic architecture gives it a somewhat eerie presence, making the church an excellent meeting point for participants of the St. John's Haunted Hike, held late on summer evenings. (See more about this attraction in the "Walking Tours" section later in this chapter.) A small museum is on-site. During July and August, you can include a stop for tea weekday afternoons (2:30 to 4:30pm) at the Cathedral Crypt Tea Room ℰ **709/726-1999.**

22 Church Hill (at Gower Street). ℰ **709/726-5677.** Free tours are available daily 10am–5pm June–Sept.

 Up in Smoke

St. John's has been the victim of three "Great Fires." The first was actually a combination of two fires that took place in November 1817 (on the 7th and 21st). Together, they caused about $4 million in damage and destroyed almost 400 homes. The second major conflagration happened in June 1946, again causing $4 million in damage. But these were just sparks compared to the biggest fire of them all: the Great Fire of 1892. From a dropped pipe in a hay stable, the flames grew to nightmarish proportions. At its height, the heat was so intense it melted glass from windows throughout the city, most notably the Anglican Cathedral. When the smoke cleared, one-third of the city's population (10,000 people) were homeless.

Government House   Completed in 1831 for the Governor of Newfoundland (the island was an independent democracy until it joined Canadian Confederation in 1949), Government House is one of the city's few architectural treasures to have survived the Great Fire of 1892. The magnificent property reportedly cost four times more to complete than the U.S. White House (built the same year), and boasts a 3.6-m (12-ft.) moat. (Which is odd, because the building is not surrounded by water!) Today, Government House is the official residence of NL's Lieutenant Governor. The lovely grounds feature flower gardens and a place to have a relaxing stroll. Guided tours are available (by appointment only) for groups of 15 or more.

Military Rd. at King's Bridge Rd. ℰ **709/729-4494.** www.mun.ca/govhouse. Free admission. Daily 9am–dusk.

Newfoundland Science Centre *(Kids*   Contagiously enthusiastic scientific presentations that will motivate kids to experiment with all kinds of gross, goofy stuff. Here, they can walk like a dinosaur, build a castle, try out the "astronaut toilet," or even race with a bubble. A small section is dedicated to insects, fossil digs, and the telephone. And the interactive Space Odyssey display is way cool (with the magic of computer simulation, you too can blast off to Mars!). Just don't use the dreaded "e" word (educational). The Newfoundland Science Centre is very much a learning experience, but what the kids don't know won't hurt them.

Murray Premises, 5 Beck's Cove. ℭ **709/754-0823**. www.nlsciencecentre.com. Admission C$6 (US$4.25) adults, C$4.25 (US$3) students and seniors, free for children under 2; C$20 (US$14.50) family. Mon–Fri 10am–5pm, Sat 10am–6pm, Sun noon–6pm.

Newman Wine Vaults   These stone and brick vaults, constructed in the late 18th or very early part of the 19th century, were used by Newman & Co. (a British wine merchant) until at least 1893—possibly as late as 1914—to age their fine port. It started by accident in 1679, when a Newman's ship had been diverted to the island of Newfoundland to escape pirates and ended up storing its precious cargo in caves during that winter. When the crew returned to England with their port the following year, they discovered that its flavor had improved dramatically. Newman then began a cross-Atlantic custom of bringing its port to Newfoundland for aging in wine cellars, and eventually in these vaults, now a Provincial Historic Site. It would be nice if visitors to the vaults were given a tiny shot of port (even if a small admission had to be charged to pay for it), but that privilege is reserved for guests of private functions. Allow yourself 20 minutes to explore.

440 Water St. (north side, just west of Springdale St.). ℭ **709/739-7870**. www.historictrust.com/newman.shtml. Free admission. June 10–Aug 30 daily 10am–4:30pm.

Roman Catholic Basilica Parish of St. John the Baptist   The twin towers of the Basilica are a striking landmark in the city and can be seen rising high above its surroundings. You are free to tour this magnificent old stone church (a National Historic Site) of Romanesque design, built between 1841 and 1855, at any time other than during mass, which is held Sunday at 10:30am, Tuesday at 7pm, Wednesday to Friday at 9:30am, and Saturday at 5pm. You are, of course, welcome to attend mass. While at the Basilica, visit the Presentation Convent (just behind the Basilica) and see the Veiled Virgin marble carving.

200 Military Rd. ℭ **709/726-3660**. www.stjohnsarchdiocese.nf.ca. Free admission for children under 12; C$2 (US$1.45) for anyone over 12 to tour the Basilica Cathedral Museum, located on the corner of Military Rd. and Bonaventure Ave. Mon–Sat 11am–4pm.

 Spa at the Monastery

If all that touring leaves you exhausted, let the **Spa at the Monastery** take you on a journey of renewal. The only facility of its kind in the province, this day spa has 40 well-trained staff eager to pamper you. The most popular treatments include the wonderful hydrotherapy (C$45/US$32) and the Ayurveda Bindi herbal body therapy (C$80/US$57), the spa's specialty. Economically priced "Vitality Day Passes" are available for C$30/US$22, giving you access to the soak pools, sauna, steam room, cardio room, and the iceberg-water plunge pool. Reservations aren't just recommended, they're essential—unless you're lucky enough to step into a cancellation.

The spa is at 63 Patrick St. (ℭ **709/754-5800**; www.monastery-spa.com). Follow Water Street out of downtown to Patrick. Hours are Wednesday to Friday 10am–8pm; Monday, Tuesday, and Saturday 10am–6pm; Sunday 11am–5pm. A boutique, salon, and cafe are on-site, where they make some dynamite strawberry smoothies.

OUTSIDE OF DOWNTOWN

Cape Spear 🎯🎯   Cape Spear is the most easterly point in North America and a National Historic Site well worth visiting because of its naturally dramatic setting. You may be amazed at how different its weather can be from that in the city—it's situated just 15 minutes and 11km (7 miles) south of St. John's, but you may feel as much as a 59°F (15°C) temperature difference. Be sure to bring a sweater or jacket along with you. Allow at least 1½ hours to tour the visitor center, lighthouse, and gift shop, more if you'd like to linger and watch for whales along the coast.

Cape Spear Rd. (heading out of town, Blackhead Rd. turns into Cape Spear Rd.). ✆ **709/772-5367.** Lighthouse tour C$2.50 (US$1.80) adults, C$2 (US$1.45) seniors and children; C$4 (US$2.90), saving $1 off the regular admission, if you purchase a double pass to visit the Interpretive Centres at both Cape Spear and Signal Hill National Historic Sites. May 15–Oct 15 daily 10am–6pm.

Fluvarium 🎯🎯 *Kids*   If you're interested in what's underwater in the local freshwater ponds, the Fluvarium is a great place to visit. Twice voted the best indoor tourism site by Attractions Canada, the octagonal design of the subterranean Fluvarium makes it an interesting place for the whole family. You'll learn about three separate and distinct freshwater habitats and see a free-range fish habitat, a deep-water display of brown trout, and many interactive displays. You're looking through a glass wall at the underwater world outdoors, so it's best not to visit immediately after a rain as the water will be cloudier and visibility poorer. Allow no less than 1½ hours to visit, more if you'd like to enjoy the hiking trails. Feeding time is at 4pm, so it's best to arrive around 3pm.

Nagle's Place (next to Pippy Park). ✆ **709/754-3474.** C$5 (US$3.60) adults, C$4 (US$2.88) seniors and students, C$3 (US$2.16) children, children under 5 free. Summer hours daily 9am–5pm; rest of year Mon–Sat 10am–4:30pm; Sun noon–4:30pm.

Fort Amherst   The former lightkeeper's house at the Fort Amherst light station has been privately restored and now houses a small museum, photo gallery, craft shop, and a lovely tea room with breathtaking view. Local military, lighthouse, and community history is interpreted in each room. The lighthouse was put into operation in 1810 and was the first on the island of Newfoundland. Fort Amherst is situated across the Narrows from Signal Hill—a reminder of just how much protecting St. John's must have needed in its early days. It takes a bit of an effort to get there, but makes for a pleasant outing.

Prosser's Rock Boat Basin. (Traffic to Fort Amherst is restricted because of the narrowness of the road and lack of parking. You can park at Prosser's Rock and walk the rest of the way. It's not a difficult walk, but be aware of it. To get there, go west on Water St. until you reach the turnoff for Cape Spear Dr., at the intersection of Leslie and Water sts. Turn left at the traffic light; go over the bridge, then turn left again. This will take you along the south side of the harbor and to Prosser's Rock.) ✆ **709/368-6102.** Admission $1. June–Sept Mon–Fri noon–8pm, Sat–Sun 10am–8pm.

Institute for Ocean Technology 🎯 *Finds*   The free tours offered by the Institute are fantastic. Most visitors wouldn't think of St. John's as a locale boasting such advanced technology, but this facility does scale-model testing on boats and ships: everything from Coast Guard ice breakers to America's Cup yachts and oil platforms. The institute has three test tanks: an ice tank and two wave tanks, one complete with a simulated retractable beach! Just as with the Marine Institute (see the listing below), a full slate of activities may not be scheduled for the day you plan to visit, so when you phone ask what's going on that day. But even if one tank is unavailable for viewing, the machine shop alone is worth the visit.

Kerwin Place, Memorial University Campus. © **709/772-4366**. Reservations required for the free tours, conducted May–Aug Mon–Fri 9am–4:30pm. Children under 10 are not permitted.

Johnson Geo Centre *★★★* *(Kids* Prepare to "ooh" and "aah." What better place than the Rock to have a world-class geology center? But this is much more than a rock exhibit. A glass-walled elevator carries you three storeys underground to the floor of the main reception hall, where you are greeted by an oversized 3-D display of the solar system. Your next stop is the Geo Theatre for a dramatic presentation (with voiceover by actor Gordon Pinsent) on plate tectonics and continental formation. From there, kids of all ages are drawn to the exposed rock wall, where conveniently placed water bottles encourage you to spray the wall—thereby revealing the nuances of the granite structure. With new displays being added all the time, you're sure to find at least a couple of intriguing surprises. Allow a minimum of 1½ hours to visit—much more if anyone in your party has a fascination with rocks.

175 Signal Hill Rd. © **866/868-7625** or 709/737-7880. www.geocentre.ca. Admission C$6 (US$4.30) adults, C$5 (US$3.60) seniors and students, C$3 (US$2.16) children and youth 5–17, children under 5 free, C$15 (US$10.80) family. June 1–Oct 15 Mon–Sat 9:30am–5pm, Sun 1–5pm; Oct 16–May 31, closed Mon.

Marine Institute Affiliated with Memorial University, the Marine Institute teaches everything from fishing techniques to marketing and canning. Free tours are conducted during the summer. You can see the world's largest flume tank where actual-size fishing gear is lowered: from the amphitheater observatory it's like looking into a huge aquarium. There's also a marine simulator room where captains are trained and tested. Computer screens at the institute can simulate various harbors from around the world, creating virtual storms and causing the floor to move while students navigate their way on the screens. Both rooms are extremely interesting if in use but not nearly as exciting if you happen to visit while nothing is scheduled.

155 Ridge Rd., Pippy Park. © **800/563-5799** or 709/778-0200. www.mi.mun.ca. Free admission. Tours conducted during the summer Mon–Fri 1:30 and 3pm. Call in advance for reservations or to see what's happening that day.

Memorial University Botanical Garden If you're curious about the local flora, you should make your way over to the Botanical Garden, situated near Memorial University and Pippy Park. It's not as spectacular a public garden as you may find in some larger centers, but it's interesting to see the province's various boreal plants tastefully arranged by theme. There are also lovely walking trails that take you down to Oxen Pond. Give yourself a couple of hours to enjoy the setting. Be warned that the maps provided of the gardens can be somewhat confusing.

306 Mt. Scio Rd. © **709/737-8590**. Admission C$3.50 (US$2.50) adults, C$2.50 (US$1.80) seniors over 65 and students with ID card, C$1 (US$.71) children ages 6–18, children under 5 free. May–Nov daily 10am–5pm.

Ocean Sciences Centre *★* *(Finds* *(Kids* Just a short 5km (3-mile) drive from St. John's you'll find the Ocean Sciences Centre, a research facility right on the Atlantic Ocean, where you can see seals joyfully frolicking in large outdoor tanks and kids can examine whale bones and small ocean creatures in an outdoor touch tank—all for free. The building itself is not open to the public (except by guided tour), as it is strictly a research facility. But plans are under way to construct a new Cold Ocean Aquarium, which will be located on the shores of Logy Bay, adjacent to the Ocean Sciences Centre. Check their website for updates. Even if you don't arrange for a tour, the outdoor exhibits are still worth the short drive.

Marine Lab Rd. (take Rte. 30 [Logy Bay Rd.] onto Marine Dr. to get to Marine Lab Rd.). ✆ **709/737-3706.** www.coldoceanaquarium.ca. Admission C$4.50 (US$3.25) adults, C$3.50 (US$2.50) children. Tours July–Aug every half-hour from 10am–5pm, less frequently May–Nov.

 Finding Your Lucky Rock

While in the area of the Ocean Sciences Centre, be sure to stop in at **Middle Cove Beach** and look for your lucky rock! Many Newfoundlanders believe that finding a stone with a complete white line (the white line is calcite) around it will bring you good luck. And finding one with a double white line (and there are some—I know because I found one!) is said to bring you double the luck.

Quidi Vidi Village Pronounced "kiddee viddee," the historical fishing village of Quidi Vidi quite literally has something for everyone. Its namesake, Quidi Vidi Lake, is the site of the Royal St. John's Regatta (see more about this in the "Festivals & Special Events" section below).

A self-guided walking trail around Quidi Vidi Lake provides information about the local history and the opportunity to enjoy the outdoors. Plan to spend most of the day in Quidi Vidi Village. It's just minutes from the modern world of downtown St. John's, yet a historical world away. Across the tiny, picture-perfect harbor, your imagination will be captured by the sheds and stages seemingly suspended from the side of a cliff. They are accessible only by boat. (*Note:* The village has no inn, but the Stagehead Restaurant serves a fine lunch.)

During your walk around the lake, take the time to tour the **Regatta Museum,** which salutes the longest-running sporting event in North America. The museum houses a selection of non-curated awards and trophies from past Regatta events.

2nd floor of the lakeside boathouse. ✆ **709/576-8058.** Call ahead as hours of operation are seasonal and subject to change.

Quidi Vidi Battery is a Provincial Historic Site where you can learn more about the military presence in old St. John's. The Battery was first erected in 1762 by the French. It was later rebuilt by the British and has been restored to circa 1812. The knowledgeable interpretive guides in period costume make history come alive.

Cuckhold's Cove Rd. ✆ **709/729-2977.** Admission: C$2.50 (US$1.80) age 13 and up. Open daily 10am–4pm, mid-June–Labour Day.

Nearby, you'll find **Mallard Cottage Antiques and Collectibles,** the oldest cottage in North America—a provincial and national Heritage Cottage. Here, you can purchase some lovely collectibles and antiques. If the door is locked when you arrive, just cross the street. The owner, Peg, lives there and will be pleased to open up for you.

2 Barrows Rd. ✆ **709/576-2266.** Open daily 10am–5pm year-round.

A Village Stay at Petty Harbour/Maddox Cove

If you don't have the time or resources to tour the outlying regions of the province, try to make it to Petty Harbour/Maddox Cove for a "village stay." It's only a 15-minute drive to the capital city, and a favorite stop for visitors touring Cape Spear.

Petty Harbour is the most picturesque part of the community, a fact recognized by filmmakers, who have used the town as a backdrop for a number of feature films *(Orca, A Whale for the Killing, John and the Missus)*. As you can tell from the number of boats around the harbour, as well as the old-time wooden wharves, this is a vibrant fishing community—and has been for more than 500 years. Even the name reflects its maritime heritage (Petty is derived from the French word "Petite," meaning "small harbour").

In addition to its fishing heritage and postcard scenery, Petty Harbour/Maddox Cove is also known as the home of the oldest hydroelectric station in the province. Because it's a working plant, however, you won't be able to tour the inside.

This is a great place to stay if you'd like to be near but out of the city, or if you're hiking along the East Coast Trail. The scenic village is just south of Cape Spear (on a road simply known as the Petty Harbour/ Maddox Cove turnoff) and has an interesting antiques and flea market shop by the town's bridge. Herbie's Olde Shoppe is a craft store worth visiting just so you can see its interior: until recently, it was a traditional, working, rural grocery.

Spend a night with Reg and Mil Carter at the Orca Inn Bed & Breakfast. Weather permitting, you can have breakfast on the deck, looking out on the harbor. Call ✆ **877/747-9676** or 709/747-9676, or visit them on the Web at www.orcainn.nf.ca for more info.

If you're a beer drinker, you can tour **Quidi Vidi Brewery,** a micro-brewery offering six great brews. The 1892 Dark Ale is fantastic, and the Honey Brown and Eric's Cream Ale are also very nice. The Northern Lager and Northern Light are pretty standard offerings. If you're looking for something really different, try the Kriek cherry beer. It's uniquely refreshing on a hot summer's day.

15 Barrows Rd. ✆ **800/738-0165** or 709/738-4040. www.newfoundlandbeer.com. C$2.50 (US$1.80) per person. Weekday tours are offered year-round and run hourly beginning at 1pm.

Signal Hill A National Historic Site offering the best view of the province's capital, Signal Hill is the city's granite guardian. Its summit is a forbidding 183m (600 ft.) above sea level, which is why its early significance centered on its role as a lookout post. The military history of this site is well explained at the informative Interpretive Centre halfway up the hill. You'd be wise to stop here and learn about the site before you head to the next level.

Try to time your visit to take in the Signal Hill Military Tattoo, held beside the Interpretive Centre 4 days a week during the summer (Wednesday, Thursday, Saturday, and Sunday), at 3pm and 7pm. The colorful artillery and military drumming display takes you back to the days when this site was of paramount importance to the safety of St. John's.

Between the Interpretive Centre and the top of Signal Hill you'll find a restored cannon battery pointed seaward, much as it was when it was necessary to protect the settlement from marauding pirates or warring nations.

At the top of the hill, you can tour Cabot Tower, the stone tower built in 1897 to commemorate the 400th anniversary of John Cabot's landing at St. John's, and the site at which Marconi received the first transatlantic broadcast in 1901. While visitors can access the roof of the Tower, it's not advisable on windy days—particularly not with children. The winds here can get very high and could literally pull a small child out of your arms.

If you're feeling really energetic, and I mean *really* energetic, you can tackle the 896-step descent that skirts the seaward side of Signal Hill. The view from the trail is breathtakingly beautiful. But don't be deceived: it's also very dangerous. If you do the complete walk, there are sections where only 1.5m (5 ft.) of terra firma and an iron chain hammered into the rock separate you from a 61-m (200-ft.) drop. Not recommended for children, pets, or acrophobics.

Signal Hill Rd. *C* **709/772-5367.** Free admission to the site. Admission charge to tour the Interpretive Centre: C$2.50 (US$1.80) adults; C$2 (US$1.43) seniors and children. You'll pay C$4 (US$2.87), saving $1 off the regular admission, if you purchase a double pass to visit the Interpretive Centres at both Cape Spear and Signal Hill National Historic Sites. 10am–6pm, May 15–Oct 15.

6 Museums & Galleries

MUSEUMS

A new state-of-the-art facility is under construction in St. John's that will house the Provincial Museum of Newfoundland & Labrador, the Provincial Archives of Newfoundland & Labrador, and the Art Gallery of Newfoundland & Labrador, all currently in separate locations and in much need of expansion. Scheduled to open in June 2004, Newfoundland & Labrador's new 14,000-sq.-m (150,000-sq.-ft.) cultural and heritage center—to be called The Rooms—will bring the province into the 21st century with an ability to showcase the many treasures that had previously been crammed into musty and outdated facilities.

The design concept for The Rooms pays tribute to the traditional lifestyle and unique language of NL. "Rooms" were buildings along the shoreline where fish were processed and where nets and other fishing equipment were stored. Another point of interest is that Fort Townshend, the site of The Rooms, is itself an archaeological treasure, as a late-18th-century strategic fortification and also once the residence and seat of early Newfoundland governors. The Rooms will be one of the only facilities in North America to incorporate an active archaeological excavation within its walls. Stay tuned to www.therooms.ca for updates.

James J. O'Mara Pharmacy Museum   This Provincial Heritage Site is a good spot to visit if you've always been fascinated by pharmacies and the dispensing of prescription medicines. This heritage drugstore was built in 1895 and is particularly interesting because of its Art Nouveau/Art Deco amalgam design. Inside, you can see a set of original drugstore fixtures made in England in 1879 that found its way to St. John's, and an assortment of antique apothecary bottles.

488 Water St. (at Brennan St.). *C* **709/753-5877.** Free admission. Open to the public 10am–5pm, June–Sept, and by appointment at other times of the year.

The Provincial Museum of Newfoundland & Labrador   Although interesting, some of the displays at this three-floor museum look tired. The first floor celebrates the natural history of the province. Highlights include a minke whale skull as well as the biggest lobster claw I've ever seen. The second floor depicts the history of the various aboriginal peoples that inhabited what is now NL, including the Dorset, Maritime Archaic, and Beothuk Indians. The third floor is devoted to the province's military and early industrial history. Allow yourself about 45 minutes in order to see all of the displays. The lack of seafaring history is disappointing, but it's to be rectified in The Rooms when it opens.

285 Duckworth St. ⓒ **709/729-2329**. Admission C$3 (US$2.15) adults; C$2.50 (US$1.80) seniors and students; free for under age 18. Mid-June–mid-Sept daily 9am–4:45pm; mid-Sept–mid-June Tues–Fri 9am–4:45pm, Sat 9:30am–4:45pm, Sun noon–4:45pm, closed Mon. Closed all statutory holidays as listed in the Fast Facts section in chapter 2.

Railway Coastal Museum 🔥🔥 *Kids*   There's something strangely compelling about trains. Whatever it is, the mystique carries over to this newest St. John's museum attraction. The centenarian stonework structure that was once the province's main railway station has been meticulously renovated to commemorate that historical era. In addition to the typical pieces you'd find in any museum (historical photo exhibits, period costumes, storyboards), here you and the kids will be captivated by the 1940s passenger train diorama as well as the automated train model. All aboard!

495 Water St. W. ⓒ **709/753-5877**. Admission C$5 (US$3.60) adults; C$4 (US$2.86) seniors and students; C$3 (US$2.15) children 5–17; free for under age 5; C$12 (US$8.60) family rate. Mon–Sat 10am–5pm, Sun 1pm–5pm, closed Mon Oct 16–May 31.

GALLERIES

Art Gallery of Newfoundland and Labrador   The provincial art gallery is the largest public gallery in the province, housing more than 4,000 works of contemporary Canadian art (but there's only a small sampling of them on display). You'll find a strong emphasis on art from across NL, including traditional and mixed media. The permanent collection features major works by nationally recognized artists as well as hooked mats made by women who live in the many outport communities throughout Newfoundland and Labrador.

You'll also find an interesting array of temporary exhibits such as "Atlantic Modern," which was organized by the Faculty of Architecture and Planning of Dalhousie University in Halifax, Nova Scotia, and the region's provincial architects' associations. The first of its kind, this is a juried exhibition of drawings, photographs, and models representing significant structures designed by architects in Newfoundland, New Brunswick, Nova Scotia, and Prince Edward Island over the last 50 years. Ask for a copy of the "Guide of Artist Studios" brochure, which gives you a list of artists you can visit in their downtown studios. The gallery will be moving to expanded premises at The Rooms in 2004.

St. John's Arts & Culture Centre, Allandale Rd. at Prince Philip Dr. ⓒ **709/737-8209**. www.agnl.ca. Admission is free; donations accepted. Year-round Tues–Sun noon–5pm; June–Sept extended hours on Fri (7am–10pm).

Christina Parker Gallery   Built in the 1930s and originally occupied as a canning factory, this somewhat funky gallery features an eclectic mix of visual art in an open, spacious environment. All the artists featured are contemporary artists from Newfoundland & Labrador. Highlights include paintings by David Blackwood, recycle art by Peter Drysdale, photographic art by Ned Pratt, and dyed silk art by Diana May Dabinett, who is responsible for the beautiful silk art hanging at the Fluvarium.

7 Plank Rd. ⓒ **709/753-0580**. www.christinaparkergallery.com. Mon–Fri 10am–5:30pm, Sat 11am–5pm.

Emma Butler Gallery This is a more traditional gallery, with a wonderful selection of classic art. Blue-chip artists such as Christopher and Mary Pratt and David Blackwood—Canada's foremost printmaker—are well represented. Blackwood's etchings provide an excellent visual history of NL. The gallery also handles several international artists from countries that include the U.S., France, and Russia. You will find many pieces by J. C. Roy, a French artist who comes to NL every year to paint. Emma will ship your purchases worldwide.

111 George St. W. (between Waldegrave and Springdale). © **709/739-7111**. www.emmabutler.com. Free admission. Tues–Sat 11am–5pm and by appointment.

Lane Gallery If you're interested in photographic art, don't miss the Lane Gallery. Don Lane, owner and photographer extraordinaire, sells and exhibits strictly his own work, but don't think that's limiting. As a native of the city, he knows where—and how—to get the best shots. His photographs of icebergs are simply breathtaking. If you're looking for a photograph to hang on your wall that will always remind you of just how beautiful this province is, drop in to visit the Lane Gallery, situated on the main floor of the Fairmont. Prices range from C$100 (US$71) for smaller prints to C$1,000 (US$710) for larger pieces.

Fairmont Hotel, 115 Cavendish Sq. © **877/366-5263** or 709/753-8946. www.lanegallery.com. Free admission. MC, V. Mon–Fri 9am–5pm, Sat 10am–5pm; closed Sun.

7 Festivals & Special Events

The atmosphere in St. John's is festive year-round, but especially so during the first week of August, when you'll find the province's three largest events—the **Newfoundland & Labrador Folk Festival**, the **George Street Festival**, and the **Royal St. John's Regatta**—happening simultaneously.

NEWFOUNDLAND & LABRADOR FOLK FESTIVAL

This festival is most rewarding because of its size. It's not like many larger festivals throughout North America where you're one very small part of a massive sea of fans, waving with excitement in the wind but all the while thinking you could have a more rewarding musical experience by watching the artists' DVDs at home.

The event generally runs the first weekend in August, beginning on the Friday night and concluding with singing of the **"Ode to Newfoundland"** on Sunday evening. The Ode was the national anthem of Newfoundland when it was an independent nation, and was written by Sir Cavendish Boyle while he was Britain's Governor of Newfoundland between 1901 and 1904.

Most of the entertainment is top-notch local, and of a bluegrass or Celtic nature. There are booths where you can purchase the performers' music, as well as watch artisans blowing glass and turning woodcrafts. Others are selling pottery, jewelry, dyed silks, and T-shirts. Reasonably priced food can be purchased at booths on-site, and of course there's the expected beer tent, where you can purchase beer, wine, or coolers. You can't take your alcoholic beverage out of the beer tent (nor can you bring in your own), but you can see the stage from inside the open-sided tent.

Bannerman Park (Military Rd. is the gate entrance). © **709/576-8508**. www.sjfac.nf.net. Regular weekend pass C$40 (US$28.68) adults, C$20 (US$14.34) seniors; evening and afternoon sessions C$10 (US$7.17) adults, C$5 (US$3.58) seniors; free for children age 12 and under accompanied by an adult.

GEORGE STREET FESTIVAL

One word best describes the George Street Festival—*wild!* If you don't like crowds, loud music, and lots of noise, best not to visit George Street during the first week of August. That's when you'll find 25 bands playing on the street and in the 20 clubs that occupy this two-block stretch of rowdydom. But if you *do* like great music—and standing shoulder-to-shoulder with your fellow enthusiasts—check it out!

Not just for the 19-to-25 crowd, over a 6-day period the George Street Festival provides cheap—but great—entertainment of most music types, from rock to bluegrass, country, and Celtic, and for all ages.

And you're allowed to walk freely on the street—beer in hand—until 3am. But navigating your way down the street can be tough. Not just from the amount of beer you're likely to consume, but because it's difficult to find a place to walk. It's as crowded—and rowdy—as you'll find any evening on Bourbon Street in New Orleans (perhaps except during Mardi Gras). No advance tickets required. Just show up and politely nudge your way in. The street is closed off to traffic during the festival. Ticket booths are by Trapper John's (George Street at Bishop's Cove) and at the other end of George Street at Adelaide, by the Sundance Saloon and Kelly's Pub.

George St. (between Queen's Rd. and Bate's Hill). © **709/685-9232** or 709/576-5990, or drop in to any George St. pub for a schedule of performers and additional info. Admission C$5 (US$3.60) for all ages.

ROYAL ST. JOHN'S REGATTA

This is the event of all events in St. John's. And it's the only civic holiday in all of North America that's weather dependent! It's normally held on the first Wednesday of August—if you wake up that morning and the weather is inclement, the best thing to do is turn on the radio or TV to find out whether the Regatta has been postponed. If it's on, head down to Quidi Vidi Lake and have yourself a great time.

The Regatta started in 1825 and is the oldest continuous sporting event in North America. The excitement centers on a day of fixed-seat rowing races in six-man (or -woman) sculls. The city of St. John's actually shuts down on Regatta Day. You're lucky if you can find so much as a convenience store open for business, so be prepared with camera film and whatever else you may need, as you're not likely to find it at the Regatta.

What you will find is a small lake where teams of rowers challenge one another in a series of races. You'll find dozens of food booths, games of chance, rides for the kids, and small items such as jewelry for sale. Moo Moo's homemade Newfoundland ice cream has a booth offering delicious treats. Another local favorite is the Hiscock's Wedge Fries truck from Grand Falls, NL. Make sure to try the grilled shish kabob (marinated pork cubes skewered with onions). Where else can you get a country-fair atmosphere with free entertainment, free admission, and a day's worth of inexpensive family fun within 5-minutes' drive of a city's downtown?

Quidi Vidi Lake (take King's Bridge Rd. to Lakeview Ave.). © **709/576-8921** or see www.infonet. st-johns.nf.ca. Free admission. Parking can be a problem; be prepared for a long walk. First Wed of Aug, weather permitting. Races run continually from 8:30am–6pm. The Regatta Museum is closed on Regatta Day.

8 Outdoor Activities

The city of St. John's is full of parks and a great place to enjoy the outdoors. Whether you just want to take a leisurely walk and smell the flowers or you're looking to be educated along the way, there are a number of good options from which to choose. The city is small, so seeing it on a big motor-coach tour should be a last resort. (That mode of travel is best reserved for touring other regions of the province and will be touched on in subsequent chapters.) To best enjoy the full flavor of St. John's, take a walk or a carriage ride and see the city slowly—as it should be seen.

If you're a golfer, you'll be pleased to learn that Newfoundland & Labrador has a number of fine courses and that some of them can be found right in St. John's. The best-groomed 18-hole course in the city is the Osprey (one of two courses at Clovelly), but if you want more of a challenge look to the Admiral's Green, located in Pippy Park. For a free copy of the province's *Golf Guide,* call © **866/563-4653** or visit www.golfnewfoundland.ca.

Bowring Park   Bowring Park is the city's preeminent green space. It has a river and brook running through it, ducks swimming happily about, and pigeons doing their best to make a mess of the lovely bronze statues. There's a whimsical statue of Peter Pan (it's a replica of the same statue that stands in the Kensington Gardens of London) alongside the pond that, while beautiful to look at, has a melancholy history. It's actually a memorial for a little girl who had loved the park, but who, along with her father, had been tragically shipwrecked. The park also contains a tribute to St. John's military history, with a number of commemorative war plaques to read. If you're into Elizabethan theater, time your visit to coincide with Shakespeare by the Sea, held in the park's amphitheater. Tickets are C$10 (US$7.10). Bowring Park also offers a large playground for the kids, an outdoor pool, tennis courts, picnic grounds, walking trails, and cross-country ski trails and tobogganing in the winter. Of particular note is the Ronald McDonald playground equipment for children with disabilities.

Southwest of downtown on Waterford Bridge Rd. © **709/576-6134.** No admission charge to enter the park. Daily 9am–10pm.

C.A. Pippy Park   Situated on the northwestern end of the city near Memorial University, this park features a peaceful pond where you can rent canoes or kayaks within minutes of downtown. There's a playground and mini-golf for the kids, two golf courses, camping, picnic grounds, water sports, fishing, hiking trails, a botanical garden, and the Fluvarium (see "Exploring St. John's," earlier in this chapter). You'll pass the expansive park many times on your travels in and around the city. Be sure to take the time and spend a day or half-day there, depending on your interests. There's good bird-watching around the pond, and people have even spotted the occasional moose in the park! Pippy Park is a dog-friendly place.

Take Kenmount Rd. to Thorburn Rd. or Prince Philip Dr. © **709/737-3655.** www.pippypark.com. No admission to enter the park. The grounds are open daily from dawn to dusk.

CUSTOM TOURS

Flanagan's Fancy Inc.   If you like one-on-one or customized small-group touring, Flanagan's Fancy Inc. is a company to consider. Susan Flanagan is a townie with a global perspective. She has lived in various parts of Eastern Canada, as well as Japan and Australia, but has returned home to the place she loves.

Flanagan's will customize any tour to your liking, whether it's snowshoeing to Cape Spear or special kids' tours (Susan has four of her own and knows all the kid-friendly zones). Plus, she's a rich repository of information about the history, culture, flora, and fauna of the region.

34 Shea St. (℃ **709/579-7760.** E-mail: flanagan@thezone.net. C$200 (US$142) for half-day or C$300 (US$213) for full-day tour. No credit cards. Bilingual service offered.

Scademia Adventure Boat Tour This boat tour is a must for anyone who loves tall ships, traditional Newfoundland music, and Newfoundland dogs—and who wants to get screeched! Twice voted the "Best Cruise Shore Excursion" by the cruise-ship industry, you'll soon see why. The fun-loving crew is knowledgeable and eager to please. And if you're not too shy, go ahead and get screeched. This involves reciting a silly limerick, tossing back a small shot of Newfoundland rum (also known as screech), and then kissing a piece of salt cod. The screech straight up is pretty wicked stuff, but for your reward you'll be presented with a genuine NL Purity mint—to get the taste out of your mouth—and a certificate (making you an honorary Newfoundlander) to take home and put in your photo album.

During the 2-hour sailing aboard the 27-m (90-ft.) schooner, you'll take in some great views of St. John's harbor and the Narrows. As well, you'll have the opportunity to see a variety of seabirds—and some whales, if you're lucky. Fog is common here, so good visibility can't be guaranteed, and there are often cold winds (even on a warm day), so be sure to bring along a jacket and a hat that won't get blown off.

Pier 7, Harbour Dr. (across from the Murray Premises). (℃ **800/779-4253** or 709/726-5000. www.nfld.com/ scademia. Fares C$35 (US$25.10) adults; C$20 (US$14.34) children ages 13 and under; free under age 4. Seniors get a discounted price of C$20 (US$14.34) on Mon only. DC, MC, V. Sailings at 10am, 1pm, 4pm, and 7pm daily, weather permitting from May–Sept. Wheelchair accessible.

St. John's Carriage Tours A fun way to tour the city is to hire a horse-drawn carriage. Owner Derm Duggan has a small stable of horses that he pastures on a hill overlooking Quidi Vidi Lake. The carriage will take you along your selected course (you can choose either an hour or a half-hour tour of "Old Downtown" or the "Historic East." Both are lovely routes, but depending on the time of day you take the ride ask the driver which route is less busy, as the horse understandably gets somewhat agitated in times of heavier traffic.

The horse stops at Belbin's, the oldest grocery store in St. John's, where he/ she will receive a tasty apple. (If you want to make a hit with the horse, bring along your own cut-up apple as a present to offer at the beginning or end of your journey.)

You'll find the carriage parked near the Fairmont or the Delta. (℃ **709/738-6999.** Tour prices are C$30 (US$21.51) for half-hour tour and C$50 (US$35.85) for hour tour. V. Daily 10am–midnight.

WALKING TOURS

Many companies offer reasonably priced walking tours in and around St. John's. Each service provider will appeal to a slightly different clientele, so take your pick and enjoy the walk.

- **A Step Back in Time** (℃ **709/576-8106**): If you're keenly interested in architecture, choose one of the Step Back in Time series of walks. These are marvelous, free, self-guided tours made possible by the City of St. John's. You'll walk away with plenty of useful and interesting information about the striking architecture and colorful buildings found throughout the city.

- **Boyle's Walking Tours** (© **709/364-6845** or 709/368-0202); C$5 (US$3.58); Thursdays 7:30 to 9pm by reservation only: Smiling Michael Boyle is quite the character and claims to be a direct descendant of Sir Cavendish Boyle, who wrote the "Ode to Newfoundland." Boyle offers several different themes to his walking tours, including a pub tour of the old city.
- **Haunted Hike** (© **709/685-3444**); C$5 (US$3.55) cash per person; Sunday to Thursday nights 9:30 to 10:45pm, early June to mid-Sept; no reservations required: Meet at the west entrance of the Anglican Cathedral on Church Hill. If you're not afraid to delve into the dark side and want to be spooked a little, take this evening hike with the very Rev. Thos. Wyckham Jarvis, Esq. *Note:* This hike isn't the ideal choice for children, as they may find it too scary and it runs late into the evening.
- **R&R Walking Tours** (© **709/682-7948**); C$5 (US$3.55) cash per person; 10:30am to noon, Tuesday and Thursday during August only; reservations preferred; English, German, and French service available: Choose this company if you'd like to be entertained while on tour. It's run by a couple of women who'll sing you stories about old St. John's.
- **St. John's Historic Walking Tours** (© **709/738-3781**); C$20 (US$14.34) cash for one person, C$35 (US$25.10) for two people, children under 12 free; Monday, Tuesday, Thursday, and Friday June to Labour Day; 11am to 1:30pm and 2 to 4:30pm; meet at Zachary's Restaurant, 71 Duckworth St.: If you're looking for some real insider's tips and are willing to spend a little more for them, try the St. John's Historic Walking Tours.

9 Shopping

St. John's offers some varied shopping options. You'll find several unique shops along downtown Water Street, but if you're looking for really good bargains you might have to venture away from downtown and into suburbia where the locals shop. One such suburb is called "The Goulds." This is where you'll find **Bidgood's,** one of the most comprehensive places in St. John's to shop for traditional food products (see below for more information).

If you're looking for chain stores, you'll find the larger malls in the suburbs, open daily from 10am until 10pm; Sunday noon to 5pm. There are two major malls in St. John's. The **Avalon Mall** at 48 Kenmount Road has more than 100 stores and services including movie theaters and a grocery store (© **709/753-7144**). The Avalon Mall is accessible by Metro bus routes 3, 4, 9, 14, and 15.

The **Village Shopping Centre** is at 430 Topsail Rd. and has 100 stores and services including *Sears* and *Shoppers Drug Mart.* The location is very accessible by bus if you don't have wheels. (Routes 1, 2, 5, 7, 8, 11, 12, 21, 22, and 25 all stop at the mall.) Call © **709/364-7011** for more info or check out the Village Mall's website at www.villageshoppingcentre.com.

Bidgood's   What will you find at Bidgood's? Just about everything! It's basically a family-run supermarket, but so much more. "Bidgood's Cottage Crafts" (at the back of the store) has a noteworthy collection of NL crafts and books—and at very reasonable prices. "Bidgood's Cove" is a section of the store where you will find a vast array of traditional Newfoundland foods, all prepared on-site and of the same quality you'd find in the home of a Newfoundlander. You can buy (or just look at!) such local delicacies as seal flipper pie, cod heads, and caribou or rabbit pies.

On shelves throughout the store you'll also find many local products, such as Bidgood's wonderful own jams (try the bakeapple) and a huge selection of Purity products such as the mints you get on the *Scademia* and tasty ginger cookies. There's a lunch bar in the store, where you can grab a light bite to eat in or take out. There's even a playland for the kids to keep them amused while you shop. And the store is located in picturesque dairy farm country, only a 20-minute drive from downtown.

Route 10 (just off Old Bay Bulls Rd.). *C* **709/368-3125**. www.bidgoods.ca. Open Mon–Sat, 9am–9pm; Sun 11am–5pm. MC, V.

Devon House Craft Centre   Probably the best-known craft shop in the city, Devon House offers a great selection of Newfoundland handcrafts at very reasonable prices (jewelry, sculpture, silk painting, hooked mats, model boats, and so on). It's a non-profit venture operated by the NL Crafts Development Assoc. Every product in the store has been vetted by the Association for its exceptional quality and artistic merit. Devon House is located behind the Fairmont Hotel on Duckworth Street. Don't overlook the upstairs showroom, where you'll find the larger and more eclectic pieces.

59 Duckworth St. (behind the Fairmont Hotel). *C* **709/753-2749**. www.craftcouncil.nf.ca/about/ devonhouse.asp. Open 10am–5pm, Mon–Wed and Sat; 10am–9pm, Thurs–Fri; 1pm–5pm Sun. AE, MC, V.

Downhomer Shoppe & Gallery   This is a one-stop shop where you can buy all sorts of NL videos, books, music, souvenirs, and gifts. They claim to have the world's largest collection of "Newfoundlandia," and after a few glances around the place, you'll likely agree. It's definitely worth a look. A unique offering is the *Household Almanac & Cookbook*, which provides a good assortment of NL recipes in addition to household hints and home remedies. Expect to pay C$19.95 (US$14.30) for the soft-cover editions.

303 Water St. Call toll-free *C* **888/588-6353** or 709/722-2970. www.shopdownhomer.com. Open Mon–Fri 9:30am–8:30pm, Sat 10am–6pm, Sun noon–5pm. AE, DC, MC, V.

Murray Premises   The Murray Premises is a historical building that houses a wonderful boutique hotel, the Newfoundland Science Centre, a couple of restaurants, and a small assortment of interesting shops. The Heritage Shop offers a good assortment of NL books, music, pottery, and items of clothing and jewelry. Check out Living Rooms, an attractive (but slightly overcrowded) shop that specializes in unique home accessories. And for wine connoisseurs, there's a specialty wine shop where you'll find the best selection of fine wines on the island.

5 Beck's Cove (just off the west end of Harbour Dr.). **Living Rooms Ltd.** *C* **709/753-2099**. Open Mon–Wed 9:30am–5:30pm, Thurs–Fri 9:30am–9pm, Sat 9:30am–6pm, Sun noon–5pm. MC, V, Interac. **Murray Premises Wine Store** *C* **709/753-7120**. Open Mon–Thurs 9:30am–5:30pm, Fri–Sat 9:30–9pm, Sun closed. MC, V.

Newfoundland Weavery   The Weavery has been open for business for more than 30 years and has continued to add to its offerings. Look for quality local art and crafts, including pottery, hand-knit sweaters, oilskin coats, silks, jewelry, and pewter.

177 Water St. (across from the Courthouse). *C* **709/753-0496**. E-mail: newfoundlandweavery@the zone.net. Open Mon–Wed 10am–6pm, Thurs–Fri 10am–9pm, Sat 10am–6pm, Sun 12:30–5pm. AE, MC, V.

Nonia   Nonia is a non-profit, volunteer-driven network founded by the New-foundland Outport Nursing & Industrial Assoc. (NONIA). Unique products include hand-knit baby bonnets, booties, tuques, mittens, and lots and lots of sweaters in all sorts of designs. Plus they'll do special orders on request.

286 Water St. (at George St.) ℭ **709/753-8062**. E-mail: noniahandicrafts@aol.com. Open Mon–Sat 9am–5:30pm, Sun closed. MC, V.

Wild Things   Looking for local items such as raw Labradorite (NL's provincial stone), Newfoundland pottery, or nature photography? Visit Wild Things, co-ordinator of the world humpback count. Pick up one of their brochures while you're around town, and you'll receive 10% off your purchase.

124 Water St. (near the War Memorial). ℭ **709/722-3123**. www.wildlands.com. Open Mon–Sat 9am–6pm, Sun 10am–5pm. AE, MC, V.

Woof Design   This is the place to go if you want one of those great New-foundland sweaters like Kevin Spacey wore in *The Shipping News*. Woof Design specializes in the design and production of mohair, wool, and angora sweaters and accessories. All of their sweaters are handcrafted in Newfoundland homes by independent craftspeople using domestic knitting machines. The accessory items are hand-knit, hand-crocheted, or woven.

181 Water St. ℭ **709/722-7555**. www.woofdesign.com. Open Mon–Sat 9am–5:30pm, Sun closed. AE, MC, V.

Wordplay   A must for book lovers is Wordplay, a centrally located independ-ent bookstore offering more than 100,000 new, used, and rare books. Their specialty is books on NL. Wordplay also offers public access to the Internet, so you can check your e-mail here. Check out the James Baird Art Gallery upstairs, featuring a good selection of contemporary Canadian art. Give yourself plenty of time to explore—you'll need it.

221 Duckworth St. ℭ **800/563-9100** or 709/726-9193. www.wordplay.com. Open Mon–Sat 10am–6pm, Sun noon–5pm. MC, V.

10 St. John's After Dark

St. John's may be the oldest European settlement in North America, but it has a very young population. The average age of a townie is between 35 and 44. That translates into a very active nightlife. In fact, it's said that the city has the high-est concentration of pubs per capita on the continent! You'll find great live music playing everywhere, as well as a good selection of dinner theaters and other cul-tural offerings. So don't wear yourself out during the day. You'll miss too much at night!

GEORGE STREET

This is where you want to be if you're looking for the local pub scene. Within a two-block stretch, you'll find about 20 establishments eager to draw you a pint. Keep in mind that it gets wildly busy on weekends—especially during the aca-demic year at Memorial University—so plan to arrive early if you want to get in to a certain place. *Note:* Lineups can be long on Thursday, Friday, and Saturday nights, so bring your umbrella, and in winter wear warm clothing and boots so you don't freeze. Once you get in, you're bound to have a great time no matter which of these establishments you choose.

The **Sundance Saloon,** George Street at Adelaide ℭ **709/753-7822,** is the largest facility and boasts the biggest patio east of Montreal. It's also known for its karaoke on Friday nights. **Trapper John's** at 2 George St. ℭ **709/579-9630** is a pub well known for its "screeching-in" ceremony, which allows you to become an honorary Newfoundlander. **Turkey Joe's** at 7 George St. © 709/722-5757 is for the just-turned-19 (and barely dressed) set that's heavy into rap. **Bridie Molloy's** at 5 George St. © 709/576-5990 has a great outdoor patio and traditional Irish music. **Benders on George** at 13 George St. © 709/738-3687 is basically a dance bar with DJ music Wednesday to Saturday where you can also have a friendly game of billiards. **O'Reilly's Irish Newfoundland Pub** at 15 George St. © 709/722-3735 is an institution. It's the most popular Irish pub on the strip. The music will have you tapping your toes, but you can expect to have them squished on the minuscule dance floor. **Kelly's Pub and Restaurant** at 25 George St. © 709/753-5300 has live entertainment every weekend and no cover charge.

OTHER OPTIONS

If you're looking for a quieter, more relaxing atmosphere, try the **Windsock Lounge** at 161 Water St., a downtown piano bar featuring local performers Thursday to Saturday. Call © 709/722-5001 for details.

The **Ship Inn** on Solomon's Lane (access from 265 Duckworth St.) is the most famous drinking establishment in the city. It's a rather dark but lively pub with a history that boasts many well-known writers and artists as frequent customers. The Ship Inn is known for hosting literary events such as book launches and readings, so you just never know what—or whom—you'll find when you drop in. In addition to some great food at reasonable prices, you'll find a nightly offering of live jazz, blues, reggae, rock, or folk. Call © 709/753-3870 for information.

Another unique and interesting option is the **Crow's Nest**, located next to the War Memorial (between Water St. E. and Duckworth St.). Here, you'll find a periscope from a Nazi sub as part of the decor! The only drawback is that the Crow's Nest offers very limited hours of operation: Tuesday to Thursday 4pm to 7:30pm; Friday, lunch is served from 11am to 2pm and they remain open until 8pm; Saturday 2pm to 8pm; and closed Sunday and Monday. In business since 1942, the Crow's Nest is a private officers' club, but visitors to the city are welcome to drop in. A "smart casual" dress code is in effect, with summers being a bit more flexible. Call © 709/753-6927 or see www.crowsnest.nf.ca for more info about this intriguing St. John's treasure.

How about dinner theater with a Newfoundland flavor? The best spot is the **Theatre at St. John's Lane,** 223 Duckworth St. (© 709/579-3023). For C$40 (US$28.68), you'll get a terrific production in addition to a creatively presented three-course meal. It's a popular location, so reserve your seats as far in advance as possible. *Warning:* The theater has only a window air-conditioner, so dress in layers.

The **Longshoreman's Protectorate Union Hall** at 3 Victoria St. (at Duckworth St.) shows good live comedy and alternative theater. The simple, unassuming location is known to locals as the **LSPU Hall.** The building itself has been designated a registered heritage structure, and you'll find an art gallery downstairs. The LSPU Hall offers a good selection of imported beer and provides live entertainment Wednesday through Sunday during the summer. Call © 709/753-4531.

If you like classical music, see if the **Newfoundland Symphony Orchestra** is playing while you're in town. Call © 709/753-6492 or visit www.nso.nfld.net for an online schedule of performances and corresponding ticket prices.

4

The Avalon Region

If your visit to Newfoundland allows for a mere week or so, you really only have time to see one region of the province. If it's your first visit, head for the Avalon, Newfoundland's most easterly peninsula.

The Avalon not only includes the capital, St. John's (see chapter 3 for key sites and attractions), but also is home to half the entire provincial population, whom you'll find living in the many tiny coastal communities dotted throughout this charming and picturesque region.

Early settlement patterns followed the length of these rocky shores, providing ready access to the sea. Little has changed. Fishing has been—and for the most part, continues to be— the primary activity around which the world turns for Newfoundlanders. Even for those not directly involved in the ocean harvest, the industry and its environment are a powerful social, cultural, and economic influence.

But the Avalon provides much more than a close look at contemporary human history. Here, in the annual playground of more than 5,000 humpback and minke whales, you'll be entertained by a natural marine show unparalleled by any of the world's most talented trained mammals. You'll find yourself on the verge of flight, vicariously soaring with the most spectacular seabird colony in North America. And you'll be speechless when a majestic caribou herd emerges from the dissolving fog within arm's reach of the highway.

If you want to walk your cares away, you can't beat the beauty and solitude of the 520-km (322-mile) East Coast Trail. Fortunately, you won't have to go the whole distance all at once; the trek is divided into convenient, manageable chunks.

You can paddle your way through a variety of sea kayak adventures, and dive for sunken treasure in the graveyard of the Atlantic. Or get into the swing of things on one of several professionally designed golf courses (where wayward moose and marauding fox join the challenge of sand traps and water hazards). And you'll really dig the way history comes alive at several active archaeological sites, in addition to breathtaking scenery. Yes, there's all that and more on the Avalon—if you know where to look (and you will, thanks to Frommer's).

You can get some helpful hints from the **Travel Guide** available free of charge from Tourism Newfoundland & Labrador. Obtain your copy by calling © **800/563-6353** or checking out the Web at www.gov.nf.ca/tourism.

The **Avalon Convention & Visitors Bureau** (ACVB) has information available at their booth in the St. John's airport, open from 10am to midnight, 7 days a week.

You can pick up regional brochures, maps, and information upon your arrival, or call the ACVB's toll-free line (© **877/739-8899**) to have free travel literature sent to you prior to your departure. The ACVB website provides details on local businesses and services at www.canadasfareast.com. Another good online resource for the Avalon Peninsula is www.doryload.com/avalonpeninsula.htm.

1 Getting Around

You'll generally arrive on the Avalon in one of two ways: flying into St. John's or arriving by ferry via the community of Argentia. (See chapter 2 for details on travel options, and for info on vehicle rentals.)

Once here, things can get a little confusing for—or overlooked by—the unprepared traveler. What's really deceiving is that you'll look at this relatively small region of the province on a map and think you can see it all in a day or two. I assure you . . . that's impossible. There is so much to see and do right in and around St. John's that you'll need a week just for that. To discover—and be captured by—the true heart of Newfoundland, you need to savor the small communities outside the "big city"—and this takes time.

Note: Other than the Trans-Canada Highway (#1), which has speeds of 90 or 100kmph (around 55–62 mph), the smaller regional routes have a maximum speed of 80kmph (around 50 mph), with speed limits being reduced to 50kmph (31 mph) once you enter many communities.

TOURING OPTIONS

Many of the tiny communities you'll find along the Avalon are nestled in a cove that you can get to only via the small access roads that stem off the provincial highways. You have to know ahead of time what each community offers, and search out the ones that appeal to your specific interests. Otherwise it would take several weeks just to visit them all.

If you don't drive or have a car, you may wish to take one of the package tours that arrange accommodations, attractions, and transportation for you. Many companies offer options, but the leader—which also serves as a wholesaler for many of the smaller operators—is **Maxxim Vacations** (© 800/567-6666; www.maxximvacations.com). Maxxim has a rich variety of custom-designed holidays for visitors who don't relish the uncertainty of charting what is to them virgin territory.

If you're like me, and prefer to orchestrate your own adventure—with the guidance of a good conductor—seek out the services of a qualified personal tour guide such as **Anne St. Croix.** Anne grew up on the Avalon Peninsula, has lived abroad, and is one of the most sensitive tour guides I have encountered, making sure your specific interests will be covered in any personalized itinerary she develops for you. To contact Anne, call © **709/726-5958** (e-mail anne_st_croix @hotmail.com). Her day rates for Avalon tours are C$100 (US$72.90) per person.

THE EAST COAST TRAIL

For the avid hiker, the **East Coast Trail** will be the Avalon Peninsula's most magnetic attraction. The entire trail takes you 400km (248 miles) along North America's easternmost coastline and 120km (74 miles) across the Avalon Wilderness Area. Parts of the trail are difficult, requiring overnight excursions. Other parts are easy—and short—enough for someone in moderate shape.

The trail is open year-round and extends along the coast south of St. John's all the way to Trepassey, but is considered to be "fully constructed" only as far as Cape Broyle. Phase II of the trail (between Cape Broyle and Cappahayden) has only recently been completed. The section of trail between Cappahayden and Trepassey is open but there is little or no signage. There is no fee for walking the trail, nor do you need to book a time for your journey.

Avalon Region

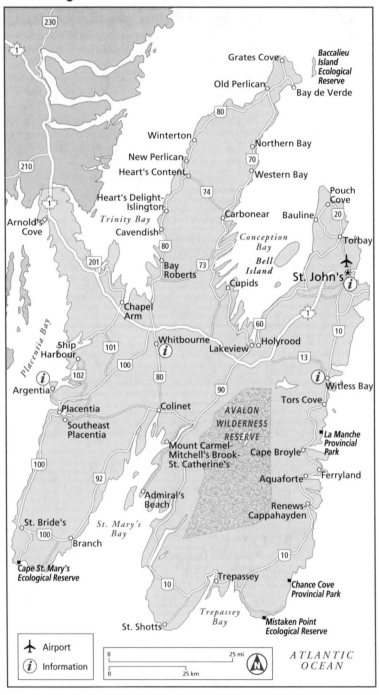

Tips **Hiking Tips**

Keep these suggestions in mind before setting out on the East Coast Trail (or anywhere in NL, for that matter):

• When hiking in damp weather, be careful when stepping over logs, as they can be very slippery when wet.

• Always bring rain gear along with you as the weather can—and does—change at whim. Also, layer your clothing so you can enjoy the sun's warmth when it comes out.

• If you have a bad back or weak knees take along a walking stick, as it helps take some of the pressure off those areas.

• Never hike alone. Always travel with at least one companion as well as an emergency pack with a flashlight and flares. And be sure to let someone know where you're going, and when you expect to return.

The most spectacular stretch is the **Spout Path,** an 18-km (11-mile) expanse rated as difficult and strenuous—and beyond my hiking abilities! You can begin at Bay Bulls or Raymond Head, with the bonus being the chance to get close to the **Spout,** a wave-driven geyser that shoots saltwater 60m (197 ft.) into the air. You'll also have the opportunity to view sea stacks (stand-alone stone pillars rising from the sea), a cast-iron lighthouse, and a couple of abandoned settlements along the way.

Your best resource for independent travel is the **East Coast Trail Association** (© 709/738-4453; www.eastcoasttrail.com). They can advise you about renting hiking equipment from any number of outfitters in the St. John's area if you don't want to bring (or don't have) your own. They also sell a comprehensive series of guidebooks on the East Coast Trail. Volume 1 covers 26km (16 miles) of the popular trail from Fort Amherst to Petty Harbour and sells for C$21.95 (US$16) with no tax, but shipping charges apply. Alternatively, for C$19.95 (US$14.61) you can purchase a set of 19 waterproof topographic maps—also available through the ECTA website.

Another good resource is **Trail Connections** (© 709/335-8315; www.trailconnections.ca), an association of accommodations and eco-tourism service providers for hikers. For a reasonable fee, a member of Trail Connections will pick you up at the airport, make bag lunches geared especially for hikers, provide bed-and-breakfast accommodations, and set you up with dinners if you desire. Daily rates for the Trail Connections service are C$75 (US$54.94) per person double, and C$120 (US$87.91) single. Five percent of their profits go toward maintenance of the East Coast Trail.

If you prefer the accompaniment of an experienced hiker, call **TrailBlazer Adventures** (© 877/368-7245; www.trailblazeradventures.com). This St. John's–based company offers a variety of options, including off-road adventures, coastal hikes, and overnight hiking adventures. Prices for half-day tours begin at C$59 (US$43.22) for adults, C$54 (US$39.56) for seniors, and C$28 (US$20.51) for children under 18. Rain gear is available for unfavorable weather, and healthy snacks are provided for all trips. TrailBlazer can even arrange hiking boot rentals.

If you plan to hike the East Coast Trail and want to do a little kayaking at the same time, get in touch with Stan Cook. He operates out of Cape Broyle, on the trail between Witless Bay and Ferryland, and his **Wilderness Newfoundland Adventures** (© **888/747-6353;** www.wildnfld.ca) is highly recommended. One- and two-person kayaks are available; there are even special kayaks that can accommodate children too young to paddle. Experienced professionals ensure beginners get thorough on-shore instruction before they head out on the water, and the sheltered environment of the harbor makes it an ideal experimental paddling ground. *Note to parents:* There are few better cures for a chronically bored teen than an oceanside view of a surfacing humpback! Prices are C$45 (US$32.96) for 2½ hours, C$65 (US$47.61) for 4 hours, and C$99 (US$72.59) for a full day.

2 The Irish Loop

ESSENTIALS
If you don't have time to see all of the Avalon, and are wondering which part to see if you only have a day or two, my recommendation would be the Irish Loop. Why? Because it has a bit of everything, including the charm of Celtic flair. Half of Newfoundland's population is of Irish descent, a heritage more prevalent throughout the Irish Loop than in any other part of the province.

You can visit the Irish Loop in the form of day trips from St. John's. For example, one day could include a visit to Bay Bulls in the morning and Ferryland in the afternoon; another day may take you to Salmonier Nature Park in the morning and St. Vincent's in the afternoon. Or you can plan to overnight at one of the interesting places you'll find along the way.

GETTING THERE
If you're coming from points other than St. John's, you can access communities along the Irish Loop by taking Highway 1 to Route 13 (the Witless Bay Line), and then heading east to hook up with Route 10 (the Irish Loop Dr.) between Bay Bulls and Witless Bay.

To reach the Irish Loop from St. John's, take Route 2 (Pitts Memorial Dr.) out of town, and then head south via Route 3, which will lead you to Route 10. You can make a slight detour onto Route 11 and stop in at **Cape Spear** (see p. 64) or **Petty Harbour** (see p. 67) along the way.

Back on **Route 10,** you'll soon come to **Bay Bulls,** possibly the best-known whale-watching site in the province. Your next stop will be at **Ferryland,** site of the Colony of Avalon, an active archaeological dig. **Cape Race** is worth a stop if you're interested in shipwrecks and the history of the *Titanic.* If you'd like to see some caribou, keep heading along Route 10 to the area between **Trepassey** and St. Shotts.

Around the coast, as the highway turns back north, you'll arrive at **St. Vincent's,** a seaside community whose waters are known as a favorite dining spot for humpback whales. At St. Vincent's, Route 10 becomes **Route 90** (also known as the Salmonier Line) and carries on to **Salmonier,** home to **The Wilds,** an 18-hole golf resort designed to complement its natural surroundings, and **Salmonier Nature Park,** my favorite nature-based family attraction. From here, you're on your way back to the city, and just 85km (53 miles) or about a 45-minute drive from St. John's. *Note:* The stretch of the Irish Loop from St. Vincent's north to the TCH is also considered part of the **Cape Shore Route,** covered in the next section of this chapter.

VISITOR INFORMATION

You should have a detailed highway map and travel literature in hand before heading out from St. John's. Once you get into the smaller communities, services are more difficult to find and they operate shorter hours. There are, however, visitor centers offering localized information at the major attractions, which include Bay Bulls, the Colony of Avalon, and Salmonier Nature Park.

GETTING AROUND

The highways within this region are excellent, though relatively narrow and notoriously winding. Don't plan to speed. Most of the way you'll find an 80-kmph (50-mph) speed limit. Stick to that for your highway driving, and allow yourself enough time to stop and enjoy the beautiful scenery and to watch for the whales and caribou along the way.

There is no public community-to-community bus system, so you'll have to hook up with a tour company if you don't have your own car.

EXPLORING THE IRISH LOOP

As you stop at the various communities that comprise the Irish Loop, you may be surprised at the very strong Irish accent of the Newfoundlanders who call this region home. Most of the people who live here are direct descendants of the Irish who settled this area hundreds of years ago. And because many of the communities have been somewhat isolated until recent times, the Irish heritage has remained vibrant and the accent kept nicely intact. Call ℂ **888/438-2898** or **709/438-2898** or visit www.irishloop.nf.ca for more detailed information about the Irish Loop.

BAY BULLS TO WITLESS BAY

The coastal town of **Bay Bulls** will probably be your first stop on your way round the Loop. Just a 20-minute drive from metropolitan St. John's, it's a vibrant community of striking contrasts: rural attitude and architecture stand side by side with a strong commercial and industrial base. It's an obvious service center for the area, with a variety of stores and services far in excess of what is needed for the just over 1,000 residents who live there. And if that weren't enough to convince you of the town's economic stability, any remaining doubts will be erased by its massive docking facility. (One of the world's largest offshore oil drill rigs was in residence for repairs at the time of my visit.)

It's not the man-made wonders, however, that attract most visitors to Bay Bulls: it's the excellent wildlife and nature-watching opportunities. A handful of tour-boat operators can take you to the **Witless Bay Ecological Reserve,** a quartet of islands just south of Bay Bulls and 5km (3 miles) offshore. The Reserve is home to more than 2½ million seabirds, including 500,000 Atlantic puffins, and is one of the best places in North America to observe whales. (See the "Outdoor Pursuits of the Irish Loop" section for details.)

Where to Stay & Dine

Elaine's B&B By The Sea ⍟   If you like kids, kittens, warm welcomes, and hearty breakfasts, Elaine's offers a charming location on .008 sq. km (2 acres) of seaside meadow, with 152m (500 ft.) of ocean frontage overlooking Bird Island and a panoramic view of the Witless Bay Ecological Reserve. Late May and early June is the prime time for iceberg watching from the backyard swing. If you're really lucky, your morning view just might include a whale waving his tail in a friendly hello.

Modest though comfortably spacious guest rooms and firm mattresses work in conjunction with the invigorating power of sea-salt air to ensure one of the most restful sleeps you'll ever have. Each room has its own ensuite.

Lower Loop Place (P.O. Box 125), Witless Bay, NL A0A 4K0. ⓒ **709/334-2722**. www.netfx.ca/elainesby thesea. 3 units; 3 ensuites. C$55–$75 (US$40–$55) double; additional person C$10 (US$7.33). V. **Amenities:** Nonsmoking facility; kitchen available to guests; beachside bonfires. *In room:* TV.

Celtic Rendezvous Cottages By The Sea ★★ *Finds*   New, immaculately
clean and fully equipped cottages with a view that pays homage to the endless harmony of surf and sky. Truly a find and an incredible sanctuary, yet just 45 minutes from St. John's. Each cottage has a huge kitchen and dining table, large sitting area, and outdoor patio. The luxury cottage comes with its own bedside Jacuzzi. One unit is wheelchair accessible. The Lookout on-site convenience store sells groceries, ice, and beer; rents movies, and has a small cafe. Plans are underway for an oceanside RV park.

I have one criticism, and it's one I hold for most cottage resorts (it just stands out more here because everything else is so conducive to a retreat environment). There isn't enough separation between the cottages; while independent, they are side by side without any vegetation or privacy fences in between. That subtle visual separation would make a world of difference.

Route 10 (take Bauline East turnoff). ⓒ **866/334-3341** or 709/334-3341. Fax: 709/334-2560. www.celtic rendezvouscottages.com. 5 units. C$89–99 (US$65–72) double, weekdays; C$249 (US$183) double, for the luxury cottage. DC, MC, V. **Amenities:** Coin-operated laundry; playground; oceanside BBQs for guest use; pets allowed. *In room:* TV/VCR, complete kitchen facilities, hairdryer, iron.

La Manche Provincial Park   For overnight and/or day use, La Manche
Provincial Park offers excellent hiking, canoeing, swimming, and bird-watching opportunities. Highlights are a suspension bridge and the abandoned fishing village of La Manche (destroyed by a tidal wave in 1996). Each of the 70 campsites has a picnic table, fireplace, garbage can, and parking. Drinking-water taps and pit toilets are located throughout the park. You will, however, have to stock up on supplies before you arrive, as there is no convenience store on-site. Nor are there shower or laundry facilities. Although it once had a reputation as a preferred hangout for inebriated teens, things have quieted down so that La Manche is again family-friendly. *Note:* swimming is unsupervised.

Route 10 (53km/33 miles out of St. John's). Mailing address: 33 Reid's Lane, Deer Lake, NL A8A 2B1. ⓒ **800/563-6353** or 709/685-1823. www.gov.nf.ca/parks&reserves/la_manche.htm. Unserviced lots C$9/night (US$6.60); subject to change. MC, V. Closed Sept 16–May 15. **Amenities:** Trout angling; day-use facilities; drinking taps & pit toilets located throughout the park; hiking trails; interpretation program; outdoor freshwater swimming; picnic sites; playground. Chopped firewood can be purchased.

The Captain's Table Restaurant ★   A three-time favorite with *Where to Eat
in Canada*, the Captain's Table has a well-deserved reputation for consistently good food. Among the fast-food staples of hamburgers (made from fresh meat), french fries (homestyle, not frozen), and chicken fillet strips (their own recipe), you'll find a trove of seafood treasures—like the best fish and chips *and* the best pan-fried cod on the Avalon. Not to mention the meal-maker chowder overflowing with cod, shrimp, and scallops. For maximum satisfaction, top it off with a slice of bumbleberry pie or warm apple dumpling à la mode. Forget counting calories—you're on vacation!

Irish Loop Highway (Rte. 10), Mobile, NL. ⓒ **709/334-2278**. www.captainstable.nf.ca. Open Apr 1– (Canadian) Thanksgiving, daily 11:30am–9pm. Main courses C$7.95–$16.95 (US$5.83–$12.43). MC, V.

(Fun Fact **From Legendary Hero to Legendary Food**

Arthur Jackman, co-owner and head chef of the Captain's Table Restaurant, is the great-grandson of Captain William Jackman, an accomplished
mariner born in 1837. Captain Jackman is remembered, however, not for
his considerable navigational prowess but for an unbelievable act of
bravery. It was October 9, 1867, and Captain Jackman was sealing off the
Labrador coast when a sudden storm forced him to head for land. After
safely guiding his vessel and crew ashore, Captain Jackman (driven by
some unknown impulse) headed out into the gale to go for a walk. He
soon spotted a schooner run aground on a reef several hundred meters
from shore. Calling for help, but without waiting for it to arrive, Captain
Jackman dove into the frigid North Atlantic waters. Twenty-seven times
he made the harrowing journey to the beleaguered vessel, each time
returning with one of its passengers on his back. The last passenger, a
woman, was already deathly ill and immobile in her cabin when Captain
Jackman insisted that she, too, would be saved from the sea. She lived
just long enough to thank him for his kindness.

FERRYLAND/AQUAFORTE

With almost 400 years of European settlement to its credit, **Ferryland** is one of
the oldest and most historical communities in the province, and also the site of
an ongoing excavation of a 17th-century colony. It's a unique archaeological dig
in that a small community of residents lives in the midst of the pick and shovel
activity. (See a detailed description of the Colony of Avalon in "Outdoor Pursuits of the Irish Loop.")

Although Ferryland doesn't have an abundance of visitor services, the focus
here is on quality—not quantity. It was the first NL community to receive the
"SuperHost" designation. SuperHost is a service-oriented training program
offered by Hospitality Newfoundland & Labrador; a visitor can expect a higher
level of service from a provider that's awarded this designation. See www.ferry
land.com for more info about the community's services.

A few kilometers farther south along Route 10, at the outermost tip of a scenic fjord, is where you'll find the community of **Aquaforte.** Unlike early settlers
who faced the challenge of a harbor too deep for anchorage and distant fishing
grounds, you'll find this a most hospitable place to visit. It's a good place to stop
for the night if your visit to the dig site keeps you late into the day or if you
choose to take in some of the great evening entertainment in Ferryland put on
by the Southern Shore Folk Arts Council.

The Southern Shore Folk Arts Council (© 709/432-2052; www.ssfac.
com) provides a variety of entertainment in the Ferryland area. The **Shamrock
Festival** is held the fourth weekend of July, offering lively music with traditional
Irish/Newfoundland flavor. And each summer, from June through September,
the **Avalonia Dinner Theatre** holds performances at the Colony of Avalon on
Tuesday and Friday nights. For C$30 (US$22), you get a three-course meal and
entertainment in a historical setting.

Where to Stay & Dine

Downs Inn ⚑   By the time you leave Downs Inn, you'll be wondering if owners Aiden and Dianne Costello are psychic—that's how good they are at anticipating their visitors' needs. You might even think they're getting divine direction from the former occupants of this well-maintained, Victorian-style, three-storey waterfront property (it used to be a convent). But no, the full breakfasts, private baths, and laundry service aren't the work of supernatural advisors. Host Aiden is the local tourism development officer, and he's well versed in the little extras that can transform a comfortable stay into an unforgettable experience—like the cozy warmth of a fireplace, or an unobstructed ocean view. And if you're not sure what else you'd like to see or do along the Irish Loop, don't be afraid to ask for Aiden's recommendations. He is, after all, the expert.

Route 10 (P.O. Box 15), Ferryland, NL A0A 2H0. ✆ 877/432-2808 or 709/432-2808. E-mail: acostello@nf.sympatico.ca. 4 units, 2 ensuites. C$55–$75 (US$40–$55) double; additional person C$10 (US$7.33). V. Open May 1–Dec 1. **Amenities:** Laundry service; tea room; nonsmoking; full breakfast; TV room.

Hagan's Hospitality Home B&B   The house isn't an architectural masterpiece, nor will the decorating scheme win any awards, but everything beyond that is extraordinary. Both in portion and flavor, the food epitomizes homemade perfection. And there's a standard of cleanliness here that would put an army barracks to shame. But even that pales in comparison to the warmth and friendliness of your host, the delightful Rita Hagan. Her perpetual smile and musical brogue more than make up for any splendor lacking from her listed amenities. With a mug of tea in your hand and one of her timeless stories in your ear, you'll feel as privileged as royalty. And the location is perfect if you're on your way from Ferryland to Trepassey, or if you're hiking the East Coast Trail.

If you don't like sharing a bathroom, be sure to ask for one of the rooms that has a private bath.

Route 10 (General Delivery), Aquaforte, NL A0A 1A0. ✆ 709/363-2688. www.haganshospitality.com. 3 units, 2 ensuites. C$60 (US$44) double; rollaway cots C$10 (US$7.33) additional; 10% discount for seniors. No credit cards. Rate includes welcome lunch on arrival and full breakfast. **Amenities:** Laundry facilities; TV in public room; room service.

The Colony Café ⚑⚑ *Finds*   A dining experience with continental flavor, located in the midst of the Colony of Avalon's archaeological dig. The building, previously occupied as the Ferryland fish plant, was supposed to have been a simple coffee shop. Customer demand forced those modest plans to be upgraded to a full-service restaurant (seating for 60), replete with attractive pine interior, custom-painted historical mural, and the services of professional French chef Christian Houle. He specializes in seafood, with a particularly tender touch for cod (this mild fish is easily overpowered by excessive accoutrements). A tantalizing whiff of a passing bowl of chowder will have you salivating for more. Give in to temptation. I guarantee you won't be disappointed. Reservations are recommended.

Route 10, Ferryland. ✆ 709/432-3030. www.ferryland.com/colonycafe. Lunch about C$7 (US$4.50); dinners C$7.95–$19.95 (US$5.83–$14.63). MC, V. Open May–Sept Mon–Thurs 11am–8pm, Fri–Sun 10:30am–8:30pm.

TREPASSEY TO SALMONIER

Midway round the Irish Loop, you'll come to the small fishing village of **Trepassey,** a good place to stop for the night if you find yourself at Mistaken Point late in the day (Mistaken Point is the only place in the world where Precambrian animal fossils are so abundant that they cover exposed areas the size of tennis courts). The location is somewhat remote, but there are advantages to that: you're right in the heart of caribou country. *Warning:* Be aware that this area is prone to heavy fog, so be careful when driving, as the animals frequently cross the road.

The area between Trepassey and Salmonier along Route 90 runs adjacent to the **Avalon Wilderness Reserve,** home to the most southerly herd of woodland caribou in the world. Imagine my surprise when a break in the fog revealed dozens of them so close to the road I had to take the zoom lens off my camera. I was even tempted to do a Kevin Costner "dances with caribou" impersonation. Luckily, I remembered that these are wild animals and wisely refrained from becoming a hood ornament on some bull's antlers.

Another claim to fame for Trepassey is that it's the spot where Amelia Earhart launched her cross-Atlantic flight in 1928. The town has a small museum with a commemorative display featuring photos of the famous aviator during her visit to the town, as well as details of her historic flight.

Rounding Trepassey Bay, you'll pass through the community of St. Vincent's. Be sure to stop here if you'd like to take in some land-based whale watching (yes, the water gets *that deep, that close* to shore).

Further along Route 10 to Route 90, you'll arrive at **Salmonier,** where you'll find a good number of outdoor pursuits, including the **Salmonier Nature Park,** the **Wilds Resort & Golf Course,** and salmon fishing. *Note:* Route 10 becomes Route 90 at the community of St. Vincent's. Route 90 joins up with the Trans-Canada Highway near **Holyrood,** for a quicker route back to St. John's. (See more about Holyrood in "Conception Bay & Marine Drive," later in this chapter.)

Where to Stay & Dine

Northwest Lodge Bed & Breakfast   Hosts Harold and Marie Pennell offer safe, clean, and economical accommodations in a family environment. Marie is noted for her homemade jams (and her cooking in general), while Harold has loads of stories about his days as a lighthouse keeper at Cape Race and Cape Pine. Although comfortable, the rooms alone won't lure you here (they're almost filled to capacity by a bureau and double bed). You'll be far more impressed by the leaping salmon in the nearby river, as well as the chance to get up close and personal with the resident caribou herd.

Route 10, Trepassey. ⓒ **877/398-2888** or 709/438-2888. www.bbcanada.com/bbnorthwest. 4 units. C$45–$60 (US$33–$44) double; rollaway cot C$10 (US$7.33) extra. MC, V. **Amenities:** Nonsmoking; wheelchair accessible; BBQ pit. *In room:* TV.

Salmonier Country Manor   Also known as the Convent Inn in tribute to its former occupants (the Presentation sisters, a holy order), this beautifully renovated convent melds understated luxury with meditative serenity. All 7 guest rooms are tastefully decorated in a warm country style (solid wood furnishings, toe-curling area rugs) and have elegantly appointed ensuite bathrooms. The best room in the house is the Florence Room: picture yourself sipping on champagne by candlelight in the double Jacuzzi, then basking in the warmth from your in-room fireplace—all the while being serenaded by the bubble of the Salmonier River as it flows below your window. Now that's my idea of paradise!

Reservations are a must if you want to dine at the inn's licensed dining room (it's a fixed menu, so you'll want to inquire in advance about what's being served), situated in what was once the convent chapel. I'd highly recommend a dinner performance here of "Christmas and the Mummers." It's a fun and informal "time," or party, that includes a traditional Newfoundland Christmas dinner, local entertainment, recitations, and a visit from wildly costumed characters known as mummers.

The inn is located just an hour from St. John's (via the Trans-Canada Highway), but while here you're a world away from traffic and the modern world. You're also near Cataracts Park and walking trails that will allow you to enjoy the quiet beauty without distraction. Children over the age of 7 are welcome; pets are not.

Route 90 to 93, Mount Carmel (take Rte. 93 turnoff at St. Catherines). 💰 **866/521-2778** or 709/521-2778. http://manor.infotechcanada.com. 7 units. C$89–$109 (US$65–$80). MC, V. No small children. Closed mid-Dec–early May. **Amenities:** Dining room; nonsmoking rooms (smoking permitted on front deck). *In room:* TV, ensuite baths.

Trepassey Motel & Restaurant As is to be expected from the price, this is a reliable overnight stop if all you need are clean sheets, a roof over your head, and a shower in the morning. That said, its location at the approximate halfway point around the Irish Loop makes it the ideal sojourn after an exhausting day of touring. You'll awaken refreshed and eager to continue your previous explorations. *Tip:* Treat yourself to breakfast in the motel restaurant. Not only is the food reasonably priced and well prepared, but the dining room's floor-to-ceiling windows provide a view that'll be the highlight of your stay.

Route 10 (111–113 Coarse Hill), Trepassey. 💰 **709/438-2934.** 10 units with private baths, including one family housekeeping unit. C$55–$64 (US$40–$47) double. MC, V. **Amenities:** Restaurant; laundry facilities; nonsmoking rooms. *In room:* TV, no phone.

The Wilds at Salmonier Resort & Golf Course 👁️ Ample accommodation choices await you at a resort geared more to golf enthusiasts than luxury-seeking travelers. (Details on The Wilds golf experience can be found in the section "Outdoor Pursuits of the Irish Loop.") You can choose from one of 40 standard hotel-style rooms, or one of 18 self-contained fully equipped cabins. I recommend the cabins. The hotel is nice if you don't mind bearing witness to assorted noises from your neighbors during the night. Even the suites, though spacious, are somewhat disappointing because of their nondescript furnishings. Considering the resort setting, I expected it to have a stronger character.

The two-bedroom self-contained cabins provide more privacy and are a better choice for families or small groups wanting to be together. Ever try to entertain a couple of young children in a hotel room? You can only hide in the bathroom for so long. Plus, you can bring pets to the cabins, and a shared barbecue area is available where you can cook when it's nice outdoors. *Hint:* The cabins book up early, so try to reserve at least 6 months in advance.

The Wilds is set on the beautiful Salmonier River, and nestled in a hilly, wooded area. Among the swimming pool, the golf course, and nearby Salmonier Nature Park, you'll have plenty of opportunity to enjoy the great outdoors. And the complimentary supervised kids' program (for ages 5 to 14) means you'll be able to have some time to yourself. For the under-5 set, experienced babysitters are available at C$6.50 (US$4.76) an hour.

Warning: There have been problems with the groundwater in this region; when we stayed at the resort, a boil-water order was in effect. The hotel supplied us with bottled water in the room but didn't advise us of the problem at check-in, and we missed the small notice that had been left on the desk in our room. Luckily, no one took ill. The staff told us that the order was simply a precautionary measure, but it's my opinion that they should ensure each guest is personally told of such a situation to prevent any misfortune.

Route 90, Salmonier Line (Hwy. 1 to Exit 35). © **866/888-9453** or 709/229-5444. www.thewilds.nf.net. C$89–$129 (US$65–$95) double; C$89.00 (US$65) country cabins. AE, DC, MC, V. Open May 1–Oct 30. **Amenities:** Restaurant, lounge; outdoor heated pool; 18-hole golf course, golf academy; children's program, babysitting. *In room:* TV, coffeemaker.

OUTDOOR PURSUITS OF THE IRISH LOOP

The Bay Bulls to Witless Bay Ecological Reserve ✪✪✪ is a favorite destination for bird-watchers, whale enthusiasts, and lovers of the great outdoors. Plan to spend at least a half-day here. To reach the Reserve, continue south past Bay Bulls along Route 10 to the community of Witless Bay. There, several local tour boat operators can carry you to within viewing distance of the four islands that make up the Reserve. Each of the following service providers is listed here because of certain unique characteristics, but others are around if the choices below are booked to capacity.

Gatherall's Puffin & Whale Watch (© **800/419-4253** or 709/334-2887; www.newfoundland-whales.com) is the company to choose if you like catamarans. Because the boat travels at high speed, you spend less time getting to and from the best viewing sites, and more time watching the whales and puffins. There's enough seating for 100 passengers in the main, heated cabin, but if you prefer the wind in your hair you can stand outside on the top deck. Gatherall's provides a shuttle service from St. John's for those without transportation. The 90-minute boat trip operates May through October, with up to six daily departures. The only negative is their overly complex pricing structure: C$46 (US$33.74) for adults, C$39 (US$28.61) seniors and CAA/AAA members, C$33 (US$24.21) post-secondary students with valid ID, C$20.50 (US$15) youth 10–7, C$16 (US$11.74) children 5–9, and C$8 (US$5.86) children 1–4; no charge for infants less than 1 year.

O'Brien's Nautical Experiences (© **877/639-4253** or 709/753-4850; www. obriensboattours.com) has been described as one of the best tourism bargains in Canada, even receiving a thumbs-up from rocker David Bowie. It's like getting two events for the price of one: a world-class marine adventure and a heck of a party too. O'Brien's popular 2-hours-plus tour takes you aboard a two-level, 14-m (46-ft.) passenger vessel where you'll hear—and sing along to—lively Irish Newfoundland folk music; drink screech; have lots of fun; and get to see whales (I saw a mother swimming protectively alongside her breaching calf), puffins, and icebergs in season. The main decks of the boats are wheelchair accessible. Cost is C$45 (US$33) adults, C$37 (US$27.14) seniors, C$34.50 (US$25.31) post-secondary students, C$21 (US$15.40) ages 11–17, C$15 (US$11) ages 4–10, and free for children under 4.

O'Brien's also has smaller boats and kayaking adventures. If you prefer smaller boats, a 2-hours-plus Zodiac marine safari will get you close to the Spout, sea caves, sea stacks, and more. Zodiac trips cost C$60 (US$44) per person, with no applicable discounts. Floater suits are included. This trip is not recommended for really young kids unless you're sure they can sit still for 2½ hours. Morning, afternoon, or evening guided kayaking adventures are also not recommended for children under 10 unless they will be sitting in the lap of a parent (remember that this is for more than 3 hours). Kayaking adventures include all supplies and a half-hour of on-land instruction, so even beginners can try it. The price is C$55 (US$40) per person; no discounts apply. All prices include tax.

Tips St. Vincent's for Great Whale Watching

The tiny village of **St. Vincent's** ⭐, in the beautiful Peter's River Valley, is the place to be between June and August if you want to see humpback whales **lunge feeding**. The whales launch their bodies right out of the water—mouths wide open—and fill themselves with capelin (small fish similar to smelt, which are a favorite dinner for the whales). The whales like it here because the water is deep even close to shore, and these conditions attract more capelin. More capelin, more whales.

Nature being nature, you can't be promised that you'll see the whales feeding if you come to St. Vincent's. But they've been doing so with some regularity the past few years, so if you're patient the chances are good. To help you pass the time while you wait for the whales, a food stand sells souvenirs and serves fish and chips right on the beach.

You can also spend an hour at the **Fisherman's Museum**. It may be a stroll down memory lane for the locals, but it's quite the eye-opener for visitors. See an example of the **Newfoundland Thermos**—a bottle wrapped in a sock that would contain the fisherman's special blend of hot tea mixed with hooch. You can examine all sorts of artifacts from a traditional fisherman's home. Stroll through the main-floor kitchen, parlor, parish room (which houses many religious artifacts from the Catholic Church), and the arts-and-crafts display. On the second floor (not accessible to those who have difficulty with stairs), you can visit the tool room, where you'll see tools used by pioneer settlers.

The museum is on Route 90, across from the visitor center and town hall ((*C*) **709/525-2540** or 709/525-2798), open July through August daily 10am–5pm. The town has one gas station and a convenience store, but no accommodations. *(Note:* Route 10 becomes Route 90 at St. Vincent's.)

Colony of Avalon ⭐⭐   Give yourself a half-day to get immersed in the history of this living archaeological dig. The Colony of Avalon is an independently run National Historic Site with a world-class interpretation center. Watch the 8-minute video and then take a self-guided tour to see artifacts from the first successful planned colony in Newfoundland, settled in 1621 by Sir George Calvert (who later became Lord Baltimore).

You're then ready to take a 1½-hour guided tour (or a more leisurely self-guided tour) of the .018 sq. km (4-acre) former colony. You'll learn about the world's first flushable toilet (we have clogs to thank for artifacts found in the "pipe") and walk on the oldest cobblestone street in British North America. Visitors are welcome to view the second-floor lab where the cataloging and reconstruction of artifacts takes place. An on-site gift shop sells local crafts and reproductions of 17th-century items from the colony, and the **Colony Café** serves great meals in a historical setting. *Warning:* The Colony of Avalon is often hit with strong, cold winds: be sure to bring along a jacket.

Route 10, Ferryland. (*C*) **877/326-5669** or 709/432-3200. www.heritage.nf.ca/avalon. Admission C$5 (US$3.66) adults, C$3 (US$2.20) seniors & students; C$10 (US$7.33) family. Mid-May–mid-Oct daily 9am–7pm.

Mistaken Point Ecological Reserve   Getting to Mistaken Point is a full day's effort from St. John's, but well worth the trip. If you're into fossils, you'll appreciate the area's key importance to paleontologists as the home of 620-million-year-old trilobite fossils (the oldest multi-celled fossils in North America, and the only deep-water marine fossils of this type found in the world).

It's a couple of hours' drive from St. John's (and about an hour past Ferryland) to the Portugal Cove South turnoff, 25 minutes in from the highway, and then a 45-minute hike from where you park your car to the fossil bed. At present, the fossil site has no guided tours, so you're on your own.

Mistaken Point: Route 10 (at Portugal Cove South). ℭ 709/635-4520. www.gov.nf.ca/parks&reserves/ecolres.htm. Accessible year-round during daylight hours, weather permitting. Free admission.

⸢Fun Fact⸣ Graveyard of the Atlantic
_____

With its perpetual fog and rock-studded shore, it's no wonder the area of the southern Avalon around Cape Race is called the **"Graveyard of the Atlantic."** Records show 365 ships have gone down between Renews Harbour and Cape Pine. Cape Race is in the center between these two points. If you're interested in maritime history, be sure to visit the **Cape Race Lighthouse,** operating since 1856. It has the largest lighthouse lens in North America. You can tour the lighthouse (including the lens housing at the top of the tower) and its museum for C$3 (US$2.20). In the museum, you'll find a Marconi replica, as well as an extensive _Titanic_ display, highlighting the Cape Race connection to the doomed ship, which sank in 1912 after colliding with an iceberg on its maiden voyage. This is where the S.O.S. signal from the sinking luxury liner was received. Although the lighthouse is automated there is a lightkeeper in residence at Cape Race, and students provide interpretive services in the summer. To make advance arrangements for your trip to the lighthouse, contact Catherine Ward, ℭ **709/438-2451.**

Salmonier Nature Park ⸢★★★⸣ ⸢Kids⸣ ⸢Finds⸣   This park is a prime example of what a 21st-century zoo should be. It's a peaceful and calming nature reserve operated by the provincial Wildlife Division. Because it's a rehabilitation facility for injured and orphaned birds and animals you'll find the guest list to be constantly changing—the goal of the park is to release as many of the creatures as possible back into the wild. For those who will never be able to survive the wild again, the park serves as a comfortable hospital or retirement home.

As you stroll along the park's 2½ km (1½ miles) of wheelchair- and stroller-friendly boardwalk, you'll see moose, lynx, owls, bald eagles, and Arctic fox in specially developed enclosures that represent their natural habitat. Approximately 100 species of birds, 15 species of mammals, and 175 species of plant have been recorded in the park—including the pitcher plant, NL's provincial flower. Benches are strategically situated along the way so you can rest, enjoy a snack, or just marvel at nature. Allow at least an hour for your visit.

Route 90 (12km/7.5 miles south of the Trans-Canada Hwy., and about a 1-hour drive from St. John's if you take the direct route). ℭ 709/229-7888. www.gov.nf.ca/snp. Free admission (donations accepted). Open June 1–Labor Day daily 10am–6pm; Labor Day–(Canadian) Thanksgiving (second Mon in Oct) Mon–Fri 10am–4pm.

The Wilds at Salmonier River ★★ *Moments*   An 18-hole golf course that has made the greatest of efforts to preserve the native woodlands, here long before we decided it was fun to whack a small white ball around with a shiny club. You'll find waterfalls and small creeks running throughout the course, and if you're lucky you just may see a moose along the way. The big brown fellows have been known to hang around the 16th green and the woods around the 7th hole.

The Wilds has an environmentally sensitive wetland. If you lose your ball in one of these areas (marked with signage) you're prohibited from trying to retrieve it. The front nine is very challenging, with a hazard on every hole.

Because it's only minutes from the Salmonier Nature Park, one parent can take the kids to the park while the other has a round of golf. Better yet, if you're staying overnight at The Wilds you can avail of the child-care program so that everyone gets to play.

The Wilds at Salmonier Resort & Golf Course, Route 90 (Hwy. 1 to Exit 35). ℂ **709/229-9453**. www. thewilds.nf.net. C$31.30–$43.43 (US$22.96–$31.86) for 18 holes; C$27.83 (US$20.41) for power cart (taxes not included). Full-service restaurant and pro shop. (See Trepassey area lodgings for resort listing.)

3 Cape Shore

ESSENTIALS
You're likely to find yourself driving at least part of the **Cape Shore Route** if you plan on visiting **Cape St. Mary's,** the best bird-watching spot in the province. Even if you're not an avid birder, you'll be awed by the number of gannets that inhabit Bird Rock. In fact, the symbol for the Cape Shore Route is one of our fine feathered friends, because this region is a birder's paradise.

The Cape Shore Route (which includes routes 90, 92, and 100) overlaps with the Irish Loop from St. Vincent's (where Route 10 becomes Route 90) north to join up with the Trans-Canada Highway (Route 1) near Holyrood.

Tips **Navigating Newfoundland**

It can be confusing driving around Newfoundland, as you'll often find that a street or highway starts out with one name or number, and then changes without notice. That's why it's critical you have a detailed high-way map before heading out on any road trip in the province.

GETTING THERE
To get to the **Cape St. Mary's Ecological Reserve** from St. John's, take Route 1 (Trans-Canada Highway) west to the Route 90 turnoff. Then head south on Route 90 past the Salmonier Nature Park (see the detailed description in the preceding section) to the Route 92 turnoff at St. Catherines. Follow Route 92 south until you get to Branch, where Route 92 becomes Route 100, and follow that to the Cape St. Mary's Ecological Reserve. When you're coming from St. John's, the 175-km (108-mile) drive should take you between two and three hours, if you don't stop along the way.

Note: The provincial travel literature tells you it will take only 2 hours, but it took us nearly 3 hours on our first trip out from St. John's to Cape St. Mary's. The road is narrow with lots of hairpin curves through gorgeous hilly country-side. It's not just difficult driving—you won't *want* to rush! The coastline along this stretch of Route 100 is scenic. The cliffs climbing up from the shoreline remind me of the Hana region of Maui (Hawaii), and also of the rugged coastline of British Columbia on Canada's West Coast.

If you've just come off the ferry at Argentia and your first destination is Cape St. Mary's, head south 75km (47 miles) along Route 100. It's a lovely coastal drive, and you'll be there in about an hour. If you're heading from Argentia to St. John's, take Route 100 north to the Trans-Canada Highway (Route 1), which will take you directly into the heart of the city.

VISITOR INFORMATION

If you arrive in this region by way of ferry from Nova Scotia, you're likely to find yourself arriving at **Argentia.** The Visitor Centre in Argentia (© **709/227-5272**) is right at the ferry terminal and open hours that coincide with the ferry's arrivals and departures. You can pick up brochures and information about the Cape Shore Region here or at the Visitor Centre at nearby Cape St. Mary's (© **709/277-1666**). Information about the region is also available by calling the **Cape Shore Loop Tourism Association** at © **709/227-5456**.

WHERE TO STAY & DINE

Tourist accommodations and services are not as developed along the Cape Shore Route as you'll find in neighboring regions, mainly because fewer communities are along the way, with virtually nothing along Route 92 from North Harbour to Branch. The community of **St. Bride's** is the largest one nearest to Cape St. Mary's and it is still very small.

You'll find a greater variety of services on Route 100 in the communities of **Argentia** and **Placentia,** including **Fitzgerald's Pond Park**—a nice RV stop on the Argentia Access Road off Route 100 (© **709/227-4488**), with unserviced lots at C$10 (US$7.33). This is a former provincial park that has been purchased by the same people who own Bird Island Resort.

Bird Island Resort ✦ *Kids*   This is an award-winning family resort with spectacular oceanfront property that's as easy on your eyes as your pocketbook. The two-bedroom efficiency units offer full kitchen facilities equipped with all the dishes, glasses, and appliances you could need—so you don't have to worry about the expense of a restaurant. And the mattresses have the supportive elasticity of trampolines (a definite bonus, according to the kids—not that my little darlings did any jumping!). There's also a well-stocked convenience store on-site, which comes in handy when you realize you forgot the ketchup for the hamburgers, and a fitness center to help you stay in shape for your day at the on-site beach. The Mannings, who own and operate the place, are a considerate family who pay attention to the details that make Bird Island Resort such a popular establishment. If you've been here once, you'll want to come back. This is the closest accommodations to Cape St. Mary's.

Route 100 (Main Rd.), St. Bride's. © **888/337-2450** or 709/337-2450. www.birdislandresort.com. 20 units, including 15 cottages. C$49 (US$36) standard double room; C$79 (US$58) efficiency units. AE, MC, V. **Amenities:** BBQ and horseshoe pits; fitness center; mini-golf; laundry facilities; sunset deck. *In room:* TV, some have kitchenettes.

Seaside Bed & Breakfast ✦   This is not your standard B&B. Along with the expected amenities of private baths, cable TV, and hot breakfasts, there's an unsupervised outdoor pool with a 15-m (50-ft.) waterslide, as well as an indoor games room where you can play pool, table tennis, darts, or even pinball. And here's welcome news for people whose digestive systems don't react favorably to different kinds of water (a lot of rural areas have well water that isn't chlorinated): Seaside uses bottled spring water in its cooking and for drinking. All five guest rooms have a sparsely furnished rustic charm that is offset by a postcard-perfect waterfront view overlooking the Southeast Arm. Surprisingly, there are no in-room phones.

Route 91, Southeast Placentia. ✆ **709-227-2825.** www.angelfire.com/nf/seasidebandb. 5 ensuite units. C$60–70 (US$44–51) double. V. **Amenities:** Outdoor covered swimming pool with waterslide; games room with pool table, table tennis, darts, and pinball machine; exercise equipment. *In room:* TV, no phone.

EXPLORING THE CAPE SHORE
CAPE ST. MARY'S ECOLOGICAL RESERVE ✸✸✸

If you're like me and are thrilled by the presence and power of nature, visiting Cape St. Mary's, on the southwest tip of the Avalon Peninsula, is a must. Just east of St. Bride's, you'll arrive at the Cape St. Mary's Interpretive Centre, where you can familiarize yourself with the types of birds you'll be seeing. Then you're off on a hike over uneven terrain. It will take you 15 minutes if you're a fast walker, 30 minutes if you take the time to appreciate the sights along the way.

As you near **Bird Rock,** a spectacular 61-m-high (200-ft.) sea stack, you'll see—and hear—the 24,000 northern gannets, 20,000 common murres, 2,000 thick-billed murres, 20,000 kittiwakes, and 300 northern razorbills that make Cape St. Mary's the most accessible seabird sanctuary in North America. You'll be standing high atop a rock roughly equivalent in height to Bird Rock itself, and close enough to touch many of its feathered inhabitants. Even though you're close enough to make physical contact, you should refrain from doing so—don't forget, they are wild animals.

Be sure to bring a jacket, hat, and non-slip footwear for the hike. And remember that this is a site to protect wildlife—not humans—so be sure to hang on to small children when you are hiking near the edge of the cliff. You'll also want to be extra cautious when the fog rolls in (it can get so thick that visibility is reduced to 3m (10 ft.).

It's a visual treat, but unfortunately not accessible to those with walking disabilities. I would still recommend a visit to bird lovers who may not be able to hike the trail but would be gratified at seeing the very interesting Interpretive Centre. As well, the slow drive along the access road gives you a long-distance view of Bird Rock.

The Interpretive Centre is open May 1 through October 8, and offers guided tours. You can take a self-guided hike to Bird Rock year-round.

Route 100 (follow the signs 15km/9 miles east of the community of St. Bride's, and take the Cape St. Mary's Ecological Reserve access road). ✆ **800/563-6353** or 709/277-1666. www.gov.nf.ca/parks&reserves/capestmarys.htm. Interpretive Centre and self-guided tour to Bird Rock C$4 (US$2.93) adults, C$2 (US$1.46) for children, and C$10 (US$7.33) families. Guided tours to Bird Rock C$5 (US$3) per person, and include a visit to the Interpretive Centre. You can walk the trail to Bird Rock for free. Open May 1–May 30 & Oct 1–Oct 8 daily 9 am–5pm; June 1–Sept 30 daily 8am–7pm.

ARGENTIA

Argentia, the former U.S. naval base and current Marine Atlantic ferry terminal, is 131km (81 miles), or about a 90-minute drive, from St. John's along Route 100 to the Trans-Canada Highway (Route 1).

If you time your visit right and happen to be in the area on the first weekend of August, you'll catch the annual Argentia **Community Day Celebrations.** There are also a couple of year-round attractions that may interest you. For war buffs, Argentia is home to the **International Museum of the Atlantic Allies** (© **709/227-5797**), in honor of the American naval base that was operational here during World War II. For hikers, the **Backland Trails** offer 20 km (12 miles) of groomed walking trails. Call © **709/227-5502** for more info.

PLACENTIA

The historical community of Placentia will give you a sense of the international tug-of-war waged over control of this new world more than 400 years ago. The Spanish originally settled the area in the 1600s. But the French soon took control, and the settlement grew to become the French capital of Newfoundland. Today, the remains of France's 17th-century fortress at Castle Hill are all that is left of the French presence once so strong here.

Situated on the edge of town (follow the signs from Placentia), the **Castle Hill National Historic Site** features the remains of French and English fortifications from the 17th and 18th centuries and is operated by Parks Canada (© **709/227-2401**; www.pc.gc.ca/lhn-nhs/nl/castlehill/index_e.asp). Unless you happen to be in the area, or arrived in the province via Argentia, I wouldn't recommend making the journey specifically to visit Castle Hill. It's a long drive and the attraction isn't as impressive as some other more readily accessed sites—Signal Hill in St. John's, for instance.

Admission is C$2.50 (US$1.83) for adults, C$2 (US$1.46) for seniors 65 years and over, C$1.50 (US$1.10) for youth 6–16, and free for children under 6. Family rate of C$6 (US$4.40). The visitor center is open June 15–August 31 8:30am–8:30pm; May 15–June 14 and September 1–October 15 8:30am–4:30pm.

4 The Baccalieu Trail

ESSENTIALS

Baccalieu may seem an odd word to find in Newfoundland. However, it's actually a derivation of an old Spanish word for cod fish, and once you've spent any time in NL you soon realize that cod is king to this province.

The Baccalieu Trail extends between Trinity and Conception bays on the Avalon Peninsula. The western access to the route is near **Whitbourne,** at Route 80 following the coast of Trinity Bay, and extends north at **Grates Cove** before continuing south along the coast of Conception Bay as Route 70 and ending at the quaintly picturesque town of **Brigus.**

Brigus is one of those places best explored on foot—especially the heart of the community, with its numerous shops and cafes. Except for the pavement, you'll think you've stepped back in time. You'll walk beneath the arching branches of aging trees gracefully overhanging the narrow streets. You'll explore the gentle paths meandering over stony escarpments and nod to the locals as they go about their daily business around immaculately maintained old-style homes, some flanked by the ordered rows of vegetable gardens.

Between Whitbourne and Brigus, you'll find a multitude of fishing villages with enchanting names such as Heart's Content, Heart's Desire, Heart's Delight, Dildo, Cupids, and Blow Me Down. Each bend of the coastline brings with it a different personality. Indeed, this driving loop takes in many interesting, scenic, and historical places. Give yourself 2 or 3 days to enjoy it at a pleasant pace.

The **Baccalieu Trail Tourism Association** has an office at Unit 1, 4 Pikes Lane in **Carbonear** (© **709/596-3474**; http://collections.ic.gc.ca/baccalieu

trail), the area's largest service center. There are four highway exits off Route 70 to Carbonear, where you'll find a regional hospital, Wal-Mart, banks, and other services.

WHERE TO STAY

The Brittoner Bed & Breakfast *Value* This beautifully restored 160-year-old saltbox-style home in the heart of Brigus is not flush with amenities, but its location makes it perfect for sightseeing. The B&B is conveniently located near Hawthorne Cottage (former home of famous Arctic explorer Captain Bob Bartlett) and the Olde Stone Barn Museum. There are hiking trails nearby, tennis courts across the street, and a deck that's the perfect setting for a delicious outdoor breakfast. It overlooks a lovely pond that's home to a playful family of ducks.

Brigus is a 45-minute drive west of St. John's along the Trans-Canada Highway (Route 1), and a 1½-hour drive from St. John's along the slower Route 70.

Route 60, 12 Water St., Brigus. (C) **709/528-3412.** www.bbcanada.com/4385.html. 3 units. C$50–$60 (US$36.68–$44) double. No credit cards. Closed Nov 1–Apr 30. **Amenities:** Laundry facilities; nonsmoking rooms; pets allowed; picnic area; playground.

Fong's If you prefer a standard motel room as opposed to a B&B, Fong's (in Carbonear) is a good place to choose while touring the Baccalieu Trail. Fong's has it all—a motel, restaurant, banquet room, and lounge all wrapped up into one very nice facility. Guest rooms are spacious with large windows and full bathrooms. It's conveniently located right off the highway, near the edge of town and across the street from Wal-Mart.

143 Columbus Dr. (off Rte. 70, 45km/28 miles off the Trans-Canada Hwy.), Carbonear, NL A1Y 1A6. (C) **709/596-5114.** www.fongs.nf.ca. 16 units. C$60–$64 (US$44–$47) double. AE, DC, MC, V. **Amenities:** Restaurant, lounge; outdoor swimming pool. *In room:* TV.

Inn By The Bay *★★* This is an exquisite waterfront B&B in the historical fishing village of Dildo, named one of Canada's 10 prettiest towns. The inn, built in 1888, was recently acquired by Todd Warren, an enterprising young man with extensive experience in the hospitality industry. It shows, because Todd doesn't miss a beat. The finest of feather duvets and pillows adorn the tastefully furnished rooms. And each room has a private bath as well as its own decorative personality.

Todd's abilities as a chef make the meals at Inn By The Bay a real treat. In addition to the full breakfast, specialties such as mussels served in a caramelized sauce are an example of the gourmet dinners guests can enjoy for an additional C$25 (US$16) per person. You'll dine on those gourmet goodies (or afternoon tea or cocktails, if you prefer) in sumptuously civilized surroundings in the Inn's beautiful verandah sunroom.

If you'd like to make a short trip to Dildo Island to take part in an archaeological dig, or maybe need some assistance booking one of the other area tours, Todd is more than happy to assist. Dildo is situated on the southern tip of the land finger separating Trinity Bay from Conception Bay, and is just an hour from St. John's International Airport and 35 minutes from the Argentia ferry terminal.

78 Front Rd. (Rte. 80 to Exit 28 and then 12km/7 miles to Dildo), Dildo, NL A0B 1P0. (C) **888/339-7829** or 709/582-3170. www.innbythebaydildo.com. 6 ensuite units. C$59–$129 (US$43.28–$95) double. Ask about seasonal discounts. AE, DC, MC, V. Closed Jan 1–Apr 15. **Amenities:** Nonsmoking facility; laundry facilities. *In room:* TV/VCR.

NaGeira House Bed & Breakfast Inn ⍟   About an hour's drive from St. John's (via the Trans-Canada Highway to Route 70), you'll find the full-service community of Carbonear and this welcoming B&B, a registered heritage structure. NaGeira's gives you a wide choice of distinctively decorated rooms. One room has an in-room whirlpool bath; another has a mahogany four-poster bed. And all rooms have down duvets and private bathrooms. The exquisite woodwork sets the tone for a quiet and relaxing stay, complemented by the inn's fireplaces and library. The quiet location and exemplary service make this a great place to stay while in the area.

7 Musgrave St. (off Rte. 70 and also accessible from Rte. 74 if coming across the peninsula from Heart's Content), Carbonear, NL A1Y 1B4. ⓒ 800/600-7757 or 709/596-1888. www.nageirahouse.com. 4 ensuites. C$89–$149 (US$65–$109) double. AE, MC, V. **Amenities:** Restaurant; lounge. *In room:* TV.

WHERE TO DINE

You'll get wonderful meals at the locations listed above, but if you're looking for a snack, light meal, or picnic lunch, here are a couple of reasonably priced options that are worth checking out.

Country Corner Eatery & Ice-Cream Parlour   While exploring Brigus, drop in to the Country Corner for lunch. If you just want a less filling meal, they make excellent cod chowder. The chowder combo gets you a delicious bowl of chowder and a serving of blueberry crisp, along with a beverage and a tea biscuit. They also sell a nice assortment of souvenirs and gifts.

14 Water St., Brigus. ⓒ 709/528-1099. C$3.95–$9.95 (US$2.89–$7.30) AE, MC, V. Call for hours.

Kountry Kravins 'n' Krafts Coffee Shop & Craft Store   This is a quaint little coffee shop that serves reasonably priced lunches inside at a few tables or outside on the small deck overlooking **Dildo Bay.** They'll also make you a picnic lunch to enjoy along the road. They have a fairly limited light lunch menu and the offerings (particularly the sandwiches) aren't great, but the setting is picturesque, the owners are friendly, and it's worth stopping in at least to see the terrific selection of local crafts they have for sale.

Route 80, Front Rd., Dildo (across the street from the Interpretive Centre). ⓒ **709/582-3888.** Lunches for around C$5 (US$3.66). Call for hours.

EXPLORING THE BACCALIEU TRAIL

Baccalieu Island Seabird Ecological Reserve   Baccalieu Island Seabird Ecological Reserve is largely inaccessible due to its steep, high cliffs and treacherous shoreline. The reserve itself contains Baccalieu Island, located off the tip of the northwest Avalon Peninsula near the tiny outport of **Bay de Verde.**

Baccalieu Island is the largest seabird island in Newfoundland & Labrador, measuring approximately 6 km (3.72 miles) long and 1 km (.62 mile) wide. Between June and August, the island is home to 3 million pairs of Leach's Storm-petrel, the largest colony of these birds in the world. Eleven seabird species breed on Baccalieu Island. You can learn more by visiting the Baccalieu Island exhibit, for a nominal fee, in the **Heritage House** in Bay de Verde (ⓒ **709/596-3474**).

Route 70, Bay de Verde. ⓒ **709/635-4522.** www.gov.nf.ca/parks&reserves/baccalieu.htm. Free admission. Open May 1–Sept 30.

Dildo Fisheries Interpretation Centre A surprisingly impressive heritage site, considering the diminutive size of both the facility and its host community. Inside, you'll find a historical account of Dildo Island as well as the Dorset Eskimos and other native peoples who once inhabited this region. There's also an interesting lifestyle section and display of the local inhabitants of the sea. Outside is a replica of a giant 8.5-m-long (28 ft.) squid that was found in these waters.

Most of the items on display have been donated by members of the community. A half-hour should be sufficient to tour this facility.

Route 80, Front Rd., Dildo. (✆ **709/582-2687**. Admission C$2 (US$1.46) adults, C$1 (US$.73) children. Open May 1–Oct 30 Sun–Sat 9am–6pm, closed Mondays.

Grates Cove Rock Walls National Historic Site The tiny outport of Grates Cove is at the very northern tip of the land finger separating Trinity Bay from Conception Bay. Here you will find examples of the old rock walls once used to separate and protect small private gardens. Hundreds of these rock walls are still intact and are plainly visible to anyone walking through the community. Grates Cove is also where you will find information about the Cabot Rock, a large rock bearing inscriptions that some claim were carved by John Cabot himself in 1497.

Note: Grates Cove has no restaurant—or even a place to get a cup of tea (unless you're lucky enough to be invited to the home of one of the locals). Apart from the rock walls and a small art studio on the Main Road, there is really very little to see or do here. There is no signage to provide an interpretation of the rock walls, nor are there guided tours. They are, however, an interesting (and free) viewing spectacle.

Route 70, Bay de Verde (adjacent to Baccalieu Island Seabird Ecological Reserve). (✆ **709/587-2326**. Free admission.

Hawthorne Cottage National Historic Site Built in 1830, Hawthorne Cottage in the lovely community of Brigus is one of the few remaining examples of the picturesque cottage *orné*—translated from French, this means it's nicely decorated. But it's more than that. The home once belonged to Captain Bob Bartlett (the world-famous Newfoundland-born Arctic explorer) and contains interesting artifacts from Bartlett's journeys to the Arctic during the early 20th century. As you walk through the house, you'll listen to recordings that explain the importance of fishing and sealing to Brigus residents around that time. You'll also see local period artifacts and textiles in their original setting, including the various upstairs bedrooms and kitchen. Personally, I was amazed at how small the rooms seemed in comparison to how big the home appeared on the outside.

Be sure to visit the lovely commemorative sculpture in the shape of a ship's sails that has been erected in honor of Bartlett on the harbor near the Brigus Tunnel.

Route 60 to Irishtown Rd., Brigus. (✆ **709/528-4004**. www.historicsites.ca. Admission C$3 (US$2.20) adults, C$2.50 (US$1.83) for seniors, C$2 (US$ 1.46) children 7–16, free for children 6 and under, C$7 (US$5.13) family rate. Open May 15–June 27 daily 10am–6pm, June 27–Labor Day 10am–8pm, Labor Day–Oct 31 10am–6pm. Wheelchair accessible.

Avondale Railway Station Museum ✯ *Kids* Just south of Brigus on Route 60 you'll find a gem of a museum located in Newfoundland's oldest railway station, circa 1864. It features five static railway cars, including a snowplow, CN A913, diesel locomotive, baggage/kitchen car, a working dining car, and a caboose. What excites most rail fans about Avondale is that it is the site of one of the last remaining railway tracks in all of Newfoundland and a prime example of the old narrow-gauge track. In the summertime, the museum runs a few small railcars on the track for kids and their parents over the 3km (almost 2 miles) of narrow gauge.

Route 60, Avondale Access Rd. ⓒ 709/229-2288. www.manl.nf.ca/avonrail.htm. Open July 1–Aug 31 daily 8am–8pm. Free admission. Gift shop.

Heart's Content Cable Station   A provincial historical site commemorating the importance of the transatlantic cable that made communications between Europe and North America near-instantaneous. After the failure of two earlier attempts, a permanent transatlantic telegraph cable was landed here in 1866. The station houses equipment and interpretive displays that explain the role Heart's Content has played in the world of communications for nearly 100 years. I was fascinated by the replica of the original Victorian cable office, as well as the storyboards describing how engineers of the day were able to overcome the many difficulties associated with laying a sub-sea electrical cable between the two continents.

Route 80, waterfront, Heart's Content. ⓒ 709/583-2160. Admission C$2.50 (US$1.83) for ages 13 and up. Open June 15–(Canadian) Thanksgiving daily 10am–5:30pm; closed Labor Day–(Canadian) Thanksgiving 1–2pm.

NaGeira Theatre Festival ⓚ ⓥ𝘢𝘭𝘶𝘦   If you like informal, outdoor theater, you'll really enjoy the beautiful seaside setting of **Carbonear's** summer performances, held each July and August. They use a number of different venues; some are indoors and some are outdoors, but all present a perfect backdrop to the variously comic, dramatic, and satirical offerings of the day.

Route 70, Carbonear. Visit the Rebel Island Theatre Company's Festival Box Office in the Trinity Conception Square. ⓒ 877/696-7453 or 709/596-1608. www.rebelisland.com. Tickets C$12 (US$8.80) adults; C$9 (US$6.60) seniors and kids under 14; C$30 (US$22) for the dinner theater, and several other price options available. MC, V.

Rodrigues Winery Tours   Not far from Whitbourne, in the neighboring community of **Markland,** you'll find Newfoundland's only kosher winery. It's surprising to find that there are indeed wineries in Newfoundland, and even more impressive to learn that the Rodrigues Cottage Winery has won several awards with its fine vintages.

A variety of wines are made from local berries such as bakeapple, partridgeberry, blueberry, and other special blends. I especially liked the bakeapple and partridgeberry wines for their tartness. You can take a tour of the small winery and see how they use modified milk and Pepsi containers to make their unique-tasting wines. Sample the different varieties and take some home as a tasty souvenir. The winery is a 45-minute drive west of St. John's.

Route 81, Markland (just south of Whitbourne). ⓒ 709/759-3003. www.rodrigueswinery.com. Free tours given year-round. Sept 4–June 30, Mon–Fri 9am–4:30pm; July 1–Sept 3, daily 9am–4:30pm.

5 Conception Bay & Marine Drive

ESSENTIALS

The territory encompassing Marine Drive to Conception Bay South represents a region that is relatively small yet rich in maritime history and spectacular scenery. I recommend you make the journey to **Bell Island,** an enjoyable 20-minute ferry ride from the community of Portugal Cove.

Marine Drive will take you north of St. John's along the coast to the northern stretches of Conception Bay. Following Conception Bay south of St. John's, you'll find yourself in the aptly named community of **Conception Bay South,** the region's largest commercial center. And at the very southernmost tip of Conception Bay is the pretty little town of **Holyrood,** a good place to stay if you're looking for economy accommodations from which to do day trips.

GETTING AROUND

Driving northeast of St. John's along Route 20 (Torbay Rd.) and then Route 30 (Logy Bay Rd. continues on to become both Marine Dr. and Middle Cove Rd.), you can be quickly out of the city and at the beach (think beach rocks, not sand). **Middle Cove Beach,** the **Ocean Sciences Centre,** and **Logy Bay** are covered in chapter 3, in the "Outside of Downtown" section under "Exploring St. John's" (the beach is only 5km [3 miles] from the city).

If you take Route 40 (Portugal Cove Rd.) northwest from Route 1 (TCH), you'll end up in the twin communities of **Portugal Cove** & **St. Phillips,** and still be just a 15-minute drive from St. John's. The Portugal Cove Ferry Terminal is where you catch the Bell Island Ferry. The ferry, which carries passengers and vehicles, can't be booked in advance—it's filled on a first-come, first-served basis.

Conception Bay South is a much larger, full-service community of about 20,000 people, accessible by taking Route 61 off Route 1 (TCH). Conception Bay (the actual body of water) was named by the Spanish in the 1700s in honor of a religious holiday relating to the Immaculate Conception. The Bay has a colorful history, and was home to pirates during the 17th and 18th centuries. **Kelly's Island,** just offshore from Conception Bay South, was a popular stopover for pirates and is the rumored hideaway of buried treasure.

You'll find the Conception Bay area to be a splendid outdoor retreat, offering spectacular scenery and an abundance of marine life. The **Trans-Canada Trail** runs along the banks of the beautiful bay, where you can see colorful sunsets, majestic icebergs, and playful whales. Conception Bay South is also home to the **Royal Newfoundland Yacht Club,** the largest yacht club in the province. Yacht races are held in Conception Bay throughout the year, attracting participants from around the world. Call © **709/834-5151** or visit them on the Web at www.rnyc.nf.ca.

With three shipwrecks piled on top of one another in shallow water offshore, Conception Harbour offers terrific diving opportunities. Just be aware that the clarity of the water changes when the algae are in bloom.

Just a bit farther south you'll come to **Holyrood,** a picturesque community at the junctions of routes 90, 62, and 60. Its location makes it a convenient place to lay your head while touring around the Avalon.

PORTUGAL COVE TO HOLYROOD
WHERE TO STAY & DINE

Beach-Side B&B ♠   Sunny Conception Bay South is said to have the best weather on the Avalon, so if you're as affected by the weather as I am, you might like to choose this location. Situated just 10 minutes from St. John's, the Beach-Side B&B is a great location if you don't have a car but would still like to stay outside the city, as the B&B offers guests free pickup from St. John's Airport and pickup at the Argentia Ferry Terminal for a nominal fee.

All guest rooms are newly constructed, have private baths, and are tastefully furnished. The spacious Oceanview Celebration Suite has a double Jacuzzi and private deck overlooking the ocean. In addition to the standard breakfast fare, you'll also be treated to local specialties that include toutons (rounds of fried bread dough), moose or caribou sausages, and salt fish (when available). Don't be surprised if your hosts, Pat and Jerdon Reid, ask you to join in a friendly Newfoundland sing-along—it's a happy and musical household. While in town, be sure to take in a performance of the "Kelligrews Soiree." (See more about the *Soirees & Times* series of performances in the Appendix.)

77 Gully Pond Rd., Kelligrews, Conception Bay South. ℂ 866-834-0077 or 709/834-0077. www.beach side-bb.nf.ca. 4 ensuite units, 1 suite. C$69–$130 (US$50.63–$95.37). C$10 (US$7.33) for additional person. Ask about off-season discounts. V. **Amenities:** Full traditional breakfasts; laundry facilities; nonsmoking rooms; computer on-site for guest use; fireplace on beach; adjacent to Trans-Canada Trail for hiking and biking; restaurants, fishing, and golf 15 minutes away. *In room:* TV, dataport.

Dogberry Hill B&B ★★★   Haute ambiance and breathtaking vistas combine with impeccable service and distinctive decor for an unforgettable experience. This inn is the epitome of graciousness, with a friendly bilingual staff and a private country setting close to the city. Situated on an incredible 2-ha (5-acre) property with beautifully landscaped gardens, the Dogberry Hill B&B offers beautiful views of Bell Island and Kelly's Island. Each guest room has a distinctively different personality featuring tasteful custom furnishings. I recommend you take the virtual tour to ensure you choose the room that best suits your style (I'd pick the one with the footed soaker tub—decadent!).

The culinary experience at the Dogberry can be just as satisfying as the visual. One of the owners is from Newfoundland and the other from France, so you'll be offered the best in local and European cuisine. The Dogberry Inn B&B is a highly recommended location for those willing to pay a little more than expected but eager to receive the absolutely best accommodations and food in the area.

Alfred's Drung off Dogberry Hill Rd., Portugal Cove–St. Philip's. ℂ 709-895-6353. www.dogberryhill.com. C$95–$175 (US$70–$128). AE, MC, V. 4 units. **Amenities:** Authentic regional and French cuisine prepared on request. *In room:* Ensuite baths, Jacuzzi and soaker tubs available, ocean view, antique furnishings, high-quality French linens.

Villa Nova Bed & Breakfast *Value*   Pat and Marie Hynes have created a haven of hospitality at their cozy Villa Nova B&B. These friendly hosts enjoy making conversation and are pleased to share their wealth of local history, culture, and folklore. The peaceful seaside location along with the very comfortable mattresses and pillows are sure to help you sleep like a baby. The rooms are spacious, reasonably priced, and only 15 minutes from the city of St. John's. This is an ideal location if you have a car and are more interested in touring the Avalon than staying in the city.

31 Baird's Lane, Manuels, Conception Bay South. To get there: Take TCH westbound (Rte. 1) Exit 41 onto Manuels Access (Rte. 2); take Manuels exit to Route 60; turn right onto Greenslades Rd., take 1st left onto Baird's Lane. ℂ 888/315-3141 or 709/834-1659. 3 units. C$55–$68 (US$40–$50). **Amenities:** Full breakfast; nonsmoking rooms; walking distance to sea kayaking, boat charters, and scuba diving (they can book for you). *In room:* Shared bathrooms and ensuite.

⌒*Tips* **Money-Saving Tip on Accommodations**

Staying close to but outside the city limits can save you—not only on the basic rates, but also on taxes. Smaller facilities with three rooms or fewer are not required to charge tax, so you save yourself an additional 18% off rates that are (in some cases) already lower than within the city.

EXPLORING CONCEPTION BAY
BELL ISLAND

The largest of several islands in Conception Bay, Bell Island measures about 9km (5½ miles) by 3½ km (2 miles). There's quite a bit to see and do on the island, including diving, bird-watching, hiking, and touring. Be sure to take note of the mining murals that adorn many of the town's buildings. Visit www.bell island.net for detailed information about services on Bell Island.

To get to Bell Island, take Route 40 to get to the Portugal Cove Ferry Terminal. It costs C$5 (US$3.66) to get over to the island by ferry for a driver and vehicle, C$4.50 (US$3.30) for seniors, and C$3 (US$2.20) for each additional passenger. The trip takes only 20 minutes, and the ferries run frequently during the summer, less often at other times of the year. There are permanent residents of Bell Island who regularly commute to St. John's to work—so the service is dependable, but it can still be influenced by the weather. It's recommended not to travel by ferry during the early morning or late afternoon rush hours in order to avoid lineups. You can reach the Bell Island Terminal at ✆ **709/488-2842** and the Portugal Cove Terminal at ✆ **709/895-3541**. See www.bellisland.net for the online ferry schedule.

Lance Cove at Bell Island is where you can see firsthand evidence of World War II. It was here on September 5, 1942 that German U-boats sank two Canadian ships, the *Lord Strathcona* and the *Rose Castle*, along with many other British and French ships during the war. Two of these were the British *Saganaga* and the French *PLM 27,* where 69 lives were lost. Efforts are being made to protect the wreck sites.

No. 2 Mine & Museum   While on Bell Island, you can take a tour of the abandoned **No. 2 Mine.** From 1895 until 1966, more than 78 million tons of iron ore were mined here, the world's largest submarine iron ore mine. The mine's museum contains interesting artifacts as well as masterful photos taken by world-famous photographer Yousuf Karsh. Karsh, who is known for his uncanny ability to portray the inner character of his subjects, has captured on film the grit and determination of Bell Island's iron-ore miners.

No. 2 Mine & Museum, Bell Island. ✆ **709/488-2880**. Take a virtual tour online at www.bell island.net/no2mine. Open June–Sept daily 11am–7pm. C$7 (US$5.13) adults, C$6 (US$4.40) seniors, C$3 (US$2.20) children under 12. C$2 (US$1.46) for museum tour only.

Scuba Diving   Lance Cove on Bell Island is an excellent place for divers to explore shipwrecks and take a closer look at torpedoed ore carriers. You'll also discover the abundance of native marine life. The main company to call is **Ocean Quest.** Their 11.5-m (38-ft.) Cape Islander, the *M/V Ocean Quest,* is known for its seaworthiness and stability on the open ocean and is equipped with a 135-hp Ford Senator diesel engine. It is Canadian Coast Guard–certified for 20 passengers. Safety equipment includes a life raft, onboard oxygen, and an outboard powered inflatable tender. Other amenities include a fully equipped galley, barbecue, fresh water, and restroom facilities. The comfortable layout includes a dive platform for easy diving access and a flying bridge for sightseeing.

Foxtrap Marina, Conception Bay South. ✆ **866/623-2664** or 709/685-4565. Book online at www.ocean questcharters.com. If you're new at scuba diving, try their "Discover Scuba" program. You'll get 1 hour of supervision from a qualified instructor for C$50 (US$36). You must provide your own wetsuit. If you're an experienced diver, you can get five open-water dives for C$250 (US$183). There are a number of other options.

5

The Eastern Region

The Eastern Region of Newfoundland & Labrador is the smallest region of the province, but it would be a mistake to equate the depth of its attractiveness to its diminutive size.

On the northernmost tip of the region, at the top of the **Bonavista Peninsula,** you'll find the twin communities of **Trinity** and **Bonavista.** Bonavista is the fabled landing spot of old-world explorer John Cabot, while Trinity is renowned for its historically accurate architectural restorations.

Turning to the region's polar opposite, the **Burin Peninsula,** you'll discover a seemingly barren area that is really a treasure trove of glacial deposits and the favored stomping grounds of 16th-century pirates and privateers. Their modern-day equivalents can be found in the rum-runners who still smuggle bootleg hooch from the French colonies offshore.

Yes, France's border actually extends this far across the Atlantic, to the tiny islands off the south coast of Newfoundland—**St. Pierre** and **Miquelon.** You can get there by plane, or via passenger ferry from the town of **Fortune** at the foot of the Burin Peninsula.

Clarenville is the region's figurative center of gravity. It's roughly halfway between the Bonavista and Burin peninsulas, and is the main service center for the area. For that reason, it's not so much a destination as it is a base for exploring the rest of the region.

Although we've said elsewhere that we're generally following the same regional divisions as the provincial tourism guide, that's not entirely true in this section. The provincial tourism guide stops the Eastern Region boundary at Port Blandford, but we're stretching it as far west as Glovertown. Why? Because you're more likely to tour this area from a Clarenville base than from the doubly distant town of Grand Falls–Windsor. So, even though it's separated from the rest of the region by the wilderness expanse that is **Terra Nova National Park** (the park is not covered here; you'll find it in chapter 8), don't forget to include the northwest section in your itinerary. That's where you'll find the province's largest water/amusement park.

1 The Discovery Trail

From roadside vendors of hand-picked seasonal berries, to a singularly unique railway loop (the only one of its type in North America), to a replica of a 500-year-old sailing ship, this is indeed a journey of discovery. Easily accessed from the Trans-Canada (Route 1), the Discovery Trail is a mostly straight highway drive, except for discretionary digressions into communities of interest. It extends northeast from the Trans-Canada, 114km (71 miles) from Clarenville to Bonavista. Although you can easily make the return trip in a single day, you'll really need at least 2 days to enjoy the multitude of services and attractions you'll find here.

Eastern Region

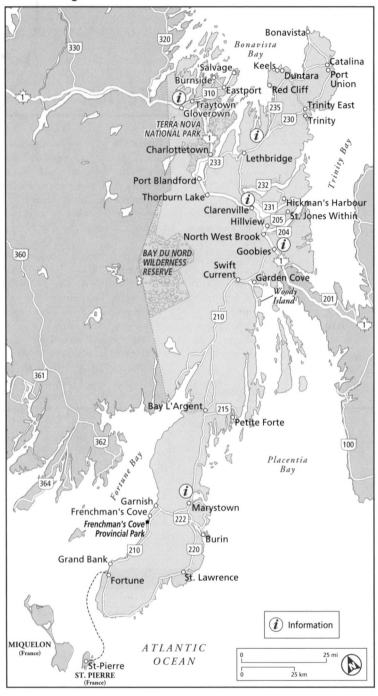

ESSENTIALS
GETTING THERE
If you're touring the province from east to west, Clarenville is a 2-hour drive from St. John's (189km or 117 miles) and a 1½-hour drive from the Argentia ferry terminal. For those entering the Eastern Region from the west, the Trans-Canada Highway (Route 1) takes you right to Port Blandford, just an hour's drive southeast of Gander. About 32km (20 miles) south of Port Blandford, you'll arrive at Clarenville.

There are three entrances to the Discovery Trail from the Trans-Canada: Route 230A at Clarenville, Route 230 at George's Brook, and Route 233 at Port Bland-ford. I recommend the central exit, Route 230, because it offers the fewest opportunities for you to get lost (it's as simple as turning left at the first intersection).

VISITOR INFORMATION
You'll find visitor information in Clarenville at the office of the **Discovery Trail Tourism Association,** 54 Manitoba Dr. (*©* **709/466-3845;** www.thediscovery trail.org), or call the Clarenville Area Chamber of Commerce (*©* **866/466-5800**).

You'll also find visitor information pertinent to the Bonavista Peninsula at the **Trinity Interpretation Centre** in Trinity (*©* **800/563-6353** or 709/464-2042), open daily during the summer months 10am to 5:30pm, and at the **Ryan Premises National Historic Site** in Bonavista (*©* **800/213-7275** or 709/468-1600), open mid-May through mid-October 10am to 6pm. Information is also available at the other Provincial and National Historic Sites in the area.

GETTING AROUND
Roads throughout this region are in comparatively good condition (not really an endorsement when you consider the potholes and their black-patch spawn that dominate so many of the province's highways). There's room for improvement as well in the placement (I should say absence) of highway signage. You won't get lost, but you may have to backtrack for missed turns. For example, I was caught off guard while driving along Route 230 to Trinity because Route 239 (which takes you right into Trinity) appeared without warning. But aside from that, if you follow Route 230 from beginning to end it'll carry you to Bonavista and back again to the Trans-Canada.

Tip: Within the historical communities of Bonavista and Trinity, park your car and travel on foot. Not only does the diminutive size of these towns make for an enjoyable walking tour, but you'll find that the narrow breadth of the streets (paths, really, in some sections) makes driving a less-than-pleasurable experience. *Warning:* Be aware that children may be playing on or very near the highway: extra caution is advised when traveling along the smaller routes. We were startled to find some kids playing basketball—complete with a portable hoop—right on the highway!

EXPLORING THE DISCOVERY TRAIL
While you'll undoubtedly head to the anchor attractions of the Discovery Trail, there are other, less well-known points of interest that also deserve attention. Like the enticingly named Tickle Cove (after Bonavista, it's thought to be the oldest settlement on the Peninsula), or James Leo Harty House in Duntara (a prime example of a traditional outport home, built by the great-grandson of the village's founder). There's also Elliston—the root-cellar capital of the world. Although they look like fairy dwellings, root cellars are merely holes dug into the

side of a hill for winter storage of dried meats and root crops. Encased as they are by the hill itself, with roofs of grass and wildflowers, you won't recognize a root cellar from any angle except front-on. That's when you see the door. Another not-so-main attraction is Port Union, the only union-built town in North America. Sir William Coaker established the town in 1916 in an attempt to ensure fishermen were paid a fair price for their catch. The moral of the story: you're on the Discovery Trail, so don't restrict yourself to the roads most traveled.

Nor should you limit yourself to summer touring. The weather of early fall (September through to mid-October) is generally very favorable, requiring just a light jacket and pants. You won't want to come here after the end of October, however, as many of the attractions and even accommodations close for the winter.

(Moments **Ghosts of Days Gone By** ✸✸✸

A common theme in Newfoundland & Labrador culture is the dreaded necessity of having to leave someone or something you love (usually for economic reasons). In certain cases, entire towns have been abandoned. Such is the case with Woody Island. Except for a handful of die-hard residents, this once-prosperous community of 400 became a ghost town after the provincial government's resettlement programs of the 1960s.

A 40-minute sail across the waters of Placentia Bay to **Woody Island Resort** will bring you as close as a visitor could possibly come to understanding the indestructible connection that ties Newfoundlanders to their anchor, the Rock. While you'll stay in a fully equipped tourist lodge, the circa-1950s furnishings, tufted bedspreads, and aging linoleum make the experience as authentic as possible.

You may at first marvel that anyone would want to live so far away from the rest of the world, but you'll soon come to understand the Newfoundlander's love of place. Your first stirrings of empathy come to life with resort owner Loyola Pomroy's stories of days gone by (Pomroy was born on another resettled island—Merasheen—38km [24 miles] south of Woody Island). Then, standing beside the cracked stone monuments and simple wooden crosses of uncles, parents, children, and sisters long gone but not forgotten, you feel the magnetic pull of this land. You smell it in the smoke of your beachside bonfire. It seeps into your bones as you hike in the footsteps of families and friends who will never again tend to their sheep or vegetable gardens. It becomes part of you with every breath of salt air and every glimpse of naked foundation. By the end of your 2-day tour, you may well find yourself on the upper deck of the *Merasheen*, fixated on that final glimpse of departing land, unexpected tears of bereavement mingling with the ocean spray.

East of Clarenville, exit Route 1 at Goobies, follow Route 210 to Route 210–13, Garden Cove. The 13-m (42-ft.) cabin cruiser *Merasheen* carries passengers from Garden Cove to Woody Island. ✆ **800/504-1066** or 709/364-3701. Fax: 709/745-4937. www.woodyi.com. Reservations required. 22 units, 7 bedrooms have a double and a single bed, 4 rooms have just a double bed, and 11 rooms have 2 single beds. C$109–$149 (US$80–$109) per person, HST extra. All-inclusive package including transportation to and from Garden Cove, one night accommodations, meals, and entertainment. Open end of April to end of October. Nonsmoking facility. AE, MC, V. **Amenities:** private and shared bathrooms; large dining room; communal fireplace, parlor, patio; paddleboats, rowboats, and horseshoe games.

CLARENVILLE TO PORT BLANDFORD

For those preferring to stay in a full-service community, Clarenville is a large (by Newfoundland standards) center and the home of roughly 5,000 residents. It has an airstrip, hospital, banks, a couple of fair-sized shopping malls, and other major services.

About 5 minutes along the Trans-Canada northwest of Clarenville, you'll find **White Hills Ski Resort** (eastern Newfoundland's premier cross-country and downhill ski resort). Continuing along the same route, you'll come to Port Blandford, situated on beautiful Clode Sound and home to **Twin Rivers Golf Course,** a spectacular Robbie Robinson/Doug Carrick–designed 18-hole course ranked among the top 30 in Canada. The course is affiliated with the Terra Nova Golf Resort, listed later in this chapter.

WHERE TO STAY & DINE

Clarenville Inn 🎃🎃 *Kids*   This is a family-oriented facility easily recognized by the larger-than-life inflatable crustacean flanking the front lawn (except during the winter months, when Larry the Lobster goes into hibernation). Mom and Dad can relax in the reclining chairs poolside while kids frolic in the water, shoot a few hoops, or romp over the adjacent playground equipment (all enclosed by a privacy fence). Then, after a busy day of doing as little as possible (you're on vacation, remember), retire to the cozy comfort of your room. Here you'll find all the standard features of a well-appointed inn: working area with chair; barely sufficient closet storage; and an expansive makeup counter/sink area separate from the full bathroom. Surprises include the absence of an iron and ironing board (available on request from the front desk) and the inclusion of a curling iron (first time I've seen that).

Winchester's Dining Room 🎃, the Clarenville Inn's on-site restaurant, is above average for a hotel dining room. For several years running, the restaurant has been named the "Best Place to Eat Off the Avalon" (meaning, not on the Avalon Peninsula) by the *Newfoundland Herald,* a local magazine. Lunch prices average C$10 (US$7.33), dinners C$15 (US$11). Specialties of the house include seafood and prime rib.

Route 1, Clarenville. 🕐 877/466-7911 or 709/466-7911. Fax: 709/466-3854. www.clarenvilleinn.ca. 63 units, including 1 suite. C$85–$145 (US$63–$107) double. AE, DC, MC, V. **Amenities:** Full-service restaurant; lounge; outdoor heated pool; video rentals; ATM; nonsmoking rooms; custom golf packages; kids stay & eat free (subject to certain conditions). *In room:* TV, coffeemaker, hairdryer, and curling iron.

St. Jude Hotel 🎃🎃   Almost directly across the blacktop from the Clarenville Inn is the St. Jude Hotel. While the former is ideal for the traveling family, this hotel caters to travelers with disabilities and business travelers. Not only is the entire hotel wheelchair friendly (all doors and corridors are wide enough for a wheelchair, the second and third floors are accessible by elevator, and a guest wheelchair is available at the front desk if needed), but there's also a specially designed room for people with physical disabilities. Located on the first floor, it's larger than the standard guest rooms, and has hand rails in the bath and next to the taller-than-normal toilet. For the corporate traveler, the in-room Internet jacks as well as the front desk photocopy and fax services are de rigueur, but the on-site audiovisual equipment (overhead projector, television, and VCR) is a bonus. That said, it's not all work and no play at the St. Jude either. You can kick back with your favorite beverage in the warm surroundings of the Republican Lounge, or pick something from the all-ages recreational reading material in the decently stocked guest library. I'd like to say you could carry a book outside to enjoy while you sunbathe next to the pool, but there's no pool. You'll have to make do with reading yourself to sleep. The single guest rooms at the St. Jude are average in every way: small worktable with chair, color TV, plain but solid furnishings, and color-matched Wal-Mart prints on the wall. For double your money, you can have the best suite in the house (complete with separate sitting room, and whirlpool built for two).

You'll find **Don Cherry's Ultimate Sports Grill** on site, a great place for a quick, reasonably priced lunch. Between 11:30am and 3pm each weekday, you can get a wide range of satisfying lunch entrees for C$7.25 (US$5.35). Dinners range from C$11 (US$8) for two small chicken breasts to C$22 (US$16) for a 16-oz. steak. *Hint:* In the evening, the atmosphere at Don Cherry's becomes more sports bar and less restaurant—making it the ideal location for a basket of wings and a cold beer while watching the game on a big-screen TV.

Route 1, Clarenville. (C) **800/563-7800** or 709/466-1717. Fax: 709/466-1714. www.stjudehotel.nf.ca. 63 units, including 3 suites. C$75–$150 (US$55–$110) double. AE, DC, MC, V. **Amenities:** Restaurant & sports bar; banquet facilities; ATM; guest library; laundry facilities; business center; concession stand; nonsmoking rooms. *In room:* A/C, TV, coffeemaker, hairdryer.

Terra Nova Hospitality Home & Resort ✸ *(Value)*   If you're in the mood for genuine Newfoundland hospitality, you've come to the right place. There are accents so thick and so studded with motherly endearments, you'd almost think you were staying in a private outport home—especially when you smell the fresh-baked bread (to heck with Atkins!) and oven-roasted turkey. As homespun as it is, it's also a very professional, full-service resort with three distinct accommodation options. You can choose from the economical B&B, the more luxurious suites at the resort, or the four-season, self-contained cottages (all three are located on the same property, right on the highway as you turn in to Port Blandford).

The winterized (no drafts!) 2-bedroom cabins are excellently maintained and spotlessly clean, completely lacking the musty odor that comes with so many resort cottages. With a little squeezing, two families could share one of the cottages by using the pullout sofa bed. I suggest you put the kids on the sofa bed—the lighter you are, the less noticeable the foundation.

The main feature of the B&B has nothing to do with its 6 guest rooms, Master Suite, or bathroom facilities. It's the sauna—small, yes, but still a sauna. And you can use it no matter which room you rent. For just C$55 (US$40) a night, you can sweat the small stuff, then retire to your private bath to soak your cares away (standard size—not Jacuzzi—tubs, unless you book the Master Suite).

The resort is the suite-est of the three, containing 3 double-bed suites, one king-size and one queen-size. Both of the latter have their own ensuite Jacuzzi.

Route 1, Port Blandford. (C) **888/267-2333** or 709/543-2260. Fax: 709/543-2241. www.terranova.nfld.net. 19 units. B&B: C$45 (US$33) single, shared bath. C$55 (US$40) double, private bath. Cabins: C$95 (US$70). Inn: C$110–$125 (US$80–$92). C$8 (US$5.86) additional for cot in room. AE, DC, MC, V. **Amenities:** Restaurant; nonsmoking rooms; wheelchair accessible; nearby golf, hiking, and cross-country ski trails, national park. *In room:* Inn rooms have satellite TV, telephone. Some have air-conditioning, fireplaces, and Jacuzzis. Cabins have full kitchen, one with microwave and hot tub.

Terra Nova Golf Resort ✸✸ *(Kids)*   If you love to golf and you have kids, the Terra Nova Golf Resort is a wonderful vacation destination. Twin Rivers, the resort's 18-hole golf course, has been voted one of the top 30 in Canada, and the lodge's children's program (included with the room rates) is so good, the kids won't want to leave! The program includes games, supervised swimming, treasure hunts, and craft-making as well as supervised lunches.

Even if you don't use the program, you can still take advantage of the outdoor heated pool, walking trails, playground equipment, tennis court, basketball court, and mini-golf. *Tip:* Bring your own racket and balls. You don't pay for time on the court, but there is a charge for racket rental—and tennis balls are a couple of dollars more here than in a Clarenville department store. *Another tip:* Unless you're in a ground-floor room with outdoor access, don't forget to bring a wrap. Guests aren't permitted to walk around the lodge in just their swimsuit.

Since none of the guest rooms come with cooking facilities (even the efficiency units have just a fridge and microwave, no stove), you'll probably eat at least one meal in the on-site restaurant. But don't worry, they don't take advantage of their culinary monopoly. The surroundings are business-casual elegant, with an easy-on-the-eye golf-course view and thick wooden beams running overhead to remind you you're in a lodge. The reasonably priced food is tasty and well portioned (although they seem to run out of breakfast danish on a regular basis).

Guest rooms are nicely furnished in a solid, rustic style (no Queen Anne spindles!), and notably soundproof, considering the number of children you'll find scurrying about. *Warning:* There's a C$75 (US$55) fine for smoking in a nonsmoking room.

Route 1, 3rd exit to Port Blandford if you're arriving from the south. ℂ 709/543-2525. Fax: 709/543-2201. www.terranovagolf.com. Open May–Oct. 95 units, including 5 suites. C$99–$120 (US$72–$89) double; C$155–$219 (US$114–$162) suite; C$109–$209 (US$80–$154) efficiency. AE, DC, DISC, MC, V. 18 holes of golf cost C$36–$43 (US$27–$32) without a cart. **Amenities:** Full-service dining room & pub; outdoor heated swimming pool; 2 golf courses; golf school; mini-golf; tennis courts; fitness room; complimentary children's recreation program; babysitting; guest laundry; playground, basketball, volleyball, soccer; nature trails; nonsmoking rooms. *In room:* A/C, TV, alarm/clock radio, room service, coffeemaker, iron. Efficiency units have microwave, but no stove.

 Calling All Grease Monkeys

If you can't resist the roar of high-performance, plan to spend a Saturday or Sunday afternoon at the **Clarenville Dragway.** Granted, it's not the lush surroundings of Monte Carlo, but that's no reflection on the intensity of the competition. Every second weekend from early June to early September, performance-vehicle enthusiasts congregate on this paved airstrip 14km (8.5 miles) up the Bonavista Highway (don't ask me why they call it the Clarenville Dragway, since it's not actually in Clarenville). You'll see dragsters racing pro street cars, and the emerging sport compact class going head-to-head with Harleys. There's even something called a racing sled; it's a snowmobile on wheels. Only in Newfoundland! *Tip:* Bring a picnic lunch and moist towelettes, even a cushion if you have it. The on-site facilites include wooden bleachers for spectator seating and those horrid blue portable washroom cubicles. For the latest racing schedule, call ℂ **709/749-6831** or go online to http://home.thezone.net/~pnicol/nor index.html.

HISTORICAL SITES TRINITY ✦✦✦

It's sure to be love at first sight in Trinity. Here you'll find a passionate regard for the past embodied in an almost unanimous community-wide celebration of historically accurate home restoration. From the picket fences, vertical slider windows, vegetable gardens, and distinctive signage, it's obvious that Trinity takes pride in its history. And why not? It was a crucial pioneer settlement in the province, with some of the first clergy, doctors, and professional tradesmen in Newfoundland.

⟨Tips⟩ Best Seat in the House

For the best possible view of Trinity, stroll over to Courthouse Road, behind the Royal Bank. Climb the hill, following the hiking trail to the top, where you'll be rewarded with an incredible view of Trinity Bay. Do it just before sunset, when the soft pre-dusk lighting produces picture-perfect colors. It's a 20-minute hike to the top—I'm mildly asthmatic, and I made it without difficulty—and it will leave you with a visual memory to last a lifetime.

WHERE TO STAY & DINE IN TRINITY BIGHT

Campbell House ✦✦✦   A first-class hospitality home that epitomizes traditional styling and old-world refinement. Campbell House was built more than 150 years ago in conventional saltbox form (a popular Newfoundland house design, the saltbox features a main rectangle-shaped front section with gabled roof, sloping down to a single-storey appendage out back). Its roadside appeal is further enhanced by the expert horticultural skills of owner Tineke Gow, a microbiologist originally from Holland.

Once inside, you'll love the exposed brickwork in the dining area and be drawn to touch the crockery displayed in the open-face cupboard (back away from the blue-patterned serving tray—it's a hand-painted antique). Moving to the upstairs bedrooms (each has its own private bathroom, but not all are ensuite), you'll delight in the low-by-today's-standards ceilings and the romance of old-fashioned washbasins. With the four-poster bed, fireplace, bureau, and cheval mirror, some people might think the rooms crowded, but I prefer the term "cozy."

If you like the atmosphere at Campbell House but require more privacy, you'll want to stay at one of Gow's other Trinity properties: Dover House and Kelly House. Both are heritage-style vacation homes with similar amenities to those you'll find at the main house. Dover is the more "feminine" of the two properties, with dainty floral-patterned wallpaper and comforters. Kelly House has a more dominant color scheme, and a sleeker, Euro-design kitchen.

Because of the delicacy of the antique furnishings, neither pets nor children under 7 are allowed. Not that you'd really want to bring them here anyway—there's too much work involved in keeping sticky fingers and wagging tails away from the various heritage bric-a-brac.

Route 239, Trinity, Trinity Bay. ⓒ **877/464-7700** or 709/464-3377. www.trinityvacations.com. Open May 1–Oct 31. C$99–$225 (US$72–$166). AE, DC, MC, V. **Amenities:** Gourmet breakfast; wine cellar; laundry service available; book & video library; Dutch & French spoken. *In room:* Amenities and rates vary considerably, depending on whether you're taking a B&B room, suite, or one of the vacation homes. Packed lunches available on request for C$12 (US$8.80); full dinners for C$30 (US$22) per person.

Eriksen Properties ✦✦   An haute-atmosphere establishment that couldn't decide if it wanted to be a high-class B&B or a gourmet restaurant, so it became both. Originally the home of a 19th-century merchant, the Eriksen Properties shows what it was like to live in outport high society 200 years ago. Furnished with authentic period pieces, including Victrolas and handmade washbasins, this two-storey Mansard-style home deliberately evokes Victorian charm. But the real extravagance is in the fine-dining room, where gourmet treats are served with classical flair (think of succulent scallops in a white wine sauce and a piano concerto softly filling the background). No reservations; seating is on a first-come, first-served basis.

Route 230, Trinity. © **877/464-3698** or 709/464.3327. www.trinityexperience.com. 7 units. C$70–$125 (US$51–$92). Each additional person or rollaway cot C$15 (US$11). AE, MC, V, Interac. **Amenities:** Full complimentary breakfast; full-service restaurant; TV, VCR, & phone in common area; nonsmoking rooms (smoking allowed on patios). Restaurant: Lunches C$4–$8 (US$2.93–$5.86), dinners C$13–$20 (US$9.60–$14.76). Open May 1–Oct 31 daily 8am–9pm.

Fishers' Loft Inn ⟡⟡⟡   It's a 5-minute road trip outside Trinity proper to the favored destination of visiting movie stars. Both Dame Judi Dench and Kevin Spacey stayed at Fishers' Loft during filming of *The Shipping News*. With good reason: on the exterior it fits in well with the local architecture, but inside it has the world-class flavor you'd expect from its cosmopolitan owners. John and Peggy Fisher are from England and Ottawa, Ontario, respectively. The former professional restorers (they were involved in the reconstruction of Toronto's Adelaide Court Theatre) brought their talents to Port Rexton in 1990, when they decided to turn their summer home into a year-round residence. Their handiwork is evident in each of the distinctive guest rooms, all of which have a big-screen view of the mini-islands scattered along the shore of Trinity Bay. The quilts and simply styled furnishings hint at old-world austerity, but the down-filled duvets are pure luxury where it counts the most.

The royal treatment becomes even more evident in the dining room, where the in-house cooks work under the tutelage of consulting chef Todd Perrin. (Perrin is a freelance chef; his culinary artistry has graced the tables of The Church Restaurant in Stratford, Ontario, and the Canadian Pacific Lodge at Kananaskis.) Together, they create unique menus that are several steps ahead of the fare you'll find in most inns this size: carrot-ginger soup with fresh French bread, grilled chicken with lime mayonnaise and roasted vegetables, and frozen meringue cream with a partridgeberry coulis. *Tip:* Breakfast and a 5-course dinner is approximately C$100/night (US$74) per couple, over and above the room rate. Splurge—this is the place you've been saving for. *Hint:* Daily menus are fixed, so call ahead to see what's being served.

Mill Rd., Port Rexton. © **877/464-3240**. www.fishersloft.com. Open May 15–Oct 31. 12 units. C$98–$150 (US$72–$110). C$15 (US$11) for additional person. AE, DC, MC, V. Breakfast C$7–$10 (US$5.13–$7.33), dinner C$32 (US$24). **Amenities:** Gourmet dining; bar. *In room:* TV w/VCR available on request, dataport, ensuite baths, down duvets.

Village Inn ⟡   Village Inn offers a traditional inn atmosphere where guests are encouraged to socialize with their hosts rather than hide away in their rooms. If, after a busy day of touring and a satisfying meal, you're ready to relax but not quite ready for bed, head down to the living room. That's where you'll find owners Dr. Peter Beamish and wife Christine, along with other guests and any friends who happen to visit, engaged in lively conversation. Whales tend to be a popular item for discussion, and no wonder. Beamish is a Ph.D. biologist who has been studying whales for 30 years. If you're really keen on the oceanic behemoths, you can listen to his lectures on communications research with the whales or watch a film or slide show. From June through October, you can take it a step further by going out in Beamish's boat for an experience you'll never forget. (See the "Outdoor Pursuits" section for details on the Ocean Contact whale experience.)

Guest rooms at the Village Inn have old-style beds, handcrafted Newfoundland quilts, folk furniture, and hardwood floors. All rooms have ensuite or private bathrooms. It's a kid-friendly environment without the abundance of breakables you'll find in so many other establishments. Ask about special deals for their 3-, 5-, and 7-night packages. The dining room serves traditional Newfoundland favorites and will also cater to special needs on request.

Taverner's Path, Trinity. ⓒ **709/464-3269**. www.oceancontact.com. 8 units in inn and 4 in adjacent guest house. C$69–$85 (US$51–$63). C$10 (US$7.33) each additional person. MC, V, Interac. **Amenities:** Two dining rooms; pub; library with collections on whales and whale research; nonsmoking; Internet access, fax machine; piano, games, TV, & VCR in common room; children welcome; ample parking; knowledgeable guides; hiking trails nearby. *In room:* AM/FM radios, private baths.

 Camping in Trinity Bight

If you prefer natural over man-made history, pitch your tent at **Lockston Path Provincial Park**—a provincially run campground with 36 semi-serviced and 20 fully serviced sheltered campsites, as well as a freshwater beach for swimming. The lower-numbered campsites are closest to the beach, while numbers 41 to 56 have the advantage of looping around a wheelchair-accessible comfort station with laundry and shower facilities as well as a dumping station. Lockston Path Provincial Park is approximately 6km (less than 4 miles) from Port Rexton on Route 236—about a 15-minute drive from Trinity. The woods grow close to the road on this unpaved route, so keep a sharp eye out for four-legged pedestrians.

Route 236, Port Rexton. ⓒ **800/563-6353** or 709/464-3553. www.gov.nf.ca/parks&reserves. C$18 (US$13) for serviced lots and C$11 (US$8) for unserviced. MC, V. Open May 15–Sept 16, weather permitting. **Amenities:** Boat launch; comfort station; picnic and day-use facilities; dumping station; laundry facilities; outdoor swimming; pit privies; drinking water (taps); playground; hiking trails; fishing; activity center. Firewood available at check-in for C$4 (US$2.93) a bundle.

EXPLORING TRINITY

Begin your Trinity Village visit at the **Trinity Interpretation Centre** (ⓒ **709/729-0592**). Here you'll get a one-page map naming each of the significant sites (convenient in a town where so many of the buildings look like heritage structures). From there, your next stop should be the Lester-Garland Premises, located in the former general store. Take a look at the original 1896 ledger to see the names and purchases made by residents of the time. Hiscock House, a 1910 restoration, represents a typical merchant's household, complete with fancy furnishings. Next door to that is a craft shop that closes at 5:30pm, so try not to arrive too late in the day or you may be disappointed. *Note:* The historical experience is so well integrated within the community it's easy to forget that people really live here. When you see someone hanging out clothes or eating supper, remember they're not historical interpreters—they're residents. Say hello, but respect their privacy.

The various historical sites are open 10am to 5:30pm during the summer months. *Tip:* Some are Provincial Historic Sites and others are managed by the Trinity Historical Society and Trinity Trust, so you can't buy one pass to get into everything. The Interpretation Centre, Lester-Garland Premises, and Hiscock House are run by the province and can be seen under one package price of C$2.50 (US$1.83) for those 13 and over. The Trinity Museum, Green Family Forge, Court House, and Lester-Garland House (this is different from the Lester-Garland Premises) are run by the Trinity Historical Society and Trust and will cost you another C$2 (US$1.46) per person (over age 12) to see. Unless you're staying in the area for several days and have lots of time, or are really interested in the details of local history, I think you'll get enough out of the three provincial sites—which you can see in about an hour.

Kids All Aboard!

For a trip on the longest mini-train ride in North America, head to **Trinity Loop**. It's an amusement/activity park centered around a bona fide miniature train—a CN 802 replica—and a 2,000-m-long (1.2 miles) track that drops 10.3m (34 ft.) from beginning to end. The 10-minute trip is the highlight of the park, especially as you look out over the pond as you cross the bridge. I could have done without the wooden cartoon character cutouts nailed to various trees, but the kids made a game out of who could spot them first. In addition to the train, you'll also find aqua water trikes, rowboats, pedalboats, kayaks, bumper boats, a Ferris wheel, mini-golf, and a railway museum built in—what else?—railway cars. Trinity Loop is located on Route 239, follow the signs south of the Trinity Village turnoff. Visa and MasterCard accepted, Interac available. There is no day pass: you pay as you ride. Both the train and the Ferris wheel are C$3 (US$2.20) adult, C$2.50 (US$1.83) child. Water rides range from C$5–$6 (US$3.66–$4.40) per half hour.

NIGHTLIFE

A trip to Trinity wouldn't be complete without treating yourself to a performance of the **Rising Tide Theatre** (© **888/464-3377;** www.risingtidetheatre. com). Between June and October each year, the company puts on a number of performances in an outdoor seaside venue. It costs C$14 (US$10.26) for one of the regular plays in the program, and C$29 (US$21) for the dinner theater. You'll find the Rising Tide box office in the Trinity Arts Centre (prices are before 15% HST).

Rising Tide's prime offering is the **Trinity Pageant** ⊛, the anchor event of Trinity's Summer in the Bight Theatre Festival. Actors move from one historical site to another throughout the town, telling a story as they go. There are times when the wind and passing traffic overwhelm the actors' voices, but these impressive improv artists usually find a way to integrate such minor technicalities into the script. The pageant is held from early July until Labour Day on Wednesday, Saturday, and Sunday. Tickets are just C$10 (US$7.33).

If you're not into live theater but love live music, put on your dancing shoes and shuffle over to the only bar in town: **Rocky's Place** (© **709/464-3400**), just up the road from Campbell House. On Wednesday evenings during the summer, fiddler Kelly Russell and folklorist Tonya Kearley get together here for Dance Up (a lively mélange of folk music and step-dancing). While you're welcome to sit back and enjoy the show, audience participation is a given. Don't worry about not knowing the steps—the music itself has a way of telling you how to move.

 Random Passage

If you're a movie buff, you've probably already seen the movie *The Shipping News* and know that it was filmed in Trinity Harbour. But another well-known Canadian production was filmed just 14km (less than 9 miles) from Trinity, up Route 239. *Random Passage,* the international-hit miniseries, was filmed in nearby **New Bonaventure.** Based on the novels *Random Passage* and *Waiting for Time* by Bernice Morgan, the site includes a number of early-1800s houses, a church, school, and fishing stages and flakes (wooden structures upon which fish was traditionally dried and salted). With its weathered gray dwellings and denuded spruce trees for fencing, this recreated settlement depicts the hardships of living in a world without running water or electric heat, physically cut off from the world, dependent on a merciless sea for its people's livelihood.

Set tours run from approximately mid-June through Oct 15 9am–7:30pm and cost C$6 (US$4.40) for adults, C$4 (US$2.93) for seniors, C$3 (US$2.20) for children 5–16, and C$14 (US$10.26 for families).

OUTDOOR PURSUITS

If you're looking for a more active adventure than you'll find at the local museum, invigorating outdoor activities are easy to find. You can charter a yacht, go sea kayaking or hiking, or study the whales with one of the most knowledgeable whale experts Newfoundland has to offer.

Atlantic Adventures Boat Charters & Tours   Set sail for an all-in-one yachting adventure, whale-watching tour, dinner theater, and port explorer. Your host Art Andrews (former CBC radio personality) invites you for a 3-hour nature cruise aboard his 14-m (46-ft.) ketch-rigged Trawl'R Sailer. It's a glorious feeling to be standing on the forward deck, feet braced on the plank floor, hands gripping the railing and all 60 sq. m (642 sq. ft.) of sail stretching to catch the wind. With each graceful dip of her prow, you feel the salty sting of pure freedom. You may even find yourself in the company of a curious humpback or minke as you head into one of the narrow harbors leading to an abandoned fishing port. The 1-hour dinner cruise is limited to 12 people, but should really be no more than 8 in order to comfortably accommodate elbow room and the characters who entertain you while you dine.

Route 230, Trinity Harbour. ☎ **709/464-2133.** www.atlanticadventures.com. May–Oct. 3-hour nature cruise C$40 (US$29.50) per person; dinner cruise C$69 (US$50.63) per person. MC, V.

Mag-Ami Kayaking   No-frills kayaking at its best. You won't be treated to fancy feasts or trained entertainers at Mag-Ami—just the opportunity of a lifetime to get eye-to-eye with whales, water, and seabirds. Nick and Wanda Donovan are expert instructors with a talent for making even the most apprehensive beginner comfortable with a paddle. You'll soon find yourself gliding across the ocean, changing direction with a shift of your weight or a turn of your shoulder.

Sure, you can rent the kayak and go out on your own, but for just a bit more money you can go on an excursion with an expert guide. They'll show you the best places for sea caves, whale feeding grounds, and icebergs (in season), as well as abandoned settlements. If you head out on the full-day excursion, you'll be treated to an authentic Newfoundland "boil-up." *Tip:* Bring along extra footwear (as your feet tend to get wet in the kayak) as well as a warm jacket and sunscreen. Even when the air is chilly, the sun reflected off the water can give you a painful burn.

Tours depart from Trinity Bay. Call ☎ **709/466-2451** or 709/464-7538 for reservations. http://magami kayaking.tripod.com. Mid-May–Sept. Half-day tour C$50 (US$36.68); full-day tour C$90 (US$66). Rentals: C$10/hr. (US$7.33); C$40/day (US$29.50); C$100/weekend (US$74). No credit cards.

 Enjoying a Newfoundland Boil-up

Boil-ups are a traditional Newfoundland way to enjoy a sunny summer afternoon—the equivalent of the North American picnic with sandwiches and lemonade or iced tea. But in Newfoundland, the beach boil-up gen-erally includes boiling the kettle for a cup of tea and having a bun or slice of homemade bread with it.

Ocean Contact Ltd. ⋆⋆ If you're looking for the best possible interactive whale experience in Trinity Bay, you'll find it through Dr. Peter Beamish, Ph.D. His "Ocean Contact" concept offers unique opportunities in human–whale interaction as you take part in active research. The whales come so close to Beamish's 8-m (26-ft.) rigid hull inflatable you'll practically be able to touch them. This is a tad scary when you're in a Zodiac, but you can trust that the man knows what he's doing, as he hasn't lost a passenger yet!

One thing I especially like about Ocean Contact is that they don't overfill the Zodiacs like some other tour operators I've been with. The boats hold 24 people, but Beamish generally doesn't put more than 12 onboard at a time. This gives you room to maneuver if you're trying to get that perfect picture of a nearby whale. There are four sailings daily, but I'd recommend the early-morning cruise, when the wildlife is generally most active, or the evening cruise, when you can enjoy a lovely sunset amid frolicking whales. Beamish and his wife, Christine, also own and operate the **Village Inn** in Trinity.

Trinity. ☎ **709/464-3269**. www.oceancontact.com. C$55 (US$40) adult; C$45 (US$33) ages13–15; C$35 (US$26) ages 4–12. MC, V, Interac. June–Oct daily departures.

Hiking the Discovery Trail If you're into hiking, you'll really enjoy the Dis-covery Trail. Not to be confused with the Discovery Trail referred to earlier in this chapter, which is a driving route, this is a series of groomed coastal trails that retrace the footpaths traditionally used by early European and aboriginal settlers. You can hike along rocky outcrops 30m (100 ft.) above sea level, visit the aban-doned communities of Kerley's Harbour and British Harbour, or listen to the music of a water-caressed sea stack. Several of the trails are less than 5km (3 miles) in length, to a maximum of 17km (10½ miles). All trails have direc-tional signage and maps available for purchase.

Hike Discovery, P.O. Box 3300, Clarenville, NL A0E 1J0. ☎ **709/466-3923**. www.thediscoverytrail.org/hike discovery/index.html. To order the "Hike Discovery" booklet, send C$7.50 money order or check payable to the Discovery Trail. In St. John's you can purchase the guidebook for C$6 (US$4.40) at Outfitters on Water St.

BONAVISTA 🟊🟊

In addition to being the site where *continental* Europeans first touched North American soil more than 500 years ago (the Vikings were here first; you can read about that in chapter 7), Bonavista is an almost full-service community. It has a hospital, pharmacy, gas station, and banking services, but little in the way of accommodations (apart from a couple of B&Bs and a small motel). That being the case, it's best to think of Bonavista as a half-day excursion from Trinity, or Trinity–Bonavista as a full-day trip from Clarenville.

 ### "O Buena Vista!"

These were the words uttered by Italian explorer Giovanni Caboto (aka John Cabot) on his first sight of Cape Bonavista on June 24, 1497. He and his 20-man crew had been sailing into the unknown for 5 tense weeks, wondering if at any minute they were going to fall off the edge of the Earth. They were on a mission, funded by King Henry VII of England, to investigate whatever lands they might find by sailing west from Europe across the Atlantic. The underlying hope was that they would discover a shorter passage to the Far East. Instead, Cabot found a new-founde-lande teeming with fish reportedly so plentiful they filled a net at a single dip. Whether Cabot's cry of "O buena vista!" (Oh beautiful sight!) expressed his appreciation for the view, or relief that he and his near-mutiny crew had finally found land, remains shrouded in history.

EXPLORING BONAVISTA

A leisurely 3km (less than 2 miles) past the town of Bonavista is Cape Bonavista, site of the red-and-white-striped **Cape Bonavista Lighthouse** 🟊🟊🟊, a Provincial Historic Site. Interpreters dressed in 1870s costume will guide you through this beautifully restored facility, with its 9-m-high (30-ft.) central stone tower (housed inside the building). The attention to historical detail is exquisite, from the warmth of the kitchen woodstove to the toys in the children's bedroom. After viewing the living quarters of the former lighthouse keeper, his assistant, and the assistant's family, you head up the steps to the top of the tower. From here, you can see puffins flitting around nests burrowed into the granite cliffs. Allow your eyes to trace the rust-tinted rock as it lowers to meet the sea, then follow the vast expanse of ocean until it fades into the horizon. The view is magnificent, but you may still be disappointed—it's all just for looks these days; an automated light is mounted atop a metal tower constructed alongside the lighthouse.

When you're finished the inside tour, take an hour or two to explore the marshy grounds around the site itself. Climb to the hill above the parking lot, where you'll discover a miniature pond and sandpipers searching for insects in the mud while bluebells tinkle in a light breeze and a whale snorts in the distance. Turn to the left and walk across the barrens to the municipal park, where you'll find a statue of John Cabot. Along the way, you may be lucky enough to sight the low-growing orange-red berry known as the bakeapple. Also called a cloudberry, it grows only in this province and Norway.

Cape Bonavista Lighthouse: Capeshore Rd., Cape Bonavista (end of Rtes. 230/235). ⓒ **709/468-7444.** Open mid-June–(Canadian) Thanksgiving, daily 10am–5:30pm. C$2.50 (US$1.83) for age 13 and over. Same admission gets you into the Mockbeggar Plantation.

(*Fun Fact* **Getting to Know the Puffin**

The official feathered mascot of Newfoundland & Labrador is the puffin, a penguin-sized bird roughly 30cm (12 in.) tall with a large white face and prominent, colorfully striped beak. Also known as the "sea parrot," puffins are excellent swimmers and divers. Their flying, however, is decidedly less graceful.

Located on the tip of the Bonavista Peninsula near the Cape Bonavista Lighthouse is **Dungeon Provincial Park,** a natural scenic wonder. The Dungeon is a collapsed sea cave with a natural archway carved out by sea action. It looks like someone—or something—literally sucked the land down into the ocean through the dual "straws" formed by the arches. Situated on what is locally known as "Backside," on a scenic but bumpy gravel road (approximately 2km/ 1 mile off Rte. 235), complete with pasture land for horses, cows, and sheep, a trip to the Dungeon makes for a nice diversion.

Dungeon Provincial Park: Bonavista, Route 230 to Route 235. ( ) **709-635-4520.** June 1–Sept 30. Picnic sites and pit toilets are available for day users. No camping.

Down at the harbor, you can board but you can't sail on a 20th-century reconstruction of the 15th-century *Matthew,* John Cabot's ship. The 30-minute tour, led by costumed interpreters, provides a fascinating insight into the trials faced by Cabot and his crew as they sailed the wild waters of the Atlantic in the very close quarters of a 19-m (63-ft.), three-masted, wooden caravel. Imagine yourself as one of the 21 people who lived and worked on just such a ship for the 5-week crossing—manually pumping the bilge, struggling for sleep, surrounded by caged livestock, living on salt fish and ale—and you'll come a lot closer to understanding why Cabot was so grateful to see Bonavista.

Matthew Reconstruction: Bonavista Harbour. ( ) **877/468-1497.** www.matthewlegacy.com. C$3.50 (US$2.58) adults; C$3 (US$2.20) seniors; C$1.75 (US$1.20) ages 6–16; free for under 6; C$8 (US$5.86) family rate. Open May–Oct daily 10am–6pm. Give yourself at least an hour to tour the new Interpretation Centre, ship, and gift shop.

Although it's 300 years old, the most recent half-century is responsible for **Mockbeggar Plantation**'s Provincial Historic Site status. In March 1946, two of the most important political figures of the day met here to plot strategy for the upcoming referendum that would decide whether Newfoundland joined the Canadian Confederation. Gordon Bradley and Joseph R. "Joey" Smallwood agreed that, if successful in getting a majority vote in favor of Confederation, Smallwood would become premier and Bradley would become Newfoundland's first cabinet minister in Canada's federal government. Aside from being silent listeners to secret political machinations, the walls of Mockbeggar show how the upper class of the time lived, offering quite a contrast from the very basic lifestyle common to most residents of the fishing villages. Highlights include a stained-glass window inside the main house that depicts the *Matthew,* as well as an old-fashioned carpentry shop and cod liver oil factory.

Mockbeggar Plantation: Mockbeggar Rd. ( ) **709/468-7300.** www.nfmuseum.com. C$2.50 (US$1.83) admission for 13 and over. This admission also gets you into the Bonavista Lighthouse. Open mid-June–Thanksgiving daily 10am–6pm.

A Unique Shopping Opportunity

While at the Ryan Premises, check out the unique wooden furnishings and collectibles handcrafted by Mike Paterson of **Newfoundland Outport** ⚒, a company based in nearby Upper Amherst Cove. If you're intrigued by Paterson's display of period reproductions at the Ryan Premises, drive down Route 235 to his shop and see his range of products from C$25 to $3,000 (US$18.45–$2,214). Call ℭ **709/445-4341** for shop hours or to request a copy of their catalog.

There's nothing grand or ostentatious about the **Ryan Premises National Historic Site** ⚒⚒, a cluster of five white, red-trimmed, wooden structures with sharply angled roofs on the Bonavista waterfront. And that's exactly why you should include them on your itinerary! The understated drama of their purpose-built design gives new life to the daily interactions of 19th-century fishermen and merchants. When you walk through the former offices, look at the figures logged on the old ledger. Fishermen would sell their fish to the merchant and get paid in goods from the company store, owned by the same merchant to whom they had sold their fish. Rarely did this barter system work to the fishermen's advantage, with more than one of them going to an uneasy grave because they died indebted to the merchant.

As you wander around the site, you'll encounter plank floors and sawdust, thick-beamed building supports, and the unmistakable scent of salt fish. You'll watch videos, read storyboards, and speak to costumed reenactors demonstrating how the fishery brought Newfoundland & Labrador into the global economy hundreds of years before e-commerce, NAFTA, or the WTO.

Ryan Premises: Route 235, Bonavista Harbour. ℭ **800/213-7275** or 709/468-1600. Open May 15–Oct 15 10am–6pm. C$3.50 (US$2.58) adults, C$3 (US$2.20) seniors, C$1.75 (US$1.20) children, and C$7 (US$5.13) family rate. Gift shop on-site; restaurant next door. Ask about the live performances put on by the Rising Tide Theatre. Theater tickets should be reserved in advance.

 Lunch with a View in Bonavista

Skipper's Café ⚒⚒ *Value*   Next to the Ryan Premises is as close to the water as you can be without getting wet. It offers a lovely, unobstructed view of Bonavista Harbour, coupled with a traditional food menu at reasonable prices. The seafood chowder may seem a tad expensive, but it's well worth it—with hearty chunks of salmon, cod, scallops, and shrimp. The cod au gratin is similarly noteworthy. The cod is caught locally, giving you an unbeatable fresh flavor topped with plenty of bubbling cheddar. Skipper's has a full liquor license, and boasts local Newfoundland wines as well as friendly service. To get to Skipper's, follow Route 235 to 42 Campbell St., Bonavista (next to Ryan Premises). ℭ **709/468-7150.** Open June 1 to September 30, 10am to 10pm. Lunches range from C$3 to $8 (US$2.20–$5.86). MasterCard and Visa accepted.

2 The Heritage Run

It's a long and lonely drive for most of the Heritage Run, 198km (124 miles) from the time you turn off the Trans-Canada at Goobies to Grand Bank on the southwest coast of the Burin Peninsula. It's a tedious journey over relatively flat land, with a sameness of scenery underwhelmingly punctuated by gray-brown boulders. But wait—move in for a closer look. Those aren't just rocks. They're glacial erratics, 10,000-year-old footprints of the last ice age.

That's the way it is in much of Newfoundland & Labrador: even the most ordinary detail can take on new significance if you know how to look at it. You could allow yourself to be bored because it doesn't have the bustle of New York City or the architectural treasures of Italy. Or you can open your eyes to the natural understated glamor of the place, thrilling in the simple things. Like the line of birch mirrored in a ripple-free pond. Or the circling flight of a bald eagle on the hunt. And a people who'll smilingly acknowledge your presence, often stopping in the middle of whatever they're doing to say hello and help you on your way. The Burin Peninsula throbs with under-acknowledged beauty. Whether or not you see it is up to you.

ESSENTIALS

GETTING THERE

The entrance to the Heritage Run (also referred to as the Burin Peninsula Highway) is at Goobies, 162km (101 miles) west of St. John's. If you're traveling east to west across the island, take the left turn onto Route 210 just past the Irving station (watch for the giant statue of Morris the Moose out front). Route 210 will take you all the way to Marystown, the largest community on the Burin Peninsula. Past Marystown, there's a looped highway that takes you to the coastal communities around the foot of the Burin Peninsula (see the map on p. 104).

VISITOR INFORMATION

Information about sites along the Heritage Run is available from the **Heritage Run Tourism Association,** which has an office in Marystown at 1 Centennial Rd. in the lighthouse-shaped building located at the entrance to town (© **709/279-1887**). The office is open from mid-June to mid-September daily 9am to 9pm. You'll also find visitor information centers in Goobies at the Irving Service Station, at the intersection of routes 210 and 1 (© **709/542-3239**), and in Fortune (© **709/832-3031**) near the waterfront Customs Office. Hours at this location coincide with the St. Pierre ferry schedule.

Visitor information for the French islands of St. Pierre and Miquelon is available from **St. Pierre Tours Ltd** and **Lake's Travel Ltd.,** which share an office at 5 Bayview St. in Fortune (© **800/563-2006**). St. Pierre Tours Ltd. also has an office in St. John's at 116 Duckworth St. (© **888/959-8214**). *Note:* When visiting the islands, you must have proper passports and documentation just as though you were visiting France. This wasn't always the case: the stricter border crossings are another consequence of September 11, 2001.

GETTING AROUND

You'll find far fewer services for visitors in this region than on the Discovery Trail. Be sure to plan ahead and pack snacks or a lunch, especially if you're traveling in the evening or on a Sunday, when services may be closed. The same advice goes for filling up your gas tank. Don't assume that just because you'll soon be arriving at a village that there is a gas station there, or that it will be open if you're arriving outside of daytime business hours.

It's also important to note that visitors with limited mobility are best off not planning a trip to the French islands; they offer few wheelchair-accessible services.

EXPLORING THE HERITAGE RUN

Divided into four sections, the Heritage Run begins with Route 210, which extends all the way to Marystown, the region's major center on the east coast of the Burin Peninsula. This part of the route is known locally as **Mariner Drive.** The connecting route from Marystown south through routes 222, 221, and 220 to the community of Epworth, near Burin, is known locally as **Captain Cook Drive.** The portion of Route 220 that takes you around the bottom of the peninsula is known as **Captain Clarke Drive.**

The segment of Route 220 that takes you to Fortune (where you catch the ferry to the French islands of St. Pierre and Miquelon) and nearby Grand Bank is appropriately known as the **French Islands Drive.** It's all a bit confusing—with the route changing its name and number with nearly every bend in the road—but apart from a couple of very short side routes that branch off from Route 210–220 it's all one road and you can't get lost.

Approximately 60 percent of the peninsula's 28,000 residents live in one of the five major communities of Burin, Fortune, Grand Bank, St. Lawrence, and Marystown, the communities discussed in this chapter.

 Cod Fishing and the Grand Banks

You may have heard of the "Grand Banks" off the southeast coast of Newfoundland, once considered the richest cod fishing grounds in the world. The town of Grand Bank on the west coast of the Burin Peninsula was named in honor of the region's fishing heritage, much of which is well-explained in the Southern Newfoundland Seamen's Museum (see "Area Attractions" later in this chapter).

If you'd like to see just how dangerous fishing on the Grand Banks can be, watch the George Clooney movie *The Perfect Storm*. The film depicts the tragedy faced by so many longliner fishing boats that never made it back from a trip to the fish-filled waters. It's based on the book *The Perfect Storm: A True Story of Men Against the Sea*, by Sebastian Junger, about Grand Banks fishermen from Gloucester, Massachusetts.

GOOBIES TO MARYSTOWN

As you begin your journey along Route 210, you'll leave the fast pace of the Trans-Canada Highway at Goobies, a small community of 250 residents just 162km (100 miles) northwest of St. John's. Goobies is your gateway to the Burin Peninsula.

Marystown, the major regional commercial center of the Burin Peninsula with nearly 7,000 residents, is farther along, at 306km (190 miles) west of the capital city. It doesn't sound that far, but if you look at the map you'll see it isn't a straight drive. Follow the Trans-Canada Highway (Route 1) northwest until you get to Goobies, and then head southwest along Route 210 to Marystown.

WHERE TO STAY & DINE

You aren't going to find much in the way of accommodations or restaurants between Goobies and Marystown. Which means you either eat at the Irving Restaurant in Goobies (it's typical Irving, with clean bathroom, booth seating, slow service, and filling food at a reasonable price), or you wait for the bigger selection in Marystown. *Tip:* While you can function on low fuel for a few hours, your car can't. It's a good idea to fill your tank in Goobies before beginning the next 144km (90 miles) to Marystown.

Dock Point B&B *Value*   Here are exceptional surroundings for a fraction of what you'll pay in more populated areas. Except for the excessive greenery in the dining area (sit by the window and you'll feel like you have a fern growing out of your head), the rest of the furnishings are exquisite: antique mahogany beds and desk and a gorgeously ornate fireplace with extensive brass trim. The grounds are similarly spectacular, with an abundance of lilies and other floral varieties that had me green with envy! Ultra bargain.

Route 210. 16 Kings Rd., Marystown. (*C*) **709/279-4570**. www.dockpoint.ca. 2 units. C$50–$55 (US$36.68–$40). Additional person $10 (US$7.33). V. **Amenities:** Nonsmoking rooms; complimentary breakfast; shared bathroom. Gift/antique shop, golfing, tennis courts, walking trails, and shopping nearby in Marystown.

Five Bays Lodge   If you've made your way as far as Goobies (about a 1½-hour drive from St. John's) and would like to stay for the night before you head farther along the Heritage Run, there is a small, full-service lodge that might fit the bill. The Five Bays Lodge will give you a comfortable place to lay your head and get a good home-cooked meal in a casual, friendly, and rustic atmosphere. The guest rooms—although clean, with comfortable beds and private, 3-piece bathrooms—are best suited for a brief stopover. If you're looking for something fancier, you're best off continuing down the Burin Peninsula.

Route 1, Goobies. (*C*) **709/542-3444**. Fax: 709/542-3445. 13 units. C$49.95–$59.95 (US$40–$44). AE, MC, V, Interac. **Amenities:** Restaurant; pub; billiard tables; video lottery machines. *In room:* Private bath, satellite TV, telephone.

Golden Sands Resort *Kids*   Not to be mistaken for the 5-star Shangri-la Golden Sands Resort in Malaysia, this family getaway has seen better days. Many of the cabins need extensive upgrading, both in furnishings and electrical power supply. It's a shame, because the Golden Sands has a lot to offer the vacationing family—most especially a beautiful sandy beach that's just over a meter (4 ft.) deep for hundreds of meters offshore. There's just been a change of ownership, however, so it's hoped the new managers will bring this resort back up to the standard it held 10 years ago. *Warning:* Be careful wandering into the woods, especially near the cabins. We inadvertently discovered a wasp's nest while retrieving a soccer ball. *Tip:* Bring a first-aid kit in case of encounter with aforesaid wasps.

Route 210. Winterland Rd., Marystown. (Take Route 222 3.2km [2 miles] past the Route 210 junction. Follow gravel road 1.6km (1mile) to the resort.) (*C*) **709/891-2400**. Open June 15–Sept 3. 18 units. C$65–$75 (US$48–$55). MC, V. **Amenities:** Waterslide; boat rentals; fishing; laundry facilities; games arcade; trackless train; mini-golf; convenience store; restaurant with takeout; freshwater lake; sandy beach; campground. *In room:* TV, phone, full kitchen.

Hotel Marystown *❋*   Part of Atlantic Canada's City Hotels chain, the best thing about the Hotel Marystown is its location—you're just 70km/43 miles (about 40 minutes) from the St. Pierre ferry, and Marystown is a central point for exploring the Burin Peninsula. Bilingual service is offered and the hotel has a pretty good restaurant (see below). The guest rooms themselves are standard for the brand (bland decor, comfortable beds, desk)—if you've seen one, you've seen 'em all.

Route 210. 76 Ville Marie Dr., Marystown. ℂ **800/563-2489** or 709/279-1600. www.cityhotels.ca. 131 units. C$55–$99 (US$40–$72). AE, DC, MC, V, Interac. **Amenities:** Banquet/meeting facilities; P.J. Billington's Restaurant; lobby bar, lounge, saloon; room service; air-conditioned public areas; business services; laundry/valet services; pets allowed; walking distance to mall. *In room:* Private, 3-piece bathrooms, kitchen facilities in efficiency units.

P.J. Billington's Restaurant

Decorated with a theme corresponding to the colorful rum-running history of the Burin Peninsula area, Billington's has a casual, relaxed, and friendly atmosphere. The best value of the day is at breakfast: you can have a complete breakfast with toast, hash browns, scrambled eggs, bacon, sausage, juice, and tea or coffee for C$3.99 (US$2.93).

Route 210. Hotel Marystown, 76 Ville Marie Dr., Marystown. ℂ **709/279-1600**. Open Mon–Sat 7am–11pm, Sun 8am–9pm. C$5–$20 (US$3.66–$14.76). AE, DC, MC, V, Interac. Designated smoking and nonsmoking areas. Reservations not required, but appreciated.

Kilmory Resort & Trailer Park ★★★

You'll pay more here than for the standard rent-a-cabin, but it's worth it. Kilmory Resort is the absolute, unequivocal, best cottage getaway in the province. Private decks, a well-maintained modern playground, overstuffed furnishings, and floor-to-ceiling pine interiors all contribute to the perfection of your stay. It's a pastoral idyll of cozy log chalets and camping in a quiet, private setting overlooking Piper's Hole River and the Bear's Folly Mountains. Be sure to take a trip to the top of the hill overlooking Swift Current as the view is spectacular—especially in the fall, when the foliage changes color. If you enjoy winter sports, Kilmory Resort is a great place for snowmobiling as well as cross-country and downhill skiing—making it the most beautiful resort to stay at on the Burin Peninsula, any time of year. The one thing I didn't appreciate occurred on my most recent attempt to stay at Kilmory, when the reservations clerk laughed at me for trying to make a last-minute weekend booking. Sure they're booked months in advance, but they could at least sound regretful that they couldn't squeeze me in!

Route 210, Swift Current. ℂ **709/549-2410**. www.kilmory.nf.ca. Cabins open year-round. Camping from May 20–Oct 15. 17 cottages. C$84–$159 (US$62–$117) double; additional person C$8 (US$5.86). 11 semi-serviced campsites C$18 (US$13); 6 fully serviced sites C$20 (US$14.76). AE, MC, V, Interac. **Amenities:** Boat and canoe rentals; dumping station; electrical hookup (15 & 30 amp); sewer hookup; shower/washroom facilities; water hookup; heated pool in summer; snowmobile and ski rentals in winter.

Wong's Palace Restaurant

It's like a fish out of water: a genuinely authentic Chinese restaurant in the Newfoundland heartland. It doesn't look the part, but just wait until you taste the chow mein—you'll think you're in the middle of Chinatown. Wong's is a fully licensed restaurant offering both Canadian and Chinese (primarily Cantonese) fare. Prices are very reasonable, with traditional Chinese dishes like their highly recommended chow mein starting at C$6.35 (about US$4.69) and a la carte dishes such as steaks, chicken, and seafood going for around C$14 (US$10.26).

Route 210. McGettigan Blvd., Marystown. ℂ **709/279-3773**. Open 11am–10:30pm Sun–Thurs; 11am–11:30pm Fri–Sat. C$6.35–$14.25 (US$4.69–$10.53). MC, V, Interac. Reservations not required. Casual attire.

EXPLORING MARYSTOWN

One of the most prominent features of Marystown is Kiewit Offshore Services, the largest marine fabrication and outfitting facility in the province. Mortier Bay, which leads into Marystown Harbour, is one of the largest natural harbors in the world, at 2,300 by 250m (7,544 by 820 ft.).

Moving farther down the road, you'll find there are two shopping malls in Marystown, complete with banks, supermarkets, a liquor store, pharmacy, and department store. The town's recreational facilities include an indoor swimming pool, a municipal park, track and field facilities, and a stadium.

The **Marystown Museum** (✆ 709/279-1462), on Ville Marie Dr., is open from early June to late September. The displays include numerous local artifacts (for example, glass floats, ship models, and a "gob stick"—you'll have to visit to find out what that is!) and provide an interesting interpretation of the area's history.

BURIN TO BAY L'ARGENT

With so much wide-open space, you may be surprised to learn that the Burin Peninsula is actually a small area. Just 161km (100 miles) in length and 40km (25½ miles) at its widest point, it would take you only a couple of hours to drive around the loop from Marystown if you didn't stop to see the sights. But if you enjoy space and breathtaking scenery, give yourself time to enjoy it.

Detouring off the major Route 210–220 arm of the Heritage Run onto secondary Route 221, you'll arrive in **Burin,** a community of about 3,000 residents. The region boasts quite a colorful seafaring history. The famous navigator and cartographer Captain James Cook spent five summers navigating the coast of Newfoundland between 1763 and 1767. His goal was to create the first accurate maps of the area, complete with sailing directions and advice on safe anchorage. Captain Cook used one of the best vantage points in the Burin area to keep an eye out for smugglers, illegal French fishing boats, and French and American mercenaries called privateers. The **Captain Cook Lookout** in Burin bears the explorer's name.

Just past Burin, you'll arrive at **St. Lawrence.** If you're interested in soccer be sure to stop here—the community has named itself the Soccer Capital of Canada because of its excellence in the sport. The St. Lawrence Laurentians have taken home more championships than any other community its size in the country.

Rounding the bend along Route 220, you'll arrive at **Fortune,** most noteworthy for being the departure point for the **St. Pierre/Miquelon** ferry. It's hard to believe that the Burin coast is just 24km (15 miles) from France's only North American territory. The passenger-only ferry runs daily between July 1 and Sept 2, and costs C$75 (US$55) for adults and C$37.50 (US$27.72) for children age 2 to 11 years for a same-day return trip. Parking is available in Fortune.

Next to Fortune is **Grand Bank,** home to roughly 3,000 residents. The community is most noteworthy because of its connection to the Grand Banks fishery, excellently depicted in the murals that adorn the Southern Newfoundland Seamen's Museum.

As you head north back up Route 210 you'll come to the turn-off for Route 212, which will take you to the community of **Bay L'Argent,** where you can catch the passenger ferry to **Rencontre East** and **Pool's Cove,** two isolated outports of Central Newfoundland—if you're *really* looking to get off the beaten path! While Pool's Cove is accessible by road, the 1-hour, 45-minute passenger ferry is the only way into or out of Rencontre East, home to 215 people. It's a land of lush green hills, gravel roads, fishing boats, wooden wharves, and a single B&B. For just C$40 (US$29.50) per night double, you can stay in the home of Margaret and Fred Mullins, a 5-minute walk from the ferry ✆ **709/848-3226.** The ferry travels back and forth between Bay L'Argent–Rencontre East–Pool's Cove several times per day. One-way fare is C$3.50 (US$2.58) per adult and C$1.75 (US$1.30) per student, child, senior, and regular commuter. For more information, call © **709/895-3541** or visit the ferry schedule website at www.gov.nf.ca/FerryServices/schedules/O-rencontr.stm.

When you arrive in Bay L'Argent to continue your return journey back up the Burin Peninsula, remember this is the last community along the Heritage Run until you're back up to Swift Current, so gas up before you head out.

(Finds A Little Bit of France, Just Off the Coast of Newfoundland

Saint-Pierre et Miquelon is a tantalizing tidbit of France—242 sq. km (93 sq. miles) to be exact—just 75 minutes away by ferry from Fortune, a short flight from St. John's, and an even shorter one from the Burin Regional Airport in Winterland.

Roughly 7,000 French-speaking citizens live in the French territory, many of whom also speak English. The narrow streets are lined with colorful houses, and you'll find the assorted boutiques, the French pastry shops (*Ah, les croissants! Les baguettes! C'est magnifique!*), and the wonderful restaurants worth the trip. You'll need to be on full alert as you walk through the shopping district, as the Minis seem to race along at a speed out of proportion to their size.

You can take day trips to St. Pierre by ferry, or you can plan for a longer stay so as to better soak up the French joie de vivre. Just make sure you confirm and re-confirm, as the hotels have been know to overbook and then cancel reservations at the last minute.

Call St. Pierre Tours at © **800/563-2006** to arrange a package stay. There are many touring options, including bus, mini-train, bicycle, and horseback. For independent travel, call St. Pierre Tourism © **800/565-5118** (English service) or 011/508-41 23 84 for French service. The comprehensive website, www.st-pierre-et-miquelon.com, is fully bilingual and will provide you with interesting current affairs as well as the history of the islands.

Note: Remember that St. Pierre time is 30 minutes ahead of Newfoundland time. This is important when you're catching the ferry to return to NL. You'll also find getting around on the islands expensive. Think France. Canadian money is accepted, but all prices will be quoted in euros. At press time, C$1 = 0.644€, very close to the conversion from C$ to US$.

WHERE TO STAY & DINE
Frenchman's Cove Provincial Park ✦   This is a quiet, picturesque, family-oriented facility with all the amenities you'll need for a memorable camping experience—except a shower. It's located on the west side of the Burin Peninsula on Route 213. It has a pebble beach, quiet pond, marsh and stream, excellent bird-watching, interesting geological formations, and (gasp!) a 9-hole, par-36 golf course. The on-site Grande Meadows Golf Course is a Robert Heaslip design that requires more accuracy than distance off the tee. (I can just see all the golf enthusiasts out there suddenly lobbying for a camping vacation.)

The campground is ideal for trailers and has a new comfort station as well as lots of small trails for hiking.

Route 210 to 213. Frenchman's Cove, Fortune Bay. ℂ **800/563-6353** or 709/826-2753. www.gov.nf.ca/parks&reserves/frenchmans_cove.htm. 76 sites. Call for rates. MC, V. Open May 15–Sept 16. **Amenities:** Day-use facilities; drinking water; picnic sites; pit privies; outdoor swimming; playground; fishing; boat and cabin rentals.

Grand Fairways Resort   If you want the golf, but not the tent, it's just a 5-minute walk to Grand Fairways' fully equipped 2-bedroom chalets with tasteful, rustic styling and handcrafted furniture. You'll also find a pullout couch for additional sleeping quarters. Each cabin has a gas barbecue and private lot with a large grassed backyard. There is one fully accessible wheelchair unit. Be sure to bring all the supplies you'll need, as there is no on-site confectionery.

Route 210. Frenchmen's Cove, Fortune Bay. Toll-free ℂ **866/826-2400** or 709/826-2400. www.geocities.com/grandfairwaysresort. 6 units. C$85 (US$63). AE, DC, MC, V. **Amenities:** Fully equipped kitchen; private bath; TV w/VCR.

Long Ridge Cottages   If you can't get into the Long Ridge Cottages, try the Grand Fairways Resort and vice versa: accommodations-wise they are quite similar. Like Grand Fairways, these are fully equipped 2-bedroom housekeeping units. The main difference is the view. Grand Fairways has a more private, wooded setting, while Long Ridge offers spectacular ocean views from less private cabins. The cottages are fully winterized and open year-round, making them an excellent four-season retreat. Accommodations are spacious and very modern, with pine log interiors. There are hiking and ATV trails nearby, and it's just minutes to freshwater swimming and golf.

Route 210 to 213. Long Ridge Place, Garnish. ℂ **709/826-2626** or 709/826-2104. www.longridge cottages.com. 4 units. C$72–$82 (US$53–$61). AE, MC, V. **Amenities:** Color cable TV; electric heat; full bath; patio, barbecue; play area.

The Thorndyke Bed & Breakfast 👍👍★   Historical character comes to life on the walls of this old sea captain's home. Built in 1917 by Captain John Thornhill, the home is named after one of Thornhill's fishing schooners. When completed, the Captain didn't host a housewarming party—he hosted a wall-signing party. To this day, you'll find the signatures of early-20th-century sea captains scribbled on the Thorndyke's wall. The house is an excellent example of Queen Anne architecture, with a "widow's walk," or belvedere, on the roof that guests are allowed to use. Back in the seafaring days, wives of the fishing captains would stand on the roof to watch for the flags of the incoming schooners. While the kitchen is thoroughly modern, the rest of the house is maintained in its original condition. You'll find evidence of that early-1900s character in the antique furnishings and four-poster beds gracing most of the 8 guest rooms, and especially in the bridal suite with its canopy bed and brass-fitted claw-foot tub. And being served with genuine crystal glasses really brings home the elegance of a more refined time. Don't take that the wrong way: this isn't a stiffly formal establishment. You can come and go as you please at the Thorndyke (there's no curfew), even make yourself a late-night snack in the kitchen. The catch is that you might have to share with Potter, the Thorndyke's English springer spaniel mascot.

Route 210. 33 Water St., Grand Bank. www.thethorndyke.com. ℂ **709/832-0820**. 5 units. Open May 1–Sept 30. C$50–$90 (US$36.68–$66). V. **Amenities:** Full breakfast; satellite TV, DVD; nonsmoking.

AREA ATTRACTIONS

Burin Heritage Museum   This museum is an impressive facility, with 15 display rooms that pay tribute to the community's interesting past. It has a gallery for art and traveling exhibits, a craft shop and tea room, and is open from the May 24 (Victoria Day) weekend through early October, 10am until 6pm, with extended hours during July and August to 8pm. © **709/891-2217**. Visit them on the Web at www.burincanada.com.

Echoes of Valour   is the name of the memorial built to commemorate the tragic 1942 event when the *USS Truxtun* ran aground at Chamber Cove during a violent storm. The memorial can be seen near St. Lawrence Town Hall on Memorial Drive. The **US Memorial Health Centre,** built from donations of thanks on behalf of the U.S. sailors, contains an interpretive display of the naval disaster and heroic actions of the local people who rescued 186 sailors from death. Call the St. Lawrence Town Hall at © **709/873-2222** for more information.

Southern Newfoundland Seamen's Museum   54 Marine Dr., Grand Bank (© **709/832-1484**). Here you'll find a large collection of models and paintings of the schooners so important to the heritage and settlement of this region. It will take you at least an hour to see all the exhibits—more if you're really into fishing and seafaring history. On the building you'll find the largest mural in Atlantic Canada, depicting a 1930s Newfoundland fishing village. The museum is open from early May through mid-October daily from 9am until 4:45pm.

St. Lawrence Miner's Memorial Museum   Route 200, St. Lawrence (© **709/ 873-2222**). This facility will teach you about the difficult life of a Newfoundland miner through its interesting display of artifacts and photos from the 20th century. Open year-round, daily from 9am until 9pm.

⟨*Kids*⟩ Splashtacular! 🎢🎢

Before you say goodbye to the Eastern Region, give the kids a treat by spending a day at the largest waterpark in the province. **Splash-n-Putt Resort** borders the Trans-Canada Highway just west of Terra Nova National Park in the community of Glovertown. And except for some overly aggressive go-kart drivers (they must think they're at the Clarenville Dragway), it makes for great family fun. There's a 91-m (300-ft.) waterslide, 18-hole mini-golf, half-kilometer go-kart track, miniature go-kart track, electric bumper cars, bumper boats, swimming pools, and a kiddies' recreation complex. A Splash Pass day pass (including 2 go-kart rides, 3 bumper car rides, 2 bumper boat rides, and unlimited use of all other park activities) costs C$28.70 (US$21.21) plus HST. *Tip:* Try going to the park after 5pm, when you can buy an evening pass for C$14.78 (US$10.92). For more information, call © **709/533-2541** or go online to www.splashnputt.com.

6

The Central Region

If all you see of the massive land mass between Gambo and Springdale is what you glimpse from behind your windshield on the Trans-Canada Highway, you're going to be disappointed. For 2½ hours, it's nothing but spruce, birch, pine, scattered ponds, and boreal bog. So if you're planning to just drive straight through, pack a pillow and designate another driver. But consider yourself warned: that nap may cost you the experience of a lifetime.

The Central Region is the largest region on the island of Newfoundland. You'll see almost none of it from the Trans-Canada, even though this is where you'll find the most densely populated centers, like Gander and Grand Falls–Windsor.

The international airport town of **Gander** made world news following September 11, 2001. With significant help from its neighbors, this community of 10,000 played host to almost 7,000 stranded air passengers—the greatest number at one time on Canadian soil.

An hour west of Gander is **Grand Falls–Windsor,** population 20,000. This tidy town is best known for two things: its pulp and paper mill, and the excellent salmon fishing. The **Salmonid Interpretation Centre** explains the life cycle of a salmon, and if you time your visit for mid-July you'll catch the fabulous 5-day **Exploits Valley Salmon Festival.**

But while these two main service centers are bigger, they aren't necessarily better than what you'll find slightly

north of the Trans-Canada. Less than 100km (63 miles) to the right of Route 1 (assuming you're driving east to west) is an abundance of natural treasures.

The **Kittiwake Coast** (stretching from Eastport to Laurenceton), and especially the town of **Twillingate,** is known for the numerous icebergs that can be seen just offshore—most frequently in May and June. The thrill of kayaking among these great castles of the sea provides an outdoor experience that's hard to duplicate. There are also white sand beaches, perfect away-from-it-all picnic spots, a town cobbled together by inter-island bridges, and even an ancient aboriginal campsite. The **Boyd's Cove Beothuk Interpretation Centre** illustrates the daily life of the semi-nomadic Beothuk natives who once inhabited this region.

If you'd like to meet the island's modern-day native population, visit the **Miawpukek Mi'Kamawey Mawi'omi** (Conne River Tribal Nation). The reserve is about 160km (100 miles) south of Bishop's Falls, at the mouth of one of the best salmon rivers in the province.

Finally, of note in the Central Region are the isolated fishing communities that make up its **South Coast.** Communities like **Harbour Breton, Hermitage, Francois** (pronounced "Franceway"), and **Grey River.** The first two towns are accessible by road if you travel south off Route 1 at Bishop's Falls onto the **Coast of Bays** (Route 360, which branches into routes 361, 362, and 364). To reach the latter two more remote communities (Francois and Grey River), you have to travel from town to town along the South Coast by passenger ferry.

1 Gander

The story of Gander's founding is a classic tale of putting the cart before the horse. A world-class international airport was built here in 1938—before anyone lived here! Residents, services, and accommodations came later. Even though the town has since expanded in size and raison d'être (it's now one of the main service centers in the region), much of its history and cultural character remains entwined with the transportation industry.

American Jim DeFede has written an excellent book (*The Day the World Came to Town: 9/11 in Gander, Newfoundland*) that follows Gander residents and stranded passengers through the heartwarming experiences immediately following the terrorist attacks of September 11, 2001. In stark contrast to the tumult affecting the U.S., a uniquely Newfoundland-style act of kindness was put forth through the collective effort of local service organizations, church groups, and countless individuals who opened their homes to complete strangers. This inherent generosity of spirit is what makes Newfoundland such a uniquely attractive destination.

ESSENTIALS
GETTING THERE
Outside of St. John's, Gander is the transportation hub of the province. You'll need to travel Route 1 and pass through Gander whether you've come off the ferry at Port aux Basques in the Western Region and are heading toward St. John's, or are making your way west toward Gros Morne from Argentia or St. John's. It's a straight drive from either direction, so you couldn't get lost unless you tried. You can also fly directly to Gander International Airport—car rentals are available at the airport. See www.ganderairport.com for information.

VISITOR INFORMATION
There is a Visitor Information Center in Gander on Route 1 that is open from Victoria Day weekend (May 24) to October 30 daily 8:30am to 9pm. Call ℭ 709/256-7110 or visit the community's website at www.gandercanada.com.

A limited amount of visitor information is also available at Gander International Airport. Call ℭ 709/256-6677 to reach the Information Desk.

GETTING AROUND
It'll cost C$9 (US$6.60) for a taxi to take you the 5km (3 miles) from the airport to where you'll find most of the hotels and services. If you plan on driving yourself around town, ask for a municipal road map at the information desk. There are only five main thoroughfares in Gander (plus the Trans-Canada, which borders the town), with side streets intersecting one or more of them — you'll be navigating like a pro in no time.

WHERE TO STAY
Next to St. John's, Gander has the highest density of hotel rooms in the province. In addition, you'll find a good selection of restaurants and other services for travelers. That said, you won't come across the assortment of charming historical properties that are in St. John's or some of the smaller heritage communities.

Comfort Inn   The units may be somewhat sterile, but you can always count on the chain to provide clean, comfortable guest rooms at reasonable prices. This location is no exception. It's a modern two-storey building, offering drive-up rooms and some very spacious kitchenette units. There is an elevator for easy access, and free deluxe continental breakfast is included in the rates. Pets are welcome. Plus, the Comfort Inn is home to Jungle Jim's Restaurant (see "Where to Dine").

112 Trans-Canada Highway, Gander. *©* **888/256-3535** or 709/256-353. www.ganderhotel.com. 64 units. C$89–$119 (US$65–$89) double. Extra person C$10 (US$7.33). Senior's discount of 20%. Family rates available. AE, DC, MC, V, Sears, Interac. **Amenities:** Licensed restaurant; exercise facility; guest laundry; nonsmoking rooms. *In room:* A/C, TV, dataport, coffeemaker.

Country Inn Motel & Trailer Park   If you have wheels, this is a tidy, inex-pensive motel offering unremarkable rooms in a quiet country setting. On the downside, unless you really like walking you'll be stranded about a 10-minute drive from downtown Gander. There is a 60-lot trailer park on the premises and pets are allowed.

315 Gander Bay Rd., Gander. *©* **877/956-4005** or 709/256-4005. country@roadrunner.nf.net. 9 motel units. C$47.95–$53.95 (US$35.80–$40.29) double. Cots additional C$5 (US$3.66). MC, V. 10% discount for seniors, government, and corporate. **Amenities:** Complimentary continental breakfast; nonsmoking rooms. *In room:* TV. **Campground amenities:** 60 trailer sites open May 1–Oct 31. C$11–$15 (US$8–$11). Dumping station, electrical/sewer/water hookup, shower/washroom facilities, picnic area, playground, pets allowed (on leash), BBQs on request.

The Irving West Hotel *Value*   Very reasonable rates and comfortable sur-roundings combine with a prime location to make the Irving an excellent choice for the cost-conscious traveler. You really get your money's worth: spacious rooms, free continental breakfast, outdoor heated pool, and live weekend entertainment in their Legends lounge. And, when you're ready to seek action farther afield, all you have to do is walk across the Trans-Canada to the Visitor Information Centre. They'll give you all the direction you need. Pets are allowed.

1 Caldwell St., Gander. *©* **800/563-4900** or 709/256-2406. 62 units. C$56–$69 (US$40.70–$50.63) double. AE, DC, MC, V, Interac. **Amenities:** Free continental breakfast, lounge, outdoor heated pool, nonsmoking rooms. *In room:* TV.

Hotel Gander *✦*   This is the biggest and best place in town, with a location that begs a trip to the two nearby shopping malls. Not that the malls are teeming with designer clothing, but it is a welcome panacea for desperate shopaholics.

The guest rooms are comfortably appointed, with gracious bedside sitting areas that can be either convenient work spaces or cozy conversation corners. Among their 154 rooms they have just one Jacuzzi suite, and I advise you to get it if you can. Ascending the trio of pyramid steps is like climbing to paradise. And when you're fully immersed in the pulsating streams, you'll feel like you have your own personal hydro-masseuse. Afterward, you can get dressed up in your nicest traveling clothes and head down to Alcock & Brown's, the on-site eatery. It has a split personality: simultaneously fun and formal (see "Where to Dine").

100 Trans-Canada Highway (Route 1). *©* **800/563-2988** or 709/256-3931. www.hotelgander.com. 154 units. C$85–$139 (US$63–$103.81) double. AE, DC, DISC, MC, V. **Amenities:** Indoor swimming pool, spa, fitness center, limited room service, laundry facilities, nonsmoking rooms. *In room:* A/C, TV w/ pay movies, coffeemaker, hairdryer, iron.

Central Region

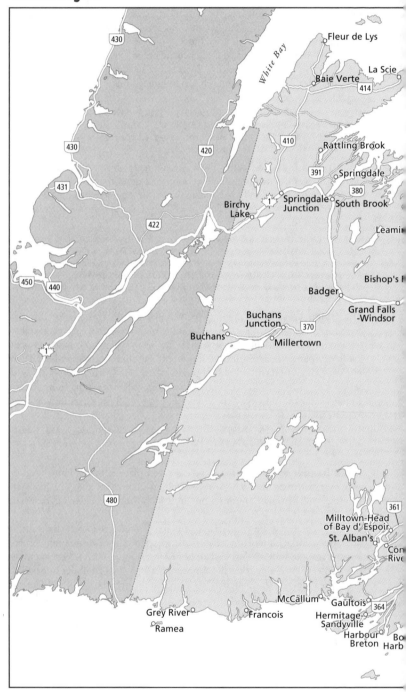

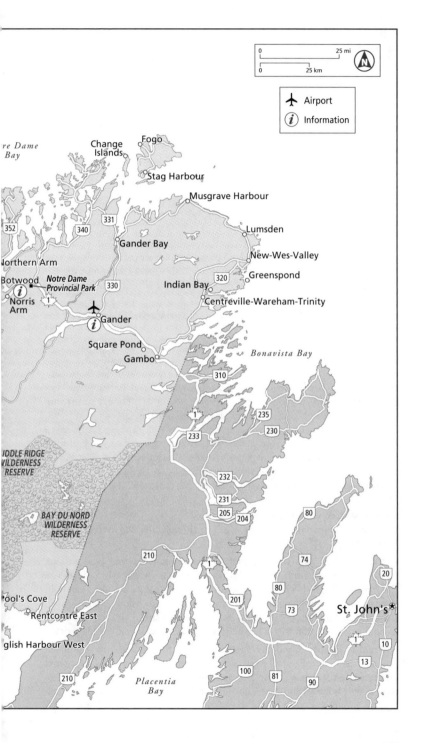

WHERE TO DINE

Alcock & Brown's Eatery ★★ CONTEMPORARY   Named after the fliers who made the first non-stop aerial crossing of the Atlantic, Alcock & Brown's is appropriately decorated with caricatures of the famous duo. The funky cartoon-character wall hangings signal an informal bonhomie that's made even more evident by the brown-paper table coverings and complimentary crayons. But wait, there's more here than meets the eye: there's also a quieter, more upscale eating area custom-made for intimate dining. The menu reflects the restaurant's dual personality, with burgers and chips sharing space with grown-up dishes like salmon in a creamy dill sauce. Make sure you leave room for dessert, especially the whimsically named Chocolate Moose. Not only is it a perfectly velvety smooth concoction, it comes with its own antlers!

Hotel Gander, 100 Trans-Canada Highway (Route 1). ✆ **800/563-2988** or 709/256-3931. www.hotel gander.com. Dinner reservations recommended. Open Sun 7am–1:30pm & 5pm–8pm, Mon–Thurs 7am–1:30pm & 5pm–9pm, Fri & Sat 7am–1:30pm & 5pm–10pm. All-day menu prices C$5–18 (US$3.66–$13.44). AE, DC, DISC, MC, V.

Giovanni's ITALIAN   A great casual place for gourmet coffees, Italian sodas, grilled panini (seven different varieties are available), pasta salads, biscotti, and other tasty treats. Giovanni's coffee shop is located in the Town Square Shopping Centre.

71 Elizabeth Dr. ✆ **709/651-3535**. Reservations not required. Open Mon–Wed 7:15am–6pm, Thurs & Fri 7:15am–10pm, Sat 9am–10pm, Sun noon–5pm. MC, V.

Jungle Jim's ★ CONTEMPORARY   Swing on in for a tasty treat—it's a jungle out there! A popular eatery with the 20-something jeans and T-shirt crowd because of its late hours, Jungle Jim's is also a great choice for casual family dining. The safari-style bamboo decor, patio lights, and stuffed jungle animals provide plenty of distractions for energetic youngsters. The extensive menu includes a variety of Mexican-style dishes (nachos, burritos, fajitas, tacos) as well as steaks, hamburgers, pasta, and salad. Try the ribs—they've been simmered in a zesty sauce to a melt-in-your-mouth tenderness and seared on the grill for a final flavor kick. You'll find Jungle Jim's on the same lot as the Comfort Inn.

112A, Trans-Canada Highway, Gander. ✆ **709/651-3444**. www.junglejims.ca. Reservations not required. Open daily from 11am–11pm. Lunches about C$8 (US$5.86); most dinners about C$12 (US$8.80). AE, DC, MC, V.

EXPLORING GANDER

Let your spirits soar in Gander. It's as easy as checking out one of these aviation attractions:

AeroSmith Inc.   You've heard of boat tours, bus tours, and even walking tours. Why not an airplane tour? It's not cheap (their Cessna 185 Floatplane charters for C$230 (US$171.78) per flight hour), but since the plane can hold three passengers you might be able to share the cost with fellow travelers. Allow a couple of hours for a decent tour—not of just the Gander area, but the entire Central region (✆ **888/999-2376** or 709/651-3222; www.aerosmithinc.com).

Festival of Flight   Gander's biggest annual brouhaha is held each year in late July or early August. It's a full week of family entertainment, much of it centered on the namesake theme. There are community breakfasts, suppers, and barbecues, as well as model airplanes, kites, and fireworks. There are even professional buskers, pub nights, craft sales, a demolition derby, and a parade. Some events are free, others charge a nominal entrance fee (✆ **877/919-9979** or 709/651-5927; www.gandercanada.com/tour/t_flight.htm).

North Atlantic Aviation Museum ✦ If you're driving from east to west on the Trans-Canada Highway, the Aviation Museum is on the left-hand side of the road as you pass through Gander. You shouldn't have any problem finding it: it's the building with an airplane tail sticking out of it! The museum is both a record of Gander's growth and a timeline for aeronautical evolution. Among the static displays and storyboards, you'll see World War II aircraft such as a Hudson Mk III, a CF-101 Voodoo Canso PBY-5A water bomber, a Tiger Moth biplane, a Beech 18S, and more. You'll even be able to step into the cockpit of a DC-38.

Route 1 (between the Tourist Chalet and the James Paton Memorial Hospital). ✆ **709/256-2923.** http://naam1.tripod.com. Open July–Aug daily 9am–9pm, the rest of the year Mon–Fri 9am–5pm. Admission C$3 (US$2.20) adults, C$2 (US$1.46) seniors and youth ages 6–17; free for children under 6.

2 Grand Falls–Windsor

There's always been an unofficial rivalry between Gander and Grand Falls–Windsor. Both communities are service centers, but they have very different personalities. Grand Falls–Windsor has fewer services for travelers, but it has a longer, stronger history as evidenced by its numerous heritage properties.

Grand Falls–Windsor is the home of Canadian actor Gordon Pinsent, who starred with Kevin Spacey in *The Shipping News.* But that's not all the town has to brag about. *Chatelaine* magazine, a popular Canadian publication, recently named Grand Falls–Windsor one of the top places to live in North America because of its community spirit, natural beauty, and friendly residents.

ESSENTIALS
GETTING THERE
Grand Falls–Windsor is the approximate halfway point between St. John's and Port aux Basques. To be exact, it's 428km (265 miles) west of St. John's, 476km (295 miles) east of the ferry terminal at Port Aux Basques, and just 91km (56 miles) west of Gander International Airport. To find it, all you have to do is follow the Trans-Canada Highway, which actually goes right through the center of town.

VISITOR INFORMATION
There's a Visitor Information Centre on Route 1 just west of Grand Falls–Windsor that is open May 1 to October 15, daily 9am to 9pm. Call ✆ **888/491-9453** or **709/489-6332,** or see www.grandfallswindsor.com for more information.

WHERE TO STAY & DINE
Carriage House Inn ✦ All it needs are a few climbing vines and you'd swear it was straight from a Norman Rockwell painting. Even without the encircling greenery, Carriage House Inn is pretty as a picture. The covered verandah, gabled roof, and 2.4-ha (6-acre) wooded property give it the presence of a cozy country retreat. Which is exactly what it is. You'll want to relax in the porch swing with a book from the library, or soak in the sun on the spacious patio deck. Inside, you can't go wrong with any of the nine nicely furnished guest rooms with varying bed sizes and amenities—all are impressively clean, with freshly scented linens and private baths. The rooms aren't air-conditioned, but they do have ceiling fans to keep you cool on a sultry evening.

Take Exit 20 off Route 1 to 181 Grenfell Heights, Grand Falls–Windsor. ✆ **800/563-7133** or 709/489-7185. www.carriagehouseinn.ca. 9 units. C$69–$119 (US$50.63–$89). V. **Amenities:** Complimentary breakfast; nonsmoking rooms. *In room:* TV, hairdryer, no phone.

Mount Peyton Hotel   It's not the only game in town, but it is the largest. The Mount Peyton is a Central Newfoundland institution that gives new meaning to "full service." Looking for a standard hotel, motel, or housekeeping unit? They have all that. In the mood for steak? They can fill that order too. You'd rather traditional home-style cooking? Once again, the Mount Peyton has what you're looking for, and more. Everything, that is, except the opulence of the Royal York. But then, do you really want to pay C$300/night for a place to sleep?

Trans-Canada Highway (Route 1) to 214 Lincoln Rd., Grand Falls–Windsor. ℭ 800/563-4894 or 709/489-2251. www.mountpeyton.com. 102 hotel units, 32 motel units, and 16 housekeeping units. Hotel and housekeeping units operate year-round, motel Apr–Oct. C$78–$118 (US$58.26–$88.14) double. MC, V. **Amenities:** Dining room, steakhouse, lounge; laundry/valet service; nonsmoking rooms. *In room:* A/C, TV w/movies and PlayStation™, coffeemaker, hairdryer, iron.

Sanger Memorial RV Park   Some people call it camping, but purists will scoff as they turn over in their sleeping bags. Why? Because it's a campground where no tents are allowed, only trailers. Sanger Memorial has a good range of amenities, including private showers and washrooms, accessible facilities, and 24-hour security. The camping lots are large and full-service, with 15- to 50-amp hookups. It's just minutes from downtown Grand Falls–Windsor.

Trans-Canada Highway (Rte. 1) Exit 20 to Scott Ave., Grand Falls–Windsor. ℭ 709/489-8780 and 709/489-7350 for off-season bookings. fred.parsons@nf.sympatico.ca. 38 sites. Open June 15–Sept 6. C$18.50 (US$13.81). Weekly rates available. MC, V.

EXPLORING GRAND FALLS–WINDSOR

There are a number of activities and events to please visitors to the Grand Falls–Windsor area: everything from hiking and fishing to snowmobiling and cross-country skiing. For information about any of the events call ℭ **709/489-0450.**

A.N.D. Company's Summer Theatre Festival   Bravo! Amateur theater so good, *you'll* be picturing the actors' names in lights on Broadway. Running from late June to the end of August, the Summer Theatre Festival features a number of enthusiastic local performers. Don't let their youthful appearance fool you: their stage presence has a maturity far beyond their years. There are both evening and daytime performances at various venues throughout Grand Falls–Windsor. The daytime shows are considerably cheaper than the evening dinner shows and offer an economical option to see a great performance for less cash.

ℭ **709/489-6560.** www.andco.nf.ca. Reservations definitely recommended. Tickets from C$10 (US$7.33) for adults and C$8 (US$5.86) for students and seniors, to C$30 (US$22) for adults and C$19.50 (US$14.56) for youths (18 and under) for the dinner theater performances.

Exploits Valley Salmon Festival   During this 5-day event, the resident population triples to approximately 60,000 (keep this in mind when booking accommodations). The festival lineup includes a salmon dinner, live music, a craft fair, and lots of family fun. The highlight of the festival is the Splash Concert, which always features well-known Canadian artists of contemporary and traditional music. Tickets for the concert are usually about C$35 (US$26.14) and are available in advance or at the gate. Call ℭ **709/489-0450** or see www.salmonfestival.com for more information.

Salmonid Interpretation Centre   Look out—there goes a flying fish! Okay, they're not really flying—but they are jumping from rung to rung on the "salmon ladder" as they try to make their way upstream to their spawning grounds. You won't want to miss this extraordinary facility, located on the Exploits River just 4km (2.5 miles) from downtown Grand Falls–Windsor.

Highlights are the underwater viewing windows, where you can see salmon in their natural habitat, and the live exhibits of brook trout, sticklebacks, and eels. The center is fully wheelchair accessible.

Cross the bridge over the Exploits River to reach the Salmonid Interpretation Centre. (C) 709/489-7350. Open mid-Jun–mid-Sept daily 8am–dusk. Seasonal pass: C$5 (US$3.66) adults, C$3.50 (US$2.61) youth 16 years and under, free for children 5 and under. Daily pass: C$3.50 (US$2.61) adults, C$2 (US$1.46) youth.

3 The Kittiwake Coast

Many communities along the northern coast were isolated until as recently as the 1960s, when causeways were constructed between the Twillingate, Change, Chapel, and New World islands to the mainland.

The best-known community along the north coast is **Twillingate,** a picturesque haven for viewing the many icebergs that float into Notre Dame Bay. It has about 5,000 residents and numerous services, including a regional hospital.

En route to Twillingate you'll come to the village of **Musgrave Harbour** and the coastal stretch to **Lumsden,** where you'll find Newfoundland's best beach. A few kilometers farther along, you'll arrive in **Newtown.** It's known as the "Venice of Newfoundland" because it's built on a series of tiny islands joined by bridges.

Those interested in mining will find a gem of an attraction at the **Baie Verte Peninsula Miner's Museum.** And if you're intrigued by native history, be sure to check out the **Dorset Soapstone Quarry** at **Fleur de Lys.** Both these attractions are located north of Route 1 on Route 410.

ESSENTIALS
GETTING THERE
Several routes run north of the Trans-Canada Highway (Route 1) to the communities along Notre Dame Bay. If you leave the Trans-Canada at Gambo for Route 320, you're in for a leisurely coastal drive that'll take you past Newtown and the Barbour Living Heritage Village, not to mention the beach at Lumsden and other assorted outport settlements. If you continue along Route 320, it becomes Route 330 at Cape Freels. Keep going until you reach the intersection at Gander Bay, and you'll have a choice between returning to Gander along Route 330 or continuing north to Twillingate, Fogo Island, and Change Island. On the return trip, take Route 340 back to the Trans-Canada (stopping to see the Boyd's Cove Interpretation Centre along the way). Route 410 takes you to the Baie Verte Peninsula on the northwestern tip of the Central Region. The Baie Verte Peninsula is covered later in this chapter.

VISITOR INFORMATION
Information about the entire Central Region can be obtained from the Central Newfoundland Tourism Association (call (C) **888/491-9453** or see www.central newfoundland.com). The Kittiwake Coast Tourism Association is another useful resource that can provide information about the northeastern part of the Central Region, including the Notre Dame Bay area. Call (C) **709/256-5070** or visit their website at www.kittiwakecoast.com.

For information specific to the Twillingate area, contact the Regional Visitor Centre in Newville on Route 340 (call (C) **709/628-7454** or see www.twill ingate.com). This location is open mid-May through mid-October, daily 9am to 9pm.

TWILLINGATE, STAR OF THE NORTH COAST ☆☆

During the 1800s, Twillingate was the most active and prosperous seaport on the North Coast. Even today, you'll find a broader range of services here than in many of its neighboring communities.

If you're keen on seeing the largest icebergs, the best time to come is late spring, early summer. If you're most interested in whales, the summer months provide your best chances. So if you come in late June or early July, you just may catch a glimpse of both these natural wonders floating about in Notre Dame Bay.

Twillingate is an Anglicized version of the community's original French name, "Toulinguet," which is also the name of a group of islands off the French coast near Brest. The French fishermen evidently saw a similarity between their home-land and this lovely Newfoundland community.

Fun Fact **Nightingale of the North**

Born in Twillingate in 1867, Georgina Ann Stirling was the daughter of Ann Peyton and Twillingate's first doctor, William Stirling. The clarity of her powerful soprano voice was apparent at a young age and her wealthy father sent her first to Toronto and later to Paris to train as an opera singer. Under the stage name Marie Toulinguet, she became one of the most famous singers of her time, performing in Italy, Washington, and New York. Tragedy struck at the peak of her career in the form of a serious throat ailment, thus ending her operatic dreams. She returned to Twillingate, where she lived until she died of cancer in 1935. A 2-m (6 ft.) stone monument near St. Peter's Church marks her burial spot.

WHERE TO STAY & DINE

BlueWater Lodge & Retreat ☆☆ *Finds*   It's like finding the pot of gold at the end of a rainbow. This true retreat location, owned and operated by Win-nifred and Gary Sargent, pays homage to four-season outdoor enjoyment. In winter, spring, summer, or fall, BlueWater Lodge can arrange activities for it all—like canoeing and scuba diving, kayaking and hiking, or snowshoeing and snowmobiling.

After a busy day of roaming, retire to the coziness of the lodge's dining room for a satisfyingly simple feast made from fresh produce and seasonal berries (included with your room rate). Toast your day with a glass of fine wine while watching the crimson farewell of a fading sun magnified in the still waters of the nearby lake. Before turning in for the night, sit by the magnificent stone hearth in the common area, where you'll also find a piano in case you're in the mood for a sing-along. Finally, snuggle into a fluffy duvet for the most stress-free sleep you'll ever have. *Tip:* This is not a family vacation destination; BlueWater caters to adult visitors. *Note:* BlueWater Lodge is about an hour's drive from Twill-ingate; it's 3km (2 miles) east of the Notre Dame Junction on the Trans-Canada Highway.

Route 1, 3km (nearly 2 miles) east of the Route 340 Notre Dame Junction. ☎ **709/424-4600**. www. relax-at-bluewater.ca. 10 units. C$125 (US$92) double. AE, MC, V. **Amenities:** Dining room, lounge. *In room:* Ensuite bath.

Cabins by the Sea *(Kids)*   The price is definitely right for these spacious, taste-fully decorated, 2-bedroom family getaways. The location is fantastic, with pic-nic tables outside each cabin and recreational facilities just a short walk away. By foot, you're 2 minutes from the Lions Club Playground, and 3 minutes from the indoor swimming pool in the Twillingate Recreation Centre. One of the cabins is wheelchair accessible. No pets allowed. *Warning:* Watch children closely, you're just 30m (100 ft.) from the ocean.

11 Hugh Lane, Twillingate. (*C*) **709/884-2158**. www.cabinsbythesea.com. 7 units. C$65–$70 (US$48–$51) per unit. AE, MC, V. **Amenities:** Housekeeping units; BBQs available on request. *In room:* TV.

Dildo Run Provincial Park Campground   The amenities are typical of all provincial parks throughout Newfoundland & Labrador: each of the 55 camp-sites comes with picnic tables and fire pits. Drinking-water taps are conveniently located throughout the park, as are some less-than-fresh pit toilets. *Tip:* Ask for a campsite that's away from a pit toilet. You don't want to be caught in a downdraft.

Facilities aside, it's the location that gives every provincial park its character. In this instance, the lovely seacoast setting offers the opportunity to see growlers and "bergy bits" (iceberg chunks that might float ashore), as well as whales. You can also see quite a few of the 365 islands in Dildo Run from the lookout point. This is a wonderful location for kayaking and canoeing.

Route 340, Virgin Arm. (*C*) **800/563-6353** or 709/629-3350. www.gov.nf.ca/parks&reserves. Open May 31–Sept 16. 55 sites. Call for rates. MC, V. **Amenities:** Day-use facilities; pit privies; showers, drinking water (taps); dumping station; laundry facilities; picnic sites.

Toulinguet Inn Bed & Breakfast   Location! Location! Location! Conve-niently situated in the center of Twillingate, Toulinguet Inn B&B is a short dis-tance from a coin laundry, bank, restaurants, walking trails, and boat tours. All this, plus an ocean view. Inside this traditional 1920s Newfoundland home you'll find a kitchen replete with antique collectibles; my personal favorite is an old-fashioned cast-iron stove. There are two spacious queen units and one smaller room with twin beds; all three have private bathrooms.

Toulinguet's welcoming character also deserves attention. From the minute you pull into the driveway, it's like you're a long-lost friend or favorite cousin. You feel it in the radiant greeting at check-in, you smell it in the just-washed sheets upon the bed, and you taste it with every bite of your homemade break-fast muffin. Smoking is permitted outside, on the porch, in the garden, or on the second-storey balcony. This is a popular location, so be sure to book ahead as far as possible.

56 Main St., Twillingate. (*C*) **877-684-2080**. www.toulinguetinn.ca. Open May 1–Sept 30. 3 units. C$65 (US$48) double. **Amenities:** Continental-plus breakfast; laundry facilities for small fee; nonsmoking rooms. *In room:* Private bath/shower.

EXPLORING TWILLINGATE & NOTRE DAME BAY

On the eastern side of the North Coast, you'll find a small peninsula that is home to a cluster of tiny outports along Route 330 (from Route 320). If you have the time to explore, you'll find some interesting pursuits along the way.

Barbour Living Heritage Village *(★)* *(Finds)*   Perched along the weathered shore of Newtown (listed as New-Wes-Valley on the map) is a recreated circa-1900 fishing village. The sights and sounds as well as the look and feel of the Barbour Living Heritage Village proclaim its historical authenticity. The buildings represent the prosperous mercantile premises owned by the Barbour family, which played an important role in the local sealing industry. In addition to the Barbour family buildings, the Village includes a Methodist schoolhouse, craft shop, restaurant, visitor information center, sealing interpretation center, theater, art gallery, stage with fish flakes, liver factory, and other smaller buildings.

Live theatrical performances are held during July and August. The actors' accents tend to be exaggerated Newfoundland, so you may have some problem understanding the dialogue. Dinner, which approximates a traditional potluck meal, is a serve-yourself affair featuring such items as cod au gratin, fish-n-brews, beet salad, mustard salad, potato salad, ham, turkey, caramel tart, partridgeberry pie, and Jell-O. The theater, restaurant, and craft shop are wheelchair accessible.

Route 330 to Newtown. © 709/536-3220. Open June 15–Oct 15 daily 10am–6pm. C$5 (US$3.66) adults, $4 (US$2.93) seniors 65 years+, C$3 (US$2.20) ages 5–18; free for children under 5, C$12 (US$8.80) family rate. Theater performances are an additional C$7.50 (US$5.50) adults, C$7 (US$5.13) seniors 65 years+, C$3 (US$2.20) ages 5–18, free for children under 5, C$18 (US$13.44) family rate.

Boyd's Cove Beothuk Interpretation Centre   Little is known about these reclusive island inhabitants, because—unlike other native groups—they avoided Europeans. Boyd's Cove has particular significance because it offers more evidence about their way of life than any other site on the island. Among the items recovered at the archaeological dig are iron nails that have been refashioned into arrowheads and other tools. The nails weren't the result of trade, but of Beothuks scavenging through the debris left behind by seasonal European fishers. The life of these now-extinct people (the last known Beothuk died in 1829) is depicted in the construction and contents of the wigwam-shaped Interpretation Centre, as well as along the 1½km (less than 1 mile) groomed trail leading you past the excavation site of several Beothuk houses that date between 1650 and 1720.

Route 340 to Boyd's Cove. © 709/656-3114. www.heritage.nf.ca/aboriginal/beo_boydscove.html. Open June 1–Thanksgiving daily 10am–5:30pm. C$2.50 (US$1.83) age 13 and up; free for children 12 and under.

Fishermen's Museum   A short distance past Newtown is Musgrave Harbour and its Fishermen's Museum. You'll find this location especially interesting if you've been to Port Union (see chapter 5's "Discovery Trail" section). This two-storey, oversized fishing shed was built in 1910 by Sir William Coaker, founder of the Fishermen's Protective Union. The Fishermen's Museum has an interesting collection of artifacts related to the fishery (like a fish-splitting table and weighing machine). Outside, you'll see a fascinating mural depicting the way fishing traditions have progressed from past to present.

Route 330 to Marine Dr., Musgrave Harbour. © 709/655-2119. Open late June–Sept 2 daily 11am–7 pm.

Long Point Lighthouse   Another must-see in the Twillingate area is one of the last manned lighthouses in the province—the Long Point Lighthouse, built in 1876. Long Point is situated just north of town on Route 340. The lighthouse is no longer open to the public, but is still worth a look because of its dramatic setting, especially if you arrive around sunset when its red-and-white stripes take on new, softer shades. Across the parking lot from the lighthouse you'll find the **Long Point Interpretation Centre,** home to an exhibit explaining the connection between the area's natural and human history, as well as a small gift shop and tea room.

Route 340, north of Twillingate. © 709/884-5755 or 709/884-2247. Open mid-May–mid-Oct daily 9am–9pm.

OUTDOOR PURSUITS & EVENTS

The Fish, Fun & Folk Festival 🕹   Folk-music enthusiasts will want to mark their calendars for the last full weekend in July, when Twillingate is home to one of the largest and best established folk festivals in the province. Activities include a parade, beach bonfire, helicopter rides, craft sale, and of course lots of great music and fellowship. Unlike many other folk festivals, this one's musical entertainment takes place indoors—meaning it won't be affected by inclement weather. Prices vary per activity. Call 📞 **709/884-2678** or visit www.fishfun folkfestival.com for more information.

Red Indian Adventures 🕹   Here you'll find adventure tourism at its finest, combining first-class guides and dazzling scenery in an unforgettable epic journey. Experience the thrill of whitewater rafting as you battle the surging waters of the Exploits River, surfing past black bear and moose in their natural habitat. Plus, it's full family fun—the ultimate antidote for teenage ennui. Sea kayaking and canoeing options are also available. *Note:* The company is based out of Grand Falls–Windsor, so book your Twillingate adventure in advance.

Tours take place at various locations throughout the Exploits Valley. 📞 **709/486-0892**. www.redindian adventures.com. Kayaking: C$95 (US$70) per person for day tours and C$235 (US$175.44) per person for overnight tours. Rafting & canoeing: C$75 (US$55) for day tours and C$195 (US$144) for overnight tours. Prices include tax.

Twillingate Island Boat Tours   Set sail with Cecil Stockley, the self-appointed "Iceberg Man of Twillingate." Stockley has been chasing bergs for 20 years and says he has a sixth sense that enables him to track the sometimes-elusive sea castles. This is a smaller vessel than you'll find used by the competition, but "Cec" takes a more educational approach to his tours, making this the best choice for anyone who wants an in-depth interpretation of what they are seeing. The 2-hour boat tours run three times daily.

50A Main St., Twillingate. 📞 **800/611-2374** or 709/884-2242. www.icebergtours.ca. C$30 (US$22) per adult, C$15 (US$11) for children 15 and under. MC, V. Departures May 1–Sept 30 daily 9:30am, 1pm, and 4pm.

4 The Baie Verte Peninsula

It doesn't have an abundance of services or attractions, but what it does have is worth seeing—especially the **Baie Verte Miner's Museum,** located in Baie Verte, and the **Dorset Soapstone Quarry,** located 28km (17 miles) up the road in Fleur de Lys. Because it's a 2-hour trip from Grand Falls–Windsor to Baie Verte, you should plan to stay the night in the area so you can take in the two main attractions as well as spend a few hours cruising along the coast.

ESSENTIALS
GETTING THERE

Take Route 1 to Route 410 to arrive on the **Baie Verte Peninsula** and the community of Baie Verte. A few kilometers farther and you reach the end of Route 410, where you'll find Fleur de Lys. This tiny hamlet is approximately 89km (55 miles) north of the Trans-Canada Highway (Route 1) and about 2½ hours from Corner Brook.

VISITOR INFORMATION

There is a regional Visitor Information Centre in Baie Verte (📞 **709/532-8090**) right on Route 410 at the junction of Route 412 as you enter town. This is the same building that houses the Miner's Museum. It is open daily during July and August, from 9am to 9pm.

Conne River Mi'kmaq Reserve

For an experience unlike any other on the island, visit the Miawpukek Band in Conne River—180km (112.5 miles) from Grand Falls–Windsor on Route 360. They are a proud, independent, visionary people, reveling in their native heritage while simultaneously embracing modern society. You may be surprised—even disappointed—by the bungalows, retail stores, cars, trucks, and ATVs. Don't be. Underlying these 21st-century appendages is a deeply rooted respect for the land and each other. You see it in the design of their native crafts, and you hear it in the tales of their unique customs (like planting trees in lieu of headstones as a way to remember a lost loved one). Time your visit to coincide with the annual **Powwow**, a 4-day event usually held early in July. It combines sacred ritual with tribal dance as well as communal feasting and elder wisdom. Non-natives are allowed to participate in most ceremonies. Free camping and trailer sites are available on the Powwow site on a first-come, first-served basis. There is no entry fee to the Powwow, but participants are asked to contribute to the daily potluck feasts. For more information, visit Conne River online at www.miawpukek.nf.ca.

WHERE TO STAY

Bailey's Dorset Country Inn   Located in the center of Baie Verte, this newly renovated inn has 8 rooms, each with a private bath, and a delightfully homespun atmosphere. Your host, Pearl Bailey, will do everything she can to make you feel comfortable—so you'd better not come here if you don't like being pampered. The common area lounge has a TV. No pets allowed.

Route 410, Baie Verte. ✆ **709/532-8075**. 8 units. C$58–$72 (US$43.31–$52.46) double. AE, MC, V. **Amenities:** Full complimentary breakfast; coin-operated laundry facilities; nonsmoking rooms. *In room:* TV.

EXPLORING THE BAIE VERTE PENINSULA

Baie Verte Miner's Museum ⊛   You won't have to dig too deep to find this goldmine of information about the region's rich mining heritage. The building is immediately evident because of its distinctive double A-frame shape. Inside, there's a simulated mining tunnel leading to the museum, which contains an interesting collection of artifacts that date back to the first European mine built here in 1860. Among the things you'll see outside the museum is the first train in the province, once used for the now-defunct Terra Nova mine.

Route 410 to Baie Verte. ✆ **709/532-8090**. Open June 15–Aug 31 daily 9am–8pm. Museum: C$2 (US$1.46) adults and C$1 (US.73¢) children 6–17.

Dorset Soapstone Quarry ⊛   At the northernmost tip of the northernmost community on the Baie Verte Peninsula, you'll find a little-known Provincial and National Historic Site. But don't mistake its obscurity as a measure of its worth: the Dorset Soapstone Quarry is an incomparable link to the people who lived here more than 2 millennia ago. Inside the Interpretation Centre you'll see examples of the soft-stone cooking pots used by the Dorset natives. Then, after a brief journey along a friendly walking trail flanked by waving wildflowers, you can see the quarry site where the Middle Dorset people carved out pots and lamps. Here you'll see archaeologists at work as they continue to uncover artifacts. *Note:* Look, but don't touch. Rather than accidentally destroy archaeological evidence, watch from the designated viewing platform.

There are several hiking trails around the site, ranging from easy to difficult. It will take about 2 hours to tour the quarry site and an additional 2 hours to hike one of the four trails. The Interpretation Centre/Museum doubles as a community computer center, where you can check your e-mail.

Route 410. © 709/253-2126. http://ezc.ca/webs/ez_web.asp?user=soapstone. Open mid-May–mid-Oct daily 6am–8pm. Computer hourly rates C$2 (US$1.46).

5 The South Coast

The South Coast of the Central Region—also known as the **"Coast of Bays"**—is unknown to most visitors because of its inaccessibility. Route 360 will take you into the area, but you have to take a small ferry if you want to visit many of the tiny outport communities, as they are not accessible by road. It's isolated, primitive, beautiful, and totally unspoiled by commerce and tourism.

ESSENTIALS
GETTING THERE
You can reach selected communities along the South Coast only via Route 360, which runs south of the Trans-Canada Highway (Route 1) just east of Bishop's Falls. As you get closer to the South Coast, Route 360 branches out into routes 361, 362, and 364.

 Cruising the South Coast

To reach the most isolated communities along the South Coast, you'll need to drive 2½ hours along Route 360 to the town of **Hermitage**. And that's just the beginning. You'll have to park your car in this colorful hamlet to board the passenger-only ferry to **McCallum**. Every second Tuesday and every Thursday, the *MV Marine Voyager* departs Hermitage at 2:30pm for the 1½-hour ride to McCallum—a community married to land and sea by both livelihood and geography. You'll have half an hour in this picturesque place, which is barely enough time to capture it on film. But never mind, you'll have a 75-minute stopover on your return trip. At 4:30pm you're underway again, this time to **Francois** (www.francoisnf.com). It's a breathtakingly rugged village (population: 120) tucked into the shadow of 207-m-high (680-ft.) hills. There are no cars in Francois: the main street is an extra-wide wooden boardwalk. Houses are built in ascending order, with the most congested area around the waterfront and increasingly fewer dwellings as you move uphill. You'll have to spend the night here, as the ferry doesn't move down the line until 7:30 the next morning. Then you're off on a 2-hour sail to **Grey River** (www.bbsict.com/greyriv.html), another fishing village of fewer than 150 residents. You won't have any problem getting to meet the locals, as many of them have a habit of coming to greet the boat. From Grey River, you'll have to decide whether to turn back or continue on to Ramea and Burgeo. You should probably turn back, since you can access both those communities via car and passenger ferry from Burgeo in Western Newfoundland. For complete information on ferry schedules and prices, go to www.gov.nf.ca/ferryservices/schedules.stm.

VISITOR INFORMATION

Visitor information can be obtained by calling ✆ **800/205-0799** or 709/538-3552. The Coast of Bays Corporation has an informative website at www.coastofbays.nf.ca that can help with your planning.

GETTING AROUND

If you look at the map, you'll notice that the ferry hops from bay to bay along the South Coast. The ferry provides year-round passenger service, although the schedules change with the seasons. The 1½-to-2-hour ride between communities costs about C$3.50 (US$2.58) for adults and C$1.75 (US$1.30) for seniors, children, and students. Call ✆ **709/551-1446** or see www.gov.nf.ca/ferryservices/schedules.stm for more information. Unfortunately, the lack of car-rental agencies means you won't be able to drop your rental at one end of the ferry route and rent another on the other end. So, if you decide to explore these hidden gems, you'll have to return via the same route to retrieve your car.

HARBOUR BRETON

Harbour Breton is one of the largest and oldest communities along the South Coast. It has a hospital, a bank, and a beautiful beach at Deadman's Cove, where on a clear day you can see the French islands of St. Pierre and Miquelon in the distance. Information can be obtained by calling ✆ **709/885-2354** or by visiting the community's website at www.townofharbourbreton.nf.ca.

WHERE TO STAY & DINE

Southern Port Hotel ⚐   This facility is so flawlessly organized and charmingly operated, you'll think you've walked into a fairy tale. And in a way, you have. The on-site bar and grill is named for a trio of real-life star-crossed lovers with a woeful story of double-cross and deceit. The hotel is a new, single-storey, fully accessible facility overlooking the town. Each of the clean, comfortable, and spacious guest rooms comes with its own private bathroom.

Route 360, Harbour Breton. ✆ **709-885-2283**. www.southernporthotel.com. 15 units. C$69–$79 (US$50.63–$57.96) double. Additional person C$5 (US$3.66), cots C$7 (US$5.13). MC, V. **Amenities:** Dining room/restaurant; lounge; limited room service; laundry service. *In room:* TV, dataport.

WHAT TO SEE & DO

Sunny Cottage Heritage Centre   Harbour Breton is home to a wonderful 1907 Queen Anne–style home that houses displays on fishing, resettlement, and the home's original merchant residents. Guides dressed in period costumes will take you on a guided tour; in the kitchen, you'll be able to sample freshly made traditional delicacies. The harborfront setting and lovely gardens add to the charm of this attraction. Sunny Cottage currently serves as the area's tourist information center.

Route 360 to Harbour Breton. ✆ **709/885-2425**. http://muddy-hole.tripod.com. Open 9am–5pm Mon–Fri & 1pm–5pm Sat–Sun from late May–early Sept.

Tradition by the Sea Festival   In mid-July, Harbour Breton hosts a celebration of traditional life along the South Coast. The annual festival begins with a beach party at Deadman's Cove and continues with a variety of activities—such as dory races—that demonstrate the distinct culture of this area. Other highlights include traditional music, dancing, and food, games of chance, cotton candy, and festivities for the kids. Prices vary per activity.

Activities staged at various locations throughout Harbour Breton. ✆ **709/885-2354**. www.harbourbreton.com/tbts.htm.

7

The Western Region

If you're traveling in an east–west direction across the island, the Western Region is the grand finale to a wondrous adventure. If, however, this is your entry point to Newfoundland, it's an enticing prelude to an unforgettable vacation. Either way, it's a memory in the making.

Just over 200km (125 miles) west of Grand Falls–Windsor is **Deer Lake.** Aside from being the first noteworthy community you'll find as you enter the Western Region, it's also the point of decision. You either leave the Trans-Canada to follow Route 430 along the **Great Northern Peninsula,** or you stay on the Trans-Canada and head south toward **Corner Brook** and the Marine Atlantic ferry terminal at **Channel–Port aux Basques.** Before you head in either direction, delight the kids with a visit to the **Newfoundland Insectarium & Butterfly Pavilion,** the only facility of its type east of Montreal.

North of Deer Lake is **Gros Morne National Park,** a UNESCO World Heritage Site and the undisputed highlight of the Western Region (Gros Morne is covered in detail in chapter 8). In addition to picturesque fjords you'll see rock-hard evidence of continental drift, and be taken on an asphalt roller-coaster ride through the **Long Range Mountains.**

It's almost 400km (200 miles) from Gros Morne to the northern end of the Great Northern Peninsula, but it's well worth the journey. This is where you'll find **Port au Choix National Historic Site,** the known home of four distinct ancient cultures, and **L'Anse aux Meadows,** where Vikings settled more than 1,000 years ago.

Along the way, you're likely to see moose—lots of moose. This part of the Western Region is home to the largest percentage of the province's plentiful and impressively racked creatures. It's also a good place to see icebergs if you're visiting later in the summer. The Northern Peninsula is usually the last place on the island where bergs are spotted, occasionally as late as August.

About three-quarters of the way up the Northern Peninsula is where you'll find **St. Barbe**—the launch point for a visit to Labrador. (Labrador is covered in detail in chapter 9.)

If at Deer Lake you decide to continue south along the Trans-Canada Highway, you'll follow a mostly straight two-lane highway entwined with slumbering rivers and pastoral prettiness. You'll see places where the rising sun lends a morning glow to misty mountains and feel nature's gale-force power at the aptly named **Wreckhouse.** You'll encounter champion salmon fishing on the world-renowned **Humber River,** the best downhill skiing east of the Rockies at **Marble Mountain,** and the last francophone stronghold on the island on the **Port au Port Peninsula.** You'll see denuded trees and mountain-top ponds, thrilling theater, and international-class triathlon.

Allow at least a week if you want to enjoy everything between the northernmost tip of the Great Northern Peninsula and the southwesterly coastal communities of the Cabot Strait.

1 Exploring the Great Northern Peninsula

The Bonne Bay entrance to the Great Northern Peninsula is a dazzling panorama of surreal extremes: you'll scale near-perpendicular mountain heights through some of the tallest trees in the province, following a twining blacktop on what seems a perpetual climb, until a sudden final crest reverses your direction into a similarly stunning descent. All the while, your vehicle is regularly overtaken by tractor trailers, logging trucks, and speeding grannies who are obviously immune to the natural wonder.

It calms down considerably after that. As is typical elsewhere in the province, the highway follows traditional coastal settlement patterns. Virtually all settlement in the province is along the coast, a reflection of the importance of the fishery and ocean access to early settlers. From Cow Head north, the topography is mostly flat, with stands of tuckamore (trees whose growth has been stunted by wind and sea) to the right and the Atlantic Ocean to the left. Here and there you'll encounter stretches of barrens and bog, much like the scenery along the Burin Peninsula. *Warning:* The farther north you go along Route 430, the more isolated it becomes.

Moose Can Be Hazardous to Your Health

As you drive along the highway, you'll see moose silhouettes and bright-yellow signs depicting a crunched car and a moose. There's a good reason. However majestic these 450-kg (1,000-lb.) animals are to look at, they are a dangerous and mobile road hazard. More than 500 moose–vehicle accidents occur every year in the province, causing more than $1 million in damages as well as serious injury and even death.

You'd think it would be easy to spot and avoid these massive animals, but they are masters of camouflage—especially in low light. Their mottled brown coat blends so well into the foliage that you may not see one standing in the brush to the side of the road until it walks into your path.

How to Avoid an Accident:

- Moose are nocturnal. Reduce your speed, or avoid driving altogether, in the early morning and at night.
- Be extra cautious when you see moose warning signs. They signal high-risk areas.
- Scan the highway as far ahead as possible, paying particular attention to areas where trees and shrubbery grow close to the road. Use high beams whenever possible.
- If you see a moose on the highway, pull over and turn off your lights. Like deer, moose are transfixed by light. They have also been known to charge at lights, rather than run away.

PORT AU CHOIX 🍁

As the approximate halfway point between Deer Lake and St. Anthony, Port au Choix is a convenient stopover on the Great Northern Peninsula. It's one of the larger communities en route, with the highest number of services/facilities (for example, bank, post office, restaurants). You can either stop at Port au Choix

Western Region

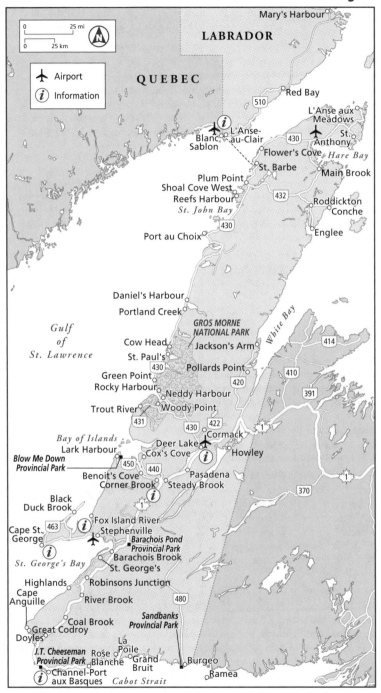

LABRADOR

QUEBEC

Mary's Harbour

Red Bay

510

L'Anse aux Meadows

St. Anthony

430

Blanc-Sablon

L'Anse-au-Clair

Flower's Cove

Hare Bay

St. Barbe

Main Brook

Plum Point

Shoal Cove West

Reefs Harbour

432

St. John Bay

Roddickton

Conche

430

Port au Choix

Englee

Daniel's Harbour

Portland Creek

GROS MORNE NATIONAL PARK

White Bay

Gulf of St. Lawrence

Cow Head

Jackson's Arm

414

St. Paul's

430

Green Point

Pollards Point

420

Rocky Harbour

Neddy Harbour

410

391

Trout River

Woody Point

431

430

422

Cormack

1

Bay of Islands

Lark Harbour

Deer Lake

Cox's Cove

Howley

Blow Me Down Provincial Park

450

440

Benoit's Cove

Pasadena

Corner Brook

Steady Brook

370

1

Black Duck Brook

463

Fox Island River

Cape St. George

Stephenville

Barachois Pond Provincial Park

1

St. George's Bay

Barachois Brook

St. George's

Highlands

Robinsons Junction

Cape Anguille

River Brook

480

Coal Brook

Sandbanks Provincial Park

Great Codroy

Doyles

J.T. Cheeseman Provincial Park

La Poile

Rose Blanche

Grand Bruit

Burgeo

Channel-Port aux Basques

Ramea

Cabot Strait

Scale: 0 — 25 mi / 0 — 25 km

✈ Airport

ⓘ Information

145

for lunch before continuing up the coast, or stay overnight to visit the Point Riche Lighthouse and the site where archaeologists are uncovering evidence of ancient native cultures.

ESSENTIALS
GETTING THERE
Port au Choix is about 13km (8 miles) off of Route 430, and 230km (143 miles) north of Deer Lake. Both the main highway and the paved access road are in good condition, but you won't find a lot of services along the way—so be sure to tank up and have a few snacks with you before heading out. It's a 2½-hour drive from Port au Choix to St. Anthony.

VISITOR INFORMATION
There is a Parks Canada Visitor Center at the Port au Choix National Historic Site, located a few kilometers from town. The center is open during the shoulder seasons of June 1 to June 14 and September 3 to October 14, daily from 9am until 5pm. During the busy season of June 15 to September 2 there are longer hours of 9am to 8pm. Call ℂ **709/861-3522.**

WHERE TO STAY & DINE
There is one motel in town as well as a B&B, a small inn, and a couple of good restaurants—making it the best place to stay while in the area. *Note:* The Port au Choix National Historic Site is situated at a rather remote location, so you should plan on staying overnight if you want to enjoy the site.

Anchor Café ✶   You won't have any problem recognizing the Anchor Café— the front of the building is shaped like the bow of a boat! It's a casual, fun (albeit kitschy) establishment decorated with lobster pots, fishing nets, and a sou'westered mannequin. With such an obvious fishing theme, it's no surprise this wheelchair-friendly restaurant specializes in fresh local seafood—especially succulent shrimp and great seafood chowder. I highly recommend the blackened cod. The Anchor Café is located next to the National Historic Site Maritime Archaic Indians Burial Grounds.

Route 430. Main St., Port au Choix. ℂ 709/861-3665. Open June 1–Sept 30 8am–midnight, Oct 1–Dec 10 & Apr 1–May 31 11am–10pm. Closed Dec 11–Mar 31.

Point Riche Family Restaurant ✶   Although not as colorful as the Anchor Café, this cheerful restaurant in the Sea Echo Motel has similar nautical-style decor. They make fantastic cod au gratin, tasty cheddar-topped cod baked in a rich cream sauce and served with a fresh roll. A great choice for dinner is the Maritime Archaic Platter, offering a selection of local seafood. Unfortunately, the Sea Echo uses an average-quality frozen orange juice and an edible-oil product for their coffee whitener, so you may be slightly disappointed with the breakfast offerings.

Sea Echo Motel, Port au Choix. ℂ 709/861-3777. www.seaechomotel.nf.net. Open daily 7am–10pm. Dinner entrees C$7.95–$16.95 (US$5.83–$12.86). Kids' menu. AE, DC, MC, V, Interac.

Sea Echo Motel ✶   There's a wise manager in charge here: the hanging plastic seafood and lighthouse replica (charming in the restaurant) are thankfully absent in the warm decor of this newly renovated motel's very spacious rooms. You'll be surprised at just how much space there is: besides the bed(s), there are nightstands, a bureau, a love seat, a table with two chairs, and still ample room to move around. It's not advertised as wheelchair accessible, but I don't think maneuvering around this single-storey structure will be a problem for travelers with disabilities. See above for a review of the on-site restaurant.

Route 430. Fisher St., Port au Choix. © **709/861-3777.** www.seaechomotel.nf.ca. 33 units. C$72–$85 (US$52.46–$63). AE, DC, MC, V, Interac. Senior and group discounts apply. **Amenities:** Full-service restaurant; lounge w/ billiard table; RV hookups to water & electricity. *In room:* TV, hairdryer.

EXPLORING PORT AU CHOIX
Port au Choix National Historic Site ★★ Archaeological findings confirm that as far back as 5,500 years ago a variety of native cultures lived in this area. The **Parks Canada Visitor Centre** has a wonderful assortment of displays about the Maritime Archaic Indians, Groswater, Dorset-Paleoeskimos, and more recent native cultures.

Don't miss the life-sized replica of a Dorset-Paleoeskimo dwelling from about 1,500 years ago. Whale bones were used to frame the structure, and animal skins insulated it from the region's harsh weather. The dramatically lit and brightly colored displays, such as the interesting assortment of stone and bone native tools, make for an entertaining and educational experience.

Port au Choix National Historic Site. © 709/861-3522. www.parkscanada.patrimoinecanadien.gc.ca/lhn-nhs/nl/portauchoix/index_E.asp. Open June 1–June 14 & Sept 3–Oct 14 9am–5pm, June 15–Sept 2 9am–8pm. C$5 (US$3.66) adults 17 to 64, C$4 (US$2.93) seniors 65+, C$3.75 (US$2.84) youth 6 to 16, free for children under 6, C$10 (US$7.33) family rate. Gift shop on-site. Guided and self-guided tours available.

 ## Walking Trails

Once you've had enough of the indoor displays at the National Historic Site, head out on one of the three hiking trails in the Port au Choix area. *Note:* These are free, self-guided walking trails.

Coastal Walking Trail At the end of the road past the National Historic Site is **Point Riche Lighthouse,** a former site of Dorset habitation. The road is paved up to the Visitor Centre but is uneven gravel between there and the lighthouse.

Dorset Walking Trail Accessible from the Parks Canada Visitor Centre, it takes you out to the Point, passing Dorset burial caves along the way. *Note:* This trail is 5km (3 miles) long and takes about 2 hours to complete, including a climb of 120 steps along the way.

Phillips Garden Walking Trail Phillips Garden is an oceanfront grassy meadow where you can faintly discern the circular foundations of some 50 native houses. On a clear day, you can see Quebec across the Gulf of St. Lawrence, some 96 km (50 miles) away. When you reach the meadow, you have a choice of either returning to the Visitor Centre or continuing on for another 3km (1.8 miles) to the Point Riche Lighthouse.

WHERE TO SHOP & STOP
Museum of Whales & Things ★ It's not every day you see a 14-m (46-ft.) skeleton of a sperm whale, but that's exactly what you'll find outside the appropriately named Museum of Whales & Things. It's not a large building or a particularly well-organized exhibit, but every nook and cranny holds something

with a story to tell. This eclectic collection, located at the entrance to Port au Choix, is the work of local artisan and entrepreneur Ben Ploughman.

Route 430 to 24 Fisher St., Port au Choix. ☎ **709/861-3280.** www.studiogargamelle.nf.net. Free admission; donations accepted. MC, V. Open June 1–Sept 30 Mon to Sat 9am–5pm, Sundays by appt.

Studio Gargamelle *Finds*   If you're looking for a unique gift to bring home, stop by the Studio Gargamelle (adjacent to the Museum of Whales & Things), run by "lath art" specialist Ben Ploughman. Don't know what lath art is? Then visit Ploughman's studio and see his 3-D wood art for yourself. His unique style depicts local life in colorful wooden squares patched together in a quilt-like fashion. The lath art is relatively expensive, at C$200 (US$146) for a small piece up to C$2,000 (US$1,460) for a large piece.

Studio Gargamelle also has unique items for the more budget-minded traveler. Take a look at the "Viking critters" that sell for C$15 (US$11) each. These comical fellows are made from a scallop shell, a mussel shell, moose hair, and a lobster claw, providing a one-of-a-kind reminder of your NL adventure.

Route 430 to 24 Fisher St., Port au Choix. ☎ **709/861-3280.** www.studiogargamelle.nf.net. Free admission. MC, V. Open June 1–Sept 30 Mon–Sat 9am–5pm, Sundays by appt.

ST. BARBE

The most noteworthy aspect of St. Barbe is that it's the departure point for the ferry to Blanc Sablon on the Quebec–Labrador border. You probably won't stay here overnight unless you're catching an early morning ferry, but if you are you'll find a nice motel and dining room conveniently located right at the ferry terminal.

ESSENTIALS
GETTING THERE

St. Barbe is on Route 430, a 75-minute drive north of Port au Choix. If you're heading to the Labrador Straits, you'll need to get to St. Barbe to catch the ferry. (See "Getting There: Arriving by Sea" in chapter 2 for information on the Woodward Group, which operates the ferry across the Strait of Belle Isle. See chapter 9 for detailed information on the communities of the Labrador Straits.) All vehicle sizes are permitted on the ferry, but if you don't want to take your RV you can park it by the terminal in a secured parking lot. Call ☎ **709/877-2272** for details. It's about 125km (78 miles), or a 1½-hour drive, from St. Barbe to St. Anthony.

VISITOR INFORMATION

A very limited amount of regional information is available at the ferry terminal, which is open only shortly before each ferry is due to arrive or depart. It's better to pick up travel literature at other visitor centers in the region.

WHERE TO STAY & DINE

Dockside Motel & Cabins *↙*   The Dockside Motel is virtually connected to the ferry terminal, making it extremely handy if you're taking the early-morning ferry. Though white-glove clean, the motel's sparsely decorated guest rooms are obviously intended for overnight stays rather than long-term vacation ambiance. You may hear truck engines running outside your window around 6:30am, when large vehicles start to line up for the ferry. The Dockside Motel has a very good restaurant that is tastefully decorated with linen tablecloths—something you don't see much of in these parts.

Route 430 to Labrador ferry terminal, St. Barbe. ℂ **709/877-2444**. www.docksidemotel.nf.ca. 15 motel units; 10 cabins. C$56–$70 (US$42.50–$51) double. AE, DC, MC, V, Interac. **Amenities:** Full-service restaurant, pub. *In room:* TV. Cabins are fully equipped and have private entrances. **Docker's Diner** is open daily 6am–9pm in summer & 8am–8pm the rest of the year. Dinner entrees offer generous portions and are reasonably priced at C$6.25–$15.95 (US$4.74–$12.10).

WHAT TO SEE ALONG ROUTE 430

Bird Cove Archaeological Dig   A few kilometers before St. Barbe you'll pass the turnoff to a cluster of archaeological dig sites at Bird Cove. (Watch carefully, as there's just a small sign.) The dig sites are a 5-minute drive off of Route 430 and a very short walk from the parking lot. In addition to the anthropological findings (there's evidence here of Beothuk, Dorset-Paleoeskimo, and Maritime Archaic Indians), you'll see displays of local rocks, fossils, and whale bones in the museum portion of the centre. The Interpretation Centre, museum, and boardwalk are wheelchair accessible; the dig sites are not. Ask about the Learning Vacation Program (only C$37 [US$27.14] a day, lunch included).

Route 430, Bird Cove. ℂ **866/247-2011**. www.bigdroke.com. Admission to Interpretation Centre & museum is C$3 (US$2.20) adults, C$2.50 (US$1.83) seniors, C$2 (US$1.46) students 6–17. Additional C$3 (US$2.20) for guided tour of the archaeological dig sites. MC, V, Interac. Open June 1–Aug 31 9am–9pm, Sept–Oct 9am–5pm.

Borealis Crafts & the Labrador Lookout *(Finds)*   Further along Route 430, near the tiny outport of Shoal Cove East (not to be confused with Shoal Cove, which is on Rte. 430–36), you'll pass the **Borealis Craft Cooperative.** It's an economuseum, presenting a wonderful opportunity to purchase handicrafts made by local artisans.

I bought a small but unique whalebone face for C$45 (US$33), carved by Abiel Taylor, who also has a shop in Raleigh on Route 437 (ℂ **709/452-3386**). (Raleigh is home to the **Burnt Cape Ecological Reserve,** ℂ **709/729-2424,** where you'll find some very rare flora, including the Burnt Cape Cinquefoil. Local interpreters give guided tours.) Aside from the aesthetic value, I really like Taylor's carvings because they're affordable, small, and very lightweight, making them a fabulous gift idea that won't weigh you down.

Next to the building is a viewing platform complete with telescope, where you can see the Point Amour Lighthouse across the Strait of Belle Isle in nearby Labrador.

Route 430, Shoal Cove East in the Straits Development Association Building. ℂ **709/456-2123**. Open summer Mon–Fri 8am–6pm, Sat noon–5pm. Spring and fall open Mon–Fri 9am–4pm. MC, V.

 Creating New Money from Old Traditions

Economuseums use traditional manufacturing techniques or know-how in the production of goods and services. They provide income for skilled craftspeople while instilling cultural pride and preserving a way of life that might otherwise be forgotten. Products available might include knitted goods, quilts, and handcrafted wooden furniture. In addition to being retail outlets, economuseums are frequently staffed by the artisans themselves—offering interested visitors the opportunity to learn about the history and process used to manufacture the products on display.

Flower's Island Museum   If there's one thing you'll learn about Newfound-landers, it's that they're a very determined, resilient people. You'll find an inspir-ing example of that robust willpower in Nameless Cove, home to the Flower's Island Museum. This small museum was created by a high-school student, Christopher Mitchelemore, who didn't want a multi-generation family home to go to waste. Instead, he gathered as many artifacts as he could (some are as much as 200 years old) and developed the interpretive program to go with them. Based on initial response from the more than 450 visitors who stopped by his museum during its first year in business, Christopher says he plans to expand the prop-erty by adding a mini-golf course, gift shop, and concession stand.

Route 430, Nameless Cove. (C) **709/475-4241**. Open June 15–Sept 12, Mon–Sat 10am–6pm, Sun 2–8pm. C$2 (US$1.46) adults, C$1.50 (US$1.10) children 4–12. Free for under 4.

ST. ANTHONY *

Known as Newfoundland's northern capital, St. Anthony is located at the mouth of horseshoe-shaped Hare Bay, near the tip of the Great Northern Penin-sula. Isolated from the rest of the province by sheer distance, the community is primarily visited by travelers wishing to explore nearby L'Anse aux Meadows National Historic Site.

St. Anthony is a pleasantly scenic destination combining remote appeal and historical ambiance with a good range of modern services. You'll find a hospital, a small shopping mall, a pharmacy, a bank, a few nice places to stay and eat, vehicle servicing and rentals, Viking-themed boat rides and activities, as well as a nearby airport. A winter visit to St. Anthony allows for lots of outdoor fun—snowmobiling, cross-country skiing, and ice fishing are very popular activities.

ESSENTIALS
GETTING THERE

St. Anthony is the second-last community on Route 430, the provincial high-way accessed from the Trans-Canada at Deer Lake. The town is a 2½-hour drive northeast of Port au Choix, almost 4 hours from Rocky Harbour (midway through Gros Morne National Park), and 5 hours from Corner Brook.

For those who wish to investigate the multi-lineal heritage and rugged land-scape of the Northern Peninsula but want to avoid the long drive from St. John's, it's an hour's flight from St. John's to St. Anthony. *Warning:* St. Anthony Regional Airport is not really *in* St. Anthony. It's about 50km (31 miles) from the town to the turnoff for the airport, and another few minutes from there to the airport itself.

Aside from driving your own vehicle or flying, there is a bus service that can take you the 493km (306 miles) from Corner Brook to St. Anthony. The **Viking Express** (C) **709/634-4710**) departs Corner Brook on Monday, Wednesday, and Saturday. The bus returns to Corner Brook from St. Anthony on Tuesday, Thursday, and Sunday. One-way tickets cost around C$50 (US$36.68).

VISITOR INFORMATION

For a complete list of services in St. Anthony, visit the town's website at www.town.stanthony.nf.ca or call (C) **709/454-0061.** There is no official visitor center in St. Anthony, but information can be picked up at the Grenfell Inter-pretation Centre located at 1 Maraval Rd., open May 20 to June 14 from 9am until 5pm, June 15 to September 30 from 9am to 8pm ((C) **709/454-4010**).

GETTING AROUND

St. Anthony Regional Airport has car rentals, so you can fly in, rent a car, and take a driving tour of the area. National Car Rentals offers competitive rates. Call ℭ **800/227-7368** or see www.nationcar.com.

Note: Be aware that gasoline prices are higher on the Northern Peninsula than you'll find elsewhere in the province. Expect to pay about 5¢ per liter (20¢ a gallon) more for gas here than in St. John's.

 Roadside Peculiarities

While driving in the vicinity of St. Anthony, you'll likely notice the garden plots alongside the highway. These are owned by private citizens who arbitrarily stake their claim and plant potatoes, beets, and other hardy crops for their own use. Occasionally a gardener will identify a plot with a flag or scarecrow, but on the whole they're not afraid of anyone pilfering their harvest.

You may also wonder why you see wood piles (most often in the shape of a teepee) standing alongside the road. This is how the local residents dry their firewood. The trees are cut and cleaned of branches and then propped together to let the sun and wind dry them out for winter burning in the woodstove.

WHERE TO STAY & DINE

Haven Inn ✪   You'll find inexpensive lodging in a recently renovated motel that unfortunately didn't include soundproofing in the remodeling. Haven Inn has good-quality standard rooms as well as premium suites with Jacuzzi and fireplace. But, as attractive as it is to have a bedside Jacuzzi, it's not quite distracting enough to overlook the hideous blue of the TV stand and desk/table (it gains an electric hue in the morning light). The above-and-beyond service of the friendly staff, however, more than compensates for whatever the inn lacks in haute design (they answered each and every question I had about services and attractions—even when it meant phoning the competition). Wheelchair-accessible rooms are available.

The Haven Inn is home to the best restaurant in town, **Cartier's Galley,** named in recognition of French explorer Jacques Cartier, who visited here in 1534 and named it "St. Anthony's Haven." You'll find a good variety of reasonably priced dishes for lunch or supper, including an on-site **Greco Xpress Pizza** takeout service, great for late-evening snacks. The pizza is good, the service is fast, and you can enjoy it in the comfort of your room.

Route 430 to 14 Goose Cove Rd., St. Anthony. ℭ **877/428-3646** or 709/454-9100. www.haveninn.ca. 30 units. C$75–$115 (US$55–$87) double. AE, MC, V, Interac. **Amenities:** Full-service restaurant; lounge w/video lotto machines; nonsmoking. *In room:* TV. Cartier's Galley open summer 7am–2pm & 5–9pm, rest of year 7am–2pm & 5–8pm.

Leifsburdir Viking Feast   If you'd like to become an honorary Viking, make a reservation at Leifsburdir, a Viking-themed dinner theater located at the end of Fishing Point Road. The feast is served by costumed animators in a reconstructed sod hut overlooking the ocean. You'll sit on wooden benches at 8-person tables while "slaves" bring you an assortment of acquired-taste food (the menu includes salt capelin, cod tongues, moose stew, and squid-fried rice). After dinner, you can participate in a mock trial at the "Althing" (Viking court). I guarantee your stomach will hurt the next day from the innumerable belly laughs caused by the raucous Viking hijinks.

Fishing Point Rd., St. Anthony. © 877/454-4900 or 709/454-4900. Call for reservations. C$32 (US$24). Open July–early Sept daily at 5pm for bar service, with dinner & ceremony commencing at 7:30 pm.

Spruce Inn Bed & Breakfast *Value* Spruce Inn boasts exceptional prices for a professional B&B (it's not just a room in a private home). Even though all rooms are nonsmoking, with private bath/shower and radio, you won't be attracted to the Spruce Inn for its amenities. Aside from the price, you'll enjoy the panoramic harbor view and waterfront proximity as well as the large, comfortable sitting room—custom-made for mingling with other guests. A light continental breakfast (home-baked bread with partridgeberry and bakeapple jam) is included in the room rate, but if you'd like something more substantial a full breakfast is available at a small additional charge.

1 Spruce Lane (off East St.), St. Anthony. © 877/454-3402 or 709/454-3402. 4 units. C$40–$50 (US$29.50–$36.68) double, C$7 (US$5.13) additional person. MC, V. **Amenities:** Light breakfast, complimentary tea & coffee; laundry service available at extra charge. *In room:* no phone.

Triple Falls RV Park Located just 7km (4 miles) from St. Anthony, this fully serviced tent and RV campground offers a freshwater beach, playground, games arcade, mini-golf, great salmon fishing, and lots of hot water in the showers. Campsites are nicely wooded and located along a scenic river. Facilities are wheelchair accessible.

Route 430, north of St. Anthony. © 709/454-2599 or 709/454-2438. 70 sites. C$12–$18 (US$8.80–$13.44). V. Open May 24 long weekend–mid-Sept. **Amenities:** Convenience store; fully serviced sites; RV dumping station; shower & laundry facilities.

Vinland Motel *★★* A modern, full-service property conveniently located in the heart of town near shopping and other services. The Vinland Motel has the most extensive list of on-site amenities in St. Anthony, including a fitness center and massage therapist. The double rooms have the bathtub and toilet separated from the sink and counter, which is convenient if you're traveling with a partner. There are some suites available as well as two fully equipped cabins. The motel is accessible to travelers with disabilities.

West St., St. Anthony. © 800/563-7578 or 709/454-8843. www.vinlandmotel.com/vinland.htm. 46 units. C$76–$108 (US$57.68–$82) double. Government, corporate, group, & senior discounts available. AE, DC, MC, V, Interac. **Amenities:** Full-service restaurant; lounge; fitness center with sauna & hot tub; massage therapist; coin-operated guest laundry; nonsmoking rooms. *In room:* A/C, TV, coffeemaker, iron. Restaurant open summer 7am–10pm, the rest of the year 8am–2pm & 5–9pm.

EXPLORING ST. ANTHONY

The historical highlight of a trip to St. Anthony is learning about **Sir Wilfred Thomason Grenfell,** a British physician who arrived here in 1892. Appalled by the desperate poverty and even more harrowing health problems (tuberculosis was rampant), Grenfell traveled the coast, healing the sick and feeding the needy.

You can find several Grenfell-related sites in St. Anthony, notably the **Grenfell Interpretation Centre.** Another part of the Grenfell legacy is at the Charles S. Curtis Memorial Hospital, where you can view the thought-provoking **Jordi Bonet Murals** in its rotunda. There is no charge to see the stone murals and no

Hero of the Northwest-Labrador Coast

Sir Wilfred T. Grenfell: "The purpose of this world is not to have and hold, but to serve." By the time Grenfell retired in 1935, at 70 years of age, the following were in operation throughout Newfoundland & Labrador as a result of his efforts: 5 hospitals; 7 nursing stations; 2 orphanages; 14 industrial centers; 4 summer schools; 3 agricultural stations; 12 clothing-distribution centers; 4 hospital ships; 1 supply schooner; 12 community centers; several cooperative stores; a cooperative lumber mill; and a haul-up slip for ship repairs.

specific hours of operation. Just stop in at the reception desk and pick up the brochure for your self-guided tour. Bonet is a Montreal artist who was commissioned in 1967 to create this tribute to Grenfell and life in northern Newfoundland & Labrador. The hospital is located at 178–200 West St. Call *©* **709/454-4010** for further information.

If you're looking for a scenic spot to just hang out and look for icebergs or whales, follow the main road in town to **Fishing Point Municipal Park** (open May 1 through October 31), where you can climb a 91-m (300-ft.) lookout to get the best view of St. Anthony Harbour.

Grenfell Interpretation Centre *✦✦*   The newly constructed Grenfell Interpretation Centre displays informative panels that aptly explain Grenfell's life and his tremendous impact on area residents. It also houses a fascinating selection of his medical tools and equipment. Although there are interpreters on hand to answer questions, the centre is meant to be a self-guided tour. A small tea shop is located on the lower level of the center. There's also a playground for the kids.

Admission to the Grenfell Interpretation Centre also includes admission to the following: the **Grenfell House Museum,** where 85% of the household artifacts are originals that belonged to the Grenfell family; the **Dockhouse Museum,** which has a display of maritime tools and artifacts; and **Grenfell Park,** where you can see a statue of the man himself. You'll need at least a couple of hours to see all the Grenfell sites.

Route 430 to 1 Maraval Rd., St. Anthony. *©* **709/454-4010.** www.grenfell-properties.com. Open May 20–June 14 daily 9am–5pm, June 15–Sept 30 9am–8pm. Call for appt between Sept 30 and May 20. C$6 (US$4.40) adults, C$5 (US$3.66) seniors, C$12 (US$8.80) family rate.

OUTDOOR PURSUITS

One of these boat operators is located right in St. Anthony, and the other is a few kilometers away en route to L'Anse aux Meadows. Choose the one that best suits your mood and interests, as they're both well-run operations.

Northland Discovery Tours *✦*   This award-winning, family-run company is on a mission to provide an experience that will be the highlight of your vacation—and do they deliver! Owner Paul Alcock (a biologist and noted conservationist) will have you crossing paths with spouting humpbacks and racing dolphins as he navigates the natural wonders of Iceberg Alley. He'll explain why some icebergs are blue, and how you can tell when an iceberg is ready to roll (*Hint:* Watch the birds). He'll even scoop a few bergy bits from the sea, giving you a taste of the purest water on Earth. Tours operate rain or shine, from late May to early October, three times daily (9am, 1pm, and 4pm).

Route 430 to St. Anthony Harbour. © **877/632-3747** or 709/454-3092. www3.nf.sympatico.ca/paul.alcock. Reservations recommended. C$40 (US$29.50) adults, C$25 (US$18) age 12–17, C$20 (US$14.76) under 12, free for children under 4. Group discounts available. Prices include applicable taxes. May 15–Oct 15 daily 8am–10pm.

Viking Boat Tours ⚡ *(Kids)*   Equally as good as the Northland Tours but in a very different way, Viking Boat Tours gives you the chance to ride in a *Knarr,* an open longboat like the one Leif Eiriksson may have sailed in when he landed in Newfoundland more than 1,000 years ago. The tours are 2½ hours long and let you have Viking-style fun while searching for icebergs, birds, and whales. To make the experience even more authentic, you can wear a traditional Viking costume and take a turn at the oar. But remember that there's no pillaging allowed in this Viking crowd—just good clean fun.

Weather permitting, there are three sailings daily: 10am, 1pm, and 4pm. Special full-day adventure tours are also available, where you have the chance to climb ashore and have a Newfoundland-style boil-up.

Route 436 to Noddy Bay, 2km south of L'Anse aux Meadows. © **709/623-2100**. www.nfld.net/vikingboat tours. June 1–Sept 1. Reservations preferred. C$38 (US$27.86) adults, C$23 (US$17) children 5–12, free for children 4 and under.

L'ANSE AUX MEADOWS

At a barren outpost on a flat headland jutting bravely into the North Atlantic, you'll find several innocuous grassy mounds that are both a UNESCO World Heritage Site and a National Heritage Site. These "mounds" are the footprints of the first European settlement in North America. Although the Viking Norsemen who first arrived on these shores more than 1,000 years ago didn't make a permanent home of what they called *Vinland,* they left evidence of their passage in the foundations of the original sod structures that once housed them.

The modern-day community of L'Anse aux Meadows offers a limited number of services. You're probably best off staying in St. Anthony and making a day trip to L'Anse aux Meadows and *Norstead,* the reenactment village located a short distance from the National Historic Site.

ESSENTIALS
GETTING THERE
L'Anse aux Meadows is 30 minutes or 40km (25 miles) north of St. Anthony (turn off Rte. 430 onto Rte. 436).

VISITOR INFORMATION
Visitor information is available at the L'Anse aux Meadows National Historic Site. Call © **709/623-2608** or check out http://parkscanada.pch.gc.ca/lhn-nhs/ nl/meadows/index_e.asp. The center is open June 1 to June 14 and September 3 to October 14 daily 9am to 5pm. During the peak visitor season of June 15 to September 2, longer hours of 9am to 8pm apply.

WHERE TO STAY & DINE
Norseman Restaurant & Gallery ⚡⚡⚡   The Norseman is rated one of the better fine-dining restaurants in the province, and for good reason. It has a great selection of wines (try the crisp, citrus complexity of the Penfolds–Adelaide Hills–Semillon 1998), the freshest seafood, and Newfoundland game. You can actually visit the wharf to pick out your own lobster (in season), and your drinks will be served with genuine iceberg ice. There's a dinner theater (C$25/US$18.45) during July and August, every Tuesday and Friday at 7pm.

Route 436, L'Anse aux Meadows Harbour. ℂ **877/623-2018**. www.valhalla-lodge.com/restaurant.htm.
Dinner C$19.95–$29.95 (US$15.57–$23.38). MC V. Open June 1–Oct 1 daily 9am–10pm. Fully licensed.

Smith's Restaurant *(Overrated)*   On your way from St. Anthony to L'Anse aux
Meadows, you'll pass through St. Lunaire–Griquet, where you'll find an attractive restaurant right on the waterfront. If ambiance is more important to you
than the quality of the food, do stop in at Smith's Restaurant. It offers an extensive menu, reasonable prices, and fairly fast service. However, I can't recommend
the food. I ordered the scallop and asparagus stir-fry, which came to the table
with overcooked broccoli and no asparagus. As well, the cod au gratin was dry
and dull. Although the desserts were reasonably priced, the cheesecake was also
dry and the crust far too thick for my liking. Although it's listed in *Where to Eat
in Canada* (2002–2003 edition), I can't support a good rating based on this visit.

Route 436, St. Lunaire–Griquet. ℂ **709/623-2539**. Lunch C$4.95–$9.95 (US$3.75–$7.30). Dinner C$6.55–
$18.95 (US$5–$13.38). MC, V. Open Apr 1–Dec 25 daily 8am–9pm. Wheelchair accessible.

Valhalla Lodge *(Finds)*   Look for these Viking-themed accommodations in a
friendly B&B with understated appeal just 8km (5 miles) before the L'Anse aux
Meadows National Historic Site. The property is situated on a quiet hill overlooking the ocean, where you can watch icebergs, whales (up to a dozen have
been seen here simultaneously), and birds. Guest rooms are warmly furnished in
Scandinavian pine with cozy quilts on the beds and exquisite reproductions
from local artists on the walls. Accommodations are fairly tight: standing
between the wall and the bed, chances are good that you'll bang into one or the
other. But it's the memory of your gracious hostess Bella Hodge and her
famously fluffy partridgeberry pancakes that will stay with you long after you've
forgotten the minor discomfort of semi-cramped quarters.

Route 436 to Gunner's Cove, L'Anse aux Meadows. ℂ **877/623-2018** or 709/623-2018 & 709/689-4825 in
the off-season. www.valhalla-lodge.com. 6 units. C$60–$85 (US$44–$63) double, C$15 (US$11) additional
for cot. Off-season discounts available. DC, MC, V. Open June–Oct. **Amenities:** Complimentary breakfast;
sauna. *In room:* Some rooms have private baths; one Jacuzzi suite.

Viking Village Bed & Breakfast ★ *(Value)*   This new B&B within walking
distance of L'Anse aux Meadows National Historic Site is as close as you can get
to Viking habitation without actually sleeping in a sod hut. Its proximity to the
wharf is an added bonus, offering the opportunity to talk to local fishermen.
The Viking theme–named guest rooms all have patio doors and balconies,
which is a lovely feature if you're visiting during summer.

A full breakfast and evening snack are included with the room rates, and the
owners will cook you a Newfoundland-style dinner for an extra fee of C$12
(US$8.80) per person. The owners will pick you up at St. Anthony airport or at
the bus stop. The same owners also run the more basic **Viking Nest B&B** with
slightly lower rates, which can be reached via the same contact numbers.

Route 436 to Hay Cove, near L'Anse aux Meadows. ℂ **877-858-2238** or 709/623-2238. www.bbcanada.
com/vikingvillage. 5 units. C$44–$58 (US$33.40–$43.31) double, senior and weekly rates in off-season. MC,
V. **Amenities:** Full breakfast; complimentary evening snack; limited room service; common-area satellite TV;
laundry service; nonsmoking facility. *In room:* Private ensuite baths.

EXPLORING L'ANSE AUX MEADOWS

L'Anse aux Meadows National Historic Site and Norstead are complementary
must-see attractions: one is a formal archaeological introduction to a 1,000-year-
old Viking habitation, the other brings the ancient Norse experience to life.
Note: All Vikings were Norsemen, but only a small percentage of Norsemen were
Vikings. (Vikings had a notorious reputation for raping and pillaging.)

L'Anse aux Meadows National Historic Site ✸✸   Embark on your Viking journey at the Visitor Centre in L'Anse aux Meadows. The details of your adventure will be revealed in a 30-minute video (offered in the theater) that details the discovery of the site by Dr. Helge Ingstad and his wife, Dr. Anne Stine. As Norwegians, Ingstad and Stine had a strong interest in determining the exact location of *Vinland,* the legendary location referenced in the Norse sagas.

After watching the video, examine the many artifacts that confirm the Vikings' presence here as far back as A.D. 1000. You'll even see a model of how the settlement would have looked when it was inhabited. From there, it's on to the real thing. A short trek along a gravel path takes you past the excavated ruins of the Viking settlement and the reconstructed sod and timber buildings that would have housed their community so long ago. Reenactors will educate and entertain you with demonstrations of their various crafts. "Gunnar" shares the secret of navigation and ship construction, "Harald" illustrates the power of forge and anvil, while "Thora" proves that Viking women are a force to be reckoned with (she plans to divorce her impractical dreamer of a husband—Bjorn, the "brains" behind the expedition—when they return to civilization).

Route 436, L'Anse aux Meadows. ✆ **709/623-2608.** www2.parkscanada.gc.ca/lhn-nhs/nl/meadows/index_e.asp. C$7 (US$5.13) adults, C$5.50 (US$4) seniors 65+, C$3.50 (US$2.60) students 6–16, free for children under 6, C$14 (US$10.26) family rate. MC, V. Open June 1–June 14 & Sept 3–Oct 14 9am–5pm, June 15–Sept 2 9am–8pm.

Norstead ✸✸✸ *Kids*   If you want to walk like the Norse, talk like the Norse, eat like the Norse, in fact become a Norseman or -woman, then you *must* come to Norstead. Located 2km (1¼ miles) from the L'Anse aux Meadows National Historic Site, Norstead is a recreated Norse trading post. Enthusiastic and knowledgeable reenactors walk you through every aspect of early Norse life on the Rock, including religion, weaponry, blacksmithing, activities in the "Trading House," the scalley (kitchen/cooking area), handcrafts such as pottery and the carding of wool, and the sleeping quarters. You'll also get a chance to see and explore a replica of a Viking *knarr,* the type of boat Leif Eiriksson used to sail across the North Atlantic back in A.D. 1000.

Norstead offers a Discovery Program that gives kids an opportunity to participate hands-on in activities carried on in the settlement. The program generally runs for 2 hours—kids can get into period costume and try baking flatbread, carding wool, and forging tools from bog iron. There are similar learning-vacation programs geared to the adult audience.

Even though Norstead closes for the winter, not everyone goes into hibernation. Ask the folks at Norstead about booking the Viking-themed snowmobile excursions that run in March. During this unforgettable adventure you'll sled the scenic region, sleep outdoors, and eat authentic Viking meals such as beef and carrot stew.

Note: Norstead is wheelchair friendly, but not fully accessible. *Warning:* The area is often cold and damp. Dress appropriately.

Route 436, L'Anse aux Meadows. ✆ **709/454-8888.** www.vikingtrail.org. C$7 (US$5.13) adults, C$6 (US$4.40) seniors, C$3.75 (US$2.84) children 6–15. Family rate of C$14 (US$10.26). MC, V. Open June 1–Sept 30 daily 10am–6pm.

WHERE TO SHOP
The Dark Tickle Company   A delicious solution to the problem of wild-berry lovers everywhere: you can pick 'em, but you can't take 'em with you (they'd perish on the way home). The Dark Tickle Company uses only

uncultivated berries (bakeapple, partridgeberry, blueberry, crowberry, and squashberry) in their lip-smacking jams, preserves, and syrups. They even have something called Drinkable Berries: natural nectar in bakeapple and partridge-berry varieties. The result is just-picked freshness in a portable package. The Dark Tickle Company also sells products worldwide via its website.

Route 436, St. Lunaire–Griquet (between St. Anthony & L'Anse aux Meadows). ℂ 709/623-2354. www.darktickle.com. MC, V. Open May 16–June 15 Mon–Fri 9am–6pm, June 16–Sept 7 daily 9am–6pm, Sept 8–Sept 30 Mon–Fri 9am–6pm, Oct 1–May 15 Mon–Fri 9am–5pm. Guided tours available on request.

Stagehead Carving Shop   Expert carver Norman Young creates interesting pieces out of whalebone, soapstone, and antler at prices ranging from C$45 (US$33) for smaller, simpler pieces to C$165 (US$125) for the larger or more intricate works of art. There are also some unique jewelry pieces for sale. All pieces, regardless of size, show a masterful blending of modern, traditional, and native influence.

Route 436, Griquet (between St. Anthony & L'Anse aux Meadows). ℂ 709/623-2407.

Finds   **Escape to Quirpon Island**

For splendid, majestic isolation, **Quirpon Island** ✫✫ stands alone. Drive to the most northeasterly tip of the Great Northern Peninsula to the minute fishing outpost of Quirpon (pronounced kar-*poon*). Now look across the harbor. Here is Quirpon Island, a half-hour boat ride farther north than any other point on the island portion of the province. Both the dock and the helideck are a striking testament to the solitude of this sanctuary. Once ashore, you'll stay at one of two sturdy dwellings located near the base of an automated lighthouse: either the former lighthouse keeper's residence or the more modern house built next door. Regardless of which building you stay in, you're guaranteed not to be bothered by cable tel-evision, clock radios, or in-room telephones. Instead, you'll spend hours contemplating the streaks and fissures of passing icebergs. Entertainment is provided by breaching, blowing humpback and minke—you may even be soaked by a spouting whale. All this, plus home-cooked meals under the hospitable care of Doris, Madonna, and Hubert Roberts. Truly a rare gem of serenity in a world of sensory overload.

From Route 436, turn right onto the gravel highway to Quirpon. A 9-m (29.5-ft.) boat will carry you to Quirpon Island. ℂ 877/254-6586. 11 units, one with private bathroom. C$200 (US$147.600) single, C$300 (US$220) double, C$50 (US$36.68) child. AE, MC, V. All meals and transportation to and from the island from the community of Quirpon are included in the price.

---

2 Deer Lake

DEER LAKE

Deer Lake is the transportation hub of the Western Region. Here, you head either north to Gros Morne and the Northern Peninsula or south to Corner Brook and the Nova Scotia ferry. The community has a population of about 5,000 residents and offers a good range of services including a regional airport. The airport is especially convenient if you fly into St. John's, drive across the province, and don't want to drive all the way back to St. John's to catch a return flight.

ESSENTIALS
GETTING THERE

If you're coming from Channel–Port aux Basques and traveling north along the Trans-Canada Highway (Route 1), it's a 3-hour drive to Deer Lake. If you're coming from the east along Route 1, there's a 637-km (395-mile) stretch of driving between Deer Lake and St. John's. And, if you're heading south from St. Anthony on Route 430, it's a 443-km (275-mile) drive to Deer Lake.

Or you can just bypass the driving altogether, and fly directly into Deer Lake airport (3km/2 miles east of town). The airport is serviced by Air Canada Jazz, Air Canada Tango, and Provincial Airlines. Four car-rental agencies have outlets at the airport.

VISITOR INFORMATION

Visitor information is available at the Tourist Chalet on the Trans-Canada Highway (60A, Route 1), located near the junction of Route 1 and Route 430. It's open mid-May to mid-October, daily 9am to 9pm (© **709/635-2202**).

WHERE TO STAY

Deer Lake Motel   Conveniently located on the Trans-Canada Highway, this newly renovated property is well situated for day excursions both north and south—which makes it ideal for skiing at Marble Mountain and hiking in Gros Morne. The on-site restaurant has a pleasant decor, quiet ambiance, and great food from an award-winning chef—he's especially gifted with thigh-thickening desserts. The dining room is thankfully free of the most common restaurant mistake: tables are spaced sufficiently far apart to allow for private conversations. Guest rooms feature standard hotel decor that has yet to show the wear and tear of previous guests. There is no charge for local phone calls.

Trans-Canada Highway (Rte. 1), Deer Lake. © 800/563-2144 or 709/635-2108. www.deerlakemotel.com. 56 units. C$68–$89 (US$50–$65) double; suites C$125 (US$92) double. AE, DC, MC, V. **Amenities:** Restaurant; lounge; nonsmoking rooms. *In room:* A/C, TV, coffeemaker; some with mini-bars, outside entrances, and hairdryers.

Driftwood Inn *(Value*   The perfect location for fast four-season fun, Driftwood Inn is affiliated with Backcountry Adventures, a company specializing in ATV and snowmobile tours. You can snowmobile all the way from Deer Lake to St. Anthony, or take part in an extreme ATV adventure through some of the wildest territory on Earth. The Driftwood Inn offers a cozy atmosphere with rustic styling enhanced by the friendly service of the super-accommodating staff. This property is near shopping and other services, and just 10 minutes from the Deer Lake Airport.

3 Nicholsville Rd., Deer Lake. © 888/635-5115 or 709/635-5115. www.driftwoodinn.net. 25 units. C$74–$89 (US$54–$65) double. MC, V. **Amenities:** Restaurant; lounge. *In room:* TV, AM/FM radio, 4-piece bathroom, telephone, some with dataport.

Humberview Bed & Breakfast *(Finds*   This is the kind of palatial home most people can only dream about: a modern, executive-style castle in an exclusive neighborhood. It's a showpiece of opulent comfort topped with crown molding and chandelier lighting. The aptly named Grand Room is 76 sq. m (820 sq. ft.) of elegant intimacy with its own sitting area and four-poster bed. Not only does the ensuite bathroom have a Grecian-style Jacuzzi flanked by twin columns, it also has a bidet! The other three rooms are named according to their color schemes. The Green Room is the most basic and compact, and it still comfortably accommodates two double beds. It would be easy to be intimidated if not for the warm hospitality of owners Bronson and Irene Short. Still, you can't help but feel you have to be on your best behavior (this is, after all, a private home—not an impersonal hotel). Rates include a full home-cooked breakfast. No pets allowed.

11 Humberview Dr., Deer Lake. ℭ 888/635-4818 or 709-635-4818. www.thehumberview.com. 4 units. C$65–$150 (US$48–$110) double, $10 (US$7.33) additional person. MC, V. **Amenities:** Full breakfast; laundry services available; nonsmoking rooms. *In room:* Private bath/shower, TV, telephone/facsimile service on request.

WHERE TO DINE

Irving Big Stop Family Restaurant ★ *Value*   I'm not normally one to eat at gas stations, but this one came recommended by a local resident and it's definitely a cut above the rest in its class. It offers good food at reasonable prices and attentive service. They have special offerings such as a "Jiggs Dinner" (corned beef and cabbage) served every Thursday for C$7.99 (US$5.85). The kids will likely be thrilled at the sight of Howley, Newfoundland's Biggest Moose—a huge moose statue located in the front of the building. *Note:* Irving bathrooms are well-known among seasoned travelers for their cleanliness.

Trans-Canada Highway (Rte. 1), Deer Lake. ℭ 709/635-2129. Extensive all-day menu. Dinner entrees from C$8–$17 (US$5.86–$13.26). AE, DC, MC, V. Open 24 hrs/day, 7 days/wk. No alcoholic beverages or smoking.

Jungle Jim's *Kids* CONTEMPORARY   This casual, safari-style restaurant is located at the Driftwood Inn but is independently run. Because of their hours, this is a great place to eat if you're looking for a late-night snack or even a meal. Specialties include stir-fry, BBQ ribs, and spicy chicken wings. The funky surroundings and children's menu make this an ideal family restaurant (a welcome change in a sea of ultra-fast food choices).

3 Upper Nicholsville Rd., Deer Lake. ℭ 709/635-5054. www.junglejims.ca. Reservations not required. Lunches about C$8 (US$5.86); most dinners about C$12 (US$8.80). AE, DC, MC, V. Open Sun–Tues 11am–11pm, Wed–Sat 11am–11:30pm. Li'l Jimmy's Pub is open Mon & Tues 5pm–midnight, Wed–Sat 3pm–2am.

EXPLORING DEER LAKE

Deer Lake (the lake) has one of the nicest sandy beaches in Newfoundland. You'll also find a lovely park and scenic walking trail in town just off Nicholsville Road, viewable from the Trans-Canada Highway. Plus, it's home to the Humber River, one of the best salmon fishing rivers in Canada. Be sure to visit **Big Falls,** where you can see the salmon jumping right out of the water. The best time to witness this natural wonder is in late June and early July.

Newfoundland Insectarium & Butterfly Pavilion ★★★ *Kids*   The highlight of Deer Lake is the Insectarium & Butterfly Pavilion, just north of town on Bonne Bay Road. If you like butterflies this place is a must-see, with many specimens, including the impressive Blue Morpho. There's also an observation hive where you can watch thousands of honeybees going about their busy day—and be a breath away from live scorpions and tarantulas (safely enclosed by thick glass). If you're one of those people who like to get up close and personal with creepy crawlies, the staff will be happy to oblige by putting a live tropical leaf insect in your hand. This is one of only two such facilities in Canada (similar to sections of the American Museum of Natural History). It comes with a nice walking trail, an ice-cream shop, and a rather unique bug-themed gift shop. An elevator facilitates wheelchair access to all three levels.

Route 430 to 2 Bonne Bay Rd., Reidville. ℭ 709/635-4545. www.nfinsectarium.com. C$6.50 (US$4.80) adults, C$5.50 (US$4) seniors, C$4.50 (US$3.30) kids 5–14, C$22 (US$16) family rate. Open July 1–Aug 31 daily 9am–9pm, Apr 25–June 30 & Sept 1–Oct 10 weekdays 9am–5pm, weekends 10am–5pm. Wheelchair accessible.

3 Corner Brook

Its proximity to the open waters of the Gulf of St. Lawrence makes Corner Brook a favorite destination for cruise ships sailing Canada's east coast. That's just one of many appealing aspects to Corner Brook's spectacular location. The community is located in a hilly lowland region surrounded by the Long Range Mountains—a continuation of the Appalachian belt stretching up from the New England states—so the natural beauty is stunning.

Corner Brook has been called the "Forest Capital of Canada," so it's no surprise to find one of the world's largest integrated pulp and paper mills here. Too bad it spoils the view of the bay slightly, but the mill provides a very important and much-needed source of employment to the community's 22,000 residents. You'll find a full range of services in Corner Brook, including a good selection of churches and the Western Region's largest hospital.

ESSENTIALS
GETTING THERE

Corner Brook is 53km (33 miles) southwest of Deer Lake along the Trans-Canada Highway (Route 1) and 218km (135 miles) north of the Channel–Port aux Basques Ferry Terminal. It's 687km (426 miles) west of St. John's.

VISITOR INFORMATION

The visitor center in Corner Brook at 11 Confederation Dr. can provide you with regional information. The center is open year-round, from June 15 to September 15 daily from 9am until 9pm, and the rest of the year Wednesday to Friday from 9am until 5pm and Saturday to Tuesday from 9am to 4pm. Call 𝄐 709/639-9792 or visit the community's website at www.cornerbrook.com.

WHERE TO STAY & DINE

There are quite a few nice places to stay and eat in Corner Brook, but we have space to list only the most outstanding. We've also included a couple of locations in nearby Steady Brook, where you'll be closer to the Marble Mountain ski resort.

The Glynmill Inn ⍟   The professional confidence of the staff and the understated dignity of the foyer tell you that this is the most prestigious property in Corner Brook. The Glynmill Inn is a traditional Tudor-style home overlooking its namesake pond, located within a 5-minute walk of downtown Corner Brook. The inn, a Registered Heritage Structure, carries an Olde-English theme throughout (think dark wood furnishings and gilded picture frames), and offers a variety of standard guest rooms as well as several styles of more spacious suites. It's also home to two good restaurants. The Wine Cellar specializes in steak and seafood and is one of the finer restaurants in Corner Brook. The decor is more elegant and the food less affordable than the casual and moderately priced Carriage Room restaurant, which specializes in traditional Newfoundland favorites. The inn has an elevator and a wheelchair ramp.

1 Cobb Lane, Corner Brook. 𝄐 **800/563-4400** or 709/634-5181. www.glynmillinn.ca. 81 units. Some rooms are pet friendly. C$75–$165 (US$55–$125) double. AE, DC, MC, V. **Amenities:** 2 restaurants; pub; fitness room; business center. *In room:* A/C, TV, coffeemaker, hairdryer, iron, ironing board, some refrigerators. Carriage Room restaurant open daily 7am–9:30pm. Wine Cellar dining room open evenings only.

Holiday Inn Corner Brook ⍟   Although Holiday Inns as a rule don't have a depth of character comparable to that of the Glynmill Inn, the Holiday Inn Corner Brook is the exception. Elegant tile floors, leather furnishings, and a dramatically curving staircase are among the features that grace the open reception areas of the hotel. Among its numerous guest amenities (oversized whirlpool, fitness facility, complimentary underground parking, and an elevator) is an indoor swimming pool—the only hotel in town to have one. All guest rooms are spacious and newly renovated, with beautifully solid furnishings and a Goldilocks-approved mattress (not too firm, not too soft, it's just right). There are also executive and king suites to choose from, as well as a special unit for guests with disabilities. The on-site Crown and Moose Pub and Eatery is a convenient dining choice that, like the hotel itself, exceeds the usual standard. It's a casual, all-day eatery; kids 12 and under eat free from the children's menu.

48 West St., Corner Brook. Ⓒ **800/399-5381** or 709/634-5381. www.holidayinncornerbrook.com. 101 units. C$92–$120 (US$67.46–$88) double. Special family & corporate rates available. AE, DC, DISC, MC, V, JCB. **Amenities:** Restaurant; lounge w/VLTs; indoor pool, fitness center, whirlpool; limited room service; Laundromat; nonsmoking rooms. *In room:* A/C, TV w/pay movies, dataport, coffeemaker, iron.

Marble Mountain Cabins ★ *Value*   These accommodations offer you the convenience of being within easy walking distance of Marble Mountain without paying resort prices. Marble Mountain Cabins are across the highway from the ski hill on the banks of the Humber River. The maroon-colored cedar-shake cottages range in size from one to four bedrooms. Amenities and services differ from cabin to cabin, with some having full kitchens and others having kitchenettes. Several have a fireplace and Jacuzzi. *Hint:* If choosing between the Studio Cabin and the 1-Bedroom Deluxe, go for the Studio Cabin. The open-concept design is more spacious than that of the 1-Bedroom Deluxe and the bathroom is nicer too. The Chalet Cabin is the most luxurious, with a cathedral ceiling, fireplace, and Jacuzzi.

A convenience store, gas station, takeout restaurant, and liquor store are within walking distance; more extensive services are 10 minutes away in Corner Brook.

Dogwood Dr., Steady Brook. Ⓒ **877/497-5673** or 709/634-2237. www.explorenewfoundland.com. 15 cottages plus 10 inn suites. C$79 (US$58) for a 1-bedroom up to C$219 (US$166) for a 4-bedroom unit; C$99 (US$72) for the inn suites. Mid-week and off-season discounts apply. Inquire about ski-pass discounts. MC, V. **Amenities:** Dining room; den with bar service; heated pool; sauna & exercise facilities; playground; laundry facilities. *In room:* Fully equipped kitchen/kitchenette, TV, some with fireplace and Jacuzzi.

MarbleWood Village Resort ★★   Here, at the foot of Marble Mountain, you'll find ultimate convenience, deluxe accommodations, and premium prices. For almost double the money you'll spend at Marble Mountain Cabins, you can ski all day from the doorstep of your very own luxury chalet. Each of the adjoining units is styled along modern, clean lines with dramatic cathedral ceiling, pine-and-marble fireplace, and private sundeck or patio. With the fully equipped kitchen (even down to the microwave and dishwasher), TV with VCR, and top-quality linens, it's like taking the comforts of home with you on vacation. *Added bonus:* While it's ideal for skiing, MarbleWood Village Resort is designed for four-season fun. You're near the Steady Brook Falls Hiking Trail, salmon and trout fishing, caving, and just 50 minutes from Gros Morne National Park. *Note:* As part of Interval International, MarbleWood Village Resort offers timeshare vacation options that are interchangeable with The Royal Caribbean resort in Cancun, Mexico and Marriott's Cypress Harbour in Orlando, Florida.

8 Thistle Dr., Steady Brook. Ⓒ **888/868-7635** or 709/632-7900. www.marblemountain.com. 24 units. C$129 (US$95) for a 1-bedroom up to C$359 (US$273) for a 4-bedroom. AE, DC, MC, V, Interac. *In room:* Full kitchen, TV w/VCR.

Strawberry Hill Resort ★★ Share a pillow with some of the world's most famous people. Originally built and designed by a pulp and paper magnate (Sir Eric Bowater) as a corporate retreat for visiting dignitaries, Strawberry Hill Resort has hosted former Canadian prime minister Pierre Trudeau as well as Queen Elizabeth II and Prince Philip. This exquisite retreat has a breathtaking location on the Humber River, where you can enjoy salmon fly-fishing right at your fingertips. Trophy salmon are caught here each year between June and October. Not only does the resort have a sauna, hot tub, some nice hiking trails, and horseshoes to amuse you, but the owners will also help you arrange boat tours and guided excursions. Guest rooms at Sugar Hill epitomize rustic luxury. Each has a king-sized bed, cozy feather duvet, and fireplace. And there's a video library available so you can enjoy movies in your room. Guest rooms in the Manor House are nice, but the chalets are newer, larger, and more expensive.

Exit 10 off Route 1 to Little Rapids. ✆ 877/434-0066 or 709/634-0066. www.strawberryhill.net. 15 units (7 rooms in Manor House & 8 chalets). Manor House: C$150–$200 (US$110–$146) double. Chalets: C$300–$400 (US$220–$293). Off-season and seniors' discounts available. MC, V. **Amenities:** Gourmet dining; hot tub, sauna. *In room:* TV w/VCR.

Thirteen West ★★ NOUVELLE Thirteen West is one of my favorite restaurants in Corner Brook—it has a really innovative menu with a wide range of offerings. This is the high-caliber kind of restaurant you'd expect to find in St. John's, and a wonderful find in a smaller city like Corner Brook. The prices, however, are also higher than you'll find in most other restaurants in town. *Note:* Thirteen West is owned by the same people who own The Cellar in St. John's, so you can expect a similarly superlative fine-dining experience.

13 West St., Corner Brook. ✆ 709/634-1300. Reservations recommended. Dinner entrees C$16–$28 (US$11.74–$20.52). AE, DC, MC, V. Open Mon–Fri 11:30am–2:30pm & 5:30–9:30pm, Sat 5:30–10:30pm, Sun 5:30–9:30pm.

EXPLORING CORNER BROOK

Corner Brook Museum & Archives A former courthouse/telegraph office/ customs house finds new life as a Registered Heritage Structure and museum. There are approximately 1,000 items in this collection, highlighting the town's forestry and pulp and paper industries as well as the lifestyle of the aboriginal people who once lived here. In addition to enjoying the intriguing black-and-white photos depicting life in Corner Brook circa 1900, you'll be captivated by the century-old artifacts (like the Nestlé floor-model hair-perming machine: it looks like Medusa on wheels). If nostalgia overwhelms you, compare the push-button modern clothes washer to the crank-handle wringer washer. It gives you a completely new perspective on the "good old days."

2 West St. ✆ 709/634-2518. www.cornet.nf.ca/web/cbmuseum/default.htm. C$4 (US$2.93) adults; C$2 (US$1.46) students age 12–17; free for children under age 12 accompanied by an adult. Open June 15–Aug 31 daily 9am–8pm, Sept 1–June 14 Mon–Fri 9am–5pm.

Marble Mountain ★★★ *Kids* In winter, snow-polished hills make the Corner Brook–Steady Brook area Atlantic Canada's best downhill skiing destination. Marble Mountain, with a peak elevation of 488m (1,600 ft.), receives about 4.8m (16 ft.) of snowfall per year (plus a man-made boost when Mother Nature needs a break). There are 34 different runs ranging from novice to expert, with 27 groomed trails and 7 mogul runs including a half-pipe and a terrain park. Marble Mountain operates 4 lifts, including a high-speed detachable quad chair, 2 more quad chairs, and a beginner's platter lift. There's even a children's program where kids get certified ski instruction as well as supervised play time in the indoor activity center. All this makes Marble Mountain a full-family-fun experience. Ski rentals are available for C$19 (US$13.93) per day, and an all-day lift pass costs C$36 (US$27). Call ✆ **709/637-7600** or visit www.skimarble. com for more information.

Newfoundland Emporium *(Finds* Sophisticated junk, antique collectibles, and Newfoundland crafts make this unusual establishment the shopping highlight of a trip to Corner Brook. Shop owner Dave LeDrew has assembled a fascinating selection of wreckage and cargo that has washed ashore after one of Newfoundland's famously horrendous storms. You can get lost in here for hours, if you've got the time.

7 Broadway Rd., Cornerbrook. ✆ 709/634-9376. www.nfldemporium.com. Open July 1–Aug 31 daily 9 am–9 pm, reduced but flexible hours the remainder of the year.

4 Stephenville to Channel–Port aux Basques

South of Corner Brook is Stephenville, a community of about 8,000 residents offering a good range of services including a Wal-Mart and a small regional airport. There's even a hospital at nearby Stephenville Crossing. Stephenville is a good base if you're exploring the lovely Port au Port Peninsula or Barachois Pond Provincial Park, both just minutes away from town. Stephenville is often of interest to American visitors, as the town is home to a former U.S. Air Base.

Channel–Port aux Basques is at the southerly end of Route 1. The community gets its name from its French heritage, as this region was originally settled by Basques fishermen who came to Newfoundland in the 1500s. Today, Channel–Port aux Basques has more than 5,000 residents and is home to a Marine Atlantic ferry terminal. The community is usually referred to as Port aux Basques.

ESSENTIALS
GETTING THERE
Stephenville is 796km (494 miles) west of St. John's, 77km (48 miles) southwest of Corner Brook, and 166km (103 miles) north of Channel–Port aux Basques, following Route 1 to Route 460 or Route 490. You can also fly directly to Stephenville's small regional airport via an interprovincial flight.

Channel–Port aux Basques is 218km (135 miles) south of Corner Brook. Most people who come here do so because of its ferry terminal. (See the "Getting There" section of chapter 2 for full details on the Nova Scotia to Channel–Port aux Basques ferry.) Unlike the utilitarian North Sydney terminal in Nova Scotia, the Port aux Basques docking area and terminal site features a romantically lighted harbor entrance and a dramatic blasted-rock approach. And, although significantly smaller in size, the Port aux Basques waterfront is more visitor-friendly than the one in St. John's. It features quaint shopping sheds and a state-of-the art outdoor amphitheater.

VISITOR INFORMATION
There is a regional Visitor Centre in Stephenville located just before the junction of Route 1 and Route 490. The center is open June 1 to early September daily from 7am until 10pm. Call ✆ **709/643-5854.** A limited amount of information can also be obtained at the Stephenville airport.

The Channel–Port aux Basques Visitor Centre is on the Trans-Canada Highway just 4km (2½ miles) from the ferry terminal; its hours coincide with the arrival and departure of the ferry. The center is open mid-May to May 31 daily from 6am until 8pm, June 1 to August 31 daily from 6am until 10pm, September 1 to mid-October daily from 6am to 8pm. Call ✆ **709/695-2262.**

WHERE TO STAY

Barachois Pond Provincial Park Campground *Kids*   Just 20km (12 miles) southeast of Stephenville is one of the most scenic and best-maintained provincial parks in NL. Glorious natural eye-candy combines with a host of family fun for an unparalleled outdoor adventure. Activities include freshwater swimming, water skiing, boating, and fishing for both brook trout and salmon. There are also two sandy beaches (one is sheltered from westerly winds, the other from easterly breezes) as well as a couple of easy-to-moderate hiking trails, the best of which is the Erin Mountain Trail. *Hint:* The section of the Erin Mountain Trail to the lower lookout is boardwalked and is excellent for families. The upper half of the trail is recommended for experienced hikers because it's a tougher climb through brush and barren rock. The park has an excellent interpretive program that includes guided walks, environmental games, and campfire sing-alongs. Plus, there's a privately owned concession area where visitors can rent water trikes and pedal boats as well as play horseshoes and mini-golf. Concession information can be found in the on-site Camper's Convenience store.

Trans-Canada Highway (Rte. 1) to Barachois Pond Provincial Park. ✆ **800/563-6353** or 709/649-0048; off-season 709/635-4520. www.gov.nf.ca/parks&reserves/barachois_pond.htm. 150 sites. C$11 (US$8). MC, V. Open May 15–Sept 16. **Amenities:** Convenience store; day-use facilities; dumping station; laundry facilities; showers; freshwater swimming; boat rentals.

Holiday Inn Stephenville   Stephenville's finest hotel is ideally situated for shopping (it's connected to the town's shopping plaza), golfing at Harmon Golf and Country Club's 18-hole golf course, and touring the Port au Port Peninsula. Guest rooms at the Holiday Inn are big enough to dance in—should you feel a sudden urge to mambo—and have air-conditioning to help you cool off afterward. Wheelchair-accessible rooms are available. The Holiday Inn Stephenville won the 2002 Torchbearer Award for outstanding quality service.

Route 460 to 44 Queen St., Stephenville. ✆ **709/643-6666.** holinn.sville@nf.sympatico.ca. 47 units. C$83–$130 (US$60.89–$96) double; family & package rates available. AE, MC, V. **Amenities:** Restaurant; lounge; nonsmoking rooms. *In room:* AC, TV, coffeemaker, hairdryer, iron.

Hotel Port aux Basques ✚   If you're looking for the closest accommodations to the ferry terminal in Channel–Port aux Basques, this is it. This personable hotel is newly renovated and modernized through the addition of several suites as well as new paint, carpet, beds, and TVs. The on-site casual restaurant specializes in generous helpings of seafood and even has a special kids' menu. Hotel Port aux Basques is within walking distance of shopping, churches, a railway heritage site, a cinema, a hospital, and recreational facilities. You're a 20-minute drive from the St. Andrews Na Creige Golf Course. The hotel is wheelchair accessible. Pets are allowed.

2 Grand Bay Rd., Channel–Port aux Basques. ✆ **877/695-2171** or 709/695-2171. 50 units. Standard guest rooms: C$79.99–$84.99 (US$59–$63) double. Suites: C$129–$149 (US$95–$109). Family, seniors, & off-season discounts available; kids stay free. AE, DC, MC, V. **Amenities:** Dining room; lounge; nonsmoking rooms. *In room:* TV, coffeemaker, hairdryer.

Spruce Pine Acres Country Inn ⭐ This is a deluxe seaside B&B 10 minutes from Stephenville. The country comfort of the rustic furnishings—even the strategically placed balconies and pure mountain air—are deliberate stress reducers. If that isn't enough to help you put the cares of the workaday world behind you, you can avail of the on-site sauna and hot tub, then head down the stairway to the ocean before partaking of a European-style picnic complete with gourmet cheeses, patés, chocolate fondue, and fine wine (it's no wonder the inn's initials spell "spa"). Each of the four standard guest rooms has a private bath with tub and shower as well as a telephone and deck access. Rates include continental breakfast and afternoon tea for two. This is a completely smoke-free facility, and pets are not allowed.

Route 460 to Front Rd., Port au Port. ℂ 877/239-7117 or 709/648-9273. www.spa.nf.ca. 5 units. C$125–$150 (US$92–$110) standard double. C$150–$195 (US$110–$144) chalet. Seniors' discount available. AE, MC, V. Open Apr 1–Nov 30. **Amenities:** Breakfast room; lounge; hot tub; sauna; fitness room; nonsmoking rooms. *In room:* TV.

St. Christopher's Hotel Situated on a hill overlooking the scenic harbor, this is the largest hotel in Port aux Basques. It has more amenities than its competition, but the rooms aren't as nice. The standard guest rooms are simply adequate. There are several more spacious suites to choose from, some with fully equipped kitchenettes. The hotel is wheelchair accessible, near the marine boardwalk, and just 1km (less than a mile) from the ferry terminal. Pets are allowed. Book as far ahead as possible if you're visiting during July and August.

146 Caribou Rd., Channel–Port aux Basques. ℂ 800/563-4779 or 709/695-7034. www.stchrishotel.com. 57 units. Standard rooms: C$99.99 (US$73.30) double. Suites: C$124.99 (US$92). Off-season discounts available. MC, V. **Amenities:** Full-service restaurant; lounge; fitness room; nonsmoking rooms. *In room:* A/C, TV.

WHERE TO DINE

Emile's Pub and Eatery ⭐ CONTEMPORARY Located within the Holiday Inn, this is the closest thing to fine dining that Stephenville has to offer (although it's not unusual to see patrons dressed in jeans and a nice sweater). Emile's has an excellent reputation for delivering reliably good food. Some of their better offerings are their homemade soups—especially the rich and chunky seafood chowder. They also make great hot wings and cod dishes and have excellent sandwich specials. Emile's has a lounge as well as a separate section for families with children. There are smoking and nonsmoking sections.

44 Queen St., Stephenville. ℂ 709/643-6666. Reservations recommended for dinner. Prices range from C$6–$19 (US$4.40–$14.40). AE, MC, V. Open Mon–Thurs 7am–10pm, Fri 7am–11pm, Sat–Sun 8am–midnight.

Harbour Restaurant ⭐ CONTEMPORARY This is a popular family restaurant (with limited parking) within walking distance of the Marine Atlantic ferry terminal and adjacent to the boardwalk shopping area. Harbour Restaurant is a combination takeout/eat-in spot with an extensive menu featuring seafood (mostly fried), home-style meals (think pork chops and mashed potatoes), and pizza. French fries are disappointingly of the frozen variety. The harbor-side window seats are an ideal vantage point for watching the ferry's arrival and departure.

Main Rd., Port aux Basques, across the harbor from the Marine Atlantic ferry terminal. ℂ 709/695-3238. Most meals under C$10 (US$7.33).

Hartery's Family Restaurant ⭐ *Value* TRADITIONAL If you're looking for a more traditional Newfoundland atmosphere and a good meal, I recommend Hartery's. They serve a large variety of dishes and are well known for their traditional "Jiggs Dinner" (boiled beef and cabbage), served every Thursday and a steal at C$5.99 (US$4.40). They also serve a very nice seafood platter for C$17.99 (US$13.44).

109 Main St., Stephenville. (✆ **709/643-2242**. No reservations required. C$5–$7 (US$3.66–$5.13) lunch; C$7–$18 (US$5.13–$13.44) dinner. MC, V, Interac. Open Mon–Fri 9am–9pm, Sat–Sun 11am–9pm.

EXPLORING STEPHENVILLE & CHANNEL–PORT AUX BASQUES

St. Andrews Na Creige Golf Course   Check out one of Newfoundland & Labrador's finer golf courses. It's on Route 407 in St. Andrews, just 20 minutes from the ferry terminal at Channel–Port aux Basques. This new, par-35, nine-hole course is situated in the beautiful Codroy Valley and offers spectacular views of the Long Range Mountains and Little Codroy River. The season generally runs from May 1 to October 31. Call (✆ **709/955-3322** or visit www.golfnewfoundland.ca for more information.

Stephenville Summer Theatre Festival   The Stephenville area has several festivals during the summer, the most popular of which is the professional theater festival that runs during July and August. The festival has won several awards and has been named one of the top attractions in its category by the North American Bus Association. Tickets for the main-stage productions cost C$17 (US$12.46) adults, C$12 (US$8.79) seniors, and C$10 (US$7.33) students with valid student card. Call (✆ **709/643-1232** for more information on the theater festival and other Stephenville events.

(Finds The Last French Stronghold

West of Stephenville along Route 460 is the **Port au Port Peninsula,** Newfoundland's only remaining French region. The original settlers were reportedly Cape Breton Acadians who moved here in the 18th century. Until the last 50 years, geographic isolation and a rural economy protected the language and customs of this small francophone population.

Each August the people of Cap Sainte-Georges and surrounding communities hold "Une Longue Veillee," a folk festival that celebrates their French heritage. In recent years this festival has attracted traditional musicians, singers, and dancers from all over the province and a host of visitors and performers from the Maritime provinces, Quebec, and the French islands of St. Pierre and Miquelon.

Things to see include **Our Lady of Mercy Church and Museum** in Port au Port West (the largest wooden structure in the province; (✆ **709/648-9236** or 709/648-2261 for more information); **Our Lady of Lourdes Grotto** in the town of Lourdes (in addition to the religious monument, the Grotto also features a beautiful flower garden and an 1800 man-of-war cannon); and **Lewis Hills** (the largest mountain in Newfoundland).

It takes 2½ hours to drive around the loop of the peninsula and back to Stephenville—if you don't stop. But if you take your time and enjoy the breathtaking cliff-hanging vistas, consider it a full day's outing. Note: There aren't a lot of services for travelers in the area. It's best to tank up before you head out, and either pack a picnic lunch or have a big breakfast that will do you until you return to your post for the night. For more information, contact the Port au Port Economic Development Association ((✆ **709/642-5831**; www.nfld.net/paped/index.htm).

Gros Morne & Terra Nova National Parks

As national parks, Gros Morne and Terra Nova share a comparable quality of service vastly superior to what you'll find in the smaller provincial day/overnight parks: showers, laundry facilities, playground areas, and bilingual French/English interpretation programs. Despite the similarities, however, Gros Morne and Terra Nova offer distinctly different vacation experiences. **Gros Morne National Park** is without question the more impressive example of untamed natural wonder. Its cloud-shrouded mountains, glacial fjords, endangered species, and granite upheaval make it an outdoor adventurer's delight. A UNESCO World Heritage Site, Gros Morne is a massive 1,805-sq.-km (697-sq.-mile) park with raw beauty. Try to give yourself at least 2 days in Gros Morne—more if you're camping or backpacking.

Terra Nova National Park is the diametric opposite of Gros Morne in terms of geographic location (it's located in the more "civilized" portion of the province, at the westernmost edge of the Eastern Region). More than that, it also presents a more subdued landscape than its western cousin. Its sandy freshwater pond, children's interpretive programs, less strenuous walking trails, and nearby urban attractions make it more appropriate as a family vacation destination. That said, it still has backcountry appeal for the more adventurous souls (serious wilderness hikers can be dropped in remote locations, returning with the aid of a map and compass).

If you are lodging in any of the communities just outside the park, a full-day tour of Terra Nova will give you a very good idea of what the park has to offer. But if you're camping, the scenery and terrific outdoor facilities can keep you occupied for a full week and more.

1 Gros Morne National Park ✹✹✹

Gros Morne is larger than life, bordered by the Long Range Mountains and tapering to 90-m (300-ft.) oceanic depths mere meters from shore. In between is an unbelievable biotic richness: old-growth forests, coastal lowlands, glacier-scarred landscapes, and a place where continents collided. The best way to really appreciate it is via a boat tour, hiking, rock climbing, skiing, or snowmobiling. In short, you have to get out there!

Unless you're the hardy type, the weather may hamper your enjoyment of the park. I spent a week in Gros Morne and it rained for half that time—which isn't unusual. Between the prevailing southwest winds and the proximity of the Gulf of St. Lawrence, there is, on average, precipitation every 2 days during the summer months. From late September (for the higher elevations) on through the winter months, that dripping wetness translates into an impressive snowfall—up to 1,000cm (393.7 in., or 32.8 ft.) in some areas, making Gros Morne ideal for backcountry skiing.

ESSENTIALS

GETTING THERE

Getting to Gros Morne is easy, especially if you're arriving from Nova Scotia by ferry in Port aux Basques. From there, it's about a 3-hour drive north along the Trans-Canada Highway (Route 1) toward Deer Lake. Even if you're approaching the park from the east, you'll follow the Trans-Canada as far as Deer Lake. The main entrance to the park is just 30km (19 miles) northwest of town along the Viking Trail (Route 430—which takes you up the Great Northern Peninsula). It will take you less than an hour to drive from Deer Lake to the park.

Deer Lake also has the closest airport to Gros Morne National Park. You can fly into Deer Lake and rent a car for your exploration of the park. (See chapter 7 for more info about Deer Lake.)

If you've flown into St. Anthony (near the top of the Northern Peninsula), it's a 372-km (233-mile) trek to Rocky Harbour, about halfway through the park. (See chapter 7 for more details about services along Route 430.)

VISITOR INFORMATION

The most comprehensive information on Gros Morne is available in the park's **Discovery Centre** (✆ **709/458-2417;** www.pc.gc.ca/pn-np/nl/grosmorne/natcul/natcul12_E.asp), situated along Route 431 near the community of Woody Point.

Parks Canada publishes a wonderful visitor's guide called the *Tuckamore* that will provide you with detailed information about services in and around the park. Request a copy by writing Gros Morne National Park at P.O. Box 130, Rocky Harbour, Newfoundland, A0K 4N0 (e-mail: grosmorne.info@pc.gc.ca).

For information about privately run services in the communities bordering the park (a number of towns, like Rocky Harbour, are fully encompassed by the park), contact Tourism Newfoundland & Labrador (✆ **800/563-6353;** www.gov.nf.ca/tourism). There is also a useful website at www.grosmorne.com that provides information about services in the area.

You can also get information at the **park entrance kiosk,** located on Route 430 near the southeastern entrance to the park at Wiltondale. The kiosk does not have a telephone and is open mid-May to mid-October daily 10am until 6pm. A **Visitor Centre** (✆ **709/458-2066**), farther along Route 430 near the community of Rocky Harbour and the road to Gros Morne Mountain, is open May 1 to December 31. Hours of operation vary according to season: May 1 to June 20, daily 9am to 5pm; June 21 to Sept 2, daily 9am to 9pm; Sept 3 to Oct 14, daily 9am to 5pm; and Oct 15 to Dec 31, Mon to Fri 9am to 4pm.

GETTING AROUND

You enter the park from Route 430, just 30km (19 miles) northwest of Deer Lake and Route 1. The road is a good paved surface, and if you follow it in a northerly direction through the park you'll be well on your way to Port au Choix and a tour of the Northern Peninsula. (See chapter 7 for details about the Port au Choix National Historic Site and other highlights of the Northern Peninsula.)

Gros Morne National Park basically has two parts: the north side of Bonne Bay and the south side of Bonne Bay, with a 1-hour drive separating the two sides. The community of Wiltondale is right in the middle, at the fork of the road where Route 431 branches out from Route 430.

Route 430 takes you northwest along the north side of the bay and along the western coast of the park, while Route 431 branches in an easterly direction to the southern side of the bay and ends at the community of Trout River. You'll need to take Route 431 if your destination is the Tablelands and camping or hiking at Lomond or Trout River Pond.

Route 431 is also the location of the park's Discovery Centre, an absolute must-see if you are to make the most of your visit to Gros Morne. Unfortunately, you have to double back along Route 431 to reconnect with Route 430 and continue your exploration of the park, as the two routes don't reconnect between Woody Point and Norris Point; they are separated by Bonne Bay. But you're not likely to mind a bit of backtracking. The vistas as you drive around Gros Morne are breathtakingly beautiful.

The weather, however, can be quite unpredictable, so be prepared with clothing for all types, and be sure to get a pre-trip orientation from a park warden before you head off into the backcountry. You'll find hiking trails for every experience level, with the most difficult being the 16-km (10-mile) trail up to Gros Morne Mountain, the highest peak in the park at 850m (2,788 ft.). *Warning:* Pay special attention to prudent food handling when picnicking, camping, or hiking the backcountry so that you're not surprised by a hungry black bear.

WHERE TO STAY & DINE

You'll be pleased by the wealth of motel, inn, and B&B accommodation choices located in communities encircled by the park but outside park boundaries. If, however, you're hoping to stay in a luxury hotel, you're going to be disappointed —there aren't any, though there is always ample room at the best lodgings of all, where amenities include pine-needle carpets and starlight canopies.

During July and August, accommodations in Gros Morne—both campsites and motel rooms—can be difficult to come by. It's best to make your reservations as soon as you know you'll be coming.

There are several decent restaurants in the area, but not as many as you might think given the size of the park. It's the nature of the destination; most people aren't here for fine dining. They prefer to picnic, barbecue, or cook their own meals on outdoor stoves.

Aunt Jane's Place   In Newfoundland & Labrador, it's a traditional measure of respect and affection to refer to older, unrelated acquaintances as "Aunt" or "Uncle." Giving the title to this 19th-century tourist home evokes that old-fashioned charm just as much as its period furnishings and simple square construction. Only one of the 5 guest rooms has one bed in the room and a private bathroom; there are two beds in each of the other 4 rooms, sharing two bathrooms between them. If you aren't interested in watching TV in the common room, you can still mingle with your hosts and other guests in the upstairs sitting room while enjoying its view of Bonne Bay. Alternatively, visit the main-floor **Sample Room**'s antiques display and gift shop, where you can browse through merchandise typical of what was sold here more than 100 years ago.

Aunt Jane's Place is run by the same people who operate **Uncle Steve's Place,** a fully equipped 3-bedroom traditional-style home, great for a small group or family.

Route 431 to 1 Water St., Woody Point. ✆ **866/453-2485** or 709/453-2485. www.grosmorne.com/victorian manor. 5 units. C$40–$70 (US$29.50–$51.30) double. MC, V. Open May 15–Sept 30.

Gros Morne National Park

Backcountry Huts

Boat Launch

Boat Tour

Campground

Cross-country Ski Trail

Ⓓ **Gros Morne Discovery Centre**

Group Campground

ⓔ **Interpretive Sign or Exhibit**

Ⓣ **Outdoor Theatre**

Pay Phone

Picnic Area

Primitive Camping

Swimming

Trail

ⓘ **Visitor Information Centre**

Wheelchair Accessible

1 Bakers Brook Falls
2 Berry Head Pond
3 Berry Hill
4 Berry Hill Pond
5 Broom Point
6 Coastal (Green Point)
7 Green Gardens
8 Gros Morne Mountain
9 Lobster Cove Head
10 Lomond River
11 Lookout
12 Old Mail Road
13 Snug Harbour
14 Southeast Brook Falls
15 Stanleyville
16 Stuckless Pond
17 Tablelands
18 Trout River Pond
19 Western Brook Pond

Trout River

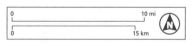

0   10 mi

0   15 km

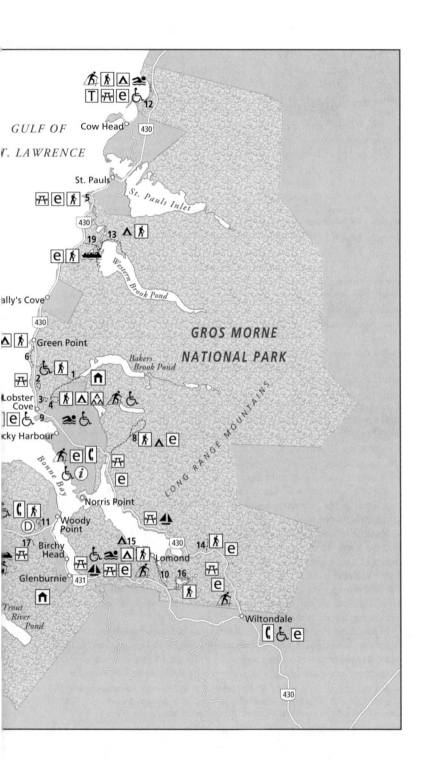

GULF OF
T. LAWRENCE

Cow Head 430

St. Pauls

5

St. Pauls Inlet

430

19 13

Western Brook Pond

ally's Cove

430

GROS MORNE
NATIONAL PARK

Green Point

Bakers
Brook Pond

6

2

1

Lobster
Cove

3 4

9

cky Harbour

8

Bonne Bay

LONG RANGE MOUNTAINS

i

Norris Point

11 Woody
Point

17 Birchy
Head

15

430

14

Glenburnie 431

Lomond

10 16

Trout
River
Pond

Wiltondale

430

Frontier Cottages The perfect location for extreme outdoor adventure, Frontier Cottages are situated at the crossroads of Gros Morne National Park. Thus, they offer the shortest route for exploring both sides of Bonne Bay. More than just a convenient exploration base, they're custom-made for outdoor fun. Stay at these fully winterized log cabins and you'll be able to start skiing and snowmobiling from the minute you walk out the door. Want to try something a little more unconventional, like ice climbing? Talk to the owners—they'll customize an expedition you'll never forget. The cabins are fully equipped and nicely decorated with pine and other rustic furnishings. There is an on-site convenience store and gas bar, craft/souvenir shop, and barbecues. Pets are allowed.

Route 430, Wiltondale. (C) **800/668-2520** or 709/453-7266. www.frontiercottages.com. 6 units. Summer: C$109 (US$80) double. Off-season: C$65 (US$48) double, C$10 (US$7.33) additional person. AE, DC, MC, V. **Amenities:** Restaurant; small playground; laundry facilities.

Middle Brook Cottages and Chalets (★★ (Kids) Families love the quality and convenience of this full-service facility (especially the playground and Laundromat). It's perfect for a day of on-site recreation or as a much-needed rest after hiking the nearby Tablelands. Both the cottages and the chalets get top marks for cleanliness and comfort with their tidy landscaped exteriors and pine-panelled walls. I especially like the chalets because of their cathedral ceilings and second-floor patio (a great place to enjoy your morning coffee and watch the sun come up).

There's a handy convenience store on-site as well as a gift shop. There's also a picnic area with barbecues and a firepit for an evening marshmallow roast. When you're not enjoying the sights and sounds of Gros Morne, you can explore the waterfall and walking trails that are within walking distance of Middle Brook.

Route 431, Glenburnie–Birchy Head. (C) **709/453-2332**. www.middlebrookcottages.com. 3 cottages, 2 chalets, 1 deluxe unit. C$99–$129 (US$72–$95) double; off-season C$65–$90 (US$48–$66) double, children under 12 free, C$10 (US$7.33) additional person. AE, MC, V. **Amenities:** Laundromat; playground; nonsmoking rooms.

Ocean View Motel (★ For those who prefer the anonymity of a motel over the forced intimacy of a B&B, this is the largest facility in the largest town in Gros Morne. It's friendly and welcoming without being as up close and personal as a smaller establishment. Guest rooms are standard motel style, although the bedding is of better quality than most. There is one housekeeping unit as well as wheelchair-accessible rooms.

Situated in Rocky Harbour, the Ocean View Motel is so close to the shore that the gentle lullaby of the surf will help you sleep at night. You may even be drawn to have a closer look, a whim easily accommodated by the steps leading from the motel lot to the beach. Or, you can stay in the comfort of the Anchor Pub and dining room, enraptured by the fading sun as it sets over Lobster Cove Head lighthouse. That's if you can draw your focus away from the superb dinner offerings, such as the just-caught lobster.

In addition to the many outdoor activities to be enjoyed throughout the park (kayaking, boat tours, hiking, skiing, snowmobiling, and so on), there is music and entertainment two to three times a week in the Ocean View's on-site pub. Further recreation can be enjoyed at the nearby public swimming complex.

Route 430 to Main St., Rocky Harbour. (C) **800/563-9887** or 709/458-2730. www.oceanviewmotel.com. 52 units. C$65–$125 (US$48–$92) double, off-season and group discounts available, C$5 (US$3.66) additional person. MC, V. **Amenities:** Restaurant; pub; nonsmoking rooms. *In room:* TV.

Shallow Bay Motel & Cabins (★ (Kids) There's something for everyone at Shallow Bay: natural wonder, peaceful solitude, and a sauna for adult enjoyment; mini-golf, heated pool, and beachcombing for the younger set. One activity both young and old are guaranteed to appreciate is the Gros Morne Theatre Festival—a powerful production of Newfoundland drama, story, and song hosted here each summer.

The property offers a choice of standard motel unit or fully equipped cabin. Both are fairly modest, although enhanced by the ocean just 5m (16 ft.) away. This is a wheelchair-accessible facility. The on-site family restaurant serves a tasty assortment of pocketbook-friendly home-style meals. The specialty of the house is lobster, but you can get it only in season, from early May to early July.

Route 430, Cow Head. ✆ **800/563-1946** or 709/243-2471. www.shallowbaymotel.com. 52 units (35 motel units, 17 cottages). C$75–$115 (US$55–$83.66) double, off-season discounts, C$8 (US$5.86) additional person. AE, DC, MC, V, Interac. **Amenities:** Dining room; lounge; outdoor heated pool; sauna; Laundromat. *In room:* TV.

 Gros Morne Theatre Festival

The Gros Morne Theatre Festival is an unforgettable experience of such rich cultural diversity, you won't be satisfied until you see it all. "All" in 2003 was 8 different productions, 3 different venues, 2 shows a night, and more than 30 professional actors, musicians, technicians, writers, directors, and front-of-house staff. Focus on the word *professional*—that's your first indication of the superior quality of these dramatic events. That, and the consistently sold-out shows. A superb example of the intensely personable plays performed during the Gros Morne Theatre Festival is *Tempting Providence*. Written by Robert Chafe, it's the haunting story of Nurse Myra Bennett, Newfoundland's own Florence Nightingale. For more than 50 years, Bennett was the only medical person on the Great Northern Peninsula. During that time she delivered more than 700 babies, extracted at least 5,000 teeth, and performed kitchen-table surgeries by lamplight. For information on the latest shows and to make a reservation, call ✆ **877/243-2899** or go to www. theatrenewfoundland. com/gmtf.html.

Sugar Hill Inn ★★★ *Finds*   One of the more luxurious places to stay while in Gros Morne (and one of the only places to have in-room air-conditioning) is Sugar Hill Inn. Most impressive is the King Suite. It features a king-sized bed, private Jacuzzi for two, and gorgeous leather couch. This room is popular—especially with honeymooners—so be sure to book early. There is also a nice cottage with queen-sized bed, Jacuzzi tub, and a private deck. Every room has hardwood floors, and most have private entrances.

The Sugar Hill Inn offers gourmet dining in its full-service restaurant. Specialties of the house include fresh local seafood—halibut, cod, salmon, shrimp, scallops, and shark. It's one of the very few restaurants in the province where *nothing* is deep-fried. Service is by reservation only—primarily for guests of the inn. But call anyway—they may have an opening for the single 7:30pm dinner sitting.

Route 430 to Norris Pt. Rd. ✆ **888/299-2147** or 709/458-2147. www.sugarhillinn.nf.ca. 6 units. C$76–$172 (US$55.70–$126.76) double. Off-season discounts apply. C$15 (US$11) additional person. AE, MC, V. Closed Nov & Dec. **Amenities:** Licensed dining room; bar; hot tub; sauna; laundry facilities; nonsmoking rooms. *In room:* A/C, TV.

CAMPING IN GROS MORNE

A good number of visitors come to Gros Morne to camp and thus to fully appreciate the great outdoors. All campgrounds within the park boundary are administered by Parks Canada and are well maintained.

Lomond Campground   Just down Route 431, 17km (10.6 miles) south from Wiltondale at Lomond, you'll find a full-service campground, the closest one to the main park entrance. This campground is ideal for people interested in fishing and boating and is popular with local residents. The area was once a logging community, and two groomed trails follow old logging roads. The campsites have lots of open, grassy spaces, and offer outstanding views of Bonne Bay, the Lomond River, and Killdevil Mountain.

Route 431, Lomond. ℂ **709/458-2417**; off-season 709/458-2059. www2.parkscanada.gc.ca/pn-np/nl/
grosmorne/index_E.asp. 29 sites. C$15.25 (US$11.70); C$3.25 (US$2.49) per firewood bundle. AE, MC, V,
Interac. Open mid-May to mid-Oct. **Amenities:** Running water; dumping station; washrooms with showers;
swimming; boat launching/docking facilities; fireplaces; kitchen shelters; picnic tables; fishing; hiking;
playground.

Shallow Bay Campground   Located near Cow Head (home of the Gros Morne Theatre Festival), this is the northernmost campground along Route 430, just before the northern entrance/exit to the park. The grassy campsites, sheltered from northwesterly winds by a protective stand of tuckamore, are a hop, skip, and jump from a 4-km-long (2½-mile) white sand beach—ideal for swimming and building sand castles. There is a trail that links the campground to the day-use area and a small outdoor theater for campfire programs.

Route 430 to Cow Head. ℂ **709/458-2417**; off-season 709/458-2162. www2.parkscanada.gc.ca/pn-np/
nl/grosmorne/index_E.asp. 50 sites. C$15.25 (US$11.70) for unserviced sites; C$3.25 (US$2.49) for firewood
bundle. AE, MC, V, Interac. Open mid-June to mid-Sept. **Amenities:** Dumping station; running water; showers;
fireplace; kitchen shelter; picnic tables; playground; swimming; theater; fishing; hiking.

Trout River Campground ✦   Campsites at Trout River are larger and more sheltered than in some other parts of the park and provide awesome views of the Tablelands and Trout River Pond. The drinking water is good, but it's still not a bad idea to filter it. This is a popular spot because of the nearby beach, boat tour, and boat launch. Although the most isolated campground in the park (excluding the primitive campsites), it's also the best base for exploring the Tablelands, the Green Gardens area, and the community of Trout River.

Route 431, Trout River. ℂ **709/458-2417**; off-season 709/458-2162. www2.parkscanada.gc.ca/pn-np/nl/
grosmorne/index_E.asp. 33 units. C$15.25 (US$11.70) for unserviced sites; C$3.25 (US$2.49) for firewood
bundle. AE, MC, V, Interac. Open mid-June to mid-Sept. **Amenities:** Shower & washroom facilities; water;
kitchen shelter; picnic tables; fireplace; playground; fishing; hiking; sightseeing; swimming.

EXPLORING GROS MORNE

Entrance to the park can be obtained with a seasonal, 4-day, or daily pass. The daily pass costs C$7.50 (US$5.50) for adults; C$6 (US$4.40) for seniors 65 and over; C$3.75 (US$2.87) for youth 6 to 16 years; free for children under 6. Family passes are a good deal at C$15 (US$11). The 4-day pass costs $22.50 (US$17.26) for adults; C$18 (US$13.44) for seniors 65 years and over; C$11.25 (US$8.63) for youth 6 to 16; free for children under 6. Four-day family passes are an excellent deal at C$45 (US$33). Your park entrance fee gives you access to park services including the wonderful Discovery Centre.

The Discovery Centre ✦✦   Your first step to exploring Gros Morne should be the Discovery Centre on Route 431. This ultra-modern and spacious facility with comfortable lounge area and huge panoramic windows offers a spectacular view of Bonne Bay. Choose from an assortment of park activities, including interpretive programs, lectures, and guided walks.

The Discovery Centre is the best place to begin exploration of the south side of the park, which includes the Tablelands (the geological feature that helped make Gros Morne a UNESCO World Heritage Site in 1987), the beautiful Green Gardens Trail (excellent for viewing wildflowers), and Trout River Pond. You'll find some incredible interpretive exhibits about Gros Morne's geology on the first floor of the center and an art exhibit that changes regularly on the lower level.

Run collaboratively by the park and the Art Gallery of Newfoundland & Labrador, an artists-in-residence program offers lectures and workshops by artists whose work is displayed at the Discovery Centre. You can also watch the artists at work, and maybe even purchase a permanent remembrance to hang on your wall at home.

Plan to spend a couple of hours at the Discovery Centre before heading out on the trail. The 5-km (3-mile) Lookout Hills Trail begins at the Discovery Centre and takes a half-day to complete. This moderately difficult trail offers the best view of Bonne Bay and the Tablelands.

Route 431 near Woody Point. ☎ **709/458-2417** or TDD 709/772-4564. Open mid-May to mid-Oct daily 9am–5pm; summer, Wed & Sun until 9pm. Your entrance fee to the park gets you into the Discovery Centre.

Lobster Cove Head Lighthouse ⊛   This dramatic lighthouse has marked the marine approach to Rocky Harbour and the entrance to Bonne Bay since 1897. What's unique is the cast-iron structure of this lighthouse, one of the first of its kind to be built by Victoria Iron Works of St. John's. The setting of the lighthouse against a rocky backdrop has made it a photo favorite for visitors to the area. See www.lorneslights.com/NF/nf105.html for a nice online photo.

The Canadian Coast Guard now operates an automated light from the lighthouse. The former keeper's house is open to the public as an interpretive historical exhibit about the various peoples who have inhabited this coast over the past 4,000 years. It also explains the seasonal fishery's importance to the region. The road to the lighthouse is marked and the lighthouse itself is visible from the highway. A 2-km (1¼-mile) trail leads from the lighthouse to a rocky beach that's best explored at low tide.

Route 430, Lobster Cove Head, near Rocky Harbour. No telephone. Open June to mid-Oct daily 10am–6pm. Your admission to the park also gets you into the interpretive exhibit.

The Tablelands ⊛   This geological wonder just south of Woody Point on Route 431 has gained worldwide recognition for its contribution to the understanding of plate tectonics. For this barren orange-yellow moonscape, Gros Morne National Park was declared a UNESCO World Heritage Site.

The Tablelands are an excellent example of plate tectonics, in which 470-million-year-old ultramafic rock was brought to the Earth's surface as a result of faulting. In plain English, it means that this is what the world would look like if you turned it inside out (the Tablelands were once several kilometers below an ancient ocean). A 4-km (2½-mile) self-guided hiking trail off Route 431 takes about 1½ hours to get to the Tablelands. *Note:* All rocks, minerals, and fossils found within national parks are protected and must be left as found. The collection of specimens for research or educational purposes requires a permit, which you must apply for well in advance of your visit because of the extensive application review process.

Tableland Boat Tours   If you're not able to hike but would still like to see the Tablelands, at Trout River you can take a 2½-hour boat tour and view this natural wonder from the comfort of a wheelchair-accessible boat. The boat dock is very close to the parking lot. There are three departures daily, but—like everything in Newfoundland—departures are always weather dependent.

Route 431, Trout River Pond day-use area. © 709/451-2101 for reservations and information. June 15–Sept 15. During June & Sept, there is only a 1pm sailing. In July & Aug, there are 3 daily sailings: 10am, 1pm, 4pm.

Western Brook Pond 🏵🏵🏵   If you have only one day in the park, you'll probably want to visit the Discovery Centre in the morning and take a boat tour of Western Brook Pond in the afternoon. You'll have a 2½-hour narrated cruise through some of the most spectacular scenery you've ever seen.

Western Brook Pond isn't what we traditionally think of as a pond. It's a 16-km-long (10-mile), 165-m-deep (541-ft.) inland fjord created during the Glacial Epoch. There's one point in the tour when the captain pauses 1m (3 ft.) from the base of a waterfall to declare that you are floating on water 91.44m deep (300 ft.). *Warning:* This is not a tour to take if you have mobility problems. You must park your car at the Western Brook Pond trail head, and then embark on a 3-km (nearly 2-mile) hike along the boardwalk to where you catch the boat. It's not a difficult hike, but it will take you approximately 40 minutes each way, and longer if you walk very slowly.

Western Pond Boat Tours: Route 430, Rocky Harbour. © 709/458-2730 for reservations. C$33 (US$24.21) adults; C$15 (US$11) youth 12–16; C$8 (US$5.86) children under 12. During June & Sept, there is only a 1pm sailing. In July & Aug, there are 3 daily sailings: 10am, 1pm, 4pm. If you pay at the **Ocean View Motel** in Rocky Harbour, you can use AE, MC, V, Interac. If you pay at the boat dock, come prepared with cash or traveler's checks. Departures are weather dependent. Bring rain gear.

GROS MORNE OUTDOOR ACTIVITIES
INDEPENDENT SKIING

There are some pretty amazing cross-country skiing opportunities in Gros Morne. If you're a beginner, the backcountry skiing will be best suited to your abilities: the terrain is more gentle, with rolling hills and no steep inclines. Skiing on the Tablelands is comparable to skiing on glaciers with steep terrain and better left for the advanced skier. The alpine terrain of the Long Range Mountains is also best suited to those with advanced skills.

GUIDED PACKAGES

Whether you're looking to do some skiing, guided hiking, sea kayaking, backpacking, or snowshoeing, you should put yourself in the hands of an experienced outfitter—especially if this is your first visit to Gros Morne. **Gros Morne Adventures** will customize a tour for you any time of the year. If your primary focus is on hiking, try the Gros Morne Explorer, a combination of coastal and mountain hiking that runs June through September. Over the course of a week, you'll hike a number of the park's best trails. Plan to cover 10 to 16km (up to 10 miles) per day, up elevations of 700m (2,300 ft.) over uneven surfaces.

Guided kayaking programs range from 2½ hours to a full day. You can also rent single or double kayaks and go off on your own if you're an experienced kayaker. Bonne Bay is a great place for sea kayaking because of the calm, sheltered waters. It's common to see whales, bald eagles, terns, mink, mergansers, and kingfishers throughout the summer. Winter programs include backcountry skiing and snowshoeing adventures. Gros Morne Adventures specializes in the telemark style of skiing, similar to the bent-knee Norwegian. The scenery is awe-inspiring, the snow is plentiful, and moose and caribou are often spotted as you make your way along.

For your overnight accommodations, Gros Morne Adventures chooses established properties to suit the individual client's preferences and pocketbook. All guides have at least 15 years' experience and are CPR and wilderness trained and certified, in addition to having avalanche awareness and safety training. The company's website will provide you with a full range of prices and options.

9 Clarke's Lane, on Norris Point off Route 430. ✆ 800/685-4624 or 709/458-2722. www.grosmorne adventures.com.

2 Terra Nova National Park ✦✦

Terra Nova (meaning "new land") is Newfoundland's first and more accessible national park. The main visitor center is located just 240km (149 miles), or about a 3-hour drive, northwest of St. John's, and about 76km (47 miles) southeast of Gander.

If you were to give them human personalities, Gros Morne would be an extreme sports enthusiast while Terra Nova would be the family guy driving a minivan. But while Terra Nova doesn't possess the striking scenery you'll find in Gros Morne, it is still a beautiful park with great camping and some excellent naturalist programs. If you have just 2 weeks in Newfoundland, you can probably see Terra Nova, the Avalon Region (including St. John's), and the Eastern Region (ends just outside Terra Nova) without feeling too rushed.

ESSENTIALS
GETTING THERE
Terra Nova National Park is conveniently located along the Trans-Canada Highway (Route 1), so if you're driving across the province you'll go straight through it. It's located in the Eastern Region about 80km (50 miles) northwest of Clarenville.

There are four paved access points into the park. Access to the most southerly part of the park can be gained from Port Blandford, in the northwestern part of the Eastern Region. (See chapter 5 for details about the Eastern Region and Port Blandford.)

Access to the southeast part of the park can be gained at Charlottetown, while entrance to the northern part of the park can be gained from two locations: near Traytown off Route 310, or off Route 1 just south of Glovertown.

VISITOR INFORMATION
You can obtain visitor information for the park at **Salton's Marine Interpretation Centre** (✆ 800/213-7275 or 709/533-2801) in Newman Sound, the hub of Terra Nova National Park. The center is generally open from mid-May until (Canadian) Thanksgiving in early October. Hours are 9am until 9pm in summer, and 10am until 5pm in spring and fall.

There is no visitor information available at the Charlottetown or Traytown entrances to the park, and it will take you 15 minutes to drive to the Marine Interpretation Centre from the Charlottetown entrance. Visitor information is also available at a kiosk at Square Pond (the northern entrance off Route 1), open July and August, daily 9am until 5pm.

For general information about Terra Nova, visit Parks Canada's website at www.pc.gc.ca/pn-np/nl/terranova. Here you will find the very detailed fee system for entrance to Canada's national parks, including Terra Nova. *Note:* You don't need a Parks Canada vehicle pass if you're just driving through the park and do not stop.

If you're planning to tour the park, you'll need to purchase an entrance pass. There are daily, 4-day, or seasonal passes available. The day pass costs C$4 (US$2.50) for adults; C$3 (US$2) for seniors 65 and over; C$2 for youth 6 to 16; free for children under 6. The family rate is C$8 (US$5). If you're camping and plan on staying at least 3 days, the 4-day pass might be best for you: C$12 (US$7.70) for adults; C$9 (US$5.75) seniors 65 and over; C$6 (US$3.85) youth 6 to 16; and free for children under 6. There is a family rate of C$24 (US$15) for the 4-day pass.

The park's visitor's guide, *Terra Nova Sounds* (available on request), will be quite useful in planning your visit and choosing which trails and campgrounds are best suited to you.

You can obtain general information about most communities near the park and private services available in and around the park from the Kittiwake Coast Tourism Association. Call them at © **709/256-5070** and ask for a copy of the *Kittiwake Visitors' Guide,* or visit them on the Web at www.kittiwakecoast.com.

GETTING AROUND

Getting around Terra Nova by car is easy, as the Trans-Canada Highway (Route 1) dissects the park from north to south. The road is good, also making it relatively easy traveling for the cyclist. In July and August, this road has heavy traffic with quite a few RVs that may slow things down a bit. But that's okay, as you should be watching your speed and looking out for wildlife. There are quite a few moose in the park, so take extra precautions at dusk or dawn, avoiding night travel if possible.

Over the past few years, Terra Nova National Park has made many of its facilities and programs accessible to visitors with physical disabilities. A heavy-duty all-terrain wheelchair is available at no charge from the park's Activity Centre. It's not motorized, so someone still has to push it, but this amenity allows visitors with disabilities to tour and enjoy many areas of the park that may otherwise be inaccessible to them.

Pocket-sized FM "Easy Listener" receivers are available for those with a hearing impairment. Close-captioned audiovisuals are shown at the Activity Centre and the Twin Rivers Visitor Centre. A TDD telephone device for the deaf is available at the Administration building.

WHERE TO STAY & DINE

Aside from topographical differences, Terra Nova also differs from Gros Morne in that it does not have a handful of small, embedded communities. Other than park-administered campgrounds and the sites near the park gates at the southern and northern access points, there are no visitor accommodations within the expanse of the park. In terms of food, there is just one snack bar, at the Salton's Marine Interpretation Centre, so be sure to either bring your own snacks into the park or be prepared to exit the park and head to one of the surrounding communities for lunch.

For motel and resort accommodations close to the Port Blandford entrance, see chapter 5. Because of its proximity to the park, and the fact that the property's main focus is on providing service to visitors of the park, a Charlottetown motel and restaurant is listed here. Other than that, Terra Nova is best suited to campers and those visiting only for the day.

Clode Sound Motel & Restaurant ✦ *(Value* You're bound to feel at home once you step through the door of this family-run establishment. Nellie Cunningham, the friendly hands-on manager, ensures you have a quality visit—whether you're dropping in for lunch, or staying with them for a week. Many small touches make the Clode Sound special. The smell of fresh bread (baked three times daily) and the apple pies made from apples grown on their property, the fresh-cut flowers on each dining table from the flower gardens that adorn the grounds, and the smiling staff—all will help make you glad you found this tiny haven along the Trans-Canada Highway (Route 1).

The accommodations are aging, but well maintained. The peaceful, yet convenient, location is what makes this property stand out. You're near Terra Nova National Park, whale- and bird-watching, sea kayaking, hiking, and golf. And you're only 2 hours from St. John's and 1 hour from Gander. Each of the fully equipped housekeeping units has access to a picnic table and barbecue pit.

Route 1, Charlottetown. ✆ **709/664-3146** or 709/664-3411 for off-season bookings. 19 units. C$65–$80 (US$42–$51) double. AE, MC, V, Interac. Open May 1 to Oct 31. **Amenities:** Licensed restaurant; bakery; heated swimming pool; tennis; hot tub; playground; nonsmoking. Winchester's Restaurant: C$6.95 (US$4.50) for great fish & chips or cod au gratin. Extensive menu. Portions are very ample. Vegetarian and local specialties. Open May to Oct daily 7am–9pm.

CAMPING IN TERRA NOVA

Camping is really the way to go in Terra Nova. They have an excellent Campfire Concert Program, with weekly concerts at the beachside campfire circle built from natural logs. And the **Junior Naturalist Club** and **Teenage Naturalist Program** ✦ have really made the park a hit with families. The junior program is geared toward kids ages 8 to 12 and the teenage program is for ages 13 to 17. Children get a chance to learn about nature in a fun, hands-on way. Visit the Activity Centre at Newman Sound Campground for more info.

In addition to the two campgrounds listed here, there are also several small backcountry campgrounds that you can access from hiking trails or by canoe. Find out more in the *Terra Nova Sounds* user's guide to the park.

Malady Head Campground *(Value* If you're looking for a secluded campground, this one provides a quiet, natural setting for campers wishing to experience nature without human frills. There are numerous hiking trails in the area and sightseeing is good on the "Road to the Beaches." One other great thing about this campground is that it doesn't book up like Newman Sound does, so if you arrive without a reservation chances are you'll still get into Malady Head. A park entry permit or seasonal pass is required to enter the campground.

Route 1 to Route 310. ✆ **866/533-3186** or 709-533-2801. www2.parkscanada.gc.ca/pn-np/nl/terranova/ activ/activ2_E.asp. 99 sites. C$12 (US$7.70). AE, MC, V, Interac. Open July 1 to Sept 4. **Amenities:** Wooded sites; heated washrooms with flush toilets; wheelchair accessible; playground; individual site firepits; kitchen shelters; hiking trails; saltwater beach nearby.

Newman Sound Campground ✦ This is by far the largest campground in the park, with 356 campsites, and it's my recommended destination as it's fully serviced and has treed lots. Only 66 of the sites are fully serviced with electricity, so if this is a requirement be sure to book as far in advance as possible. A park entry permit or seasonal pass is required to enter the campground. Check-in time is 1pm. Call ahead to guarantee a late arrival. Check-out time is noon. Quiet hours are enforced beginning at 11pm. You can camp here year-round, but the electricity is turned on only from May through October.

Terra Nova National Park

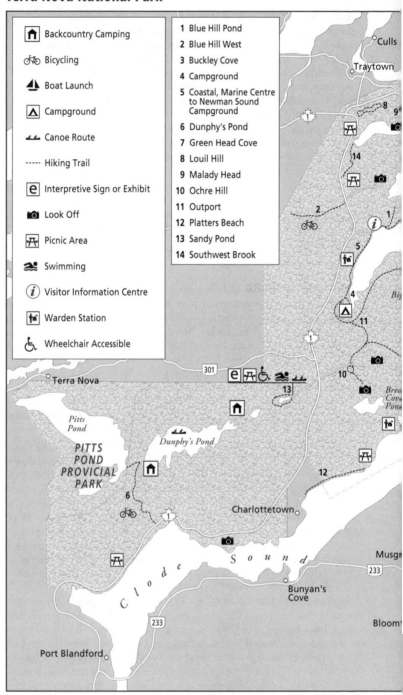

Legend symbols:

- 🏠 Backcountry Camping
- 🚲 Bicycling
- ⛵ Boat Launch
- ⛺ Campground
- ～ Canoe Route
- ----- Hiking Trail
- e Interpretive Sign or Exhibit
- 📷 Look Off
- 🎪 Picnic Area
- 🏊 Swimming
- (i) Visitor Information Centre
- 🏠 Warden Station
- ♿ Wheelchair Accessible

1. Blue Hill Pond
2. Blue Hill West
3. Buckley Cove
4. Campground
5. Coastal, Marine Centre to Newman Sound Campground
6. Dunphy's Pond
7. Green Head Cove
8. Louil Hill
9. Malady Head
10. Ochre Hill
11. Outport
12. Platters Beach
13. Sandy Pond
14. Southwest Brook

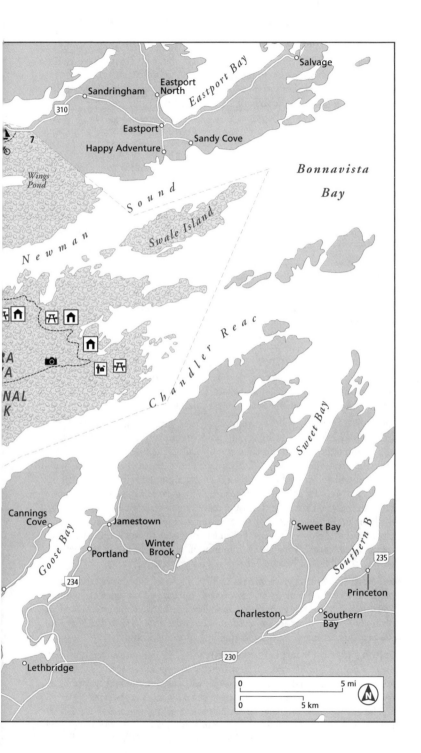

Newman Sound is ideally located near the Marine Interpretive Centre and just 30km (19 miles) from the east entrance of the park. If you like organized activities and full-service camping, Newman Sound is the better choice for you. The camping reservation system allows you to reserve your site ahead of time, but there is an additional charge of C$7 (US$4.50) for this service.

Route 1 to Newman Sound. ✆ **866/533-3186** for reservations Campground open April 9 to Oct 6 8am–4:30pm. General enquiries ✆ 709/533-2801. www2.parkscanada.gc.ca/pn-np/nl/terranova/activ/ activ2_E.asp. 356 sites. C$14–$18 (US$9–$11.50). AE, MC, V, Interac. **Amenities:** heated washrooms with showers & flush toilets; wheelchair accessible; grocery store; snack bar; Laundromat; dumping station; playground; community firepits; kitchen shelter; hiking trails; interpretive programs; kids' activity center; outdoor theater; campfire programs.

EXPLORING TERRA NOVA

The landscape of the park varies from the rugged cliffs and sheltered inlets of its coastal region (which takes in Clode Sound and Newman Sound, fjords that are extensions of Bonavista Bay), to the rolling hills of the boreal forest and the bogs and ponds that jointly make up the park's inland region. Terra Nova's "Fingers of the Sea" provide many scenic vistas and give the park about 200km (124 miles) of shoreline.

Blue Hill   If you're not into hiking or formal tours, a couple of highlights to see while in the park are Blue Hill and Sandy Pond (see description below). Blue Hill is the highest point in the park, at 199m (653 ft.). You must take a short, somewhat washboarded, gravel road to get here, which may be difficult for RVs and low-riding vehicles. But once at the top, you'll get a lovely view of the finger fjords. If you're feeling energetic, take the short drive to Ochre Hill, the site of an ancient volcano, and climb the lookout tower for another great view of the finger peninsulas and the Marine Interpretation Centre.

Coastal Trail ⊛   If you like hiking, you're in luck. Terra Nova has 100km (62 miles) of hiking trails with various levels of difficulty, as well as three mountain biking trails. One of the nicest hiking trails is the 9-km (5½-mile) Coastal Trail that runs from the Marine Interpretation Centre to Newman Sound Campground and will take you about 3 hours. About halfway along, you'll pass by Pissing Mare Falls—not spectacular by any means, but a soothing place to listen to the water trickling down the rocks as you relax on a bench and smell the fresh air. Depending on the time of your visit, you may see the dogberry in bloom and the "old man's beard" lichen hanging from the trees. Old man's beard is also called "traveler's joy"—it's an indication of clean air in the areas where it grows. It's edible, but beware—it acts as a natural laxative!

Edible Trail   You can actually take an "edible trail" hike with a park interpreter, where poisonous plants are pointed out and edible ones are sampled. You'll learn that the leaves of the corn lily taste like cucumber, but that the plant's blue-colored berries are poisonous and were once used to dye blue jeans. Register for the hike at Salton's Marine Interpretation Centre.

Salton's Marine Interpretation Centre ⊛   An impressive facility situated just off Route 1 in Newman Sound. This is worthy not only as a stand-alone attraction, but also as the place from which you'll catch a boat or kayak tour, and from where you can access one of the nicest hiking trails in the park.

The Centre offers bilingual service and has three main areas: the wet lab, the theater, and the marine exhibit. The marine exhibit is great for children, as they can learn about and touch various live marine creatures in the touch tank. They can even conduct an experiment in the wet lab with guidance from an interpreter. There is also a children's activity center, gift shop, grocery store, and a very good snack shop (with outdoor patio) at the facility. Give yourself about 1½ hours to tour the complex before you head out and explore.

(*C*) **800/213-7275** or 709/533-2801. Open mid-May to end of June & Sept 1 to early Oct 10am–5pm, July & Aug 9am–8pm. Admission is free once you have purchased a park pass.

Sandy Pond   This is the place to be on a hot sunny day. Here you'll find a sandy beach safe for swimming and water sports. The water is shallow, so it's great for small children. And you can rent boats and surf bikes—a surfboard that you bicycle on. Boat rentals cost C$5 (US$3) for a half-hour and C$26 (US$16.65) plus tax for a full day. You can pay with Visa or cash. There are also ice-cream sales and a small concession at the beach that's open mid-June to Labor Day daily 10am to 6pm.

OUTDOOR PURSUITS

As with other parts of Newfoundland, much of your Terra Nova visit will be determined by your interests and the weather. As Newfoundland has "weather with an attitude," your plans may have to be altered without choice and with little advance notice.

Ocean Watch Boat Tours (*★*)   This is a highly recommended activity, should you be lucky enough to get out on the boat. Sailings are occasionally canceled due to high winds. The captain is Ian Stroughair, whose motto is "It's better for you to be onshore wishing you could have gone out, than to be out there wishing you were onshore." It's nice to be in good hands, and Stroughair is certainly knowledgeable about the area.

Ocean Watch boat tours provide an educational experience that enables you to see parts of the park you can't see from shore. Depending on the time of your visit, you will be able to spot and learn about icebergs, whales, bald eagles, and other wildlife. *Tip:* The 9am tours are the best time to see humpback and minke whales. Ocean Watch's boat, The *M/V Northern Fulmar*, is a modern 11-m (35-ft.) fiberglass Cape Island–style passenger vessel, built to the specifications of and fully inspected and certified by the Canadian Coast Guard Safety Branch.

Route 1 to Newman Sound. (*C*) **709/533-2971** or 709/533-6024. www3.nf.sympatico.ca/oceanwatch. Catch the boat by the Marine Interpretive Centre. C$40 (US$26) for adults, C$20 (US$13) for kids 11 and under. 2-hr. afternoon tours (at 1pm & 4pm) cost C$32 (US$20) for adults, C$16 (US$10) for kids. MC, V, or traveler's checks. Open mid-May to Oct 31. Daily tours mid-June to Labor Day; off-season by reservation only.

Terra Nova Adventure Tours (*★*)   If you prefer a more active tour of the park, take a sea kayaking tour with this company, which operates out of the Marine Interpretation Centre. Guided single and double kayak tours are offered, with all necessary equipment and instruction included. The sheltered waters of Terra Nova are an excellent place to kayak, as conditions are generally quite calm. If you're experienced and prefer to go out on your own, the company will also rent you a kayak to use as you wish.

Route 1 to Marine Interpretation Centre, Newman Sound. (*C*) **888/533-8687** or 709/533-9797. www.terra novaadventures.ca. C$45 (US$29) adults, C$35 (US$22) youth. There are also full-day and weekend packages available. Daily rentals with full gear provided for C$45 (US29) for a single kayak and C$55 (US$35) for a double kayak. Tours operate May–June & Sept–Oct by reservation only. 2 tours daily during July & Aug 10am & 1:30pm.

9

Labrador

Labrador is Canada's last undiscovered frontier and North America's most pristine wilderness. In a word association game, it would likely be coupled with "cold," "snow," and "ice." The slightly more enlightened might add "fjords," "bakeapples," and "permafrost." All of which are true, but just barely hint at the complexity that is Labrador.

Its nickname is **The Big Land**—a moniker it well deserves. Physically, it dwarfs the island of Newfoundland by a ratio of 2:1. It covers a distance of more than 1,080km (670 miles) from north to south and 839km (520 miles) from east to west, for a total land mass of **294,330 sq. km** (114,789 sq. miles). Looking at it another way, it's almost identical in size to the U.S. state of Arizona but has a population of just **30,000 people** (compared to Arizona's 4.78 million).

Within that epic terrain are natural and man-made wonders of immense proportion: the **highest mountain range** east of the Rockies; one of the **world's longest runways;** 7,800km (4,875 miles) of coastline; world-class nickel and iron-ore deposits; the **largest caribou herd** in the world; and the world's largest underground hydroelectric project at **Churchill Falls.**

It is simultaneously simple and mysterious, a place of ancient civilizations but few people, a land of glacial conditions and temperate breezes. Here, engineers have achieved numerous record-setting feats, but there isn't a fully paved highway.

Most visitors come to Labrador because they long for a back-to-nature experience untainted by excessive commercialism. No one comes here expecting a glitzy nightlife or Caribbean-style sun and sloth (if they do, they need to switch travel agents).

The most densely populated communities of Labrador are Happy Valley –Goose Bay and the twin towns of Labrador City and Wabush. This is where you'll find the largest quantity of services (banks, hotels, restaurants, and so on), but even here your choices are limited.

Labrador City and **Wabush** are in western Labrador, not far from the Quebec–Labrador border. They grew in response to mining operations by the Iron Ore Company of Canada. Between them, they have a combined population of 11,400 people (Labrador City is home to four-fifths of them).

Happy Valley–Goose Bay (often referred to as Goose Bay) is both a coastal community and an inland town—although in the Labrador interior, it's also accessible by sea via Lake Melville. Home to 8,000 people, Goose Bay is the transportation and service hub of Labrador.

The remaining 10,000 inhabitants live, for the most part, in scattered coastal communities. The largest of these are **L'Anse au Loup** (population 610, across the Strait of Belle Isle from the Great Northern Peninsula); **Port Hope Simpson** (population 500, it's 200km [125 miles] of gravel road north of L'Anse au Loup); **Cartwright** (population 620, close to Eagle River and the best salmon fly-fishing in the world); **North West River** (population 600, 35km [22 miles] from Goose Bay via a rare portion of paved highway); **Hopedale** (population 625, site of Moravian Mission Museum, accessible only by coastal boat and air transportation); and **Nain** (population 1,200, the largest Inuit community in Labrador, again accessible only by coastal boat and air transportation).

1 The Labrador Straits ✦✦

The Labrador Straits stretches over nine coastal communities from L'Anse au Clair to Red Bay. Approximately 2,300 people inhabit this 80-km (50-mile) strip of southeastern Labrador (closest to the island of Newfoundland and the St. Barbe–Blanc Sablon ferry). This is the section of Labrador you'll be most likely to visit if you're planning a Newfoundland *and* Labrador vacation.

Be prepared for cold, damp weather along the Labrador Straits—whichever season you're traveling. Even in summer, the average temperature is a lowly 10°C (50°F) because of the cooling effect of the iceberg-carrying Labrador Current. It flows in a southerly direction past the east coast of Labrador and Newfoundland, except that Labrador, unlike southeastern Newfoundland, doesn't receive the warming benefits of the Gulf Stream. In sheltered areas that deflect the Labrador Current's onshore breeze, summer temperatures often rise to 25–29°C (78–85°F).

ESSENTIALS
GETTING THERE

You can take your car on a ferry from St. Barbe on Newfoundland's Great Northern Peninsula to Blanc Sablon, Quebec, driving north from there to the Labrador Straits. Alternatively, you can fly Air Labrador, Provincial Airlines, or Aviation Quebec–Labrador into the regional airport in Blanc Sablon, just a few kilometers southwest of L'Anse au Clair. You can also drive into Labrador from Quebec, drive 526km (329 miles) from Labrador City to Happy Valley–Goose Bay, then board a ferry for Cartwright and drive the final 406km (254 miles) from Cartwright to L'Anse au Clair. *Warning:* Not only is it an extremely long, isolated drive, but most of the Trans Labrador Highway is a two-lane gravel road—especially treacherous in the winter or after heavy rain.

 Understanding the Labrador Flag

The unique personality and heritage of Labrador is well depicted in the three horizontal bars of its flag. The top bar shows the twig of a spruce tree on a white background. This represents the three cultures that primarily make up the region's population—the Innu, the Inuit, and the settlers (or Europeans)—and how they have made a livelihood in harmony with the snow.

The middle bar of forest green represents the green and bountiful land, and the bottom blue bar represents the abundance of water in the region and how the many rivers, lakes, and seas have served as highways for the people and brought them a harvest of fish and wildlife.

Labrador

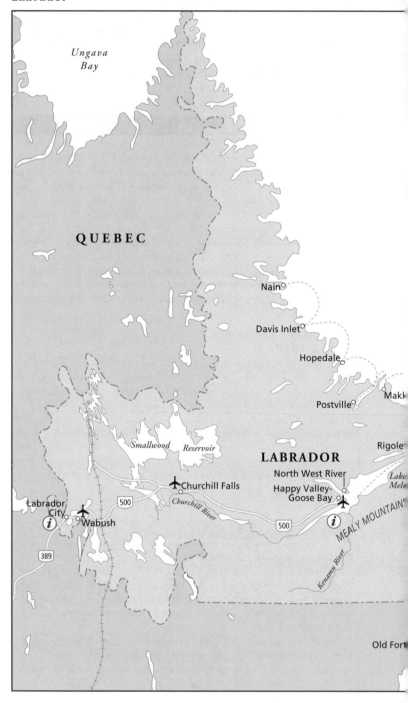

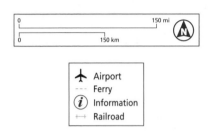

0   150 mi
0   150 km

✈ Airport
--- Ferry
ⓘ Information
↔ Railroad

A T L A N T I C
O C E A N

Hamilton Inlet

○Cartwright

510

Charlottetown○
514 ○Pinsent Arm

Mary's Harbour○ ○Battle Harbour

510 ○Red Bay

ⓘ✈
Blanc○○L'Anse-au-Clair
ablon
it of Belle Isle
○St. Barbe

Fun Fact **What Time Is It?**

Labrador is home to two time zones. The Labrador Straits operate in the Newfoundland time zone, a half-hour ahead of the rest of Labrador in the Atlantic time zone. Quebec is in the Eastern time zone, an hour behind the Atlantic time zone. So, if it's 4:30 in Red Bay, it's 4:00 in Happy Valley–Goose Bay and 3:00 in Blanc Sablon.

VISITOR INFORMATION

Information about the Labrador Straits can be obtained in L'Anse au Clair at the **Gateway to the Straits Visitor Centre** (� 709/931-2360), located in a restored building formerly occupied by St. Andrew's Anglican Church. It's right on Route 510 and open June through September, daily 10 am to 5 pm. A helpful online resource for this region is www.labradorstraits.net.

GETTING AROUND

It's only 78km (48 miles) of paved highway from the ferry terminal in Blanc Sablon to Red Bay, but there's so much to see that it'll take you a full day to travel the whole road. Set aside another full day to see Battle Harbour (once a regional commercial center, the former community has been reconstructed as a heritage site). To get there, you drive to Mary's Harbour, 65km (40 miles) past Red Bay (where, unfortunately, the paved highway ends) along Route 510. From Mary's Harbour, it's a half-hour boat ride to Battle Island, home to Battle Harbour.

Warning: Don't be surprised if you come across two cars halted side-by-side on the highway. Locals often stop in their tracks upon recognizing a neighbor, roll down their windows, and start chatting. It may take them a moment or two to finish a thought and pull aside in order for you to pass, so smile and be patient, remembering that you're now on Labrador time.

WHERE TO STAY

Forget the golden real estate rule "Location, location, location"—it doesn't apply here. The communities of the Labrador Straits are so close together, and of such similar personality (all have beautiful seaside locales and even more charming residents), that there is little visible difference between them. Instead, make your accommodation selection(s) based on style and amenities.

Hospitality homes are more common on the Labrador Straits than they are in other parts of Newfoundland & Labrador. A hospitality home brings back the simple roots of what B&Bs originally were: a basic bedroom in someone's house and a breakfast for a reasonable price. In general, expect to get less (that is, usually no in-room phone or private bath) and pay less than you would in a commercial establishment. Properties having 3 rooms or fewer for rent are not subject to the 15% combined provincial and federal tax (HST), saving you even more. Larger homes with more than three bedrooms for rent will generally fit under the bed-and-breakfast banner and are subject to the HST tax.

Basinview Bed & Breakfast One of only two places to stay in Red Bay, this modern home is the residence of Wade and Blanche Earle. It's an inviting waterfront property, open year-round. The home has a large sitting room with a great view where guests can enjoy satellite TV and have access to the telephone. Blanche will even cook you a real Labrador-style dinner such as caribou stew or pan-fried cod for an additional C$12 (US$8.80). Here's the rub: Rooms that have the best views have access to a shared bath only, and rooms that have a private bath offer no view. Guests staying in the basement rooms have to use the washroom on the main floor of the house.

145 Main Highway (Rte. 510), Red Bay. ⓒ **709/920-2002**. 5 units. C$45–$50 (US$33–$36.68) double. **Amenities:** Continental breakfast; laundry facilities. *In room:* No phone.

Battle Harbour Inn ⓕ   This is as close to luxury accommodation as it gets in Battle Harbour (even without private bathrooms, in-room phones, or TVs). This imposing two-storey inn was once the home of a merchant—outport high society. You get a flavor of that former glory in the antique furnishings, commanding hilltop location, and higher-than-average room rates. Early in the season, you'll be happily distracted by the sight of passing icebergs as you contemplate the meaning of life from this historical property's wraparound porch. A general store and wharf facilities are within walking distance. A meal for two is included in the double room rate; specialties of the house are crab, salmon, trout, char, and smoked fish products produced on-site.

Battle Island. ⓒ **709/921-6957** or 709/921-6216. www.battleharbour.com/accommodations.html. 8 units. C$100–$150 (US$74–$110) double. V. Open June 1–Sept 30. **Amenities:** Meal included with room rate; shared bathroom. *In room:* No phone, no TV.

Beachside Hospitality Home   You'll discover hospitality that's short on frills, long on warmth, in the welcoming home of Norm and Gloria Letto—walking distance from the L'Anse au Clair beach. The three guest rooms provide good value in terms of cleanliness and comfort, but only one has a private bathroom (with a Jacuzzi, no less!). For an additional C$10–$15 (US$7.33–$11) per person, Gloria will be pleased to cook you fish casserole or some other Labradorean dinner favorite. And if you ask nicely, Norm may get out his accordion for an after-dinner sing-along. Guests have access to the telephone, the kitchen, and a private entrance.

Route 510 to L'Anse au Clair. ⓒ **877/663-8999** or 709/931-2053. 3 units. C$38–$45 (US$28–$33) double, C$10 (US$7.33) additional person. MC, V. **Amenities:** Complimentary breakfast; full dinners available on request; nonsmoking rooms. *In room:* No phone.

Grenfell Louie A. Hall Bed & Breakfast ⓚⁱᵈˢ   A Registered Heritage Structure, this B&B was originally a nursing station started by Lady Grenfell who, in 1946, donated the funds to build it. It was named after her friend, Louie A. Hall. Unlike some heritage sites (those with atmospheres as welcoming as a mausoleum), this is an enchantingly nostalgic building filled with curious antiques, old-fashioned radiators, and a resident dog. It's an ideal place for families, because the upstairs attic has been converted into a guest unit with two double beds and lots of play room for the kids. All guest rooms are nice (they're each named for a different nurse who once worked here), but amenities vary: some have private baths; others share. *Hint:* Be careful getting in and out of bed: the charmingly sloped bedroom ceilings can give you a nasty bump if you're not careful. Guests can order full breakfasts and other meals in the dining room for an additional charge. A complimentary shuttle service is offered from Blanc Sablon.

Route 510 to 3 Willow Lane, Forteau. ⓒ **709/931-2916.** www.bbcanada.com/1345.html. 6 units. C$42–$58 (US$30.96–$43.31) double. Additional charge for more than 2 people; family rates available. **Amenities:** Complimentary continental breakfast; laundry facilities. *In room:* No telephone.

Lighthouse Cove Bed & Breakfast   Although called a B&B, this is actually a hospitality home, emphasis on hospitality. I can't imagine anyone being more welcoming than owners Rita and Cecil Davis. Cecil is a retired fisherman with simultaneously funny and poignant stories of how he made his living from the sea. His ancestors were granted this cove from the King of England back in 1922, so in effect L'Anse Amour is a private cove—and very special to the Davis family that today is its sole inhabitant.

Rita is the shining light of Lighthouse Cove. From the moment you enter the door, you'll feel like your visit is the highlight of her day. With a little encouragement, she'll tell you about life in L'Anse Amour—including the story of how, in 1922, the family was able to retrieve six mahogany dining-room chairs and a piano from the *HMS Raleigh*—hung up on a sandbar just offshore—before it broke up and sank. A continental breakfast is included with your room rate. Additional meals are available on request at an additional charge. Keep your fingers crossed that Rita makes you her delicious chocolate brownies. All guest rooms are fairly compact, but completely spotless and very tidy. There are no private baths.

Route 510 to L'Anse Amour Rd., L'Anse Amour. ✆ 709/927-5690. E-mail: lighthousecovebedandbreakfast @yahoo.com. 3 units. C$40 (US$29.50) double. MC, V. **Amenities:** Complimentary continental breakfast. *In room:* No phone. (1km from the Point Amour Lighthouse; 3km [almost 2 miles] off of Route 510 on a gravel road.)

Northern Light Inn ✦   With 49 standard hotel rooms, 5 suites, 5 newly renovated housekeeping cottages, and 10 fully serviced RV sites, the Northern Light Inn is the largest accommodations option along the Labrador Straits. This clean, cozy, and cheerful place has something to please just about everyone: laundry facilities, wake-up service, in-room phone, coffee shop, licensed lounge, craft shop, and ATM. A nearby indoor swimming pool makes it a perfect location for water recreation. It has no elevator, however, so be prepared to struggle up steep stairs with your suitcase to the upper-floor rooms. *Hint:* Ask the helpful staff for information about snowmobile adventures. They'll be happy to arrange a package for your winter visit. *Tip:* Even if you don't stay overnight at the Northern Light Inn, treat yourself to a meal in the on-site Basque Dining Room (see "Where to Dine" for a review). Open daily from 7:00am to 10:00pm, its menu is an eclectic mélange of roast capelin, caribou burgers, Forteau Bay scallops, tortillas Espanola, and Basque chicken. Reservation not required.

Route 510, L'Anse au Clair. ✆ 800/563-3188 or 709/931-2332. northernlight@nf.sympatico.ca. 69 units (including 10 serviced campsites). C$70–$120 (US$51–$89) double. AE, DC, MC, V. Weekly rates and seniors' discounts available. **Amenities:** Dining room; Greco Xpress pizza service; coffee shop/lounge; laundry facilities. *In room:* A/C, TV, some fully equipped housekeeping units, limited room service.

Pinware River Provincial Park Campground   In stark contrast to the many barren areas of the Labrador Straits, Pinware River Provincial Park is a fertile, beautifully forested area bordering the estuary of a good salmon and trout river. (Check with park wardens before you cast; the salmon and trout fisheries are regulated.) Because of the shelter offered by the thick stands of spruce, fir, and birch, summer temperatures here climb considerably higher than in the more open coastal stretches. Pinware Park comes equipped with vehicle parking, picnic tables, drinking water, bathroom facilities, and firepits. A major plus of this campground is its proximity to a sandy beach, where you can enjoy unsupervised swimming (if you dare take a dip in these sub-arctic waters!).

Route 510 to Pinware. ✆ 800/563-6353 or 709/927-5516. www.gov.nf.ca/parks&reserves/pinware.htm. 15 unserviced sites. C$9 (US$6.60) per night. Campsites can be reserved at an additional cost of C$5 (US$3.66) per call. MC, V. Open May 24 long weekend–mid-Sept. **Amenities:** Picnic table; fireplace. Pit toilets & drinking-water taps are accessible throughout the park. You can purchase firewood at the check-in point for C$4 (US$2.93) per bundle.

Whaling Station Cabin *(Value* Inexpensive, modest accommodations ideal for a traveling family or four adults. This 10-year-old cabin is a fully equipped, 2-bedroom unit (double bed in each room) with full bath (tub and shower) and cable TV. It's comfortable both early and late in the season because of the heat from the hot-air furnace. It's just a short walk from here to the Red Bay National Historic Site and other attractions and services. Pets are allowed. The same owners operate the on-site Whaler's Restaurant (see below for review). Note: There's only one cabin, so book early.

Route 510 to Red Bay. ℂ **709/920-2156.** 1 unit. C$65 (US$48). MC, V. Open May–Oct. **Amenities:** Dining room. *In room:* TV.

WHERE TO DINE

You won't find any fancy restaurants in the Labrador Straits, but you *will* find some of the best food you'll ever have the pleasure of eating. Every place I stopped in served ample portions of well-prepared food at very fair prices.

Basque Dining Room ⍟ CANADIAN   This casual restaurant, located in the Northern Light Inn, is listed in *Where to Eat in Canada,* and I concur with the favorable rating. They specialize in seafood and traditional Labrador dishes, and serve up some excellent versions of standard Canadian favorites. I found their homemade hearty vegetable soup to be a steal at C$2.29 (US$1.74) per bowl. It was filled with chunks of vegetables, chicken, and beef. I also enjoyed the charbroiled chicken and barbecue baby back ribs combo (again, good value at C$15/US$11). Good food, reasonable prices, and accommodating service.

Route 510, L'Anse au Clair. ℂ **800/563-3188** or 709/931-2332. northernlight@nf.sympatico.ca. Reservations not required. Dinners C$7–C$20 (US$5.13–US$14.76). AE, DC, MC, V. Open daily 7am–10pm.

Partridge Garden Restaurant ⍟ CONTEMPORARY   Located on the second floor of the Blanc Sablon ferry terminal, this casual restaurant is a cut above the standard cafeteria fare you find at most such venues. Here, you get to enjoy a well-cooked meal in comfortable surroundings. The dining room offers a great view of the Strait of Belle Isle, where you can watch the ferry approaching or leaving the wharf. You can get live lobster right out of the tank and a lobster-claw dinner. There are also very reasonably priced lunch specials. The adjacent Upper Deck Pub has a pool table.

Blanc Sablon Ferry Terminal, Blanc Sablon, Quebec. ℂ **418/461-2287.** Reservations not required. Lunch: C$4–$9 (US$2.93–$6.60). Dinner: C$13–$23 (US$9.60–$17). MC, V. Open daily during ferry season (usually May 1–Jan, depending on ice conditions).

Sea View Restaurant ⍟ TRADITIONAL   A full-service dining room offering home-style meals and local specialties that include bakeapple crepes, some incredibly hearty seafood chowder, caribou rouladen, and unique desserts such as screech parfait and partridgeberry Baked Alaska pie, available only by special request. Don't be surprised when they serve you dry, cold dressing with your hot turkey sandwich, as this is the way they serve dressing in Labrador. The ample and tasty turkey meat makes up for that. The restaurant is located near the ferry terminal and airport in Blanc Sablon.

33 Main St., Forteau. ℂ **866-931-2840** or 709/931-2840. www.preserves.nf.ca for information about *Labrador Preserves* made on-site. Lunch: C$4–$9 (US$2.93–$6.60). Dinner: C$12–$20 (US$8.80–$14.76). Special kids' menu. AE, MC, V, Interac. The restaurant is open year-round (weather permitting) 9am–midnight.

Whaler's Restaurant ★ *Value* LIGHT FARE Whaler's serves what are arguably the best fish and chips anywhere in the province. The Chalupa fish and chips is listed as a snack on the menu, but you'll get two generous fillets of cod along with home fries and coleslaw. The fish is delicately coated with a light, spicy coating and not greasy at all. The fries and coleslaw are also good, making this quite a meal for under C$9 (US$6.60). The restaurant is casual and can be noisy when the tour groups arrive by bus. A small gift shop at the front of the restaurant sells an assortment of souvenirs, including some lovely Labrador jackets.

Route 510 to Red Bay. ⓒ **709/920-2156.** Lunch: C$5–$8 (US$3.66–$5.86). Dinner: C$9–$18 (US$6.60–$13.44). MC, V. Open daily 8am–10:30pm.

EXPLORING THE LABRADOR STRAITS

Communities of the Labrador Straits are very close together and situated along a single roadway. You'll get off the plane or the ferry just over the Quebec–Labrador border in Blanc Sablon (meaning "white sand"), and then head northeast along Route 510. If you happen to fly into Blanc Sablon (or even if you don't, but have time to drop in to the airport), take a few minutes to look at the arrowhead display, housed in a wall-mounted case. It's interesting to see the different shapes and sizes of arrowheads that have been found in the area.

Driving northeast along Route 510, the first community you'll come to will be **L'Anse au Clair.** This—like all other communities on the Labrador Straits— is small (less than 300 residents), but it has the largest hotel in the area.

Just north of L'Anse au Clair is **Forteau,** a slightly larger community that offers a couple of interesting shopping opportunities and a good restaurant. Each of the communities along the Labrador Straits is so close to the next one, you really won't know when you're leaving one and entering another until you see a sign with a different town's name!

Your next stop along the Straits Highway is **L'Anse Amour** (meaning "Cove of Love") and **Point Amour.** L'Anse Amour is the 15-person community next to Point Amour, where you'll find the Point Amour Lighthouse, the tallest lighthouse in Atlantic Canada and the second tallest in all of Canada. It's also where you'll find the earliest known funeral monument in North America—a 7,500-year-old Maritime Archaic Burial Mound.

Just north of L'Anse Amour, you'll find **L'Anse au Loup,** the largest community on the Straits. L'Anse au Loup offers a good range of services for local residents including a credit union, library, public swimming pool, sports complex, and a fish-processing plant. It's also home to the annual Bakeapple Folk Festival, the largest annual event on the Labrador Straits. You won't find many services in L'Anse au Loup for travelers, and are better off overnighting in one of the neighboring communities. You'll find an assortment of motels and B&Bs in virtually all of the other points on the map along Route 510, as well as a campground and three fishing camps at Pinware River Provincial Park, situated between West St. Modeste and Pinware.

Red Bay ★★ *Finds* is an amazing community. During the 16th century, this remote Labrador outpost was the whaling capital of the world (this was, of course, before so many species of these mammoth mammals became endangered). Today, the essence and importance of that bygone whale fishery are eloquently explained through the interpretive presentations at the Red Bay National Historic Site. But don't limit your explorations to the formal site. The community itself has a story to tell through its location and topography.

Picturesque rocks protrude peacefully out of the water in the harbor, and an eerie half-sunken ship lurks in the fog just offshore behind the Orientation & Interpretation Centre. I had the very best fish and chips throughout my travels in Newfoundland & Labrador at Whaler's Restaurant, and also found some unique shopping opportunities. What more can you ask from a tiny outport community of just 300 residents?

Red Bay is formally the end of the Labrador Straits, and it's where the paved road ends. But there is one point farther up the coast worth mentioning. **Battle Harbour** *★★* has been designated a National Historic District and, as the only intact salt fishing village left in the province, is well worth a visit if you have an extra day or two to spare.

You need to drive as far as Mary's Harbour, 65km (40 miles) north of Red Bay along Route 510. *Note:* The road from Red Bay to Mary's Harbour is gravel and not ideal for low-riding vehicles. You'll then take a 30-minute boat ride to Battle Island, where you'll find the island outport of Battle Harbour. The boat leaves from the government wharf in Mary's Harbour during the summer months daily at 10am and departs Battle Harbour for the return voyage at 3pm. Cost for the round trip is about C$40 (US$25.50) per person, and you pay at the Riverlodge Hotel (*©* **709/921-6948**).

The tiny community of Battle Harbour has been restored by the Battle Harbour Historic Trust and is similar in setup to the Ryan Premises of Bonavista. (See chapter 5 for more information about the Ryan Premises and Bonavista.) These 230-year-old buildings tell you the history of the local fishery and how Battle Harbour was once the hub of Labrador.

The mercantile salt-fish premises at Battle Harbour were originally established by the firm of John Slade & Company of Poole, England in the early 1770s. Salt fish is cod that has been cleaned, split, salted, and dried; this is how fish was stored in the days pre-refrigeration.

The population of Battle Harbour increased quickly after 1820, when Newfoundland fishing schooners adopted the community as their primary port of call and declared it the capital of the Labrador floater fishery. The term "floater fishery" refers to migratory Newfoundland fishermen who fished the bountiful Labrador waters each summer and returned to their permanent homes in Newfoundland each fall.

A highpoint for the community occurred in 1892, when Dr. Wilfred Grenfell of Britain arrived in Battle Harbour. A year later he built Labrador's first hospital here. (See more about Dr. Grenfell in chapter 7's section on the Great Northern Peninsula.) If you're interested in the history of Battle Harbour, be sure to ask the staff on the ferry coming over from St. Barbe if they'll play the Battle Harbour video for you in the passenger day-use area.

Keep in mind that there are no activities to do here other than exploring the small community—and stepping back in time. If you like more action and a faster pace, Battle Harbour may not be for you. But if you like the idea of peace and solitude, there is the Battle Harbour Inn on the island where you can spend the night. The inn has cozy woodstoves to keep you warm and oil lamps to give you light.

Route 510 to Mary's Harbour. Arrange boat to Battle Island at the Riverview Hotel in Mary's Harbour. *©* **709/921-6216**. www.battleharbour.com. Open June 1–Sept 30. Air Labrador offers flights into Mary's Harbour: *©* **800/563-3042** for more information.

WHAT TO SEE AND DO ON THE LABRADOR STRAITS

Gateway to the Straits Visitor Centre ✸✸   Heading east from Blanc Sablon, the first Labrador community you'll come to is L'Anse au Clair, where you'll find the Gateway to the Straits Visitor Centre, operated by the Labrador Straits Historic Development Corporation. This center will provide you with information on the entire region. Because you're so close to the Quebec border, you'll also find information here about the Lower North Shore of Quebec. The center, in a restored 1919 church, has an extensive selection of visitor information. There is a complete set of menus from local restaurants, literature on attractions and other services, helpful and friendly bilingual staff, assorted historical photos, local craft samples, natural treasures from the sea (including a good selection of shells), and some very impressive fossils of 500-million-year-old archaeocyathid and 1-billion-year-old Precambrian granite found in the area of the Point Amour Lighthouse. Now that ought to impress any student of geology!

Route 510, L'Anse au Clair. ✆ **709/927-2360.** Free admission. Open June 1–Sept 30 daily 10am–5pm.

Labrador Straits Museum ✸   Heading east toward L'Anse au Loup on Route 510, you'll arrive at a small museum and gift shop operated by the local Women's Institute. If you're interested in purchasing local handicrafts (primarily of the knitted or crocheted variety), or in finding out how women of the area lived before the modern world was opened up to them, you'll find this an informative stop. Artifacts include tools, weapons, items from the L'Anse Amour Burial Mound, and an English ship's head.

Route 510 between Forteau & L'Anse au Loup. ✆ **709/931-2067.** C$2 (US$1.46) admission for adults; children under 12 free. Open mid-June to Sept daily 9am–5:30pm. Wheelchair accessible. Items purchased in the craft shop are tax exempt.

L'Anse Amour Burial Mound   As you make your way back toward Route 510 on the Point Amour Lighthouse gravel road, watch for a small plaque and pile of stones on the side of the road. It's the L'Anse Amour Burial Mound, a National Historic Site documented as the oldest native ritual burial site discovered in North America. An interpretive sign explains that archaeologists believe this is a 7,500-year-old Maritime Archaic Indian burial mound containing the remains of a 12-year-old child and several ritualistic artifacts.

Point Amour Lighthouse Provincial Historic Site ✸✸✸   Walking the 127 steep steps to the top of the tallest lighthouse in Atlantic Canada is a worthwhile journey for anyone who doesn't have bad knees or a fear of heights.

The costumed interpretive staff have a sense of humor: they've set up "Fun Factoids" at each level of the lighthouse tower to divert your thoughts from the stress of the 33-m (109-ft.) vertical climb. And a chair at every second level enables you to rest if you need to. This is one of only four Imperial Towers erected by the Government of Canada to protect ships traveling between Canada and England.

It took 3 years (from 1854 to 1857) to complete the 2-m-thick (6½-ft.) walls of the lighthouse. The primary layer comprises locally quarried limestone covered first by brick and then wooden shingles to protect the mortar from disintegrating in the sea air. The lighthouse was first illuminated in 1858 and was manned until 1995, when it became automated.

Inside the old lighthouse keeper's house, informative panels explain the region's naval history and all aspects of early life here. There are also some fascinating maps from the National Archives of Canada.

From the top of the lighthouse, you'll be rewarded with a magnificent view of Forteau Bay and a 500-million-year-old archaeocyathid fossil bed in the rock below. Take note that Point Amour was the site of a Marconi wireless telegraph station from 1904 until 1965. Give yourself 2 or 3 hours to explore the lighthouse exhibits and hike the trail.

Route 510 to L'Anse Amour Rd., Point Amour. (The lighthouse is about 3km [2 miles] off Route 510 on a fairly good gravel road.) © **709/927-5825.** Guided tours of the lighthouse cost C$2.50 (US$1.83) for ages 13 and up. Open mid-June to early Oct daily 10am–5:30pm. Closed Labor Day to (Canadian) Thanksgiving 1–2pm.

(Fun Fact Cove of Deaths

In times of heavy fog, even the strongest light can't help ships avoid the treacherous rocks at Point Amour. Eight shipwrecks have occurred here, including that of the *HMS Raleigh,* pieces of which can still be found along the nearby coastline. The original French name for this location was L'Anse aux Morts, meaning "Cove of Deaths."

Red Bay National Historic Site ★★★   Like Basque whalers of old, you'll be immediately drawn to Red Bay Harbour—the present-day location of the Red Bay National Historic Site. Several buildings are under the administration of Parks Canada; you'll pay a fairly hefty entrance fee, but it's well worth it. Pay at the Visitor Reception Centre (also called the Orientation Centre) at the top of the hill and watch the 30-minute video that explains the history of the Basque whalers who once populated this bay.

This building also offers a remarkable display of a *chalupa,* a 400-year-old preserved and reconstructed wooden whaling boat surrounded by the mandible of a 5.3-m (17½-ft.) bowhead whale. The bowhead is a member of the "right whale" family, so named because they were the *right* whales to slaughter for the best oil.

The Visitor Interpretation Centre, located down the hill at the waterfront, contains artifacts from the Basque whalers and one of their ships, the *San Juan,* which was loaded with about 1,000 barrels of whale oil when it sank in Red Bay Harbour during a storm in 1565. The wreck of the *San Juan* was discovered in 1978 and subsequently dismantled by underwater archaeologists. Part of its hull is on display in the Grand Hall at the Museum of Civilization in Ottawa, Ontario. You can see a replica of the San Juan (built to a scale of 1:10) in the Visitor Reception Centre.

If you step out the back of the Visitor Interpretation Centre, you can get a good look at the *Bernier,* a half-sunken French ship that went down in the same spot as the *San Juan!* It provides an eerie reminder that other shipwrecks are well preserved in Red Bay due to the coldness of its water. You can take a small boat past the *Bernier* and across the channel to **Saddle Island,** where you can embark on a self-guided walking tour of 16th-century Basque gravesites and primitive native archaeological sites.

Route 510 to Red Bay Harbour. © **709/920-2051.** www.pc.gc.ca/lhn-nhs/nl/redbay/index_e.asp. C$7 (US$5.13) adults, C$5.50 (US$4) seniors, C$3.50 (US$2.58) ages 6–16, free for children under 6. There is a family rate of C$14 (US$10.26). Open mid-June to mid-Oct daily 9am–5pm; during July & Aug until 8pm. You pay C$2 (US$1.46) additional for the boat ride to Saddle Island, which runs daily 9am–6pm.

Red Bay: World Whaling Capital

Did you know that the first industry established on Canadian soil was a seasonal whale-oil factory in Red Bay? During the 16th century, Red Bay was the largest whaling port in the world, and from 1550 to 1600 it was bustling with more than 1,000 Basque fishermen from France and Spain who came here to slaughter thousands of whales for the valuable oil made from their blubber.

The bloodshed was so intense that the waters of the bay would be red with whales' blood. It is thought that this scene provided the origin for the name of the village. The whale oil was stored in casks and transported to Europe by ship, where it was sold for a high price. It was primarily used for lighting lamps during the late Middle Ages.

UNIQUE SHOPPING OPPORTUNITIES

Ash Cottage   Once you've finished your exploration of Red Bay National Historic Site, drop in on Robert "Bud" Fowler. He's a craftsman who operates Ash Cottage, a small shop offering handmade wooden gifts and souvenirs. You'll find a unique selection of wooden fridge magnets, Christmas decorations, and other useful items that won't break the bank. Fowler's workshop is located just a stone's throw from the harbor and the Red Bay Visitor Reception Centre.

35 West Harbour Dr., Red Bay. ℂ **709/920-2071**. Open June 15–Sept 20 daily 9am–9pm. No credit cards accepted.

Forteau Bay Pottery & Studio ✦   If you like unique handcrafted pottery, be sure to visit the small shop right on Route 510 owned and operated by Tracy Keats. Keats is extremely creative, offering original items such as pendants with implants of local leaves and themed drinking mugs such as the Viking Knarr. In addition to her personal studio, Keats's work is on display in several shops throughout the area.

69 Main St., Forteau. ℂ **709/931-2160**. E-mail: tgkeats@yahoo.ca. Most items C$10–$28 (US$7.33–$20.50). MC, V, Interac. COD for mail orders. Open May–Dec daily 9am–6pm.

Labrador Preserves ✦   You can buy more than just lunch at Sea View Restaurant in Forteau: you can also purchase a selection of jams, syrups, and preserves direct from the manufacturer. Stelman Flynn is owner of Forteau Food Processors Ltd., the parent company that caters the food on the *Apollo* ferry and also puts out an assortment of tasty products under the name Labrador Preserves. The products are made in the shop right behind the Sea View Restaurant, so you know you're getting them fresh and for prices lower than you may pay in gift shops throughout the area.

33 Main St., Forteau. ℂ **866-931-2840** or 709/931-2743. www.preserves.nf.ca. C$4.50–$7 (US$3.30–$5.13). AE, MC, V, Interac. Open year-round (weather permitting) daily 9am–midnight.

OUTDOOR PURSUITS

Bakeapple Folk Festival ✦   Held the second weekend of August, when the local bakeapples (also known as cloudberries) are ready to eat, the Bakeapple Folk Festival is an area favorite. This regional festival has been running for about 25 years and offers 4 days and nights of traditional music, dancing, games, and displays, as well as great food. The Labrador Fisherman's Union Shrimp Company sponsors a delicious seafood reception on opening night with a wide array of seafood. Another highlight of the opening ceremonies is the Square Dance.

Family Day, held on the Friday, is popular with kids and always features a well-known children's entertainer. On Saturday and Sunday you can enjoy musical performances by a variety of local artists, and browse the booths for information, games, food, and crafts. Throughout the weekend there's a selection of local food served including moose burgers, fish and brewis (a traditional meal of salt cod cooked with hard bread that has been soaked overnight in water), roast capelin, and a tasty selection of bakeapple desserts.

Note: The Bakeapple Festival represents the opening of the bakeapple-picking season. There are many bakeapple marshes alongside the highway and directions to them are freely given at information centers, gas stations, and local stores.

ⓒ **709/931-2545** or see www.labradorstraits.net/festival.shtml for info on current prices and events. A festival wristband costs C$5 (US$3.66) and provides you with admission to all events except the adult dance on Saturday night, which is an additional C$5, and the teenage dance on Thursday night, which also costs C$5.

⌒ Fun Fact   What's a Bakeapple?

Bakeapples, also known as cloudberries, are similar in shape to raspberries and blackberries. They're red when they're green (unripe), turning a soft golden-orange when they're ripe. Picking bakeapples is backbreaking labor: they grow close to the ground, single berries on a short stalk. But they're well worth the effort. The flavor of these succulent northern beauties is unlike anything else you've ever tried. Then again, you're probably better off *not* developing a taste for them. There are only two places in the world where you can find bakeapples: Norway is one, Newfoundland & Labrador is the other.

Beachcombing   If you're interested in beachcombing, you should investigate the beach at Red Bay. You won't find large or colorful seashells like you will in more tropical places like Sanibel Island, Florida, but Red Bay does have some nice seashells that you can take home as cheap and attractive souvenirs. A good place to look for whale bones is Schooner Cove Trail, a relatively easy 3-km (nearly 2-mile) hiking trail that runs along L'Anse au Loup Bay. (You access the trail from Route 510, just west of L'Anse au Loup.)

Hiking Trails   Overfall Brook Trail, which is accessed at Forteau and runs along Forteau Bay, is more difficult and less accessible than the Raleigh Trail but will reward you with a great view of the Point Amour Lighthouse and a lovely waterfall. Whether you're beachcombing or hiking, you'll probably want to take along some insect repellent, as the bugs can sometimes be fierce. (Mosquito netting wouldn't go unused.) The **Raleigh Trail** ✦ begins at the Point Amour Lighthouse and follows the shoreline past pieces of the *HMS Raleigh,* a 12,000-ton light-cruiser that sank here in 1922. Pieces of live ammunition and cordite can still be found being washed ashore and in fishers' nets. The Royal Canadian Navy gets the job of safely detonating any ammo found.

As you hike your way along the trail, you'll pass fossil beds, small but scenic waterfalls, crowberry patches, bakeapple plants (the berries ripen in August), and tuckamore—the wind- and sea-stunted spruce providing some greenery to this otherwise treeless land. If you like horseback riding, ask the staff at the Gateway to the Straits Visitor Centre in L'Anse au Clair or the interpreters at the lighthouse whether they're still running the trail rides, which were initiated as a pilot project to find out if there is enough interest to continue. Cost for children is only C$3.50 (US$2.56) for a 10-minute ride.

Gull Island Charters   This company, situated in Red Bay, offers customized boat charters and tours of the area. This is the same company that does the scheduled run to Saddle Island for Parks Canada daily between 9am and 6pm. Gull Island Charters does charter tours on demand. Short, ½-hour runs are possible throughout the day if there are whales or icebergs around. Longer runs are possible in the early morning (before 9am) or in the evening (after 6pm). The maximum number of passengers is 6.

16 East Harbour Dr., Red Bay. ℃ 709/920-2058. Charter rates for the boat are C$80 (US$58.60) per hour.

Pinware River Provincial Park ⚜   is situated in the scenic Pinware River Valley, where you'll find beautiful waterfalls, a nice beach for unsupervised swimming, challenging kayaking for experienced paddlers, great salmon and trout fishing, hiking trails, and a picnic area for day use. There is an unserviced campground in the park. (See the "Where to Stay" section for details.)

You'll also find the trees here to be noticeably taller than in points west. If you have time to take a walk on the wild side, Pinware River Park is a nice place to spend a couple of hours, and longer if you like to fish or camp. Do bring your insect repellent or clothing with mosquito netting, as you'll find there are quite a few (many more than you might expect!) airborne residents of the park anxiously awaiting your arrival.

Route 510 to Pinware. ℃ 800/563-6353 or 709/927-5516. www.gov.nf.ca/parks&reserves/pinware.htm. Park entrance fee: C$4 (US$2.93) vehicle daily permits, C$16 (US$11.74) vehicle seasonal permits. Open May 24 long weekend to mid-Sept.

WATER SPORTS
Fishing
You'll cross a bridge 9km (nearly 6 miles) from the river's mouth that offers spectacular views of the Pinware River cascading over swift rapids 21m (70 ft.) below. In the lower gorge area near that bridge are the best salmon fishing holes. This is where several sports angling camps are located. The Pinware River is a scheduled salmon river. Licenses can be purchased locally and local residents are available as guides. *Note:* It is mandatory for visitors from outside the province to be accompanied by a local fishing guide. For complete and current information on hunting and fishing regulations, licenses, and fees, contact the Newfoundland & Labrador Department of Forest Resources and Agrifoods, Wildlife Division; Labrador Office ℃ **709/927-5580**.

Tickle Tours   offers fishing and diving charters as well as sightseeing tours out of West St. Modeste. They will take you fishing for salmon, char, and sea trout. Tickle Tours uses a new-model 10-m (35-ft.) boat that can comfortably accommodate 4 guests.

Route 510 to West St. Modeste. ℃ 709/927-5017. tickletours.labradorstraits.net. These aren't pre-scheduled or packaged tours, so prices vary. Call for rates. Family rates available.

Kayaking & Canoeing
Because of the rapids, the Pinware River is best left to only the most expert of kayakers and canoeists. At present, there are no kayak or canoe rentals available in the area. For more information contact the Department of Tourism, Culture, and Recreation, Parks and Natural Areas; Labrador Office ℃ **709/927-5580**.

2 The Labrador Coastline & Happy Valley–Goose Bay

ESSENTIALS

GETTING THERE

The coastline north of Battle Harbour and the Labrador Straits area has been relatively inaccessible until recently. If you continue on the gravel road past Mary's Harbour, you can drive as far north as **Cartwright,** which is now at the end of Route 510. This road was just completed in the fall of 2002, making exploration of Port Hope Simpson, Charlottetown, Paradise River, and Cartwright possible by vehicle.

North of Cartwright, most of the Labrador coast comprises tiny outport fishing communities that are accessible only via the coastal boat operated by Coastal Labrador Marine Services. On this passengers-only boat, you'll stop at several small villages and travel as far north as Nain, a community of 1,000 residents with an interesting Inuit and Moravian history.

The farther north you go, the more icebergs you'll see (many break up or melt as they head south toward St. John's), making Cape Chidley at Labrador's northern tip the place where you're likely to see the most and largest icebergs.

Currently, however, Cape Chidley is inaccessible to the average traveler as the coastal boat only goes as far north as Nain, and the nearest airstrip is a considerable distance away at Cape Uviak. In time that is likely to change, as this rugged northern region of mountains and fjords is proposed to become **Torngat Mountains National Park,** one of two national parks being planned for Labrador.

Still considered part of this coastal region, even though it appears inland, is **Happy Valley–Goose Bay** at the mouth of Lake Melville—the lake stretches out to Hamilton Inlet and the Labrador Sea—making the community accessible by ferry (from the east), by gravel road (from the west), or by air. Happy Valley–Goose Bay has a regional airport, so air travel is the most efficient of these options.

If you decide to drive to Happy Valley–Goose Bay from Labrador West, you must travel Route 500, a gravel highway with few services other than what you'll find in Churchill Falls, the halfway mark between Labrador City and Wabush and Happy Valley–Goose Bay.

VISITOR INFORMATION

The Labrador–Lake Melville Tourism Association operates a visitor center at 365 Hamilton River Rd. in Happy Valley–Goose Bay (© **709/896-8787** or **709/896-3489;** www.happyvalley-goosebay.com), open June 1 to September 30, Monday to Friday from 8am to 8pm and Saturday and Sunday from 8am to 5pm. The center is open the rest of the year from Monday to Friday, 8am to 5pm. They'll provide you with maps and brochures as well as the most current information on services and events in the central Labrador region.

HAPPY VALLEY–GOOSE BAY

Happy Valley–Goose Bay is Labrador's hub and its largest service center. The community is strategically located at the point where Labrador's coastline is naturally split by Hamilton Inlet and Lake Melville into regions locally known as the **North Coast** and the **South Coast.**

The town of Happy Valley–Goose Bay is a rather new entity, and was formally established only in 1973. The fur trade initially brought settlers to Central Labrador and others were attracted to the region's abundance of fish, wildlife, and timber, as well as its rich soil and longer growing season. Slow growth continued until World War II.

The turning point came in 1941, when the air base at Goose Bay was built as a landing and refueling stop for the Atlantic Ferry Command. During World War II, thousands of aircraft passed through Goose Bay. The airbase continues to provide support and coordination for NATO tactical flight-training activities. Military Base "5 Wing Goose Bay" provides support to Allied, NORAD, and Canadian Forces training and operations.

The Mealy Mountains characterize the region between Cartwright and Happy Valley–Goose Bay. It is for this pristine mountainous region that one of two national parks, **Mealy Mountains National Park,** has been proposed. Following that development, it is quite likely that you will see visitor services greatly expand, similar to the communities bordering the national parks of Gros Morne and Terra Nova in Newfoundland. (See chapter 8 for more on these parks.)

 ## The Inukshuk

The North Coast is inhabited by various native peoples, including the Inuit. As you travel this area, you may see unusual rock or stone figurines shaped in the rough outline of a person. They are *Inukshuk,* an Inuit word meaning "in the image of man."

These life-like figures originally served as signposts to mark the way across barren land and to offer guidance to those who followed. They are a symbol of friendship, caring, and the strong sense of community you find in the north.

Note: Although some individual Innu, Inuit, and Métis people provide tourist services, you will not find community-coordinated aboriginal tourist experiences such as are offered in Conne River (see chapter 6). The reason is that their focus is on land claims settlements with the federal and provincial governments—when it joined with Canada, Newfoundland & Labrador's political leaders neglected to negotiate Official Indian Status for the province's native communities in the Terms of Union.

WHERE TO STAY & DINE

Aurora Hotel ⟨★⟩ If X marks the spot, then this hotel's location at the crossroads of town is a sure signal of quality accommodations. The Aurora offers the personal attention of a B&B and the professional service of a four-star property. Guest rooms and suites are nicely furnished, spacious rooms that have outgrown their smaller ensuite bathrooms. Friendly accessories, like the checkered tablecloths in the dining room and a dramatically toned red and gold-trimmed front desk, lift it beyond the realm of generic hotel decor. The Aurora is conveniently situated near the Visitor Center and is a 5-minute drive from the airport, seaport, seaplane dock, and Trans Labrador Highway. One suite is specially designed to meet the needs of travelers with disabilities.

Route 500 to 382 Hamilton River Rd. ⟨℃⟩ **800/563-3066** or 709/896-3398. www.aurorahotel.com. 40 units. C$86–$120 (US$63.40–$89) double. MC, V. **Amenities:** Full-service restaurant; lounge; business services; limited room service. *In room:* TV.

Bradley's Bed & Breakfast *(Value)*   Great value and a good location in a modern back-split bungalow. Bradley's is ideally situated for four-season fun: in summer you can walk to the nearby golf course, in winter you can snowmobile on a good trail system from right outside the door. Each guest room has a private bath and a telephone. The rooms here are HST-exempt, which is a nice bonus. E-mail and fax service are available. A full breakfast is included in the room rate.

13 McKenzie Dr., Hamilton Heights, HVGB. (Take the 5th HVGB exit off Route 500.) ℂ 877/884-7378 or 709/896-8006. www.bbcanada.com/bradleybb. 3 units. C$40–$65 (US$29.50–$48) double. V. **Amenities:** Complimentary full breakfast; laundry facilities; nonsmoking rooms. *In room:* TV.

Goose River Lodges *(Kids)*   Just a 20-minute drive from Happy Valley–Goose Bay, these two-bedroom fully equipped housekeeping cabins and an RV park in a park-like setting also boast a playground, beach volleyball, and snowmobile rentals. Cabins are clean and comfortable, with electric heat, air-conditioning, and solid, albeit mismatched, furnishings. Bedrooms and eating/sitting areas are spacious, but the diminutive bathrooms come with just a shower (no bathtub). There is a wheelchair-accessible unit. Pets are allowed on a leash.

Route 520 to Northwest River Rd. ℂ 877/496-2600 or 709/896-2600. www.gooseriverlodges.ca. 19 units (including 10 RV sites). C$85 (US$63). V. **Amenities:** A/C; TV w/VCR available; nonsmoking units; children's playground area. RV sites are well-spaced & serviced with 30-amp electrical outlets.

The Labrador Inn ✴   The Labrador Inn is the largest and most modern property in Labrador, with the typical amenities you'd expect from a hotel this size (except there's no swimming pool or fitness room). It's centrally located near the military base, just minutes from the airport and the port of Goose Bay as well as government, educational, and municipal facilities. The inn is home to the Naskaupi Restaurant (fine dining) and the Flight Deck Lounge. There is complimentary outdoor parking. The inn is close to golf, fishing, snowmobiling, and skiing. It is also wheelchair accessible.

Route 500 to 380 Hamilton River Rd. ℂ 800-563-2763 or 709/896-3351. www.labradorinn.nf.ca. 74 units. C$75–$150. (US$55–$110) double, C$10 (US$7.33) additional person. Discounts available for seniors & government. AE, DC, MC, V. **Amenities:** Dining room; military-style pub with pub menu; business center; room service. *In room:* TV, minibar.

Mulligan's Pub PUB GRUB   Because it's a club that serves food (as opposed to a restaurant that serves alcohol), you must be at least 19 years of age to enter Mulligan's. The food is great—and inexpensive. The fish and chips are superb and the Chicken Delight (grilled chicken served over a Caesar salad) is excellent. If you're looking for something different, Mulligan's also serves caribou burgers. The pub is open until 2am, but the kitchen closes at the hours below. You can still get light snacks after that.

368 Hamilton River Rd. ℂ 709/896-3038. Reservations not required. C$4.95–$11.95 (US$3.65–$8.75). MC, V. Open Mon–Sat 11am–6pm, Sun 11am–3pm.

EXPLORING HAPPY VALLEY–GOOSE BAY

The foreign visitors to CFB Goose Bay have added a cosmopolitan flavor to the community and helped its population grow to nearly 9,000. The community hosts several fun cultural events, such as the **German Hangar Fest** in July and the **Sheshatshiu Innu Etiun Summer Festival** in late August. Here are some other worthwhile events.

Labrador Canoe Regatta   The 3-day paddling event features teams from all over Labrador that compete in 6-person freighter canoe races on Gosling Lake, a 20-minute drive from HVGB. Male and female contestants paddle replicas of traditional 2-person voyageur canoes in several age-specific category races. A variety of food booths will keep your tummy from growling, and live bands provide entertainment throughout the weekend. Held the first weekend in August, there is no entrance fee. Individual booths set their own prices. Call © 709/896-5817.

Labrador Interpretation Center   This is Labrador's first provincial museum. You'll see four galleries filled with life-sized dioramas, exhibits, and archaeological artifacts that interpret Labrador's history from 9,000 years ago (when the first native peoples lived here) to today. The museum is situated on Portage Road in North West River, a neighborhood of Happy Valley–Goose Bay where you'll also find the Labrador Heritage Society Museum.

Portage Rd., North West River. © 709/497-8566. Free admission. Open June 1–Aug 31 daily 9am–5pm; Sept 1–May 30 Wed–Fri 1pm–4pm, Sat & Sun 1:30–4:30pm; closed Mon & Tues.

The Labrador Sno-Break   This event, formerly known as the Happy Goose Winter Carnival, is a week-long family-oriented winter event held the second to third weekend of March. Sno-Break is 8 days of continuous winter activities including snowmobile races, trail rides to several surrounding communities, family games, relay races, and more.

© 709/896-3489. Most activities are free. There is a small registration fee to participate in the races and trail rides. Call for specifics.

North West River Beach Festival   Labrador's largest outdoor music festival takes place near Happy Valley–Goose Bay the third weekend of July. Free live entertainment can be enjoyed right on the beach (pray for a stiff breeze, or you may find yourself doing the "Black Fly Swat" dance).

Northern Lights Museum   Check out this museum's interesting display of the region's military history, including a good collection of authentic World War II artifacts.

170 Hamilton River Rd. © 709/896-5939. Free admission. Open year-round, but call for hours.

3 Churchill Falls to Labrador West

Labrador City and Wabush are the major centers of Labrador West, the resource-rich region that stretches along the Quebec–Labrador border. Churchill Falls is the halfway point between Labrador City/Wabush and Happy Valley–Goose Bay.

Labrador City was established as a community in 1958 and now offers a full range of services including visitor information, a hospital, lodging, camping, hiking, sport fishing, golf, skiing, and snowmobiling. The 11,400 residents of Labrador City and Wabush happily embrace their sometimes harsh—what some call a two-season—climate. Winter can seem never-ending when the snow is on the ground for up to 8 months! And summer temperatures in July and August are that perfect balmy warmth that more southerly residents dream of in the midst of their heat waves.

But what both Labrador City and Wabush are best known for are their open-pit iron-ore mines, the largest of their kind in North America. The community of Churchill Falls on the Churchill River is best known for having the largest underground hydroelectric generating station in Canada (the ninth largest in the world).

ESSENTIALS
GETTING THERE

If you're coming from Baie Comeau, Quebec, on the Gulf of St. Lawrence, partially paved Route 389 will take you north to the twin communities of Labrador City and Wabush. Labrador City is less than 20km (12 miles) from the Quebec–Labrador border; Wabush is just 3km (about 2 miles) farther along Route 500 and is home to the regional airport.

The 581-km (361-mile) stretch of gravel highway from Labrador City to Happy Valley–Goose Bay is basically unserviced except for what you'll find in Churchill Falls—roughly halfway along your journey—and will take you about 8½ hours to complete. Churchill Falls is situated 238km (148 miles) from Labrador City and 288km (179 miles) from Happy Valley–Goose Bay and is pretty much the only service center you'll find midway along Route 500.

The communities at either end of Route 500 also have small airports, so you can fly into Wabush, rent a car, drive as far as Happy Valley–Goose Bay, and then fly to St. John's or a limited number of other destinations without having to drive the return route.

 Navigating the Trans Labrador Highway

Many people are surprised to discover that the majority of the Trans Labrador Highway is a two-lane, gravel road. If it's wet the road is slick and slippery; if it's dry the dust is blinding; and if it's icy or snowy, driving can be lethal. Here are some tips to make the trip a bit easier:

- Try to drive on Sundays, when there are fewer tractor trailers on the road. Even though the highway is supposedly two lanes, you don't want to be crowded onto the shoulders, which are not nearly as solid as they look.
- Never start out on the highway without a full tank of gas (an extra container in the trunk wouldn't hurt either) and a spare tire.
- Be extra cautious in winter, especially with regard to traveling close to the outer edge of the highway. What looks like snow-covered highway may just be loose snow without a solid foundation.

You can also travel to Labrador West by train via the Quebec North Shore & Labrador Railway. The train departs Sept-Îles, Quebec on Tuesdays and Thursdays. The return trip departs Labrador City on Wednesdays and Fridays. It takes 7 hours if you get on the direct route and 12 hours if you get the milk-run that stops at several communities en route. The train travels 588km (357 miles) north to Schefferville and then there is a 58-km (36-mile) spur line that will take you from Ross Bay Junction to Labrador City. The cost is about C$64 (US$47) one-way, with discounts for seniors and children. MasterCard, Visa, and Interac are accepted. You must reserve your ticket at least one week in advance and pick up your ticket the day of your travel. Call ☎ **709/944-8205.** There is no website for this company.

VISITOR INFORMATION

Regional information for Labrador West is available at the tourist chalet in Labrador City at 500 Vanier Avenue. This chalet is open year-round. From mid-June to September 1 the hours are daily 9am until 5pm. The center is open the remainder of the year from Monday to Saturday, 9am to 5pm (© **709/944-7631**).

WHERE TO STAY & DINE

Bea's B&B ★   I'm including this small B&B because it has something you won't find in too many places in Labrador—a six-person hot tub! It also has a greenhouse and is situated on a lovely property overlooking a lake. There is one single room that is nice but considerably smaller than the other unit. The larger room has a sitting area and queen-sized bed. It also has a larger bathroom complete with a whirlpool tub and massaging showerhead. Local calls are free. Bea's is close to the shopping mall.

824 Retty St., Labrador City. © **709/944-2359**. E-mail: graveld@ironore.ca. 2 units. C$50 (US$36.68) single room, C$75 (US$55) queen room. **Amenities:** Complimentary continental breakfast; full meal plan available; laundry service available. *In room:* TV w/VCR. DVD in queen room.

Carol Inn   This is a good choice if you want to do your own cooking. The Carol Inn offers 20 fully equipped efficiency units and one deluxe suite. All units are spacious and have been recently refurbished. The inn is the only Labrador City property to have air-conditioning. There is an on-site gift shop. The inn features fine dining, a family restaurant, and pub-style food as well as live entertainment.

215 Drake Ave., Labrador City. © **888/799-7736** or 709/944-7736. E-mail: carolinn@cancom.net. 21 units. C$92–$132 (US$67.46–$98) double. Senior & corporate rates available. AE, DC, MC, V. **Amenities:** Full-service restaurant; family restaurant; pub; nonsmoking rooms. *In room:* A/C, TV, kitchenette, minibar.

Churchill Falls Inn   This is the only place to stay in Churchill Falls. The property is conveniently located in the town complex. There's even a swimming pool available for guest use, a real treat for this part of the world. Being in the town complex is a good thing if you're visiting during the winter, as you can get from one place to the next without having to go outdoors.

Ressigieu Dr., Churchill Falls. © **800/229-3269** or 709/925-3211. 21 units. C$82–$92 (US$61–$67.46) double. AE, MC, V. **Amenities:** Dining room; lounge; indoor swimming pool; limited room service. *In room:* TV.

Wabush Hotel   A beautifully distinctive chalet-style property built in 1960, this hotel was formerly known as the Sir Wilfred Grenfell Hotel. It's the best hotel in the area, with spacious guest rooms, exemplary customer service, and great food. The hotel features two dining rooms specializing in Chinese and Canadian cuisine—the Chinese food is really good, something that is rare in NL. The hotel offers a complimentary shuttle service to and from the airport upon request (with sufficient notice), as well as a 24-hour reception desk.

9 Grenfell Dr., Wabush. © 709/282-3221. www.wabushhotel.com. 68 units. C$86–$93 (US$64–$68.20) double. AE, DC, MC, V. **Amenities:** Dining room; lounge; beauty salon; limited room service; laundry service. *In room:* A/C, TV, hairdryers.

EXPLORING LABRADOR WEST

Churchill Falls Hydroelectric Generating Station Tours   These are free tours conducted four times daily during the summer months and less frequently the rest of the year. The tours are about 3 hours long and are indoors, so you don't have to worry about wearing special clothing. Hardhats are provided. For security reasons, children under 8 are not permitted to participate in the tours. You must reserve a spot on a tour by calling © **709/925-3335**.

Iron Ore Company of Canada and Wabush Mine Tours The Labrador West Tourism Association offers 1-hour bus tours of the open-mine pits. Visit their booth in the Labrador Mall for further details.

Labrador Mall, Wabush. ✆ 709/944-4171. E-mail: tourism@ccrstv.net. C$10 (US$7.33) for adults. For safety reasons, children under 10 are not permitted. July 1–early Sept Wed & Sun 1:30pm. Reservations recommended.

OUTDOOR PURSUITS

The area boasts excellent hiking trails and some of the best outdoor winter fun in the province. You can cross-country ski at the **Menihek Nordic Ski Club** from mid-October to mid-May. As well, there is excellent downhill skiing at **Smokey Mountain** and many kilometers of snowmobiling trails. If you're more into spectator sports, time your visit in March for the **Labrador 120,** a dogsled race that attracts participating teams from across Canada and the United States. Contact the Labrador West Tourism Development Corporation at ✆ **709/944-4171** for more information about any events in the Labrador City and Wabush area.

If you're into hunting or fishing, call Tourism Newfoundland & Labrador at **800/563-6353** or 709/729-2830 for a free copy of their *Hunting & Fishing Guide*. Labrador is a great place for hunting black bear or caribou and trophy fishing for salmon, trout, and northern pike.

 Mush!

If your idea of fun includes being pulled more than 160km (100 miles) across frozen lakes and around mountains in –40° temperatures, guided only by fluorescent markers spaced 91m (300 ft.) apart, then you'll want to know more about the Labrador 120 Dogsled Race. Each March, teams from across Canada and the United States gather in Labrador City to take part in this annual test of endurance. Teams are composed of a musher (driver), sled, survival gear, and 10 dogs (usually either Siberian or Alaskan huskies). Guided by voice commands from the musher, the dogs leave Labrador City and pull the sled non-stop 80km (50 miles) across country to Steers River, returning by the same route after a 6-hour break. Regardless of weather, the race starts at 4pm on a Saturday and usually ends around 8am Sunday. The entry fee is C$105 (US$82) per team. For more information, contact Alex Penney ✆ **709/282-6645.**

Moments **Labrador: A Spiritual Experience**

It takes a big heart to appreciate the Big Land. You'll see "brown" ponds where the water is so clear the color comes from the sun reflecting off the rocks on the bottom. You'll see double and triple rainbows, their colorful clarity enhanced by the crisp, clean air. And you'll see the aurora borealis playing across the northern sky in flowing flames of golden-crimson-emerald light. Truly, a trip to Labrador is an unforgettable, life-altering journey.

Appendix: Newfoundland & Labrador in Depth

To really understand this unique province and the people who live here, it's important to delve into the history of the island of Newfoundland and its mainland region of Labrador. It is the history, and sense of place, that make Newfoundland & Labrador such a culturally unique destination.

Despite being the oldest European settlement in North America, it is one of the least economically developed places in Canada. History has taught the people of Newfoundland & Labrador a harsh lesson of exploitation. Time and again, they have seen the heartbreaking out-migration of their vast natural resources and human potential. From the earliest days of the commercial fishery through to iron ore development, hydroelectric power, and offshore petroleum reserves, the majority of royalties and profits from these resource extractions have gone elsewhere. Which is why the people here are so fiercely determined to maximize their indigenous involvement on the labor side (the unofficial motto seems to be "Get as much work as you can, while you can"). Even so, there are never enough jobs to go around and that's why thousands of people leave the province every year—and why so few of them return.

The competition for employment and development dollars is so intense that it has created an intra-provincial rivalry. Rural areas resent the growth of urban centers, especially the capital of St. John's. Labradorians are lobbying for provincial autonomy, feeling the benefits they receive from the provincial government are nowhere near proportionate to the wealth that is generated in the region. And native groups consider themselves at the bottom of the food chain, receiving little recognition or recompense for the land and resources that were theirs for thousands of years before European settlement.

Yet, even as they cast a cynical eye toward each other and foreign commercial interests, begging to be proven wrong in their suspicion that it's yet another scheme to take advantage of them and this marvelous place, Newfoundlanders and Labradorians are simultaneously extending their hands in friendship. The Maritime provinces of New Brunswick, Nova Scotia, and Prince Edward Island have a well-deserved reputation for being gracious and welcoming, but there is still a noticeable difference between that gregarious threesome and Canada's easternmost province. It must be the isolation. Newfoundland is an island, Labrador a remote northern locale; both are difficult to access. But instead of closing them off from the world, their remoteness makes them hungry for connections beyond their borders. They greet strangers with heartfelt smiles, warm words, and genuine curiosity. Everyone is welcomed as a person with a story to tell.

Fun Fact A Cultural Time Capsule

As you travel throughout the province, you'll marvel at the distinctive dialects. Along the Southen Shore (in the Avalon Region), it's difficult to distinguish the brogue of the Irish-born local priest from that of the local people. Similarly, there are other places where the British accent is so strong, linguists can identify the part of England from which local ancestors emigrated. Why does it sound so pure, hundreds of years after the out-migration of these early European settlers? The answer is geography —Newfoundland's island isolation protected the original cultural identity of its settlers.

1 History 101

COD IS KING No matter what tangent you go off on as you research the province's natural or sociological history, everything will always bring you back to the fishery. The abundance of fish is what undoubtedly attracted the first native inhabitants to this land of shorelines. It is also the magnet that induced European commercial interests to make an annual pilgrimage to the province's treacherous shores. The fishery is what built the province. It is also what has, in many ways, destroyed it. But Newfoundlanders are a resilient people. Despite the devastation caused by the 1992 Cod Moratorium (see "Contemporary Culture," below), the sun is still shining very brightly (metaphorically speaking) on Canada's Far East as it turns its attentions to tourism and other newly discovered jewels of the sea to feed and clothe its people.

What is also important to understand is that most of Labrador (other than the Labrador Straits and the coastal region) has quite a different history and persona than the island of Newfoundland. Inland Labrador is a land rich in wildlife and natural resources, but its history has been spotted with struggle about who owns these lands. Labrador became part of Newfoundland only in 1927, and the boundary following the Torngat

Dateline

- **1000** Leif Eiriksson and his pack of Vikings land at L'Anse aux Meadows, making them the first Europeans to unofficially discover the New-found-land.
- **1497** Explorer Giovanni Caboto (aka John Cabot) lands at Cape Bonavista aboard his ship the *Matthew*, and is recorded as the man who discovered Newfoundland.
- **1583** Sir Humphrey Gilbert officially claims Newfoundland for England, making it the first overseas Crown possession.
- **1610** John Guy establishes the first British settlement in Newfoundland. It is not successful.
- **1621** Sir George Calvert (who later became Lord Baltimore) establishes the first successful planned colony, at Ferryland.
- **1651** Oliver Cromwell of England appoints a board of commissioners to govern Newfoundland.
- **1660** The French establish the colony of Placentia and build Fort Louis to defend it.
- **1763** Labrador is annexed to Newfoundland.
- **1771** The Moravians establish the community of Nain in Labrador.
- **1774** Control of Labrador is given to Quebec via *The Quebec Act*.
- **1784** Religious freedom is proclaimed and the first Roman Catholic bishop arrives in Newfoundland.

Continued

Mountains was set to separate Labrador from the neighboring province of Quebec. In many ways, it is both physically and emotionally distant from Newfoundland, leading many in the region to argue that they should form their own provincial entity.

WHO DISCOVERED THE NEW FOUNDE LAND?

Newfoundland has a long and intriguing history. Evidence of a burial mound of the Maritime Archaic Indians dating back 7,500 years—the oldest discovered burial mound in the world—has been found in L'Anse Amour on the Labrador Straits. And archaeologists have determined that as far back as 5,500 years ago the Maritime Archaic Indians, followed by other native peoples, were living in the area of the Port au Choix National Historic Site on the Great Northern Peninsula.

It was also on this Great Northern Peninsula that Leif Eiriksson and his gang of Vikings landed in A.D. 1000. Although the Vikings did not form a permanent settlement in the newfound land or officially claim what they called Vinland, they left evidence of their community in the mounds found at L'Anse aux Meadows National Historic Site.

Next up was Giovanni Caboto, more commonly known as John Cabot, the Italian-born explorer who claimed the newfound land for England in 1497. The French and Spanish soon followed, looking for a share of the bountiful Newfoundland fisheries, and many battles ensued, with the British eventually becoming the enduring force on the Newfoundland front.

Most of the early permanent settlers to Newfoundland came from southwest England and southeast Ireland, with the majority emigrating between 1750 and 1850. And because the

- **1802** The Treaty of Amiens gives control of the islands of St. Pierre and Miquelon to France.
- **1809** Labrador is re-annexed to Newfoundland.
- **1811** Newfoundland's first lighthouse is built at Fort Amherst.
- **1825** The coast of Labrador is annexed to Quebec.
- **1834** Cape Spear Lighthouse is built to light the way for ships arriving at the most easterly point in North America.
- **1858** The first overseas telegraph message is transmitted via submarine cable from Heart's Content in Newfoundland to Ireland.
- **1866** The Trans-Atlantic telegraph cable is successfully laid.
- **1871** The Newfoundland Constabulary is formed.
- **1873** Cod fishing in Newfoundland is revolutionized with the invention of the cod trap.
- **1888** Newfoundland abandons British currency and adopts the dollar.
- **1892** The Great Fire destroys 2,000 buildings in St. John's.
- **1892** Dr. Wilfred Grenfell arrives from England to establish the Grenfell Mission.
- **1895** Iron-ore mines on Bell Island open.
- **1897** First ferry service sails between North Sydney, Nova Scotia and Port aux Basques, Newfoundland.
- **1900** Cabot Tower at Signal Hill is officially opened.
- **1901** Sir Charles Cavendish Boyle, Governor of Newfoundland, writes the "Ode to Newfoundland."
- **1901** Marconi receives the first wireless signal from England at Signal Hill.
- **1904** France relinquishes rights to Newfoundland's "French Shore."
- **1908** William Coaker forms the Fishermen's Protective Union.
- **1912** The *S.S. Titanic* sinks off Cape Race after colliding with an iceberg.
- **1924** The War Memorial is unveiled in St. John's.
- **1925** Newfoundland women get the vote by way of the Women's Suffrage Bill.

Continued

Newfoundland outports were so isolated and family groups kept tightly intact, contemporary Newfoundlanders continue to speak with a strong Irish accent in parts of the Avalon (particularly the Irish Loop), and a fainter British or Scottish accent in St. John's and throughout the rest of the island.

PRE-CONFEDERATION Prior to joining Confederation and becoming part of Canada in 1949, Newfoundland was an independent British colony with its own governor and government house. Loyalty to the mother country was particularly evident during the World Wars, when thousands of Newfoundland youth voluntarily sailed overseas to do what they felt was their duty in the war effort.

Until 1949, Newfoundland produced its own currency and postage stamps. Newfoundland stamps are still relatively common, so their value isn't extremely high, but they make a wonderful souvenir for any collector. Their variety is rich and colorful, and each stamp tells a fascinating story. As well, Newfoundland produced its own coinage and bank notes from 1834 to 1949, many of which are now quite valuable to collectors. The coin denominations issued were 1¢, 5¢, 10¢, 20¢, 25¢, 50¢, $2, and gold.

CONFEDERATION The man responsible for bringing Newfoundland—Britain's oldest colony—into Canada's Confederation was Joey Smallwood, Newfoundland's first premier. Between 1946 and 1948, Smallwood organized a number of what turned out to be very controversial and emotional debates, asking his constituents whether they were in favor of becoming a Canadian province. In 1948, the final vote was incredibly close—51% supporting and 49% opposing—which is why some Newfoundlanders still think of

- **1927** The Grenfell Mission Hospital is opened in St. Anthony and Dr. Grenfell is knighted.
- **1927** Labrador becomes an official part of Newfoundland.
- **1932** Amelia Earhart takes off from Harbour Grace on her historic flight across the Atlantic.
- **1949** Newfoundland becomes a province of Canada with Joseph Smallwood as its first premier.
- **1957** All children under 16 years of age are provided with no-cost medical care.
- **1958** Four cabin cruisers are put into service, providing isolated communities with regular visits from medical personnel.
- **1961** Forest fires force the evacuation of 9,000 people from 300 communities. A million acres and 35 homes are destroyed, but luckily there are no fatalities.
- **1963** The American military base at Fort Pepperell is closed.
- **1965** The Fisheries Household Resettlement Program is introduced to encourage residents of remote outport communities to move to larger centers.
- **1965** The iron-ore mine at Wabush, Labrador, is opened.
- **1965** Newfoundland's 500,000th citizen, Bernard Joseph Hynes, is born at 2:25am on July 30 in the Twillingate Cottage Hospital.
- **1965** Come Home Year is instituted as a major tourism initiative.
- **1966** Bell Island mine closes.
- **1966** The Newfoundland portion of the Trans-Canada Highway is completed.
- **1966** St. John's businessman Chesley Pippy donates the funds to establish Pippy Park.
- **1967** Construction begins on the Churchill Falls hydroelectric generating station.
- **1968** CN introduces a trans-island passenger bus service.
- **1969** Newfoundland introduces Medicare.
- **1969** The first ship is constructed at the Marystown shipyard.
- **1969** The Newfoundland Railway is closed.

Continued

Smallwood as a traitor, and others see him as Newfoundland's greatest contemporary hero.

CONTEMPORARY CULTURE Newfoundlanders continue to be proud of their heritage despite the devastating blow dealt to them in 1992 with the Cod Moratorium, when the cod-fishing industry was suddenly shut down. The result was massive unemployment (some estimates were as high as 60,000 people, in a provincial population of 500,000), and 12 years later the province continues to have the lowest family income, the highest unemployment rate, and the highest rate of child poverty in Canada.

However, hope is on the horizon. The biggest news in recently discovered natural resources for Newfoundland is its off-shore oil developments, *Hibernia* and *Terra Nova,* each situated more than 300km (186 miles) off the coast of Newfoundland. Crude-oil production from these two sources was enough to catapult the province ahead of all other Canadian provinces in terms of economic growth for the year 2003. The oil resources, combined with other recent mining developments, are expected to bring another positive year of economic growth for 2004.

You can become an honorary Newfoundlander at a number of attractions and local destinations by participating in a "screech-in." The tongue-in-cheek ritual varies from place to place but generally requires you to recite a silly verse, drink an ounce of the hair-raising dark rum straight up, and then kiss a piece of salt cod (or, in some establishments, a stuffed puffin), upon which you'll be presented with a certificate for a keepsake.

For those who prefer their liquor with a mixer, try screech in a "Dark 'n' Dirty," the local name given to what most other places call a rum and cola.

- **1970** The Maritime Archaic Indian burial ground is discovered at Port au Choix.
- **1972** After 23 years in office, Premier Joseph Smallwood resigns.
- **1972** The Newfoundland dog is declared the province's official animal.
- **1973** The Newfoundland fishery is booming, with an estimated value of C\$45 million.
- **1974** Dorothy Wyatt is sworn as the first female mayor for the City of St. John's.
- **1974** Newfoundland & Labrador celebrates 25 years of Confederation.
- **1976** Well-known Newfoundland politican John Crosbie is elected as a Member of Parliament.
- **1978** L'Anse aux Meadows is designated a UNESCO World Heritage Site.
- **1978** St. John's Day is celebrated for the first time, with parades, steak dinners, fish-splitting contests, and a street dance.
- **1979** Oil is discovered on the Grand Banks and the Hibernia well established.
- **1979** Progressive Conservative Brian Peckford is elected Premier.
- **1979** The Matrimonial Property Act is passed, giving women financial rights in their marriage.
- **1982** Offshore oil drill rig the *Ocean Ranger* sinks in a winter storm. All 84 lives aboard are lost.
- **1982** The provincial unemployment rate hits 20%.
- **1982** Christine Fagan becomes the first woman to head the St. John's Board of Trade.
- **1983** Construction begins on the first phase of the Trans Labrador Highway.
- **1985** Arrow jet crashes at Gander, killing 256 U.S. servicemen and crew.
- **1985** CFB Goose Bay is opened and low-level flight training begins.
- **1986** Legislation puts an end to the killing of seal pups.
- **1987** Gros Morne National Park becomes a UNESCO World Heritage Site.
- **1991** Former Premier Joseph R. Smallwood dies at 90 years of age.
- **1992** Ottawa enforces the Cod Moratorium in an attempt to replenish depleted cod stocks. *Continued*

- **1993** Prospectors Al Chislett and Chris Verbiski discover the Voisey's Bay nickel deposit in northern Labrador.
- **1994** Recreational cod fishing is reintroduced to Newfoundland.
- **1997** A public referendum results in the end of denominational education.
- **1998** The Royal Newfoundland Constabulary begins carrying firearms.
- **2001** First oil at the Terra Nova oil field.
- **2001** Brian Tobin resigns as Premier and moves to federal politics at the request of Prime Minister Jean Chrétien.

The Liberal Party chooses Roger Grimes to be their new leader, effectively making him the new Premier.
- **2002** Former Premier and Canadian Fisheries Minister Brian Tobin retires from politics.
- **2002** The province officially changes its name to Newfoundland & Labrador.
- **2003** Roger Grimes and the governing Liberal Party lose the provincial election to the Progressive Conservatives under the leadership of Danny Williams.

 ## Battle of Beaumont Hamel

Two years into World War I, the Allies planned a major offensive to break through German lines, hoping to turn the tide of war in their favor. The attack was scheduled for July 1, 1916. Miscalculating the positioning of German troops, the Allied forces ran straight into heavy bombardment from machine-gun fire. Almost 20,000 British troops died that day, but hardest hit of all was the Newfoundland Regiment. The 778 members of the Regiment were among the first wave ordered to cross No Man's Land and penetrate the German front line near the village of Beaumont Hamel. The next morning, only 68 men answered the roll call—each unacknowledged name a symbol of a lost generation for the fledgling colony. There is today a permanent memorial on the battlefield of Beaumont Hamel; it is a bronze statue of a caribou, the symbol of the Newfoundland Regiment.

 ## Native Inhabitants of Newfoundland & Labrador

Palaeo-Indians (or "ancient" Indians) lived in Labrador about 9,000 years ago. Little is known about them, but based on the scant archaeological evidence, an educated guess is that they were nomadic hunters and gatherers, living along the coast in the summer and following inland caribou in the fall.

Maritime Archaic people (descendants of the Palaeo-Indians) lived throughout the entire province from 3,000 to 7,500 years ago. They are the first known inhabitants of the island of Newfoundland. They were coastal dwellers, dependent on the sea (mammals, birds, and fish) for their sustenance.

Palaeo-Eskimos began moving into Northern Labrador about 4,000 years ago, emigrating south from Greenland. There is no evidence of direct interaction between the Palaeo-Eskimos and Martime Archaic people, but it seems logical that they would have met at some point since they occupied the same geographic areas at approximately the same time.

Included within the Palaeo-Eskimo tradition were the Groswater and Dorset cultures.

Innu, who have lived in Labrador and northeastern Quebec for approximately 2,000 years, are thought to be descendants of the Maritime Archaic people. Traditionally, they are nomadic hunters like the other aboriginal groups of Newfoundland & Labrador. They differ, however, in that they are an inland people who make sporadic trips to the coast. Animals, particularly caribou, play a strong role in Innu culture. To learn more about the modern Innu population, visit www.innu.ca.

Beothuk, the original native inhabitants of Newfoundland, are extinct. The last known Beothuk, Shanawdithit, died in 1829. It is estimated that there were fewer than 1,000 Beothuk living on the island at any one time; their population was decimated by starvation, disease, and periodic skirmishes with European settlers. It's not known where they came from, or how long they lived on the island, but archaeological evidence seems to indicate they were of Algonkian origin (similar to Mi'kmaq, Montagnais, and Naskaupi). Their main settlements were in central and western Newfoundland.

Thule people were the most recent aboriginal arrivals in Labrador, crossing the Bering Strait from Asia as late as 500 to 600 years ago. They lived in small family groups, and were nomadic hunters and gatherers. They were also known as whalers, hunting baleen whales using harpoons thrown from their umiaks (open, flat-bottomed boats) and kayaks. The Thule are the ancestors of the Inuit.

Inuit (aka "Eskimo") of Labrador are traditionally nomadic hunters and gatherers known for traveling great distances in search of food and other sustenance materials. Pre–European settlement, they ranged from Cape Chidley in northern Labrador to the island of Newfoundland. The introduction of Moravian missionaries in the mid-1700s marked a change in the Inuit's traveling lifestyle as well as the dilution of their culture through the integration of European tools and ideas. Today, the Inuit people are reclaiming their heritage and finding their own place in the modern world. For more information, visit their website at www.nunatsiavut.com.

Mi'kmaq have lived in Newfoundland for more than 200 years, with their main settlements on the island's west coast. It's not certain where they came from, or when and why they moved here, but some anthropologists have surmised that they are of Maritime (that is, Nova Scotian) origin and that their emigration was motivated by scarce resources. About 600 Mi'kmaq today live in Conne River, along Newfoundland's south coast. You can visit the band on the Internet at www.miawpukek.nf.ca.

Métis people of Labrador are fighting for recognition of their native status —both from acknowledged aboriginal groups and from non-natives. Métis are a combination of Innu or Inuit bloodlines mixed with European settlers. There are approximately 5,000 Métis living in Labrador, which makes them the largest aboriginal group in the province. You can check on their progress in the fight for official Indian status by visiting www.labmetis.org.

The Little Man from Gambo

Joseph Roberts Smallwood was born in 1900 in Gambo, a town of just over 2,000 residents located in central Newfoundland. Although small of stature, Smallwood had a larger-than-life persona. He worked as a journalist, a farmer, and a labor organizer before striking his true vocation: politics. He was convinced that Confederation with Canada was the best option for a prosperous future for Newfoundland & Labrador; his mission was to persuade enough of his fellow citizens to feel the same way. He traveled the province from one end to the other, using his impressive oratorical skill and staccato style of delivery to maximum effect. He achieved his desired goal in 1949, when Newfoundland & Labrador became the tenth province of Canada.

A particularly endearing Smallwood quirk (aside from his famous bow tie) was his habit of reiterating salient points three and four times so that they were imprinted on the minds of his listeners. He also had an incredible memory for both names and faces, often recognizing voters he had met years before and linking them to other family and friends throughout the province.

Smallwood served as Premier of Newfoundland & Labrador for 23 years. His leadership was marked by an intense drive for industrialization: his government supported rubber boot and chocolate factories as well as an oil refinery, linerboard mills (manufacturers of the corrugated layer found in the middle of cardboard), and a hydroelectric power development at Churchill Falls. Even though many of his initiatives were fated to fail, the lack of success never diminished his dream of prosperity. Until his death in 1991, he was often affectionately referred to as the last living Father of Confederation.

Fun Fact **More Than Fiddles & Accordians**

For anyone who thinks that all Newfoundland music and musicians fall under the "traditional" banner, think again. The province is teeming with all kinds of talent, ranging from pop rock to alternative to hip-hop and blues. In April 2003, Corner Brook native Christa Borden won *Pop Star: The One* (a competition similar to *Canadian Idol* or *American Idol*). And in the same year, Carbonear resident Jenny Gear was one of the top finalists in the inaugural *Canadian Idol* competition.

---

2 A Land of Bountiful Natural Resources

NATURAL RESOURCES AND THE GREAT OUTDOORS Newfoundland & Labrador is a land rich in natural resources. To commemorate this abundance, the province has designated a tree, plant, gemstone, and bird as its official representatives of nature. The provincial tree is the black spruce, which is the most common tree in the province.

Newfoundland's official floral emblem is the pitcher plant. More than 100 years ago, Queen Victoria of England chose the pitcher plant to be engraved on a newly minted Newfoundland penny. In 1954, the Newfoundland Cabinet designated this fascinating plant as the official flower of the province. This unusual wine-and-green-colored flower can be found on bogs and marshes in Newfoundland & Labrador. You can see it growing on the hills surrounding Cape Spear and in Salmonier Nature Park. The plant gets its nourishment from insects that are trapped and then drowned in a pool of water at the base of its tubular leaves. If you stick your fingers into the death pod at the base of the plant, you're likely to pull out an insect or two. Don't worry: pitcher plants don't eat humans.

Warning: You are permitted to bring some of Newfoundland's natural abundance home with you, but take note that the removal of soil or plants bearing soil from NL is strictly prohibited. Vehicles leaving the province are inspected at ferry terminals and any plants or soil found may be confiscated. Special permits may be obtained from Agriculture Canada (© **613/759-1000;** www.agr.gc.ca).

You are, however, permitted to pick the berries, and there are lots of them. The most popular of the local berries is the bakeapple, internationally known as the cloudberry. The ripened berry is an orange-yellow color, and only one berry grows on each plant. Bakeapple plants grow approximately 7 to 10cm (3–4 in.) high—so you'll have to get down pretty low to pick them, but at least they're easy to spot because of their bright color. The berries are quite unique in flavor and generally ready for picking in mid-August, when you'll see many roadside stands selling basketfuls.

Another popular Newfoundland berry is the partridgeberry, internationally known as the lingonberry and a relative of the cranberry family. Each plant produces a single dark-red tart-tasting berry that usually ripens after the first frost in September. Both the bakeapple and the partridgeberry make excellent jams, spreads, and even wines that can be purchased at various shops throughout the province.

ROCKS ON THE ROCK Appropriately, Newfoundland—nicknamed the Rock—is rich in geological resources. Mistaken Point on the Avalon Peninsula has what are thought to be the world's oldest fossils, and you can find several other great places for fossil hunting throughout the province. Tourism Newfoundland & Labrador (© **800/563-6353;** www.gov.nf.ca/tourism) offers free information about places of geological interest in the *Newfoundland & Labrador Traveller's Guide to Geology.* Newfoundland's Department of Mines & Energy (© **709/729-3159;** www.gov.nf.ca/mines&en) is a good resource for geology-specific maps and information.

Named the province's mineral emblem in 1975, *Labradorite* is one of about 20 semi-precious stones found in Newfoundland & Labrador. You may spot it at a number of locations on the coast of Labrador and on the island of Newfoundland. Labradorite is an igneous, iridescent crystalline mineral (also known as Labrador feldspar) that looks like a piece of the Labrador night sky, with the colors of the aurora borealis captured inside. It's used to make lovely pieces of jewelry that you can purchase at various stores throughout the province.

WILDLIFE Some 30 to 40 million seabirds, representing many different species, visit Newfoundland & Labrador each year. The favorite among these for most travelers is likely to be the provincial bird of Newfoundland: the Atlantic puffin, also known as the sea parrot or Baccalieu bird. Puffins are quite small compared to many other seabirds, and they're striking in appearance with their black-and-white plumage and brightly colored, rounded beaks. They're exceptionally cute to watch, because their short wings seem to have difficulty supporting their chubby little bodies. Puffins need to flap their wings repeatedly

Petroleum Power

There are two producing oil fields in the waters offshore from Newfoundland & Labrador (Hibernia and Terra Nova), with a third (White Rose) scheduled for first-oil in 2005. Between them, Hibernia and Terra Nova produce about 100 million barrels of oil annually; White Rose is expected to add another 92,000 barrels of oil per day. By the time White Rose is operational, Newfoundland & Labrador will account for about one-half of Canada's conventional light crude-oil production. And exploration activity is on the increase—meaning that there could well be even more petroleum activity on Newfoundland & Labrador's horizon.

to keep themselves in flight, lacking the grace or ease of flying exhibited by most birds. About 95% of all puffins in North America breed in colonies around the Newfoundland & Labrador coasts.

The fertile waters of Newfoundland & Labrador are home to 22 species of whales; the more common species are the massive humpbacks and the much smaller minke whales. In fact, the waters around the province have the world's largest concentration of humpback whales. Between April and October, your chances of seeing a humpback fairly close to shore are quite good nearly anywhere in the province, with numbers peaking between June and September. The province also possesses the world's largest number of salmon rivers. The Main River near Corner Brook is the first Canadian Heritage River to be so designated in the province.

Canine Companions

Each of Newfoundland & Labrador's distinct geographic entities has its own namesake dog. The **Newfoundland dog** is a large animal with long black fur and webbed feet. Some Newfoundland dogs have a splash of white across their chest. In spite of their imposing size (weighing approximately 54.4 kg/120 lbs at 12 months), these dogs have a gentle, patient temperament that makes them ideal family pets. The history of the breed is marked by tales of strength, courage, and loyalty to their human masters. An example of their heroism can be found during the 1919 wreck of the *S.S. Ethie*, when the ship's Newfoundland dog jumped into the roaring sea and carried in a line, which was then secured by people on shore. The line was the lifeline by which the shipwrecked passengers were able to reach safety.

For the first time in history, the Westminster Kennel Club awarded the 2004 Best In Show Trophy to "Josh," a Newfoundland, at their 128th Annual Dog Show.

The province's other canine companion is another water-loving dog known as the **Labrador retriever.** Although they are similar to the Newfoundland in temperament, they are about half the size and have short, straight hair. As their name indicates, these dogs make excellent hunting companions.

Only 14 land mammals are indigenous to the island of Newfoundland. Additional species have been introduced by humans—most notably the moose, which have taken quite nicely to the Rock and now number 150,000. Sufferers of ophidiophobia will be relieved to know that Newfoundland has no snakes.

However, certain land species are here in abundance. The province is home to the world's largest caribou herd, approximately 700,000 animals, at George River, Labrador. The island of Newfoundland also boasts North America's highest concentration of moose, as well as the continent's largest black bears, making the province an ideal destination for lovers of wildlife, whether you're hunting with a camera, a gun, or a fishing rod. Labrador is a great place for trophy fishing and for hunting black bear or caribou; Newfoundland offers fine moose hunting and salmon fishing. You can get a free copy of the *Hunting & Fishing Guide for Newfoundland & Labrador* by calling © **800/563-6353** or 709/729-2830.

ICEBERGS   Thinking back to the untimely sinking of the *Titanic,* we all know that icebergs can be dangerous and even fatal if their vastness and power are not respected. Nevertheless, they are awe-inspiringly beautiful, and Newfoundland is one of the best places to see the largest icebergs as they make their way from Greenland past Baffin Island and down the coast along Iceberg Alley.

The largest iceberg spotted off the coast of Newfoundland was about 13km (8 miles) long, weighed more than 9 billion metric tons, and likely took 3 years to make the journey from Greenland, where it would have calved off a gargantuan land-based glacier.

Newfoundlanders are respectful of these huge "castles of the sea," despite the fact that they're used to seeing many icebergs float by their coastline each year. They know that one of the massive missives of compressed snow can break up or overturn at any time, taking with it a boat that has ventured too close. Seabirds seem to be able to sense when an iceberg is about to roll and will fly away just before it does its dangerous dance. Remember, only 10% of an iceberg's mass can be seen above the surface of the water, and the other 90% is submerged and cannot be seen.

As the massive iceberg continues to float farther south into warmer waters, it weakens and begins to break apart into smaller, more manageable pieces. Bigger pieces that are comparable to the size of a large ship are called "growlers." Smaller chunks that may be the size of a car, a small house, or less are called "bergy bits." But for those of us who "come from away" it's equally exciting, whether we're fortunate enough to see a massive iceberg or just a piece of one in a lesser but still impressive form.

When the bergs break up into growlers or bergy bits, they become more manageable and more predictable. This natural process has created some interesting opportunities for crafty and enterprising Newfoundlanders, who have begun marketing several innovative iceberg products.

Bergy bits are harvested and broken down into even smaller bits and used as ice cubes in drinks. There's something unique about iceberg ice, because of its effervescence. Your drink will pop, crackle, and fizz when the air bubbles contained in the ice make contact with the liquid.

As well, iceberg pieces are melted down and bottled into natural iceberg water. One popular brand is Borealis Genuine Iceberg Bottled Water. Just think: you're drinking water that's more than 10,000 years old! Canadian Iceberg Vodka, bottled in St. John's, is another interesting product made from the charcoal-filtered and triple-distilled water of iceberg growlers and bergy bits and mixed with grain alcohol. The award-winning vodka has been voted the second-best vodka in the world. Leave it to those fun-loving Newfoundlanders to get a buzz out of a berg!

3 Cultural Tourism & Modern Entertainment

LIGHTHOUSES You'll find many lighthouses as you make your way through Newfoundland & Labrador. Stop in and explore, as so much about the province's history and heritage can be found in these structures. They have been protecting seafarers since 1813, when the first lighthouse was built and operated by volunteers at Fort Amherst at the mouth of St. John's Harbour. Other lighthouses were built after the formation of Newfoundland's Lighthouse Board in 1832. Most of those colorful lighthouses or their replacement structures still stand. If you visit the lighthouses of Newfoundland & Labrador—many of them National or Provincial Historic Sites—you will learn much about the fishery, the naval history and shipwrecks, and the strong people who have built this land.

The Cape Bonavista Lighthouse is of prime significance as the place where continental Europeans first landed in Newfoundland. Bonavista is the oldest fishing village in Newfoundland & Labrador, with a history going back more than 500 years. And the Point Amour Lighthouse on the Labrador Straits, first illuminated in 1858, is the tallest in Atlantic Canada. It is now automated, as are most of the lighthouses in the province, but their history remains alive and of prime significance to residents and visitors hoping to gain a deeper understanding of this seafaring province.

COME HOME CELEBRATIONS Because of the province's failing economy over the past decade, many of Newfoundland's young and educated have felt compelled to move away from the Rock in order to earn a good living for themselves and their families. The province's population has actually decreased by 7% since 1996 because of this outflow of people and the fact that Newfoundland & Labrador has a very small percentage of immigrants in comparison to the rest of Canada.

Most of those leaving the province have ended up in Ontario (because of the opportunities in commerce, science, and technology) and Alberta (for those interested in the petroleum industry, as close ties have formed between the two provinces with Newfoundland's recent involvement in off-shore drilling). It is said that the population of Grand Prairie, Alberta, now includes as many Newfoundlanders as Albertans!

You may be able to take the Newfoundlander out of Newfoundland, but you can never exorcise the spirit of Newfoundland from its people. As a result, many who have left return each summer to spend time with family and friends and to visit the place they will always call home. To commemorate this spirit, many communities throughout Newfoundland & Labrador have created "Come Home Year" celebrations, filled with all sorts of food, fun, and frolic.

─────────────────────────────────────

Fun Fact **Come Home Year**

Credit for the popularity of Come Home Year celebrations belongs to former Premier Joseph Roberts Smallwood. Although he was not the first person to advocate a Newfoundland & Labrador Come Home Year Celebration (that honor belongs to the Cabot Club of Boston, which hosted the inaugeral Come Home Celebration in 1904), Smallwood's dream was realized on a much grander scale than its predecessor. Under the leadership of Dr. F. W. Rowe, the 1964 Come Home Year coincided with the completion of the Trans-Canada Highway across the island. Because it was meant to be a major tourism promotion as much as it was a chance for homesick Newfoundlanders to return to the place of their birth, Come Home Year organizers worked with the Government of Newfoundland & Labrador to accomplish the following:

- Increase air and sea transportation to the island.
- Build four new Holiday Inns across the island, and upgrade existing guestroom facilities.
- Build 10 new provincial parks.
- Establish 10 tourist information centers and employ information officers.
- Organize numerous events, including the National Junior Baseball Finals, regattas, garden parties, contests, and a cavalcade of floats and officials to celebrate the official opening of the Trans-Canada Highway.

MUMMERING   Mummering—the art of disguising one's self and one's gender in an unusual and often outlandish costume—is still relatively common in Newfoundland. Beginning on Boxing Night (the first night after Christmas) and continuing through January 6, these 12 days of Christmas are when the mummers are out in full force. Watch for them going from house to house, usually in small groups. Mummers generally approach the house of someone they know or know of (and in small-town Newfoundland, that's not hard to do), sing a satirical song, and then expect to be rewarded with seasonal snacks and libations. If you're visiting during these days, you're in for quite a treat if you hit the streets after dark.

TARGA NEWFOUNDLAND   If your interests lie in long-distance automotive adventures, you may want to plan your visit for mid-September, when Targa Newfoundland—billed as the Ultimate North American Tarmac Rally—takes place. Targa Newfoundland is the first—and to my knowledge the only—event of its kind in North America. The annual 9-day event allows owners of historic, classic, and modern sporty motor vehicles to "drive them in the way they were meant to be driven." This leads to some challenging high-speed racing on sections of highway that have been closed off to the public.

Each vehicle competes against itself on a handicap basis as well as against other vehicles. The event won't win you any prize money, but winners do get Targa plates. At present, the course covers 2,400km (1,488 miles) of roadway around the Avalon and through the Eastern Region into central Newfoundland, with future plans to expand the Targa route. Call ✆ **877/332-2413** or 709/722-2413 for more information, or visit www.targanewfoundland.com for updates, to sign up, or to read the Targa newsletter.

ODE TO NEWFOUNDLAND   The "Ode to Newfoundland" is a song that was the national anthem of Newfoundland when it was an independent nation (prior to 1949, when it became a Canadian province). The song was written by Sir Cavendish Boyle while he was Britain's Governor of Newfoundland (between 1901 and 1904). The ode remains Newfoundland's unofficial anthem.

Ode to Newfoundland

When sun rays crown thy pine clad hills,
And summer spreads her hand,
When silvern voices tune thy rills,
We love thee smiling land,
We love thee, we love thee
We love thee smiling land.

When spreads thy cloak of shimm'ring white,
At winter's stern command,
Thro' shortened day and starlit night,
We love thee frozen land,
We love thee, we love thee,
We love thee frozen land.

When blinding storm gusts fret thy shore,
And wild waves lash thy strand,
Thro' sprindrift swirl and tempest roar,
We love thee windswept land,
We love thee, we love thee,
We love thee windswept land.

As loved our fathers, so we love,
Where once they stood we stand,
Their prayer we raise to heav'n above,
God guard thee, Newfoundland,
God guard thee, God guard thee,
God guard thee, Newfoundland.

DICTIONARY OF NEWFOUNDLAND ENGLISH   Now in its second edition, this useful tool will help you prepare for your trip to the Rock. Even though Newfoundlanders speak English, they have their own dialect that has introduced new and varied meanings for common words, and they have developed unique words of their own. These can be found in the whopping 770 pages that make up the *Dictionary of Newfoundland English,* published by the University of Toronto Press.

Any visitor to the Rock will find this book extremely useful, and any student of languages will find it extremely interesting. Some examples of what you'll discover in this bulky volume include seven different meanings for the word "cat," which includes the obvious interpretation as well as others, and some surprisingly pleasant meanings for the word "piss." The book retails for C$37.95

(US$24.30), and you can find it at booksellers mentioned in the following section of this appendix. *Note:* Not every person in every region of Newfoundland & Labrador will use words found in the *Dictionary of Newfoundland English.* Some of the recorded words and phrases are obsolete.

MUSIC AND THEATER   If you are a Canadian—or if you were fortunate enough to have seen the television broadcast of the 2002 Juno Awards (awarded by the Canadian Academy of Recording Arts and Sciences)—you'll have seen what a great job the city of St. John's did in bringing what is usually a rather dull awards ceremony to life. It was an amazing scene, with thousands of people in the streets; by contrast, when the event is held in Toronto, as it often has been, it's a much more somber affair.

Planning a celebration seems to come easily to Newfoundlanders. In simple words, they know how to party, and they certainly know how to make fabulous music. Some of the better-known acts include The Irish Descendents, Great Big Sea, The Masterless Men, and The Ennis Sisters, all known for their Celtic sound.

As well, Newfoundlanders love their live theater, and you'll find many regional festivals occurring throughout the province during summer. A new innovation to the regional productions has been added to give you an even greater opportunity to share some good times with the local people. Started in 1999, Soirees & Times gives you a chance to make the circuit and take in the best of what's offered in nearly every corner of Newfoundland & Labrador. Call Tourism Newfoundland & Labrador (© **800/563-6353**) for information about dates and prices for this year's performances. You're bound to enjoy some of the best music, theater, and food ever to come your way.

4 Recommended Books

Many books have been written about this colorful land that is rich in history, culture, and natural resources. Several of these volumes have even been turned into movies for the large and small screen. To make the most of your visit, I'd recommend reading at least a couple of the gems listed below.

Note: Some of these titles may be unavailable from your favorite local or Internet bookseller because of their limited distribution. If you encounter this problem, try Wordplay Bookstore (© **800/563-9100** or 709/726-9193; www.wordplay.com) or the Downhomer (© **888/588-6353** or 709/722-2970; www.shopdownhomer.com). Both of these outlets are located in St. John's and carry an exceptional variety of Newfoundland titles.

HISTORY/HISTORICAL NOVELS

- *The Colony of Unrequited Dreams,* by Wayne Johnston (Vintage Canada): A fantastic historical novel written by a Newfoundlander about the life and times of Newfoundland hero Joey Smallwood, and the land he so loved.
- *Curse of the Red Cross Ring,* by Earl B. Pilgrim (Flanker Press): An enjoyable novel that gives you an insight into what it was like to be a Newfoundland fisherman in the late 19th and early 20th centuries.
- *In the Hand of the Living God,* by Lilliane Bouzane (Turnstone Press): A story about John Cabot's wife and the letters that were exchanged between her and her explorer husband.
- *The Labradorians: Voices from the Land of Cain,* by Lynne D. Fitzhugh (Breakwater Books): A novel about the challenges of settling the rugged

untamed frontier, the book tells the story of mixed-race settlers and their battle to survive Labrador's harsh conditions.

- *The Millennium Book of Newfoundland & Labrador: Our First Thousand Years,* edited by James R. Thoms (Stirling Press): This book contains a timeline of the province's history from A.D. 1000 to 2000, as well as a who's who of the province, some interesting stories about its history, and lots of photographs.
- *Random Passage,* by Bernice Morgan (Breakwater Books): An enthralling novel about a young Irishwoman's 19th-century journey from England to Random Passage, a remote Newfoundland outport. The book was made into a mini-series by CBC television and is now available on video.
- *River Thieves,* by Michael Crummey (Anchor Canada): A haunting tale set in Newfoundland at the turn of the 19th century, depicting the uneasy relations between the Peyton family and the Beothuk Indians.
- *Smallwood: The Unlikely Revolutionary,* by Richard Gwyn (McClelland & Stewart): Insights into Joey Smallwood, the politician who brought Newfoundland into Confederation in 1949.
- *Voyage of the Matthew—John Cabot and the Discovery of North America,* by Peter Firstbrook (McClelland & Stewart): An account of Cabot's history-making voyage more than 500 years ago to Bonavista, Newfoundland.

CONTEMPORARY

- *All in Good Time,* by Brian Tobin (Penguin Group [Canada]): A great book for those interested in contemporary Newfoundland culture and Canadian politics. Tobin was premier of Newfoundland & Labrador at the end of the 20th century and also had a successful career in federal politics as Minister of Canadian Fisheries.
- *As Near to Heaven by Sea,* by Kevin Major (Penguin Group [Canada]): A beautifully written historical account of the many people and events that have contributed to the current-day personality of Newfoundland & Labrador.
- *The Danger Tree: Memory, War, and the Search for a Family's Past,* by David Macfarlane (Vintage Canada): A memoir about a contemporary Newfoundland family and how current events have had an impact on their lives.
- *The Day the World Came to Town: 9/11 in Gander, Newfoundland,* by Jim DeFede (Regan Books): Stories of kindness and humanity in the face of the worst act of terrorism in United States history. A close-knit Newfoundland community opens it hearts and homes to stranded airline passengers.
- *Into the Night: The Samantha Walsh Story,* by Gordon Walsh (Flanker Press): The tragic true story of Samantha Walsh, a 13-year-old Fleur de Lys girl who went missing on February 6, 2000. Her body was discovered almost 3 weeks later; she'd been murdered by a lifelong family friend.
- *Latitudes of Melt,* by Joan Clark (Vintage Canada): An enchanting novel that traces a 20th-century woman's life in a small Newfoundland outport community.
- *Newfoundland & Labrador: Insiders' Perspectives,* by James Tuck and Douglas House (Johnson Family Foundation): This compilation of 24 short essays is written by a variety of experts who call Newfoundland & Labrador home, including Dr. Tuck, an archaeologist from the Colony of Avalon. Learn more about the province's history, politics, economics, people, culture,

music, food, and natural history from people who work in the field. Because the book is in a compact format, it's also suitable for travelers to take with them. The book is also available in French under the name *Terre-Neuve et la Labrador: Perspectives locales,* and in German under the name *Neufundland und Labrador: Insider berichen.*

- *No Holds Barred,* by John C. Crosbie (McClelland & Stewart): The political memoirs of one of Newfoundland's most colorful politicians, a former federal cabinet minister who came close to winning the leadership of the Progressive Conservative Party of Canada—and the top job in the country.
- *Rare Birds,* by Edward Riche (Doubleday Canada): A humorous novel about a man struggling to make a go with an unsuccessful restaurant in a New-foundland outport. The book was made into a movie starring William Hurt that is now available on video.
- *The Shipping News,* by E. Annie Proulx (Pocket Books): A contemporary story about a troubled man coming home to his Newfoundland roots. The book was made into a movie starring Kevin Spacey that is now avail-able on video.

Index

See also Accommodations and Restaurants indexes below.

RESTAURANTS